D1594064

7.50
28W

CAMBRIDGE STUDIES IN
MEDIEVAL LIFE AND THOUGHT

Edited by M. D. Knowles, Litt.D., F.B.A.

*Fellow of Peterhouse and Regius Professor of Modern History in the
University of Cambridge*

NEW SERIES VOL. VII

EARLY
FRANCISCAN GOVERNMENT
ELIAS TO BONAVENTURE

NEW SERIES

PLATE I. Brother Elias, from an eighteenth-century engraving;
after Giunta Pisano, 1236

EARLY FRANCISCAN GOVERNMENT

ELIAS TO BONAVENTURE

BY

ROSALIND B. BROOKE

CAMBRIDGE

AT THE UNIVERSITY PRESS

1959

PUBLISHED BY
THE SYNDICS OF THE CAMBRIDGE UNIVERSITY PRESS

Bentley House, 200 Euston Road, London, N.W. 1
American Branch: 32 East 57th Street, New York 22, N.Y.

©

CAMBRIDGE UNIVERSITY PRESS
1959

Printed in Great Britain at the University Press, Cambridge
(Brooke Crutchley, University Printer)

TO MY
MOTHER AND FATHER

CONTENTS

BOOK II

THE DECISIVE YEARS: 1239–1260

APPENDICES

LIST OF ILLUSTRATIONS

The painting was at the foot of a crucifix made for the High
Altar of the Basilica, but subsequently moved out into the open,
where in the course of time it decayed, and has long since
disappeared. Cf. F. M. Angeli, *Collis Paradisi amoenitas seu Sacri
Conventus Assisiensis Hist.* (Montefalisco, 1704), 1, 32. The plate
is from F. Venuti's *Vita di Fra Elia*, 1 ed., *Magazzino Toscano
d'Instruzione e di Piacere*, 11 (Livorno, 1755), facing p. 391; cf.
p. 443. The engraving was based on an ancient copy in a picture
'posseduta presentemente dal Sig. Cavalier Bastiano Venuti
Alfieri, Patrizio Cortonese'.

Photo: Alinari

ACKNOWLEDGEMENTS

I have many obligations to acknowledge. I should like first of all to thank my parents, Dr L. H. S. and Mrs Clark, who enabled me to study, and whose interest and help have been a constant encouragement to me in my student days and since. To my husband, Professor Christopher Brooke, I owe a double debt. He has discussed problems with me, read my manuscript, helped with checking references and correcting proofs; and has compiled the index. To thank him for doing this gives me, as a wife, an especial pleasure. He has also made it possible for me to study—sometimes by helping in the house or with the children, sometimes by standing between me and the washing up. He is not in any way responsible for the opinions expressed in this book or for the mistakes contained in it, which are my own.

I would also like to take this opportunity to record my gratitude to Professor Dom David Knowles for the kindly interest he has taken in the work for this book. He was my supervisor when I was a research student at Cambridge, and he has continued to advise and help me since. I am most grateful to him too for consenting to include my book in this series of medieval studies, of which he is editor. Finally, I would like to thank all those who have helped me, especially Dr Helen Cam, Dr Walter Ullmann, the Reverend S. A. van Dijk, O.F.M.; and all those who welcomed and helped me when I was studying in Italy in 1949, especially the late Father Livarius Oliger, the late Father Michael Bihl, and the Guardian and Librarian of the convent of S. Isidore de Urbe.

R.B.B.

LIST OF ABBREVIATIONS

Acta SS.	*Acta Sanctorum Bollandiana.*
A.F.	*Analecta Franciscana* (Quaracchi, 1885–).
A.F.H.	*Archivum Franciscanum Historicum* (Florence, 1908–).
A.L.K.G.	*Archiv für Litteratur- und Kirchengeschichte* (ed. H. Denifle and F. Ehrle, 6 vols.,[1] Berlin and Freiburg-im-Br., 1885–92).
Bonav.	*S. Bonaventurae Opera Omnia* (Quaracchi, 1882– , especially vol. VIII, 1898). References by chapter (c.) and not by volume are to the *Legenda S. Francisci* (ed. *Opera Omnia*, VIII).
1, 2 Cel.	Thomas of Celano, *Vita Prima* and *Vita Secunda S. Francisci Assisiensis* (references are to the sections in the Quaracchi editions, 1926–7).
Coll. Fr.	*Collectanea Franciscana* (British Society of Franciscan Studies, 1914–22).
Eccleston	*Fratris Thomae vulgo dicti de Eccleston Tractatus de adventu fratrum minorum in Angliam,* ed. A. G. Little (2 ed. Manchester, 1951) (references specified to '1 ed.' are to Little's first edition, Paris, 1909).
Eubel, *Epitome*	*See* Sbaralea.
Expositio	See *Firmamenta.*
Fioretti	*I Fioretti di San Francesco.*
Firmamenta	*Firmamenta trium ordinum Beatissimi Patris nostri Francisci* (Paris, 1512) (Hugh of Digne's *Expositio regulae* is referred to by the fols. of this edition, *quarta pars*: cf. below, p. 221 n. 2).
4 Masters	See under *Masters.*
F.P.	A. G. Little, *Franciscan Papers, Lists, and Documents* (Manchester, 1943).

---

[1] Vol. VII (1900) is not referred to.

24 Gen. (or *Chron. 24 Gen.*)	*Chronica XXIV generalium Ordinis Minorum* ('The chronicle of the 24 Generals'), in *A.F.* III.
Golubovich	G. Golubovich, *Biblioteca bio-bibliografica della Terra Santa e dell' Oriente Francescano* (Quaracchi, 1906–).
Gratien	P. Gratien, *Histoire de la Fondation et de l'Évolution de l'Ordre des Frères Mineurs au XIIIᵉ siècle* (Paris-Gembloux, 1928).
Intentio	*S.P. nostri Francisci Intentio regulae*, in Lemmens, I, 83 ff.
Jordan	*Chronica fratris Jordani*, ed. H. Boehmer, *Collection d'études et de documents*, VI (Paris, 1908).
Lemmens	*Documenta antiqua Franciscana*, ed. L. Lemmens, 3 parts (Quaracchi, 1901–2).
Lempp	E. Lempp, *Frère Élie de Cortone, Étude Biographique*, *Collection d'études et de documents*, III (Paris, 1901).
4 Masters	'Expositio Quatuor Magistrorum super regulam Fratrum Minorum (1241–1242)', ed. L. Oliger, *Storia e letteratura*, XXX (Rome, 1950).
M.G.H. Scr.	*Monumenta Germaniae Historica, Scriptores.*
Misc. Fr.	*Miscellanea Francescana* (Foligno, 1886–).
M.O.P.H.	*Monumenta Ordinis Fratrum Praedicatorum Historica* (Rome, 1897–).
Narb. (*Diff. Narb.; Exp. Narb.*)	The Constitutions of Narbonne, 1260 (references are to chapter and section of Father M. Bihl's edition, *A.F.H.* XXXIV (1941), 13–94, 284–358; previously edited by Ehrle in *A.L.K.G.* VI, 1–138) (*Diff. Narb.*: 'Diffinitiones capituli generalis O.F.M. Narbonensis', ed. F.-M. Delorme, *A.F.H.* III (1910), 491 ff. *Exp. Narb.*: 'Explanationes constitutionum generalium Narbonensium', ed. Delorme, *A.F.H.* XVIII (1925), 511 ff.).
Opuscules	*Opuscules de critique historique* (Paris, 1903–19) (references are by fascicule, *not* by volume).

Perugia, MS.   Perugia MS. 1046 (M. 69) (the first reference is
                to the chapter in F.-M. Delorme's analysis in
                A.F.H. xv (1922), 23–70, 278–332; the second
                to the full text by the same editor, *La 'Legenda
                antiqua S. Francisci', La France franciscaine,* II
                (Paris, 1926)).[1]

P.L.   J. P. Migne, *Patrologiae cursus completus, Series
                Latina.*

Rendiconti   *Rendiconti della Reale Accademia dei Lincei, Classe
                di Scienze morali, storiche e filologiche,* serie 5a,
                xvii (Rome, 1908).

Salimbene,   *Cronica fratris Salimbene de Adam,* ed. F. Bernini
B. and H.   (Bari, 1942, 2 vols., but with continuous pagina-
                tion) (B.); ed. O. Holder-Egger (*M.G.H. Scr.*
                xxxii, 1905–13) (H.).

Sbaralea   *Bullarium Franciscanum,* ed. J. H. Sbaralea (Rome,
                1759–).[2]

3 Soc.   *Legenda trium sociorum, Acta SS.,* October, II (ed.
                1866), 723–42 (also ed. M. Faloci-Pulignani,
                Misc. Fr. vii (1898); ed. M. da Civezza and
                T. Domenichelli (Rome, 1899)).[3]

Sp. L.   *Speculum Perfectionis,* ed. Lemmens (vol. II).

---

[1] This is the earliest MS. of the collection of stories about St Francis now
commonly known as the *Scripta Leonis.* For a concordance of the various
versions, see J. R. H. Moorman, *Sources for the Life of St Francis of Assisi* (Manchester, 1940), pp. 104–7. For these stories, I normally refer to the earliest
known version (usually MS. Perugia), the *Sp. S.,* being the most available
version, and sometimes also to *2 Cel.* They are mainly the work of brother
Leo and his associates, but the proportion of them which are Leonine, and the
accuracy of our texts, are still debatable questions.

[2] Referred to by page and number, followed by the number in C. Eubel,
Bullarii Franciscani Epitome (Quaracchi, 1908—referred to elsewhere as Eubel,
Epitome) in brackets. Roman numerals refer to the *Supplementum* to Eubel's
Epitome, where revised texts of more important bulls are printed. When one
of these is quoted, the text is Eubel's. A new series of numbers starts with
each new pontificate in Sbaralea, so the name of the Pope is given in each case
(H3=Honorius III, G9=Gregory IX, I4=Innocent IV, A4=Alexander IV,
C4=Clement IV).

[3] References are given by chapter (as in the margin of *Acta SS.* and the
other editions) and section (as in *Acta SS.* and Faloci-Pulignani), but not by the
chapters of *Acta SS.*

Sp. S.   *Speculum Perfectionis*, ed. P. Sabatier, 2 vols. (British
                        Society of Franciscan Studies, XIII, XVII, 1928–31)
                        (referred to by chapter. References specified to
                        '1898 ed.' are to Sabatier's first edition, Paris,
                        1898).

Spec. Vitae   *Speculum vitae b. Francisci et sociorum eius* (references
                        are to extracts printed in Lempp—from the
                        edition of Venice, 1504—unless specifically stated
                        to be from the edition of W. van Spoelberch
                        (Antwerp, 1620)).

Verba   *Verba S. P. Francisci*, in Lemmens, I, 100 ff.

Wadding, *Annales* L. Wadding, *Annales Minorum* (2 ed. Rome,
                        1731–).[1]

(The works of St Francis are quoted by name—*Admonitio,
Epistola, Reg. Prima, Reg. Bullata, Testament*, etc.—and number
or section from the Quaracchi edition of the *Opuscula* (2 ed. 1941).)

---

[1] This seems still the most available edition, and its paging is noted in the
margin of the third edition (Quaracchi, 1931–), whose additional notes have
sometimes been used.

THE MINISTERS GENERAL, 1209-74[1]

St Francis	1209–26 (pp. 56–7)
Peter Catanii	c. 1217–21 (pp. 76–83)
Elias	1221–7 (pp. 112, 118)
John Parenti	1227–32 (pp. 118, 143–5)
Elias	1232–9 (pp. 143–5, 161 ff.)
Albert of Pisa	1239–40 (pp. 193–4)
Haymo of Faversham	1240–4 (pp. 195, 209)
Crescentius of Jesi	1244–7 (pp. 248, 255)
John of Parma	1247–57 (pp. 255–6, 270–1)
St Bonaventure	1257–74 (pp. 270–1 and n.)

[1] For the status of the first three names on this list, see below, pp. 106–22. The references in brackets are to pages where evidence for the dates may be found.

BOOK I
BROTHER ELIAS

CHAPTER I

INTRODUCTION:
THE NARRATIVE SOURCES FOR
THE HISTORY OF ELIAS

I. FRANCISCAN HISTORY AND THE SPIRITUAL TRADITION

EVER since Sabatier published his delightful and profound biography of St Francis, the lives and fortunes of the saint and his followers have been a favourite study of historians, and both Roman Catholic and Protestant scholars have contributed in no small measure to our knowledge of them. The main sources have been critically edited; many problems connected with them have been satisfactorily elucidated; and the results of detailed investigations have been fitted together to form a general picture of the Order's development. Like all students of Franciscan origins, I owe a great debt to previous scholars who have prepared the field so thoroughly and smoothed away so many of the difficulties. But the possibilities of the subject have not been exhausted. The justification for my book is that parts of the story, especially the early part, down to 1239, are in need of considerable reinterpretation; while some of the documents, especially for the years immediately after 1239, have never been thoroughly analysed.

The starting-point of my investigations has been the career of brother Elias, which is of crucial importance for the understanding of the early history of the Order, and which has been left too much at the mercy of prejudices and preconceptions. His worldliness and his apostasy, and the conflicts that disrupted the Order not long after his death, combined to turn him into a legendary and sinister figure, removed and isolated from his true context. Within the first decades of its existence the Order had experienced a radical transformation, remarkable alike for its scope, its thoroughness, and the rapidity of its completion. What in 1210 had been but a

small group of simple men, pledged to the literal observance of
the Gospel, living in voluntary poverty, and preaching penitence
to all, had by 1239–40—still more by 1260—become a large,
efficient and powerful organisation, composed predominantly of
clerics and learned men, and governed in accordance with the
provisions of a constitution which took cognisance of the details
of daily life, and which required for its enforcement a complicated
executive and administrative machinery. The Friars Minor multiplied and prospered, but by their very success failed to preserve
the integrity of the ideal that had inspired their founder. The discrepancy between profession and practice grew glaringly apparent,
and led to division within the Order, to recriminations, to persecution. The changes and modifications, then as now, were variously
regarded as desirable, criminal, or inevitable, and many were concerned to apportion the responsibility. Those who suffered in the
struggle traced the origins of their troubles back almost to the
beginning, and blamed Elias and his like as the instigators of the
tragedy.

The troubles in the Order came to a head in the early fourteenth
century, with the climax of the bitter feud between the Spiritual
and the Conventual parties in the Order. It is not too much to
say that the attitude of the controversial writers of the fourteenth
century has been responsible for most of the difficulties that are
encountered in any attempt to assess the early troubles of the
Order, and especially the character and career of Elias. The views
of the Spiritual Franciscans on the early history of the Order were
expressed most fully and coherently in Angelo Clareno's *Chronicle
of the Seven Tribulations*, written between 1314 and *c.* 1323. The
constant theme of this book is that the troubles of the author's
own day can be traced back to the very beginnings of the Order;
and that its history has been characterised by a series of persecutions, in which leading Friars and their accomplices have tried to
purge the Order of those who wished to maintain the true spirit
of the founder. Of these persecutors, the first and greatest was
Elias, and his nefarious activities began while St Francis still lived.
'The Chronicle of the Tribulations', wrote Sabatier, 'is inspired
from beginning to end with the thought that the troubles of the

Order—not to say, the apostasy—began as early as 1219.'[1] That Clareno's work was objective history, no recent writer has maintained; nor would any modern scholar hold that the issue of Spiritual and Conventual existed, fully-fledged, in the early thirteenth century. Nevertheless, Sabatier accepted the main lines of Clareno's reconstruction, and he has been generally followed. He believed that one could trace the features of this deep conflict already in the relations of Hugolino and Elias—forbears of the Conventual leaders—with Francis and his more intimate followers, men like brother Leo, whom the Spirituals themselves claimed as (after the Saint himself) their founder, and to the reconstruction of whose works much of Sabatier's life was dedicated. If it was an anachronism to call these early groups 'Spiritual' and 'Conventual', at least they might be distinguished as the party of the ministers and the party of the *zelanti*. These were supposed to stand to their more coherent successors as Whig and Tory to Liberal and Conservative. We used to be told that the English parties of the eighteenth century bore the image, faint and rudimentary, but recognisable, of the later party system. Now we are told that the parties had no existence, in the later sense, at all.

It is the contention of this book that to interpret the early history of the Order in terms of parties or of the wickedness of Elias is a mistake. The conflicts were deep-rooted and matured slowly, and it is exceedingly difficult to lay our hands on their roots and origins. Thus it is as dangerous to accept the pattern imposed on events by Angelo Clareno as it is to deny that there were any conflicts at all. What is needed is a return to the contemporary documents, to Celano and Eccleston, and a new analysis of these independent of later events and interpretations. The result is to put Elias into his setting among the men whom he never dominated to the extent that has often been supposed, and to show that the early conflicts of the Order were more complex, more interesting and more humanly probable than they appear in the classical interpretations of these years.

[1] *Vie de S. François d'Assise* (Paris, 1894 (1893)), p. cvii. I hope to deal more at length elsewhere with the influence of Angelo Clareno on Sabatier and the modern study of Franciscan origins.

The bitterness of the Spiritual writers provoked them into exaggerating, inventing and even lying, and has infected many subsequent writers, and influenced others. Those who have not shared their feelings have been as strongly moved to protest against them. Thus the biographers have taken sides in the controversy, and have been concerned rather to condemn or to vindicate Elias than to do him justice. The strictures of Lempp have been countered by the plaudits of Attal.[1] The reaction in his favour, though it constitutes an advance, has been too extreme. It is true that Elias has been the victim of animosity and invective more than he deserved. But in their zeal to clean off the layers of mud that had become attached to his reputation some have scrubbed away stains that should rightly be there. Their good offices are as quixotic as those of the man in Aesop's fable, who thought that with enough soap, water and patience he could wash away the black from the Ethiopian's skin.

The first concern of this book has been to attempt a more historical treatment of Elias, and to reach a better understanding of his personality. Previous portraits have erred because they have been too consistent, too neat, simple and uniform to be lifelike. The problem of reconciling the sources has too often been shelved —such as do not conform to the writer's impression being rejected as worthless. The solution of this problem is essential before any advance can be made, and so the opening chapter is mainly devoted to a detailed examination of the chief contemporary sources. Interpretation of the man has been based on the results of this analysis. The assessment of Elias' character is a necessary step towards the solution of a deeper problem, that of what or who was mainly responsible for the changes and modifications that the Franciscan Order underwent. The friars were a new type of religious, and the way of life held out to them by their founder was original, difficult, and even disconcerting. The brethren did not start along traditional lines, and the direction in which they would eventually move was in the early years uncertain and unpredictable. For this reason the conscious policy of individuals or

[1] E. Lempp, *Frère Élie de Cortone* (Paris, 1901); S. Attal, *Frate Elia, Compagno di San Francesco* (Rome, 1936).

groups could exercise more influence on development than would have been possible in an established or highly organised institution. Elias, as one of the first Ministers General, was in a position to promote the policy for the Order that he favoured, but as a result of his later notoriety his actual influence has been much exaggerated. This can be appreciated even within the period, down to 1239, when he held a high place in the Order's counsels. To this end the part played by other important men, particularly Hugolino and John Parenti, has been examined in detail.

Once it is realised that responsibility for the changes in the Order must lie, not at the door of one man, nor even of a small group, but of a large number of the early friars, and also that in spite of the many conflicts there was no simple division into parties within the Order, it becomes necessary to see the first ministers in a broader context. Hence the second part of this book. The work of Albert of Pisa and Haymo of Faversham was probably as vital as that of any man in the early history of the Order save St Francis himself, and there is a sense in which Haymo's death in 1244 is far more of an epoch in the Order's history than the deposition of Elias in 1239. But 1244 cannot be taken as a closing date, owing to the nature of the documents. The crucial element in Haymo's work was that he greatly developed the structure of interpretation and of the constitutions which the first two generations of friars erected over the founder's Rule. But no copy of the Franciscan constitutions survives earlier than the great codification of 1260, the Constitutions of Narbonne. Compared with the earliest years of the Order, the period 1239–60 is badly documented; but with the aid of the codified constitutions, of other fragments of evidence, and especially of the various expositions of the Rule made at this time, it is possible to reconstruct something of the constitutional story of these years, and to see the factors of change actually at work. The year 1260 forms a natural term: the changes, in many respects, were complete; the conflicts, although already deep and ineradicable, were not those which, before the end of the thirteenth century, were to divide the Order into two warring camps. A new interest begins after 1260, and this is the justification for closing with the events of that year.

But the history of the Order so far must be viewed as a whole if it is to be understood at all. A comprehensive history of the Order in its early years has still to be written; this book is not planned on so ambitious a scale. By concentrating on the documents and the themes which seem to me to illuminate the story I wish to tell, I have tried to make clear the lines along which I think the early history of the Order and its government should be reinterpreted. This is essentially a study in how a small company of beggars was translated into a great, elaborately organised religious order—not without suffering serious loss in its ideals, but without their being altered or abridged by the conscious malice of men. Clareno and Sabatier were wrong to date the 'apostasy' to 1219; but change and the conflicts it engendered were already implicit even before that date.

2. THOMAS OF CELANO

Elias left no autobiography, and found no Boswell to impress an image of his personality. Since the art is lost that enabled some of the more enterprising of our forbears to satisfy their curiosity by interviewing the dead in person,[1] we must be content to see him, not as he saw himself, but as others saw him. This circumstance deprives us of a counterweight to the undeniable prejudice of some at least of his detractors. Lacking such, we are the more bound to investigate carefully the properties and defects of those eyes through which we must look, and to compare the images they retained; it is not dangerously misleading to wear green spectacles if we know that they are green.

In any classification of the sources the *Vita Prima S. Francisci* must rank apart and first,[2] a distinction that the date of composi-

---

[1] Cf. Salimbene, *Cronica*, ed. Bernini, p. 43, ed. Holder-Egger, p. 32. 'Et cognovit papa [Innocentius III] eo manifestante, quod nigromanticus esset, et quod Toleti studuerat, et rogavit eum, quod quendam suum amicum defunctum ei resuscitare deberet, ut cum eo haberet familiare colloquium et de statu anime sue ab eo posset inquirere....Suscitavit igitur ei Besmantie archiepiscopum sub illa pompa et vana gloria, qua solitus erat venire ad curiam.'

[2] Affò in his *Vita di Frate Elia* (Parma, 1783), pp. 9 ff., was the first to recognise that *1 Celano* afforded the best account of Elias in all that concerned St Francis' lifetime.

tion of itself would justify. It was completed and approved in February, 1229,[1] and so, though not strictly contemporary with its subject, bore witness to the events of a very recent past. Writing nearly twenty years earlier than any other relevant author,[2] and being naturally unaware of Elias' subsequent fate, the author was spared the temptation to introduce reservations and distortions from a sense of shame or indignation. It is improbable, moreover, that he had any strong motive for seeking to misrepresent one to whom, after all, he referred only incidentally in a work whose avowed purpose was 'to recount in order the life and acts of our most blessed father Francis, with pious devotion and constant adherence to truth'.

Elias is mentioned six times in the *Vita Prima*, and the indications are fortunately sufficient to reveal Celano's impression and opinion of him, and, if we may trust his testimony, St Francis' also. It would seem that the saint admired his character, took pleasure in his companionship, and, at least on occasion, was prepared to follow his advice. The two were travelling together through the diocese of Narni when Elias persuaded him to speak

[1] Note to Paris Bibl. Nat. MS. lat. 3817. Dr J. R. H. Moorman, *Sources for the life of St Francis* (Manchester, 1940), p. 67, favours a slightly later date, but the arguments he brings forward have been refuted by Father Bihl, 'Contra duas novas hypotheses prolatas a J. R. H. Moorman adversus "*Vitam I S. Francisci*" auctore Thoma Celanensi, cui substituere vellet sic dictam "*Legendam 3 Sociorum*"', *A.F.H.* xxxix (1946–8), 3 ff., esp. pp. 21 ff.

[2] The *Sacrum Commercium*, dated July 1227, contains no reference to Elias. Sabatier in his Introduction to Rawnsley's Text and Translation saw in the reproaches levelled in this work against those religious who dishonoured their profession of poverty, transparent allusions to the Minister General, his personal extravagance and his Basilica, but since there is no definite evidence that Elias found opportunity to indulge himself before 1232, and since the site on which the Basilica was to be built was not procured until March 1228, his interpretation may be dismissed as unfounded and anachronistic. He was, indeed, mistaken in regarding the allegory as a polemical manifesto emanating from the group traditionally represented by brother Leo. The Lady Poverty attacks, not lax friars, but the old monastic Orders.

Julian of Speyer's *Legenda S. Francisci*, probably completed some time between 1232 and 1235 (*Analecta Bollandiana*, xix, 337–9, xxi, 156; edited by van Ortroy, *ibid.* pp. 148 ff.) depends so closely on *1 Celano* both in style and content as to deprive itself of independent historical value. Chapters 63, 65, 67–9 substantially repeat *1 Cel.* 95–6, 98, 105, 106–10, but in a condensed and colourless form.

to a woman whom he had previously healed by the power of his prayers, and were both dwelling in Foligno when it was revealed to Elias that St Francis had but two years left to live.[1] The reality and depth of St Francis' affection for him is not to be inferred solely from such phrases as 'brother Elias, whom he had chosen to act as a mother to himself and a father to all the other brothers' and 'a brother whom the saint loved with a passing great love',[2] as deeds corroborate the words. When he was lying seriously ill at Siena, Elias' coming was sufficient to produce an immediate and marked improvement in his condition,[3] and, before he died, he blessed him with an especial blessing.

I bless you, my son, in all things and through all things; and just as the Highest has increased in your hands my brothers and sons, so also I lay my blessing on you and in you for all of them. May God the supreme king bless you in heaven and in earth. I bless you as I am able and more than I am able, and what I cannot may He who can do all things. May God be mindful of your work and your toil and may you have your due when the just are rewarded. May you find every blessing which you desire and may every righteous request be fulfilled.[4]

Elias on his side displayed a real concern for the saint's welfare. It was he who prevailed upon Francis to submit to medical treatment when the entreaties of others had failed, and later, when news reached him that Francis was likely to die, he came at once to care for him.[5] The impression left is of mutual friendship, esteem and trust, and Elias appears as St Francis' close companion almost to the exclusion of those who so proudly described themselves as 'nos, qui cum ipso fuimus'.[6] That Celano admired him

---

[1] 1 Cel. 69, 109.

[2] 1 Cel. 98, 109. That this brother should be identified with Elias seems clear from the context, which bears a close literary connection with Elias' letter to the Provincial Ministers, announcing St Francis' death.

[3] 1 Cel. 105.

[4] 1 Cel. 108. For the biblical and other echoes in this passage, cf. notes to the Quaracchi edition.   [5] 1 Cel. 98, 105.

[6] Members of this group of St Francis' intimate companions, which included brothers Leo, Bernard, Giles, Masseo, Angelo and Rufino, are occasionally referred to: cf. 1 Cel. 91, 102, 109. Their names, however, are suppressed 'ipsorum verecundiae parcens'.

in 1229 can hardly be contested: the very connotation of the words he used proclaims it. Reflecting on how few had been found worthy to know of the wound in St Francis' side while he was yet alive, he wrote: 'But happy is Elias, who was worthy to see it even while the saint lived', and another time: 'The good son did what the kind father instructed him.'[1]

Before accepting this description as deserved it is necessary to discover how far Celano's good opinion is likely to have been based on direct personal contact and observation, and how far it may have been influenced by external pressure or ulterior motives. He joined the Order *c*. 1215, shortly after St Francis' unsuccessful attempt to reach Morocco.[2] For the next six years we have no certain knowledge of his whereabouts, though he probably remained in Italy. But in any case it is unlikely that he could have been more than slightly acquainted with Elias at this period, as from 1217 to 1220 the latter was in Syria.[3] He was present at the 1221 Pentecost Chapter, at which Elias presided, and was one of those chosen to accompany Caesar of Speyer to Germany.[4] When he returned to Italy is doubtful, though it may well have been in the autumn of 1223.[5] From then, until he wrote the *Vita Prima*, he at least had opportunity to know Elias, and it is perhaps worth noting that all but one of the references to Elias come in the second part, which relates in more detail the events of the last

---

[1] *1 Cel*. 95, 105. That the choice of words in these two passages does indeed serve to reveal the attitude of mind of the writer is suggested by a comparison with Julian of Speyer's rendering of the same two passages: (i) 'solus hoc frater Helias casu utcumque prospicere meruit' (c. 63). (ii) Elias' part in bringing St Francis from Cortona to Assisi is completely passed over. '...deduci se rogavit Assisium. Quo postquam pervenit...' (c. 67).

[2] *1 Cel*. 56–7.   [3] Jordan, cc. 7, 9, 14.   [4] Jordan, cc. 17, 19.

[5] In 1223 Caesar of Speyer appointed him Custodian of Mainz, Worms, Cologne and Speyer (Jordan, c. 30), and left him as his vicar when he returned to Italy (c. 31). In September of the same year the new Provincial Minister, Albert of Pisa, created the Custodies of Franconia, Bavaria, Alsace and Saxony. These were given to brothers Mark, Angelus, James and John of Piano Carpine respectively (c. 32) and, since the Custodies of Franconia and Alsace must have included Mainz, Worms, Cologne and Speyer—the towns for which Celano had been responsible—he presumably ceased to hold office then. Jordan never mentions him again in connection with the German Province, though he met him in 1230 (c. 59).

two years of St Francis' life. Both attended the ceremony of canonisation—16 July 1228—and it was then that Celano received from Gregory IX the commission to write.

These few indications of occasional proximity provide no basis for assuming any long-standing or considerable degree of familiarity between the two men. Moreover Celano himself admits that he derived much of his information from 'faithful and approved witnesses' (Prologue). Can it be that the favourable mention of Elias is but the echo of the latter's story, uncritically repeated? Such has been the view taken by those who, unwilling to accept Celano's account as accurate and at the same time admitting his integrity, have concluded that he wrote in ignorance of the real situation.[1] On this question the evidence is insufficient to allow of a categorical answer. When collecting his material he can hardly have omitted to consult Elias, and the wording of the chapters on the saint's death suggests that he had before him Elias' letter to the Provincial Ministers announcing St Francis' death; the resemblance between the texts is too close to be fortuitous.[2] But he was far from being solely dependent on his testimony, and had ample opportunity to check his facts. It is important to remember this, particularly in connection with the blessing St Francis gave before his death. Elias has been accused of falsifying the details of this in his own interest,[3] but there seems little foundation for the charge. Had he wished to emphasise his own merits he would surely have used the letter as an occasion for propaganda, but in it he boasted neither of having been privileged to see the wound in St Francis' side, nor of having received a special blessing. Therefore we should not lightly presume that what he told Celano was a deliberate misrepresentation of the truth—the presence of other witnesses and his own moderation alike forbid it.

There remains the possibility that for some reason Celano resorted to flattery. It is said that, despite the fact that John Parenti held the office of Minister General, Elias, enjoying the favour and

---

[1] Cf. Lempp, *Frère Élie de Cortone* (Paris, 1901), p. 18; Sabatier, *Speculum Perfectionis* (Paris, 1898), p. C n. 2.

[2] Cf. *1 Cel.* 108, 113, partly incorporated in *2 Cel.* 217a, and Lempp, pp. 73 n., 217 ff.   [3] By Lempp, *loc. cit.*

active support of Gregory IX, was the one really in control.[1] Celano, it is suggested, was not a free agent, but had instructions from the Pope to praise his protégé; or, if that motive will not serve, perhaps he sought to curry favour with one in a position to procure his advancement. Either of these imputations, if correct, would seriously damage Celano's reputation. Neither, however, need be accepted. They both proceed from a mistaken estimate of the relationship then existing between the principals. For, as will be shown in a later chapter, John Parenti was actually as well as theoretically the head of the Order, and Elias' sphere of control was limited to what concerned the Basilica. The fact that Gregory IX had entrusted to the latter the task of superintending the construction[2] can scarcely be taken as a sign that he wished to substitute him for the existing General. There is, indeed, no adequate evidence supporting the supposition, put forward by Sabatier and Lempp, that the Pope either interfered or intended to interfere in the internal government of the Order at this time. Hence the conditions are lacking that might have compelled or tempted Celano to go beyond the truth as he saw it.

The description of Elias to be found in *1 Celano* may then be accepted as an expression of the author's own opinion, based on acquaintance though not on intimacy. The next question to decide is to what extent it may be considered a sound opinion or a representative one. Celano was singled out to write the Life of St Francis, and that of itself is sufficient surety for the high quality of his judgement, ability and education. Moreover, his statements were not irresponsible; they formed part of a book which was officially authorised by the Pope and which was intended as a standard text for a public wider than the Order. Whether his opinions can be taken as representative is more debatable; the description of the Seraph is unlikely to have been the only point brother Leo found to criticise in the *Vita Prima*.[3] Yet whatever he

---

[1] Cf. Lempp, pp. 77–8; Moorman, *op. cit.* p. 64; Sabatier, *Vie de S. François d'Assise* (Paris, 1894), pp. L, LIV.

[2] Cf. Lempp, pp. 170–1, *Instruments*. On 29 March 1228 the site for the Basilica was handed over to Elias 'recipienti pro domino Gregorio papa IX'.

[3] Cf. Eccleston, p. 75.

and his friends may have thought, it can at least be shown that Celano's admiration for Elias was not singular or surprising— St Clare and her sister Agnes were among those who shared it. In a letter to the blessed Agnes of Bohemia, St Clare included an exhortation to her to follow the counsels of brother Elias, and to prize them above every other gift.[1] Her sister, when she had been sent as abbess to the convent at Florence, wrote to Clare, grieving at their separation, and desiring the consolation of frequent visits from Elias.[2] Their words are a striking proof of trust, and strengthen the probability that, as Celano said, Elias was indeed beloved of St Francis. Nor is theirs the only unsolicited, independent and contemporary testimony that may be cited in confirmation of his rendering of fact and character. According to Eccleston's account Gregory IX confirmed Elias' appointment as Minister General 'especially because of his intimacy with St Francis' and he called to mind this same intimacy when he was later required to absolve him from that office.[3] A further, rather unexpected, reference occurs in a book *Adversus Albigensium errores* written between 1232 and 1239 by Luke, canon of Leon and later bishop of Tuy. Among the many stories he related concerning the punishments, natural and supernatural, that had been inflicted upon heretics, he included two which he had learnt from 'that most holy brother Elias, St Francis' successor'.[4]

---

[1] *Acta SS*. March, I, 506.
[2] *A.F.* III, 177: 'Precor, ut rogetis fratrem Heliam, quod debeat me visitare saepe saepius et in Domino consolari.'
[3] Eccleston, pp. 67–8.
[4] Lucas Tudensis, *Adversus Albigensium errores* (Ingolstadt, 1612), lib. III, cc. xiv–xv: 'viro sanctissimo fratre Helia successore beatissimi patris Francisci'. Favourable mention of Elias occurs only in books and letters written before his deposition, with rare exceptions. Blessed Agnes of Bohemia joined the Poor Ladies in 1234 and St Clare's letter to her was probably written soon after. It was in any case earlier than 1239 as Elias is spoken of as Minister General. The letter from St Clare's sister, also Agnes, was clearly written some time after the foundation of the convent at Florence, as she expected trouble from the nuns on her arrival there, and was probably written after Gregory IX had allowed the convent the privilege of absolute poverty, in May 1230. The date of Luke of Tuy's book is not entirely clear. Its original editor seems to have used a MS. which combined it with Luke's work on the miracles of St Isidore (cf. his preface, ff. B IV ff.), and the implication of Luke's prologue is that the

But by the time Celano composed the *Vita Secunda S. Francisci*, *c.* 1246, Elias had forfeited this esteem. No longer considered worthy to rank among the saint's companions, he is seldom mentioned, and never by name. Such references to him as there are, instead of being friendly and open, are guarded, cold and evasive. While it is tacitly admitted that he received a special blessing, the significance of this is as far as possible minimised; and, whereas before he had been accounted fortunate to have seen the wound in St Francis' side, he is now allowed merely to have been successfully inquisitive—the connotation of the words is hostile.[1] Furthermore, the catalogue of the qualities desirable in a Minister General, put into the mouth of St Francis, conveys the impression of being, at least in part, a veiled criticism of his generalate.[2] The change amounts to an implicit recantation. How does it affect the value of Celano's evidence?

In Lempp's opinion he stood self-condemned for committing such an offence against consistency.[3] Italian scholars deny the validity of this judgement on the ground that there was reason for the change. In 1229, when *1 Celano* was completed, Elias' good name was still untouched by scandal or reproach; in 1244–5, when the material for *2 Celano* was being collected, he had, by his arrogance, impenitence and continued adherence to Frederick II,

---

Adversus Albigenses was written at the same time or soon after the miracles. This raises the presumption that the *Adversus Albigenses*, like the miracles, was written before he left Leon for Tuy in 1239. It was certainly written after 1232, since it refers to the death of a bishop of Leon in that year (lib. III, c. ix). Luke died between 1249 and 1254 (on him see *Dict. de théologie catholique*, IX, 1001–2). The book was thus probably written during Elias' generalate.

The *Legenda Neapolitana* is the chief exception to the general hostility after 1239. For a detailed discussion of its date and attitude, see below, p. 19 and n. 1.

[1] *2 Cel.* 156, 216; 138.

[2] *2 Cel.* 185–6. Cf. Moorman, *op. cit.* pp. 126–7; N. Tamassia, *St Francis of Assisi and his Legend*, trans. Lonsdale Ragg (London, 1910), p. 154 and n. 4. The description lacks the simplicity and vivid metaphor characteristic of the genuine 'verba S. Francisci'. It expresses the ideal, not of a dying saint looking to the future, but of a learned brother sensible of the lessons of the past. An analysis of its composition reveals numerous quotations from Scripture and echoes of St Gregory the Great, interspersed with allusions to Elias' misconduct. Cf. *Moralia in librum Job*, XIX, c. 28, no. 30; XX, c. 29, no. 14; XXIV, c. 34, nos. 54–5 (cited, with other references, by Tamassia, *loc. cit.*).

[3] Lempp, p. 16 n. 4.

brought upon himself a renewed excommunication, and had also been deprived of the habit of his religion. Thus the fact that admiration gave place to disapproval, far from being a proof of insincerity, should be regarded as itself an indication of Celano's essential honesty.[1] Both views require modification.

The circumstances and notoriety of Elias' disgrace may confidently be accepted as the cause underlying the withdrawal of Celano's good opinion, and afford a convincing motive for his reticence. Ashamed of him, and wishing the scandal to be forgotten, he sought to efface his memory, speaking only of 'a certain brother' or 'the saint's vicar' on the few occasions he felt it necessary to refer to him at all.[2] For the same reason he forbore to give direct public expression to his indignation, though he did not conceal it entirely—the redaction preserved in the Assisi MS. contains one outburst clearly directed against the deposed and excommunicated Minister whom St Francis had blessed.[3]

But though Celano's attitude c. 1246 is understandable in the light of Elias' contumacy, to admit this does not necessitate the further admission that his evidence is therefore reliable throughout. It is explained but not authenticated. However sufficient the provocation, the fact remains that the revised presentation of Elias is misleading. It is not merely that the tone is different; some of the facts are affected. The omission of all mention of his friendship for and care of St Francis, though hardly a grave defect in a work that only very occasionally concerned him, is none the

---

[1] Cf. D. Sparacio in *Misc. Fr.* xvii (1916), 10; S. Attal in *Misc. Fr.* xxxiii (1933), 315.

[2] 2 *Cel.* 138, 216. His reaction is likely to have been representative of that of most of the respectable, educated brothers. His example was followed by St Bonaventure (*Leg. S. Francisci*, c. 13).

[3] 2 *Cel.* 156. 'Ubi sunt qui sua benedictione felices se praedicant, et familiaritate ipsius se jactant pro velle potitos? Si, quod absit, inventi fuerint absque poenitudine in aliorum periculo in se monstrasse opera tenebrarum, vae illis, vae damnationis aeternae.'
Only two quasi-complete manuscript versions of the *Vita Secunda* have survived. They are not identical, each containing several passages not found in the other. The one here quoted is not in the Marseilles MS.; in the Assisi MS. it forms part of the text. Both MSS. date from the fourteenth century. For a detailed discussion of their differences and relationship see M. Bihl in *A.F.H.* xx (1927), 433 ff.

less an imperfection, if for no other reason than that it lessens the completeness of the portrait of the saint himself. More serious is the inaccuracy of his description of the blessing St Francis gave the brothers before he died, which both over-simplifies and confuses. In this one instance Celano has given us two accounts of the same ceremony that cannot both be correct. Are both thereby rendered suspect?

According to the *Vita Prima*[1] the dying St Francis blessed his brethren twice, on different days and in different places. While he was still in the Bishop's Palace at Assisi he called many of the brothers to him and in their presence blessed Elias particularly and affectionately, ending with a warning to all of future tribulation. Soon afterwards he was moved to the Portiuncula, and here, on the day of his death, Elias obtained from him a blessing and a pardon for all the brothers, absent as well as present. This blessing the saint did not, perhaps was not able to proclaim himself; he asked for a passage from St John's Gospel to be read aloud to him, and shortly afterwards died. According to the *Vita Secunda*,[2] however, there was only one blessing. It is not explicitly stated where this was given, but it would appear from the context to have been at the Portiuncula.[3] St Francis summoned all the brothers who at that moment were in the place, and addressed to them words of comfort and exhortation. Then he laid his right hand upon the head of each in turn, beginning with his vicar, and, having warned them all of future tribulation, blessed in those present those who were absent and those who should later join the Order. This done, he blessed bread in remembrance of the Lord and distributed it among them. Finally he asked for a passage from St John's Gospel to be read aloud to him. The few remaining days of his life he spent in praise.

Were it not that this later version contains the remark that the author had already elsewhere indicated the special significance of this blessing, it would be tempting to regard it as an additional

---

[1] *1 Cel.* 108–10.   [2] *2 Cel.* 216–17.

[3] The narrative comes quickly and smoothly to his death, which took place at the Portiuncula (*1 Cel.* 108–10), without any suggestion that he was moved during his last days.

one not hitherto described—it does not correspond to either of those in *1 Celano*, though it has affinities with both. When analysed it proves to be in the main a précis of the earlier account, but a précis in which, either by inadvertence or design, the details have been shaken together and some selected to make a new pattern, just as a woman may cut up two garments and use pieces from both to make one new one. The words of the warning concerning tribulation to come are taken, with only very slight alterations, direct from *1 Celano*, 108. The same paragraph supplies the general lines of the story: the initiative comes from St Francis, who, some days before his death, calls the brethren round him and blesses them with words and with his hands. *1 Celano*, 109–10 contributes the extension of the blessing to the absent, the implication that the place was the Portiuncula, and the fact that a certain passage from St John's Gospel was read afterwards. The opening words of this passage,[1] misquoted in the *Vita Prima*, are given correctly in *2 Celano*. These pieces of old material are joined together with some new threads. The blessing of the bread may well be a detail previously unknown to the author; the sermon and the laying of the right hand upon each brother are almost certainly 'improvements'. The last in particular is a highly improbable embellishment—it would not be easy for a blind man to touch a number of brothers sitting round him, still less so to touch them in order, beginning with his vicar. Among the material discarded is the special blessing given to Elias. It is possible that Celano had forgotten the exact details of incidents that had happened twenty years before, and was unaware that he had changed them; it is more probable that he muddled them on purpose, with the object of making Elias inconspicuous without too obviously contradicting himself.

2 Celano in this instance is thus discredited, but the manner of its exposure leaves *1 Celano* undamaged. The earlier account was written in conditions markedly favourable to accuracy, when the author had many independent informants, and no motive for misrepresentation. For the blessing in the Bishop's Palace he may have had a written source. The *Legenda Neapolitana*, though prob-

---

[1] John xiii. 1: 'Ante diem festum Paschae.'

ably not compiled till some time between 1253 and 1255, made use of a manuscript closely resembling *1 Celano*, but with variations and additions that suggest an earlier recension.[1] For the other blessing he had the authority of Elias' letter to the Provincial Ministers, written probably little more than a day after the events it describes.

The contrast between the two accounts of the blessings is a good illustration of the truth of Lempp's words: 'il faut bien que dans l'une ou l'autre des deux vies il ait quelque peu défiguré la verité'. But his further conclusion—that this automatically blackens completely Celano's reputation as an author—is not justified. The alterations and omissions inspired by shame and indignation should

---

[1] Bihl, *A.F.H.* xxi, 245: 'Tibi, inquid, fili in omnibus et per omnia benedico, *qui humeris propriis honera mea suscipiens, fratrum necessitates viriliter supportasti, et sicut in manibus tuis....*' Thus for the blessing it is slightly fuller. It also mentions by name the two brothers, Angelo and Leo, who sang the Praises of the Creatures to St Francis on the day he died. Celano, in accordance with his usual practice, rendered them anonymous.

The question when the *Legenda Neapolitana* was composed has been discussed by M. Bihl, *art. cit.* pp. 240–68, and by G. Abate, *La Leggenda Napolitana di S. Francesco e l'Ufficio rimato di Giuliano da Spira secondo un codice umbro* (Assisi, 1930). Father Bihl considers that it was written after 1253, since it quotes a miracle first recorded in the *Tractatus de Miraculis*, compiled 1250–3, and before 1266, when the use of the old Legends was proscribed by General Chapter. Abate notes that the Clares are in one place referred to as living in S. Damiano, and since in 1260 they were transferred to S. Chiara inside Assisi, it must have been written before that date. He inclines to the view that it was written much earlier, between 1230 and 1239, because it mentions Elias favourably, but this dating cannot be reconciled with the use made of the *Tractatus de Miraculis*, not then in existence. Moreover one sentence referring to St Clare suggests to me the possibility of fixing the date within narrow limits. It reads: 'Ecce domina Clara, que vere meritorum sanctitate clara erat' (Lectio 9, Bihl; Lectio 3, Abate). The past tense 'erat' implies that she is no longer alive, the title 'domina' that she was not as yet canonised. In that case it was written after 11 August 1253, the day of her death, and before 26 September 1255, the day of her canonisation. This hypothesis conflicts with none of the other evidence. The manuscript in the Bibl. Nat. of Naples was written by several hands, all mid-thirteenth century and certainly not later (Bihl, *art. cit.* pp. 241, 263). What then about the tone used towards Elias, who is usually regarded as having been universally condemned after 1239? On this point Father Bihl's remarks afford a probable solution. Elias died penitent and absolved on 22 April 1253, and there may well have been a temporary reaction in his favour within the Order. The compiler can hardly have copied down from one of his sources passages well-disposed towards Elias without thinking of later developments.

not be allowed to discredit his earlier statements. As they concern Elias the two lives are of wholly disproportionate value; the first of great worth and significance, the second almost worthless. The only positive contribution of the latter, apart from the details of how Elias contrived to see the wound in St Francis' side,[1] is its reflection of the attitude of the brothers towards him *c.* 1246, and even here the presentation is not straightforward. The hostility of that time, instead of being related to the circumstances that caused it, is antedated to the period before 1230, and linked to events with which it has no true connection. The transposition has caused much misunderstanding and confusion, though it was very natural. For in conveying his new opinion Celano was hampered by his reticence and by the scope of his subject. The facts of Elias' later career were obviously outside the limits of a book devoted to the deeds and sayings of a saint, which ended suitably with his canonisation. A knowledge of them had therefore to be presumed in the reader. They are nowhere explicitly referred to, and though there are allusions, these can only be understood in the light of information gained from other sources.[2] As a result, the feelings provoked by these facts, since they were not considered equally irrelevant, and since they were denied a proper outlet, were diverted to such of Elias' activities as were available. Thus in the *Vita Secunda* a genuine, contemporary mistrust received an anachronistic setting, and fastened on to conduct which did not deserve censure. It is the first slight indication of a tendency to blame Elias indiscriminately in all he did, a tendency which soon became pronounced and vindictive.

3. JORDAN OF GIANO

At Halberstadt in May 1262, brother Jordan of Giano dictated to brother Baldwin of Brunswick an account of the establishment and growth of the Franciscan province in Germany.[3] On this subject he was well qualified to speak, for from its very founda-

[1] *2 Cel.* 138, cf. *1 Cel.* 95.
[2] For instance, *2 Cel.* 156, which is illuminated by the account in Eccleston, c. XIII, of Elias' deposition and subsequent excommunication.
[3] Prologue.

tion he had himself shared in and helped to determine its history. He had been among those chosen to accompany Caesar of Speyer, Minister of an as yet non-existent province, and had set out, in September 1221, fully expecting to suffer martyrdom—an earlier expedition had been a total failure, and the brothers who had taken part in it had returned with many tales to tell of the rough treatment they had received at the hands of the Germans.[1] He and his companions, however, were more fortunate, and Jordan spent the rest of a long life helping to spread and consolidate the influence of his Order in Central Europe. Almost from the first he held positions of responsibility—he was guardian of Speyer in 1223, of Mainz in 1224, custodian of Thuringia from 1225,[2] vicar-provincial of Bohemia–Poland in 1241,[3] and of Saxony in 1242.[4]

His chronicle begins with the year 1207 and ends in 1262, but between these two dates the subject-matter is very unequally spaced and presented. Attention is concentrated on happenings between 1219 and 1239, the years 1207–19 being dismissed in a few lines, 1240–62 in a few pages. The narrative, which at times is brief and perfunctory, is at other times vivid, detailed and alive. What determines the degree of prominence allotted to the various events is not their historical importance, but the extent of Jordan's own knowledge of and interest in them. Thus matters of provincial and even of strictly local significance take precedence over the affairs of the Order as a whole: except when these have some special bearing on the province, or on Jordan's career, they receive only the short notice of an annalist.[5]

Securely based upon his personal experience, Jordan's chronicle, while lacking an objective standard of proportion, possesses the

[1] Cc. 17–20, 5.   [2] Cc. 32, 38, 47.

[3] The writer of two letters describing the devastation caused by the Tartars, preserved by Matthew Paris, Chronica maiora, VI, 80–1, 83–4, may reasonably be identified with Jordan of Giano (cf. H. Boehmer, Chronica Fratris Jordani, Introd. pp. lxi–lxiii).

[4] C. 71.

[5] For instance, the account of the 1227 General Chapter is given solely from a provincial angle (cc. 51–2). Among many brief notices of general import may be cited: Honorius III's confirmation of the Rule (c. 29), the reorganisation of the provincial administration in 1239 (c. 67), and the succession of Ministers General (cc. 51, 61, 66, 70, 73, 76, 77).

great merits of originality and reliability. To written sources he owes practically nothing. The lives of St Francis by Thomas of Celano and Julian of Speyer were known to him,[1] but these seldom touched his chosen field. His source *par excellence* was his memory, and this, as Little has pointed out, was remarkably fresh and accurate, particularly for the period in his middle life when his own part in important affairs had not been insignificant.[2] Indeed the earlier years remained for him more clearly than the recent past, and he might appropriate the words that Dante gave to Farinata degli Uberti:

> Noi veggiam, come quei che ha mala luce,
> le cose, disse, che ne son lontano.

Furthermore his recollections had not been allowed to rust: they had been kept bright by constant retelling to eager listeners, by whom he was with reason regarded as an authority.[3] Only in the matter of exact dates had he become, at times, uncertain, and he apologises for such errors in the Prologue. These are few in number, and of no serious consequence.[4]

The years he remembered best coincided almost exactly with Elias' period of power, and the latter's activities were too relevant to be passed over. He had decisively influenced Jordan's career when Jordan hesitated to accept his destiny,[5] and his interference in the German province had proved disastrous. There he provoked first indignation, and then active opposition, in which Jordan himself took a leading part. Consequently the actions of the General and the process by which his deposition was effected are given in some detail.[6] Nothing is said, however, of his personality or characteristics. Jordan did not choose to fill in the features, though this was not through any lack of competence to paint word pic-

---

[1] Cc. 19, 53.

[2] A. G. Little, 'Chronicles of the Mendicant Friars', in *F.P.* pp. 28–9.

[3] Prologue. The request that he would have his reminiscences written down was actively supported by the Provincial Minister.

[4] The dates he gives for the depositions of Crescentius of Jesi (c. 76), and John of Parma (c. 77), are one year out. His dating of the first ultramontane missions has provoked considerable discussion among scholars (cf. Boehmer, *op. cit.* Introd. pp. lxxi–lxxx, Callebaut, *A.F.H.* XIX, 530 ff.).

[5] C. 18.   [6] Cc. 61–6.

tures, or deficiency in observation or humour. His sketches of Nicholas the Humble and John of Piano Carpine[1] are lifelike and delightful, but not one of the Ministers General (and he mentions them all) is honoured with a single adjective. His references to them are analogous to those recording the accessions of popes, emperors and kings in other thirteenth-century chronicles, and we must stifle the wish that he had said more, since it is a condition of his worth that he enlarges only upon what he knows well. His knowledge of Elias as a man was slight—only on one occasion is it certain that they spoke to each other[2]—and his interest in him was confined to the one aspect that affected him, to Elias as an official. Nevertheless, from the facts he mentions it is possible to glean some fragments of an impression. He clearly attached considerable importance to Elias, for he refers to the part he played in the Order before as well as after he became General, and remembers the occasion of his appointment as Provincial Minister of Syria, though uncertain of what else was accomplished at that Chapter.[3] He implies, also, that St Francis had a high opinion of him, thus confirming the testimony of Celano. Not only did the saint put him in charge of the Syrian province, and choose him as one of the companions he needed when returning from the Holy Land to deal with troubles in Italy; he made him his spokesman at the General Chapter of 1221, sitting at his feet and pulling at his tunic when he wished to draw his attention to anything.[4] So closely were the two associated in Jordan's mind that in another passage he said: 'brother Caesar of Speyer came to blessed Francis or to brother Elias and was kindly received by him'.[5] Finally it transpires that Elias was a gifted preacher, for, while he was in Syria, he persuaded the learned and saintly Caesar of Speyer to join the Order.[6]

Is it necessary to make any reservations before accepting Jordan's evidence? We have it from his own mouth that he was foremost in complaining of Elias to the Pope, on behalf of the Saxon province.[7] Was he, then, too hostile to be just? Lempp took the view that he was bitterly opposed to Elias, not on any grounds of

---

[1] Cc. 47, 49, 55.   [2] C. 18.   [3] C. 7.   [4] Cc. 9, 14, 17.
[5] C. 31.   [6] C. 9.   [7] C. 63.

principle—because both really belonged to the same 'party'—but because he was the friend of Caesar of Speyer, cruelly clubbed to death by Elias' gaoler. But he saw no cause to distrust Jordan's statements on that account.[1] He was, however, entirely mistaken as to the nature and intensity of Jordan's attitude. The latter's tone when he speaks of Elias betrays no personal animosity—he hints at nothing discreditable in the way he came to power, makes no allusion to his extravagant living, and, though he wrote after his death and must have known of his disgrace, is silent on that subject also. And actually he had no reason to be bitter. The story of Caesar's death does not rest on good authority, and even if true, there are indications that he died after Elias' deposition, so Elias can hardly be held responsible for his death.[2] Jordan's opposition was provoked not by any concealed cause but by the grievances he enumerates: the financial exactions to complete the Basilica, the suspension of regular meetings of General Chapter, the scattering of his opponents, and the introduction of inordinate visitations.[3] In other words, it was founded not on dislike of the man, but on disapproval of his policy, which he regarded as harmful to the interests of the Order. Therefore, in order to estimate his value as a critic, his conception of the life and duties of a friar minor must now be considered, and fortunately his chronicle contains ample material from which to determine it.

Until 1231, when, on his return from Italy, he was given an enthusiastic welcome, which he attributed to the relics of the saint he carried with him, Jordan had not held St Francis in any especial veneration.[4] He had joined the Order as a way of life, not through personal admiration for its founder, and possessed a full share of the simplicity and joyfulness that characterised the early brethren who

[1] Lempp, pp. 20–3.

[2] Cf. L. Wadding, *Annales Minorum*, III, 21, no. 5. The conclusion was drawn by A. M. Azzoguidi, *S. Antonii Sermones in Psalmos* (Bologna, 1757), I, pp. cxvi–cxviii, who is referred to by D. Sparacio in *Misc. Fr.* XVII (1916), 4 n. 4. Cf. below, pp. 157–8 and n.

Incidentally Lempp is also wrong when he says that Jordan received information from Caesar concerning the early years of the Order (*loc. cit.*). Jordan was the first to join, being received by St Francis *c.* 1217 (Boehmer, *op. cit.* Introd. p. lviii; Glassberger, *A.F.* II, 54).

[3] Cc. 61–2.   [4] C. 59.

had a real vocation. Some of the stories that he tells about himself might pass unchallenged in a Life of brother Juniper. For instance, the Provincial Minister, Caesar of Speyer, held a Chapter at Worms in 1222, to which Jordan and the other friars at Salzburg did not go. So Caesar sent them a message that they were to come to see him if they wished. This permission so perturbed them, since they had no wishes of their own and desired to do nothing but what he willed, that they set out straightway to ask him what he meant.[1] On another occasion, when Jordan was charged with an appeal to which Gregory IX was unwilling to listen, instead of retiring as ordered, he ran gaily up to the Pope's bed, seized his foot, kissed it, and exclaimed: 'We have no such relics in Saxony', and thus secured a hearing.[2] His sense of humour triumphed over hardships as well as difficulties. When his begging met with the answer 'God berad' and no food was forthcoming, he thought, and even said aloud: 'this same *god berad* will be the death of us today!' Then, pretending to misunderstand the German reply, he succeeded in obtaining necessaries.[3] The privations of the early days had, indeed, been acute, and he still remembered, after the lapse of forty-one years, that on their journey across the Alps he and his companions had become so faint with hunger that they plucked berries from the hedgerow, but because it was a Friday they had feared to break their fast and had carried them untasted.[4] According to Glassberger, who may have got his information from Baldwin, Jordan's secretary, he set a high value upon obedience.[5] Poverty and simplicity, also, he upheld; in 1225 a deserted church at Erfurt, which had belonged to Augustinian nuns, was handed over to the Friars Minor, and Jordan was asked if they would like a cloister built. 'I do not know what a cloister may be,' he replied, 'only build a house for us near the water so that we may go down from it conveniently to wash our feet.'[6] He described himself as 'minus sapiens' and knew that his style was unpolished and his vocabulary colloquial. Yet he admired those who were learned, and spoke with pride and pleasure of the well-

[1] C. 27.
[2] C. 63.
[3] C. 27; cf. Boehmer, Introd. pp. lxv–lxvi.
[4] C. 21.
[5] *A.F.* II, 54.
[6] C. 43.

educated men who were sent to Germany from time to time.[1] But, while he valued and practised the virtues dear to St Francis, he disliked and distrusted any tendency towards exaggeration or singularity. He found the great humility of brother Nicholas of Montefeltro so trying that he could scarcely bear to be with him,[2] and he held it admirable in Gotfrid, Provincial Minister of Saxony, that he 'loved fellowship and put down singularities'.[3] It is presumably because of this last that he has been called a member of the 'conventual party' and denied a place among the 'true followers' of St Francis.[4] The label is undeserved; the saint himself never encouraged singularity, and examples of the dangers he saw in it could be multiplied from Celano's *Vita Secunda*.[5] He had, it is true, been unwilling to punish offenders himself, but the insufficiently regulated admission of postulants soon rendered strict discipline essential if the Order was to retain its good name.

Jordan had the cause of his Order very much at heart, but he was not prepared to further it by any methods. The friars who established a large and flourishing province in Germany succeeded by their good example and by living according to their Rule, as his chronicle clearly shows. He did not fail to notice that the people were more moved by visible proofs of holiness than by signs of worldly prosperity and power—they had felt more reverence for John of Piano Carpine's ass than they now felt for the persons of the Ministers.[6] His belief that Elias' policy was unwise and harmful was widely shared. Marquardus the Short contracted a serious illness as a result of his labours to overthrow Elias, and became unable to sustain the rigours of the Rule. Nevertheless the brothers of Saxony elected him as their Minister.[7] Even Gregory IX, in spite of his desire to shield Elias, admitted, when he had heard Jordan, that he had been right to appeal.[8]

[1] Prologue, and for instance c. 32.
[2] C. 47. Jordan called him Nicholas of the Rhine, but Boehmer is almost certainly right in identifying him with the Nicholas of Montefeltro, whom Salimbene described as being humble above all the men he knew (Boehmer, p. 41 n. 1).
[3] C. 72.   [4] Cf. Lempp, pp. 22–3; Boehmer, Introd. p. lxv.
[5] Cf. *2 Cel.* 14, 28, 29 (...*contra singularitatem*), 32–3, 34.
[6] C. 55.   [7] C. 68.   [8] C. 63.

Jordan is, so to say, a witness for the prosecution; but an honest, sensible and unembittered witness. His evidence carries great weight, as it represents the opinion of a true friar minor, respected and responsible in his province, whose opposition was neither petty nor ill-founded. He took no account of alleged personal misdemeanours, of which he had no first-hand knowledge, and confined his criticisms to Elias' conduct in his public, official capacity. Since he experienced this, and himself took an interest in the development and government of the Order, he was as well qualified as anyone to judge of it.

4. THOMAS OF ECCLESTON

The *Tractatus de Adventu Fratrum Minorum ad Angliam et dilatione et multiplicatione ipsorum in ea* was written by brother Thomas of Eccleston for the edification and instruction of the English brothers of his Order. For twenty-six years he had taken pleasure in noting down facts and stories connected with their history, and his chronicle, completed probably in 1258, tells of their life, teaching, progress and organisation from the time of their first landing at Dover, in September 1224, until that year.[1] His aim and his scope were thus very similar to those of Jordan of Giano; he covered almost exactly the same period, and dealt with the same subject— the foundation and development of a Franciscan province. His treatment of the theme, however, was different. He attached little importance to dates, and chose to group his material into chapters concerned with particular topics, instead of presenting it in strict chronological sequence. The internal affairs of the English province, and the fortunes of certain English friars, occupy fourteen of these chapters, but one, the thirteenth, is allowed a wider field, and treats of the Order as a whole in the persons of the Ministers General. Something is said of each of these, from Elias to John of Parma, but of them all, Elias excited the greatest interest and received the most attention. The events leading up to his return to office, and the measures taken later to depose him, are related

---

[1] Cf. A. G. Little, *De Adventu Fratrum Minorum in Angliam* (Manchester, 1951), p. xxii.

in considerable detail; his behaviour during and after his generalate is also noted, though more briefly. Occasionally, too, in other parts of the chronicle his policy or his fall seem relevant, and provoke comment.[1]

Eccleston's testimony, in so far as it concerns purely provincial matters, is exceedingly reliable. Wherever his facts can be checked by other documents, the test has proved him accurate and well-informed.[2] But the same worth has not been conceded to his account of the general history of the Order, which has, by contrast, been widely rejected. Here he could not speak at first hand, for there is no evidence to suggest that he ever left England, and he had to rely upon information supplied by others. Because of this he is dismissed by Italian scholars as a writer too far removed from the scenes he recorded to know aught of them, and who therefore repeated, uncritically though in good faith, the inaccurate and prejudiced reports of Elias' opponents, who were mostly Englishmen.[3] The German biographer, Dr Lempp, considered his account of Elias both confused and improbable, and preferred that given in the *Speculum Vitae*, on the ground that both derived from a common source, which the later compiler followed more faithfully.[4] Even the English Dr Little at one time inclined to this view, though he condemned the *Speculum Vitae* equally with Eccleston. In the introduction to his first edition of Eccleston[5] he wrote: 'On the general history of the Order he is less well informed. What he says of Elias is confused: he mixes up the

---

[1] Cf. Eccleston, pp. 29, 30, 38–40, 41–3, 49.

[2] *Ibid.* pp. xxiv–xxv.

[3] S. Attal, *Frate Elia, Compagno di S. Francesco* (Rome, 1936), p. 16. 'Ma egli stesso non è un testimone oculare e visse lontano dagli avvenimenti. Ripete delle narrazioni udite, spesso deformate dalla lontananza e dalle passioni.... Il suo racconto è però deturpato da sì gravi anacronismi da togliergli ogni valore storico nei riguardi di frate Elia.' In *Misc. Fr.* XXXVI (1936), 515 ff., replying to a review of his book by Father Cuthbert in *Collectanea Franciscana*, he repeats his rejection in stronger terms, speaking of Eccleston's 'fantasiosa narrazione del Capitolo del 1239' and describing his evidence as 'dei pettegolezzi insulsi, deformati dalla lontananza, di una grettezza pietosa, ben lontani dalla grandezza degli avvenimenti'. Among others may be cited Ing. L. Mirri, in *Misc. Fr.* XXXI (1931), 234–5.

[4] Lempp, pp. 21, 24–33, 96–100.

[5] *Collection d'études et de documents*, VII (Paris, 1909), p. xxiv.

events of 1230, 1232 and 1239. Here he was doubtless drawing on a lost source which was also used by the *Speculum Vitae* and the *Chron. XXIV Generalium*. For clarity and chronological exactitude there is nothing to choose between these three documents.' Later he so far modified his judgement as to say that although Eccleston's account of the troubles of 1230–9 sounds improbable it is nevertheless the most informed and least distorted of the three.[1]

Before examining the charges of remoteness, confusion and English prejudice it would perhaps be best to establish, as far as possible, the nature of the literary connection between Eccleston, the *Chronicle of the 24 Generals* and the *Speculum Vitae* for the period 1227–40. That there is such a connection is clearly demonstrated by a comparison of the texts. Very nearly half the words contained in the *24 Generals'* account occur also in that of the *Speculum Vitae*, and their similarity is really greater even than this implies, as there are also numerous synonyms and interchangeable phrases. The link with Eccleston is less striking, but none the less real—154 of the words in his account are used in one or both of the other versions. The *Speculum Vitae* is slightly closer to him than is the *24 Generals*, having 138 as against 109 words in common. The basic question is whether all three were derived from a common source, or whether Eccleston was ultimately the source of the other two. If there was a common source behind them, as Lempp and Little supposed, it was much better copied by the *24 Generals* and the *Speculum Vitae* than by Eccleston. The two former agree very closely in their choice of words and in their facts, and in both the manner of the presentation indicates that they were based upon a written source; whereas Eccleston, besides showing considerable verbal independence, gives at times a quite different rendering of the course of events. If he used the same written source he treated it cavalierly. The whole impression of his account, however, is that it was an original composition and not a copy, certainly not a bad copy. Perhaps, then, there was no lost source behind Eccleston; in which case the *24 Generals* and the *Speculum Vitae* depend in some way upon him, and not on an earlier docu-

---

[1] A. G. Little, 'Chronicles of the Mendicant Friars', *F.P.* p. 27; and *De Adventu*, pp. xxv–xxvi.

ment. This conclusion is confirmed by a detailed study of their respective accounts.

In form the three are distinct, but comparable. The translation, Elias' reappointment, deposition and excommunication appear in Eccleston not as separate stories, but as incidents in a continuous narrative. The *Speculum Vitae* likewise gives a narrative presentation incorporating the same themes, but here they are not smoothly joined, and their details have become mingled and sadly confused. In the *24 Generals* the four are kept apart and fitted into the framework of a much larger compilation. This last, though it may be earlier in date, represents a later stage in development than the *Speculum Vitae*, which, first published in 1504, was put together some time in the first half of the fourteenth century.[1] The relevant chapters in the *24 Generals* were written in the mid-fourteenth century, certainly before 1369.[2] The writer, identified by Wadding with Arnold of Sarano,[3] definitely made use of a confused narrative source, for, after transcribing its account of Elias' deposition in a slightly condensed and digested form, he pauses to point out its incompatibility with known facts, such as the date of St Anthony's death, and himself attempts a solution of some of the difficulties involved.[4] It is possible that he actually had before him the *Speculum Vitae*, since this work cannot be precisely dated, but there are some grounds for supposing it more probable that he worked from an earlier version, of which the *Speculum Vitae* is a very close, though not absolute copy. For instance, Arnold's source may have been a little less disjointed: the *Speculum Vitae* ends a description of a chapter meeting, explicitly dated to 1230, with a sentence beginning: 'Isti vero duo fratres, videlicet sanctus Antonius et frater Adam...' regardless of the fact that brother Adam has not previously been mentioned. The *24 Generals* introduces him properly and calls him Adam Marsh, so that it is arguable that the scribe of the *Speculum Vitae* inadvertently left out a sentence or two that were present in his original.[5] Moreover,

---

[1] Sabatier, 'Description du Speculum Vitae', *Opuscules*, VI, 299.
[2] Cf. *Chron. 24 Gen.*, *A.F.* III, pp. viii–ix.
[3] Wadding, *Annales*, VIII, 332–3.   [4] *A.F.* III, 231–2.
[5] *Spec. Vitae*, printed by Lempp, p. 165; *A.F.* III, 229.

very occasionally there is verbal agreement between the *24 Generals* and Eccleston against the *Speculum Vitae*[1]—and this cannot be attributed to direct borrowing from Eccleston.

The assertion that Eccleston was completely unknown to Arnold can be easily and adequately substantiated. The *Tractatus* contains many specific and factual details that were not absorbed into the *24 Generals*: the translation was carried out three days before it should have been; the brothers sent to request from Gregory IX an elucidation of the Rule were John Parenti, St Anthony, Gerard Rusinol, Haymo of Faversham, Leo, later Archbishop of Milan, Gerard of Modena and Peter of Brescia; proposals for the reform of the Order were put forward at a General Chapter at which seven Cardinals, as well as the Pope, were present; Elias was excommunicated by Gregory IX, etc.; it would be tedious to enumerate them all. Had any of them found their way into the *24 Generals* there would be a case for supposing direct descent, but they remained peculiar to Eccleston. Since the *24 Generals* tended to follow its sources closely this can hardly be the result of selection.[2] In determining the chronology of events, also, Arnold might have derived some assistance from Eccleston, but in fact he attempted to unravel the tangle unaided, and reached the conclusion independently that Elias' penitential growth of a beard must have preceded his reappointment and not followed his deposition.[3] Finally, if more is needed, the notices on England and Englishmen that occur in other parts of his chronicle are not taken from Eccleston. He gives a different date—3 May 1219—for the arrival of the Friars Minor in England.[4] He recounts, more dramatically than does Eccleston, the story of the great master who vowed to perform whatever he should be asked in the name of the Virgin Mary, and who, prevented by divine providence from joining the Cistercians or Dominicans, eventually became a Franciscan. But, whereas

---

[1] When dealing with the violent entry of Elias' supporters into the chapter both give 'capitulum' and 'locum' where the *Spec. Vitae* has 'cubiculum' and 'sedem'; and both use 'profiteri' in connection with Elias' belated profession of the *Reg. Bullata*, whereas the *Spec. Vitae* does not.

[2] See the close correspondence between the *24 Gen.* and the *Vita fratris Leonis* for the story of Leo breaking the collecting vase (*A.F.* III, 33–4, 72).

[3] *A.F.* III, 232.   [4] *Ibid.* pp. 24–6.

in Eccleston the master in question is Adam of Exeter, in the
24 *Generals* it is Alexander of Hales.[1] Similarly, though both attri-
bute the profession of Ralph of Maidstone, bishop of Hereford,
to a vision, the vision is not the same, and the details in the 24
Generals come from Bernard of Bessa's *Liber de Laudibus*. Haymo
of Faversham, who received Ralph into the Order, is the ultimate
authority behind both versions.[2]

Nor is it admissible that the *Speculum Vitae* was immediately
dependent upon Eccleston. The tendency to write nonsense and to
confuse the sequence of events that is eminently a characteristic of the
former, suggests that the compiler was an unintelligent and inatten-
tive copyist, who transcribed passages from his sources as faithfully
as was compatible with carelessness. The resemblance to Eccleston,
though undeniable, is not close enough to allow of even very
inaccurate actual copying: there are words but not sentences in
common, and at times indirect has been changed into direct speech.[3]

An examination of the content of the stories strengthens this
argument. The accounts of the manner of Elias' deposition, in
both Eccleston and the *Speculum Vitae*, are verbally connected and
agree also in substance. Those relating to John Parenti's super-
session have many words in common, but an entirely different
rendering of cause and effect. According to Eccleston, the Minister
General, by taking off his habit, succeeded in shaming the demon-
strators, who retired abashed; according to the *Speculum Vitae* his
action was taken as a sign of resignation. When dealing with the
translation, the *Speculum Vitae* has 'antequam fratres convenirent'
and 'fecit fieri translationem' in common with Eccleston, but is

---

[1] *A.F.* III, 218–19; Eccleston, pp. 16–17.

[2] *A.F.* III, 220–1, 679; Eccleston, p. 85.

[3] There is also the circumstance that, in the description of the General Chapter at which Elias was deposed, the part played by Haymo of Faversham in
Eccleston is played by St Anthony of Padua in the *Spec. Vitae*. It could be
suggested that the scribe expanded an initial 'A', that properly referred to
Haymo, into Antonius (cf. Lempp, p. 27; Sabatier, 'Examen de la vie de
Frère Élie', *Opuscules*, XI, 168 n.), but even if this did eventually happen there
must have been several intermediate stages before Haymo Anglicus could
become sanctus Antonius, especially as Eccleston, Jordan, Bernard of Bessa
and the 24 *Gen.* all spell Haymo with an 'H'—only Salimbene and modern
writers in French favour an 'A' as first letter.

otherwise independent. According to its version the brothers in Chapter were disturbed because Elias had anticipated the ceremony and already buried the body, whereas Eccleston would have it that the disturbance was caused by Elias' partisans seeking to reinstate him, and had nothing whatever to do with the translation. Therefore, for the 1230 General Chapter and its outcome, the two follow different traditions, and so cannot be based either one upon the other, or upon a common source. Where there are divergences the *24 Generals* takes the way of the *Speculum Vitae*, though with obvious misgivings.

The relationship between the three texts would then appear to be somewhat as follows: the *24 Generals* and the *Speculum Vitae* are descended from the original of the *Speculum Vitae* (henceforward *S.V. 1*); they are also connected with Eccleston, but not directly or through a common ancestor—their affinity is the result not of consanguinity but of marriage. The Eccleston strain has at some stage been joined to an unnamed, probably Italian, line, and, if the metaphor may be pressed still further, their descendants take some after one parent, some after the other. Thus the story of the deposition of Elias, in the later accounts, has a strong family resemblance to Eccleston, while that of the translation has inherited little from him. How far the latest representatives of the house are removed from the first cannot be exactly determined, and the number of the generations does not much signify. In its simplest form the genealogical table would be:

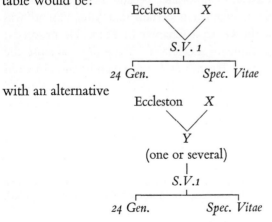

Eccleston   X

S.V. 1

24 Gen.   Spec. Vitae

with an alternative

Eccleston   X

Y
(one or several)

S.V.1

24 Gen.   Spec. Vitae

The reality and extent of the degeneration that took place is most strikingly revealed by a comparison of the chronology implied in the earliest and the latest accounts. The *Speculum Vitae* is extremely confused, as is acknowledged even by those who wish to rate it highly as a source. Eccleston, too, is said to have muddled years, people and events, but I venture to suggest that he would not have been so charged had there been no related versions calculated to ensure the perpetuation of doubt and error. What Eccleston says, in effect, is this: Elias, the first Minister General after St Francis, was succeeded by John Parenti; he in his turn was removed from office, and Elias again became General. This second substitution was due to the action of Elias' supporters, who, at the Chapter held on the occasion of the saint's translation, attempted to secure his reappointment by force. At the time, John Parenti succeeded in calling the meeting to order by taking off his habit, but the demonstration showed that he was not popular. It also temporarily alienated sympathy from Elias, but he recovered this by visible signs of penitence. Consequently, at another Chapter, John Parenti was absolved, and Elias' return received Papal approval. As General, however, he provoked widespread opposition, which at length convinced the Pope that he would have to go. He bore his dismissal badly, refused to obey the new Minister General, and was therefore excommunicated.[1] The reaction of some Italian scholars to this account is to call it grossly inaccurate. Sagui convicts Eccleston of ignorance because he called Elias the first Minister General, when it is certain that John Parenti was the first, elected at the General Chapter of 1227. He proceeds: 'What can be the value of Eccleston's accusations against the builder of the Franciscan Basilica at Assisi, when he did not even know this most important fact, the succession to the Generalate?'[2] But this argument is entirely invalid, for it is based upon a misunderstanding of Eccleston, arising out of the circumstance that his account, though coherent, is not chronological. He did *not*

---

[1] Eccleston, pp. 65–9.
[2] C. L. Sagui, *Frate Elia e la lotta fra la Chiesa e l'Impero nel tredicesimo secolo* (Assisi, 1928), p. 61; cf. D. Sparacio, 'S. Antonio di Padova e Frate Elia', *Misc. Fr.* xvii (1916), 16.

say that the Chapter held at the time of the translation happened after Elias' return to power. 'In capitulo siquidem...' clearly refers back and not forwards—after the general statement that the succession of Ministers was Elias, John Parenti, Elias, he interrupts the narrative to explain how this came about. He gives no dates, but implies the correct ones for John Parenti's period of office. The translation took place in 1230, and at the General Chapter held then John is rightly called the head of the Order; there is no mention of any election. Therefore he must have been elected at the previous General Chapter, in 1227, and it is stated that he was absolved at a later one—1232. He calls Elias the first Minister General not because he thought he was elected in 1227, but because he was among those who used that term in preference to that of Vicar to describe Elias' official position before and immediately after St Francis' death.[1]

The mistake made by these writers is a welcome illustration of the element of ambiguity in Eccleston's account. If modern scholars can so mistranslate him, it is not surprising that a medieval Italian scribe failed to grasp the proper sequence of events from his narrative, and produced a conflated, impossible version. To rearrange the sections of the story in the *Speculum Vitae*, and so produce a semblance of temporal progression, as Lempp and Sabatier have done,[2] is to treat it with more than justice and to create an entirely artificial source. If it is taken literally, as it stands, and if the implications of its statements are drawn out, it transpires that it has squeezed all the major events of Franciscan history from 1227 to 1239 into one single year—1230. It begins with Elias' preparations at Assisi for building the Basilica, records that Gregory IX laid the foundation-stone and that a marble vase for receiving offerings was put in front of the building. Leo was punished for breaking this, which so angered the brothers that at the next General Chapter they deposed Elias and elected John Parenti in his stead. The site was acquired in March 1228, Gregory laid the foundation-stone in

---

[1] For a discussion of whether Elias was Vicar or Minister General the first time he held office see below, pp. 106 ff.

[2] Lempp, pp. 24 ff.; Sabatier, *op. cit.* pp. 165 ff. Cf. also F. Tocco, *Studii Francescani* (Naples, 1909), pp. 103 ff.

July of that year, and the vase, as Leo told Giles, was by a building already 'tam excessiva'. The Chapter, then, at which John Parenti was elected could not have been in 1227, when the building was not begun, but in 1230. Elias, after his deposition, concentrated upon his building operations,[1] and summoned all his supporters to attend the next General Chapter. They forced their way into the meeting and acclaimed Elias General after John Parenti had taken off his habit and resigned. Gregory IX, who was then near Assisi, was told that the majority of the Order wanted Elias, and he confirmed their choice.[2] Then after a brief account of Elias' misdeeds as General—the extortion of money and the sending of visitors—there is another reference to a General Chapter, the only one actually dated, and it is dated 1230. St Francis' body is translated a few days before the brethren meet, and Elias, who is apparently General—so John Parenti's election and deposition were both in 1230—seeks to satisfy them by producing numerous privileges. St Anthony and Adam Marsh evade those sent to capture them and appeal to the Pope, who summons another Chapter. St Anthony makes a speech to show how Elias has misused his office, and he is deposed. Gregory then turns to St Anthony, and frees him from all official duties so that he may devote his time to preaching and contemplation. The saint died within a year and was shortly afterwards canonised. Since St Anthony died in June 1231, he must have secured Elias' deposition in 1230. So, in 1230, Elias was deposed, succeeded by John Parenti, who was then deposed, Elias returned and was again deposed. It was a memorable and eventful year indeed. There is a proverb

---

[1] The 1504 edition printed by Lempp and Sabatier reads: 'Ipso igitur regente ordinem et fratre Helia suspensum illud aedificium pomposum ecclesiae et loci Assisii viriliter prosequente....' 'Suspensum' is presumably a mistake. It should agree with Elias and not with the building operations. Spoelberch's edition, 1620, reads: 'Ipse tamen F. Helias ab officio suspensus praedictum aedificium omni conatu prosequi non destitit.' *Spec. Vitae*, part II, p. 101.

[2] At Pentecost 1230 the Pope was in Rome, in 1232 at that time he was at Spoleto. Perhaps after all John Parenti's deposition is dated 1232. It depends upon whether the scribe noticed he had dated John Parenti's appointment to 1230 instead of 1227. If that was an unintentional error, the deposition would be dated 1230. At least either his appointment or his deposition is given as occurring in that year.

which says: 'A stopped clock is right twice a day'; but though this is true, it is not to be relied upon for the time. Thus, with the *Speculum Vitae*, some of the events it places in 1230, as the translation and a General Chapter meeting, are rightly dated, but this is no security for holding it reliable in matters of chronology.

The detail of the two accounts raises an allied problem. When they are in direct contradiction, should any effort be made to harmonise them, or should one or both be rejected? There are several minor discrepancies, as for instance the order of the speeches in the Chapter at which Elias was deposed. But there are two inconsistencies which require less cursory mention if the actual course of these important events is to be established. In Eccleston the violent entry of his supporters into the Chapter meeting, though it contributed towards Elias' reappointment, did not directly secure that object; in the *Speculum Vitae* its success was immediate. If the *Speculum Vitae* intended its account to refer to 1230 it is obviously in error, for it can be proved from other sources that John Parenti was still General in the autumn and winter of that year. It was to him that Jordan of Giano came to request a new Minister for Saxony to replace Simon the Englishman, who died on 14 June 1230,[1] and he was praised by Gregory IX, who called him Minister General, in a Bull issued in December 1230.[2] If it is given the benefit of the doubt, and its account dated 1232, when a disturbance could have resulted in John's resignation, there are still some objections. The Chapter that year was held at Rieti, a small town at which it is unlikely that many brothers, except those actually summoned to the meeting, would gather. If Elias had marshalled his followers and promised that they should attend, as the *Speculum Vitae* relates, his entry would have been too patently calculated and prompted by ambition to allow of any gesture of unwillingness on his part, and would probably have provoked a storm of indignation against him. Whereas, if, as Eccleston said, the disturbance was in 1230, it could easily have possessed at least an appearance of spontaneity, for unusually large numbers of brothers had come to Assisi for the translation, and

[1] Jordan, cc. 57–8.
[2] Sbaralea, *Bullarium Franciscanum*, I, 70–1, no. G 9, 57 (74).

may well not have been under proper control. Moreover Eccleston's version receives indirect confirmation from another source. A sermon of St Bonaventure's, which has not survived, but which was known to Arnold of Sarano, made mention of John Parenti and told how, distressed by the gloss on the Rule embodied in *Quo elongati*, he had resigned.[1] The fifteenth-century chronicle of St Antonino, also on the authority of St Bonaventure, embroiders the point: 'John, the Minister General, perceiving that the rigour of the Order was somewhat relaxed, surrendered the Generalate; but remained acting General until a new appointment could be made.'[2] The significance of this is that it suggests an alternative possibility to account for Elias' return to power. Sabatier had felt compelled to accept the evidence for a disturbance in 1232 because Elias is known to have replaced John Parenti then, and because there was something questionable in the manner of his election.[3] But if the office was vacant through a resignation caused by the events of 1230 but delayed, there would be no necessity for violent measures, especially if Elias, instead of being elected at a General Chapter, which should have been held in 1233, was suggested for the post at a Cismontane Chapter held a year earlier, and confirmed in office by the Pope.[4] This would be sufficient to justify the remark of the *Chronica Anonyma* that Elias was 'non canonice electus'.[5] The suggestion that Elias owed his office directly to deliberate violence can then be discounted as one of the many calumnies later circulated against him. It may be noticed in passing that even Salimbene, who was an eager collector of his faults, hinted at nothing discreditable in the means to his promotion.

The other question is that of the year in which Elias reconciled himself to the brothers by penitence. According to the *Speculum Vitae* he retired to the hermitage at Cortona after his deposition, allowed his hair and beard to grow, put on an aged habit and appeared as a changed man. Gregory IX was so impressed by his apparent sanctity that he regretted his action in deposing him and showed him many signs of favour. After Gregory's death, how-

---

[1] *A.F.* III, 213.
[2] Cited Sparacio, *art. cit.* p. 26 n.
[3] Sabatier, *op. cit.* pp. 173 ff.
[4] See below, pp. 143–5.
[5] *A.F.* I, 289.

ever, Elias abruptly ceased his penitential practices and joined Frederick II. Comparison with independent sources reveals the large element of falsehood in this account. If Elias did show visible signs of repentance after his deposition he discontinued them not after Gregory IX's death, on 2 August 1241, but before the end of 1239. For Richard of San Germano records that he joined the Emperor by December, and celebrated Christmas with him at Pisa.[1] Nor did the Pope treat him with favour in his last years—the investigation of the validity of the absolution Elias received on his deathbed states that he had been excommunicated by Gregory IX as well as by Innocent IV.[2] As to the beard itself, there would have been sufficient time to grow one between the end of May, when he was in Assisi negotiating for blocks of stone for the building of the Basilica,[3] and December, when, at the latest, he joined Frederick, but it is unlikely that he tried so inadequate an expedient. The growth of a beard would seem too trivial to appease the strong indignation of the brothers towards him at that time. Certainly it did not succeed—Elias was not reconciled to his Order till his death—and that it did not is scarcely surprising, for already while he was General Elias had a fine beard![4] The story of penitence in 1239 cannot be substantiated. Salimbene writes: 'after he had been absolved from office he behaved neither humbly nor with patience, but went over entirely to the Emperor Frederick who had been excommunicated by Pope Gregory IX'.[5] But the sources that refute the *Speculum Vitae* confirm Eccleston. He also says that Elias retired to a hermitage and grew a beard, but he places this behaviour in 1230–2, after the brothers had been angered by his secret translation of

[1] *M.G.H. Scr.* XIX, 379.

[2] The document is printed by Lempp, pp. 179–87. It was kept in the Library of the Sacro Convento at Assisi, but could not be found when I was there in 1948.

[3] Lempp, pp. 173–4, prints a document in which Elias, 'dominus et custos ecclesiae S. Francisci', is mentioned as taking an active part in superintending the construction. It is dated 26 May 1239.

[4] Giunta Pisano painted a portrait of Elias at the foot of a great crucifix in 1236. This crucifix has disappeared, but there remain descriptions and an engraving (see Frontispiece) which depict Elias as bearded. Cf. Lempp, pp. 89 and n., 139 n. [5] Salimbene, B. p. 233, H. p. 159.

St Francis and by the disorderliness of his supporters. This is much more plausible. It allows plenty of time to grow a beard, and the beard is not known to have existed previously; it had the result of restoring Elias to favour (and to office); and the offence was not so serious that it could not be expiated by such a penance. For 1239 Eccleston's account is equally in conformity with reason and with other sources. After his deposition Elias went to Cortona, and while he was there visited a house of Poor Ladies without licence. The new Minister General, Albert of Pisa, asked him to come to him for absolution, but he refused, and departed to Arezzo, whereupon Gregory IX excommunicated him. Frederick II was campaigning in Lombardy in the summer of 1239,[1] and it would seem that Elias hoped to effect the reconciliation between Empire and Papacy that he had unsuccessfully attempted to bring about in 1238.[2] In a manifesto, written probably some time in 1239, Frederick II accused Gregory IX of offering Elias a safe conduct with the intention of having him captured. Warned of this plot at Viterbo on his way to the Curia, the ex-Minister turned back.[3] So, then, Elias did attempt to regain favour in 1239, but not by living penitently in a hermitage. Rather, his object would seem to have been to deserve praise by spectacular success as a self-appointed ambassador between the temporal and spiritual powers, which was a bold plan, but a failure.

So the *Speculum Vitae* is far inferior to Eccleston in accuracy of detail, as well as being so confused chronologically as to be valueless in matters of dating. Can any assistance be derived from the 'veramente rudis indigestaque moles'[4] of which it is composed, or is it indeed 'eine ziemlich kritik- und werthlose Compilation'?[5] It supplements the story as told in Eccleston with various additional details, some of which are demonstrably improbable or fabricated, but others, in spite of this, seem to deserve acceptance. The frequently repeated accusations that Elias obtained privileges

[1] Cf. Richard of San Germano, *Chronica*, ed. Pertz, *M.G.H. Scr.* XIX, 377–9.
[2] Salimbene, B. p. 134, H. p. 96.
[3] J.-L.-A. Huillard-Bréholles, *Historia diplomatica Frid. II*, v, part 1 (Paris, 1857), pp. 346 ff.
[4] Papini, quoted by Sabatier, *Opuscules*, VI, 301.
[5] Ehrle, *Zeitschr. für katholische Theologie*, VII (1883), 392.

contrary to the Rule and the principle of absolute poverty are
the stock charges of the fourteenth-century spirituals against the
conventuals, of whom Elias was regarded as the prototype. A
study of the Papal bulls shows that Haymo of Faversham, who
is contrasted favourably with Elias, received far more such privileges than his predecessor.[1] Yet the account of Elias' behaviour
after he joined Frederick II is substantially accurate. He did go
to Constantinople, for he brought back with him a fragment of
the true Cross, which is still preserved at the Church of St Francis
at Cortona, and he did receive absolution before he died. There
is probably an element of truth also in the statement that Elias
tried to prevent his opponents from appealing against him to
Rome, for Jordan found it difficult to obtain a hearing because
Elias had prejudiced the Pope against appellants.[2] The story of
Leo breaking the collecting vase, though impossible at the date
of which it is told, may be true of a late year of Elias' generalate,
and may have some bearing on his deposition in 1239. And though
the dating of Elias' early activities in connection with the Basilica
is misleading, he did in fact devote himself to this while he was
out of office 1227–30, as is implied by Jordan and proved by
documents relating to the construction.[3] These details in the
Speculum Vitae are most probably derived from Italian popular
sources familiar with Assisi and its great Church, and come in
part from written, in part from oral tradition. They contain a
basis of exact knowledge, but suffered such distortion in the process of transmission that they no longer have sufficient force to
defend themselves if challenged by other sources or to stand
securely alone. They can only on occasion give support to positions established by other authority.

The detail of Eccleston's account is of a very different calibre.
On some points its accuracy is established by its harmony with
independent sources. The bull *Quo elongati* confirms that the
Minister General was a member of the delegation sent to request
an elucidation of the Rule; the inquiry into the propriety of Elias'

---

[1] Sbaralea, I, pp. 285 ff.   [2] Jordan, c. 63.
[3] Jordan, c. 61: '...Frater vero Helyas factus generalis minister opus ad s.
Franciscum quod in Assisio inceperat perficere volens...'; Lempp, pp. 170–1.

absolution, that he had been excommunicated by Gregory IX and that he died penitent.[1] The valuable assistance rendered to Elias' opponents by brother Arnulf, the Papal penitentiary, was noted also by Salimbene;[2] and Jordan as well as Eccleston stated that, before the General Chapter met in 1239, brothers elected from the various provinces met to discuss measures of reform.[3] Furthermore it is remarkable throughout for its precision. Instead of saying vaguely that 'certain brothers' did this, the chief actors are named: St Anthony, Arnulf, the Papal penitentiary, Cardinal Robert of Somercote, Rainald, the Cardinal Protector, and all the members of the 1230 delegation.[4] Places, too, are given their names, even when they are not large or otherwise well-known, as Rieti, Cortona, Arezzo.[5] The translation was carried out not some days but three days early; seven cardinals were present at the 1239 Chapter; the Pope's words: 'Non est modus religiosorum iste' are remembered; after his election Albert of Pisa celebrated Mass and commented on the fact that he was the first Minister General qualified to do so; Elias was excommunicated after he had gone to Arezzo, a Ghibelline stronghold, but he was in disgrace even before then, for he had visited a house of Poor Ladies without leave and had refused to seek or accept absolution.[6] These are concrete facts that could perhaps have been taken from a written source, but there are some touches—observations on the personal bearing of individuals and on the reactions of a crowd —that can only have come ultimately from an eyewitness account. When the 1230 General Chapter was in uproar, the people outside believed it was because Elias had translated the body of St Francis before the day fixed for the ceremony, but actually it was because Elias' partisans had broken in with the intention of making him General[7]—here Eccleston is correcting the less well-informed

---

[1] Eccleston, pp. 66, 29; Sbaralea, I, 68–70, no. G 9, 56 (IV); Lempp, pp. 179–87.

[2] Eccleston, pp. 67, 68; Salimbene, B. p. 231, H. p. 158.

[3] Eccleston, p. 67; Jordan, c. 64.   [4] Eccleston, pp. 66–8.

[5] *Ibid.* pp. 67, 69. It is interesting that Ridolfi, *Hist. Seraph. Relig.* (Venice, 1586), f. 176b, also places the 1232 Chapter in Rieti, though he wrongly believed that John Parenti was re-elected then.

[6] Eccleston, pp. 65–9.   [7] *Ibid.* p. 65.

popular version that found its way into the *Speculum Vitae*. The commotion was so considerable that for a time the brothers would listen to nobody, not even to St Anthony. Lempp takes exception to this statement on the grounds that St Anthony and the other Provincial Ministers favoured the policy that Elias promoted and therefore would not have opposed him.[1] His view of party divisions and labels, however, was much too rigid—the attitude of the Provincial Ministers towards Elias at different periods of his career will be dealt with in detail in later chapters—and besides, even a supporter might be allowed to protest against such conduct as that Chapter witnessed. Both Eccleston and the *Speculum Vitae*, it will be noted, name St Anthony as a critic of Elias; Eccleston goes further and allows his criticism to be made during his lifetime. At the 1239 General Chapter Gregory IX showed the same initial unwillingness to hear ill of Elias that had made Jordan's task difficult when the appeal was moved the year before, and perhaps for this reason Haymo was plainly nervous when he began his speech. Elias, at this stage, was outwardly unperturbed, but, when he realised that Haymo's indictment was serious, he lost his self-control and cried out that he lied. When the Pope decided to depose him the joy of the brothers was 'immensum...et ineffabile'.[2]

The impression left by reading this account is, surely, that the writer of it was well and accurately informed. Who, then, were his informants? For the events of 1230 there are several people who might have told him details. It has been deduced that he joined the Order *c.* 1232,[3] and, since the *Regula Bullata* requires that postulants must be taken to the Provincial Minister,[4] he must have been received by Agnellus of Pisa. Agnellus had attended the 1230 General Chapter.[5] The visitor, John of Malvern, who brought the bull *Quo elongati* to England, may also have furnished him, indirectly, with material.[6] Then there are the five novices, who were soldiers and present at the Chapter.[7] Eccleston's refer-

---

[1] Lempp, pp. 96–7.
[2] Eccleston, pp. 67–8.
[3] Eccleston, 1 ed., p. xxii.
[4] *Reg. Bullata*, c. 2.
[5] Eccleston, pp. 4, 10.
[6] Eccleston, p. 38.
[7] *Ibid.* p. 65 (if this is the meaning of *milites novitii*).

ence to them has no apparent relevance, and their remark is oddly unexpected; it may well have been introduced because they were known to him. Albert of Pisa, who came to England in 1236, and who, as a Provincial Minister, should have been present at the 1230 Chapter, is another possibility. Eccleston was frequently in his company, tells us a great deal about him, and often authenticates examples with such words as: 'unde cum diceret frater Albertus' or 'sicut pater idem retulit'.[1] For the events of 1239, there is Haymo of Faversham, who played so prominent a part in them, and who was Provincial Minister of England 1239–40. There are, besides, the unnamed brethren who told Eccleston of the great joy that had greeted the announcement of Elias' fall.[2] England, in fact, though geographically remote from Italy, was not out of touch with her, and Englishmen, and friars stationed in England, were foremost among those who actively participated in the general affairs of the Order during and just after Elias' generalate. Though unable to write of Elias from personal knowledge, Eccleston might justly have claimed to have had recourse to 'faithful and approved witnesses'.

Finally there is the question of Eccleston's attitude towards Elias. That he was hostile to him is plainly indicated by the tone of his remarks. He returns on more than one occasion to the theme that the Order was greatly perturbed by his worldliness and cruelty,[3] and obviously shared the common view that his deposition was an occasion for thanksgiving. He regarded the type of visitation introduced by Elias as a serious grievance, and here again he voiced a widely-held opinion.[4] He also held it against Elias that he had broken the English provincial seal, stamped with a lamb bearing a cross, in a fit of temper because the brothers had presumed to ask for a particular Minister. His complaint that Elias delayed to send one for nearly a year seems childish and resentful—Agnellus died on 13 March and Albert arrived on 13 December, so the delay was hardly excessive. Besides, his name

[1] Eccleston pp. 34, 35.
[2] Ibid. p. 68: 'Factum est autem tam immensum gaudium et ineffabile, quale nunquam *dixerunt* se vidisse, qui interesse meruerunt.'
[3] Ibid. pp. 29, 51, 67.   [4] Ibid. pp. 38–40.

had been among those given to Elias as first preferences.[1] But this is the only instance of disproportionate indignation, and to say, as Goad does, that he diligently collected tales against Elias, is to exaggerate.[2]

The account of Elias' career contained in chapter XIII of the *De Adventu* is internally consistent, rich in precise information, and in harmony with other reliable sources, and these attributes far outweigh the disadvantage of its being told at second hand. For the repercussions of Elias' policy on the English province even this objection disappears, since Eccleston had personal experience of his government, and so his evidence, taken in conjunction with that of Jordan, goes far to prove that Elias, whatever his abilities, and in spite of his even admirable behaviour during St Francis' lifetime, was an unsuitable and unworthy Minister General.

5. SALIMBENE[3]

Salimbene inserted into his Chronicle, under the year 1238, a separate treatise of considerable length which he wrote 'occasione fratris Helye' and which, he tells us, 'multa bona et utilia continet'.[4] This 'Liber de Prelato' is the only contemporary work of which Elias is properly the subject, for Celano, Jordan and Eccleston referred to him only incidentally, and in some degree it fulfils its promise, for it is rich in information concerning him. The value of this, however, is impaired by Salimbene's evident and vehement prejudice. He expatiated upon Elias' faults, enumerating thirteen, allowed him only one merit—the encouragement of theological studies—and in order to illustrate and support his case employed a negative principle in selecting his facts.

His defamation of Elias has been condemned by some recent writers as morally reprehensible and therefore unworthy of cre-

---

[1] Eccleston pp. 76-7 and n. c; 78-9 and n. m.

[2] H. Goad, 'Brother Elias as the leader of the Assisan Party in the Order', *Franciscan Essays*, II, 74.

[3] Salimbene de Adam, *Cronica*, ed. F. Bernini (Bari, 1942)—(B.); ed. O. Holder-Egger, *M.G.H. Scr.* XXXII—(H.). The modern literature on Salimbene is extensive; for the most recent, cf. *A.F.H.* XLVIII (1955), 436-41.

[4] B. p. 134, H. p. 96.

dence.[1] These consider that, if he could not praise, he should at least have refrained from attacking a man to whom he owed a personal debt of gratitude. For, when Salimbene asked to be received into the Order of Friars Minor in 1238, his father, grieved and angry at the prospect of losing the son by whom he hoped yet to have an heir, tried to secure his return by argument and even by force, and also induced the Emperor, Frederick II, to write to the Minister General on his behalf. Elias, however, protected the postulant, and, that he might feel safe from pursuit, allowed him to choose his province.[2] He repaid this kindness by becoming the principal and most influential of his detractors.

Salimbene owed Elias a particular debt of gratitude and he settled it thus: he it is who is primarily responsible for all the falsehoods which have been devised and spread abroad at Elias' expense. . . . I therefore affirm that for all that concerns Elias Salimbene does not deserve the slightest credit. . . . He has lied wittingly. . . and has erected the miserable edifice of imposture which seven centuries have not yet sufficed to dissipate.[3]

Yet whatever blame should attach to him personally, his ingratitude does not automatically deprive his account of all reliability; still less does it render him responsible for all the falsehoods and calumnies that were later circulated about Elias. Salimbene wrote his Chronicle primarily for the instruction of his niece Agnes, who had entered the house of Poor Ladies at Parma, and it was never at all widely known until the nineteenth century.[4] It is improbable that it was much copied in manuscript, for only one early manuscript has survived, and that is the original itself, written, illuminated and corrected by Salimbene, with numerous marginal additions in his own hand.[5] It was occasionally referred to by writers on Italian local history, but among Franciscan his-

---

[1] Cf. Ing. L. Mirri, 'Frate Elia da Cortona—Profilo storico', *Misc. Fr.* XXXI (1931), 233–4; C. L. Sagui, *Frate Elia e la lotta fra la Chiesa e l'Impero nel tredicesimo secolo* (Assisi, 1928); E. Frati, *Figure Francescane—Frate Elia* (Pistoia, 1930); R. M. Huber, 'Elias of Cortona', *Catholic Historical Review*, XXII (1936–7), 396 ff.

[2] B. pp. 52–3, 56–7, H. pp. 39, 42.   [3] Ing. L. Mirri, *loc. cit.*

[4] B. pp. 77, 269, H. pp. 56, 187. The first edition of Salimbene was printed at Parma in 1857.

[5] B. *Nota*, pp. 939–41; B. Schmeidler, Preface to H. pp. xxvi ff.

torians Affò was the first to utilise it. Wadding listed Salimbene among the *Scriptores* of the Order, but his notices are so incorrect that he can only have known of him indirectly.[1] Therefore Salimbene can hardly have been the source of the hostile interpretation of Elias to be found in writings of the Franciscan spiritual tradition such as the *Historia VII Tribulationum* and the *Fioretti*.[2]

Salimbene wrote the 'Liber de Prelato' in 1283–4, that is to say, thirty years after Elias' death; but the lapse of time does not seem to have damaged his memory.[3] He had known Elias, being actually received into the Order by him, and had experienced his government, though not for long. The year of his noviciate, 1238–9, which he spent at Fano in the March of Ancona, was the last year of Elias' Generalate. As a recent recruit, he was probably not present at the 1239 General Chapter, to which only those brothers were admitted whose attendance was obligatory,[4] an assumption which is strengthened by his own words that he stayed at Lucca from April 1239 until 1241.[5] Elias' later conduct was known to him only by hearsay, but, as he was an eager collector of gossip, he heard and repeated a considerable amount about it.

[1] L. Wadding, *Scriptores Ordinis Minorum* (Rome, 1806), p. 213.

[2] R. M. Huber, *loc. cit.*, names Salimbene as the source of all animosity against Elias, regardless of date: Jordan, who dictated his chronicle in 1262, copies complaints concerning visitors, financial exactions, etc. directly from him, and Eccleston, who wrote *c.* 1258, was another 'who drank with avidity from the poisoned fountain of Salimbene's chronicle'. This is quite fantastic since Salimbene began to write his account of Elias in 1283.

[3] The autograph MS. of Salimbene's chronicle supplies abundant internal indications of the progress and method of its composition. It is throughout in Salimbene's own hand, in double column, with the foliation and headings put in later than the text itself. The 'Liber de Prelato' is not a separate book but an integral part of the larger work. It begins in the middle of the sixth line of the first column of f. 246v and ends on f. 278v. Salimbene inserted its title at the top of the page in the margin normally left blank. A facsimile of f. 246v, clearly showing these details, is printed at the end of Holder-Egger's edition. Salimbene fairly frequently noted the date on which he wrote a particular page. Thus f. 220 was written on 21 July 1283, f. 236 on 10 August 1283, f. 250 (the only dated folio in the section known as the 'Liber de Prelato') on 9 September 1283, and f. 287 some time in 1284. Cf. H. pp. xx ff.

[4] B. p. 231, H. p. 158.

[5] B. pp. 59, 938, H. pp. 44, ix. He saw the eclipse of the sun at Lucca in June 1239.

He had, therefore, a certain number of facts and incidents to relate from his own personal knowledge. He still remembered in vivid detail the occasion of his admission. Elias had stopped at Parma on his way to Cremona, where he was to negotiate with Frederick II on behalf of the Papacy, and, as an important visitor, he was called upon by the Podestà, a nobleman, Gerard of Corigia, with a company of knights. Elias was reclining upon a couch in front of a roaring fire, wearing an Armenian cap on his head, and when the Podestà entered he did not condescend to honour his guest by rising to greet him, but remained as he was 'ut vidi oculis meis'. Presently, while the Podestà was still in the room, and before Salimbene had changed his secular dress for the habit of religion, a dish of chicken was brought in, the gift of an abbot to Elias and the brethren.[1] Not long after he saw another gift on its way to Elias, for while he was a novice at Fano, two brethren called there, bearing with them a large salted fish, a present from the Provincial Minister of Hungary. Elias, indeed, was known to be fond of good food; he even kept a special cook, 'qui cibos delicatissimos faciebat', at the convent at Assisi, a man named Bartholomew of Padua, whom Salimbene knew.[2] Then, when Elias realised that the brothers were combining against him, he sent to all the houses, ordering that Psalm 79 (80): 'Qui regis Israel, intende...', which could be interpreted as referring to the Friars Minor, should be said daily in chapter, which was, Salimbene believed, a most unusual expedient. He wrote: 'We therefore recited that psalm before the General Chapter for a full month: which I have never seen done before or since.'[3]

The truth of a number of his statements can be established by reference to other sources. Both Jordan and Eccleston are independent witnesses to the facts that a principal grievance against Elias was his use of visitors,[4] that the opposition to him came mainly from the official element in the Order, that complaint was successfully made to Gregory IX although he tried to prevent this, and

---

[1] B. pp. 134, 137–8, H. pp. 96, 98–9.
[2] B. pp. 150, 230, H. pp. 107, 157.
[3] B. pp. 231–2, H. p. 159.
[4] B. p. 149, H. pp. 106–7; Jordan, cc. 62–3; Eccleston, pp. 38–40.

that the Pope was present at the Chapter at which he was deposed.[1]
Jordan also confirms that he held no proper General Chapters and
that, when he was deposed, constitutions were immediately drawn
up for the Order;[2] Eccleston, that he encouraged study among the
brethren, that brother Arnulf, the Papal penitentiary, was largely
instrumental in deposing him, and that Gregory IX personally
heard the votes cast for his successor, Albert of Pisa.[3] The story,
told by Salimbene, of how Elias ordered the Provincial Minister
of Bologna to be brought to him reduced to the status of a novice,
and then, when he came before him, reinstated him, is paralleled,
in Eccleston, by the incident when he broke the seal of the
English province, and afterwards sent them the Minister they
desired.[4] Both illustrate one element of Elias' character, a tendency
to sudden outbursts of anger which he later regretted. His habit
of riding a fine horse was remarked upon in Eccleston and in a
life of Bernard of Quintavalle.[5] That he joined Frederick II and
was consequently excommunicated by Gregory IX is vouched
for by Eccleston, Matthew Paris, Richard of San Germano and
the document drawn up by the commission appointed to investigate the validity of his absolution.[6] Such an accumulation of
corroborative testimony is strongly in favour of a presumption
of Salimbene's general reliability in matters of fact.[7]

Occasionally, however, his accuracy is questionable, a notable
instance being his account of Elias' parentage and early life, of
which he can have heard only at second hand.[8] His father, he

[1] B. pp. 155–7, 230–1, H, pp. 110–12, 158; Jordan, cc. 61–6; Eccleston,
pp. 67–8.   [2] B. pp. 231, 145, H. pp. 158–9, 104; Jordan, cc. 61, 65.

[3] B. pp. 145, 231, H. pp. 104, 158; Eccleston, pp. 49, 67–8.

[4] B. pp. 147–8, H. pp. 105–6; Eccleston, pp. 76, 78.

[5] B. p. 230, H. p. 157; Eccleston, pp. 67–8; A.F. III, 44 (repeated on p. 229).

[6] B. p. 233, H. pp. 159–60; Eccleston, p. 69 and n.; Matthew Paris, Chronica
maiora, III, 628; Richard of San Germano, Chronica, M.G.H. Scr. XIX, 379;
Lempp, p. 180. Richard of San Germano implies, but does not specifically
mention the excommunication.

[7] This list is not exhaustive. For instance his habit of eating alone (B. p. 230,
H. p. 157) is illustrated by the incident recorded of Bernard of Quintavalle
(A.F. III, 229). Again, Eccleston relates that at a Chapter at Genoa, probably
held in 1251, brother John of Kethene urged that Elias should be admonished
to return to the Order (p. 42 and n., cf. B. p. 236, H. p. 162).

[8] B. p. 135, H. p. 96.

wrote, came from Castel Britti, in the diocese of Bologna, his mother from Assisi. Before he entered religion he was called Bonusbaro, and he earned his living by making mattresses and by teaching young boys to read the Psalter. Elias' birthplace is still a matter of controversy, the argument being kept alive chiefly by the efforts of scholars, native to Cortona, to establish that he was born as well as died in their city. The theory that he was sprung from a noble Cortonese family, the Coppi, first gained currency in the seventeenth century; in thirteenth-century sources he is simply 'frater Helias', in the fourteenth, sometimes 'frater Helias de Assisio'.[1] In a fresco that used to be above the door of the refectory of the Sacro Convento, he was depicted among St Francis' companions as 'frater Helias de Bevilio',[2] which has been identified with a tiny hamlet, about an hour's walk from Assisi, situated on the top of a hill looking out towards Perugia. A reasonable solution of these various indications has been suggested by Fortini. Up the valley of the Tescio, upon the opposite side of Assisi from Beviglie, is another hamlet, less well-known, called Bivigliano. The name of the district it is in is Castel Britti. Salimbene, then, gave his father's place of origin its correct name, but not knowing that there was one by Assisi, he presumed it to be the Castel Britti near Bologna. The name Bonusbaro was not common in thirteenth-century Assisi. It did, however, belong to the first consul of Assisi, who affirmed the new independence of the Commune by giving judgement in the cathedral of San Rufino in the name of the Trinity instead of in the name of the Emperor.[3] Since this was in 1198, he was at least a generation older than Elias, but it is possible that he was related to him, and even that he was his father.[4] As to the circumstances of his family, nothing can be established with certainty. He may have begun humbly by teaching children and exercising a trade, but, if so, he succeeded later in acquiring a higher education, for he earned a great and widely acknowledged reputation for learning, and Eccleston

[1] E.g. *24 Gen.*, *A.F.* III, 216.

[2] F. M. Angeli, *Collis Paradisi amoenitas seu Sacri Conventus Assisiensis Historiae libri II* (Montefalisco, 1704), p. 38.

[3] A. Fortini, *Assisi nel Medio Evo* (Rome, 1940), pp. 79–81.

[4] Cf. S. Attal, *Frate Elia* (Rome, 1936), pp. 25–6.

said that he was a notary at Bologna before he joined the Order.[1]

The danger in accepting Salimbene's testimony without further investigation lies less in the possibility of actual invention than in the bias of the whole presentation. There is throughout the underlying assumption that 'brother Elias was a thoroughly bad lot',[2] who richly deserved to be deposed because of his many faults. The list of these which he proceeded to draw up shows that his hostility was grounded on personal dislike, was largely irresponsible, and even at times reprehensible. Some of the counts, as his failure to visit the provinces himself, his financial exactions, his luxurious life and his adherence to the excommunicated Emperor, are mentioned also by Eccleston or Jordan, but that on which most stress is laid is Elias' preference for laymen, at a time when there were in the Order 'plenty of goodly clerks'. His second defect was that he admitted many useless persons, that is to say laymen, into the Order, and his third that he appointed laymen to the offices of guardian, custodian and Minister Provincial.[3] Now in so doing Elias was acting strictly in accordance with the founder's will, for St Francis had never intended his Order to be exclusively or even predominantly clerical in composition.[4] Salimbene was himself aware that the impropriety of his accusation might be perceived: 'But if anyone should ask in what lay Elias' fault in receiving laymen...I answer: "quicquid agant homines, intentio iudicat omnes".' Elias' purpose was not to follow the example of Christ, who called 'not many wise men after the flesh, not many mighty, not many noble', but to collect a multitude of supporters of his tyranny. Moreover, while it was true that the Rule expressly took account of the possibility of there being lay ministers, its provision should be interpreted as having a purely temporary application to the very first years when there were insufficient priests in the Order. When clerics joined in great

[1] Bernard of Bessa, *A.F.* III, 695; Eccleston, p. 65.
[2] B. p. 148 (cf. below, p. 54 n. 3), cf. pp. 155, 232, H. pp. 106, 110, 159.
[3] B. pp. 139-43, H. pp. 99-102.
[4] Only one of the early companions, Sylvester, had been a priest. The Rule specifically envisages the possibility of priests being few (*Reg. Bullata*, c. 7).

numbers there was no longer any need of laymen, who were 'useless for hearing confessions or for giving counsel'.[1] The argument is hardly convincing, but the fact that it was thought necessary is an indication that it was Salimbene's interpretation and use of his material, and not the material itself, which was open to question.

Elias' actions, indeed, were wrong not in themselves, but because he did them. He made no general constitutions for the Order, and that was his fourth defect.[2] St Francis and John Parenti had made none either, but it is unlikely that Salimbene would have presumed to quote with reference to the saint's lifetime: 'In those days there was no king, i.e. there was no law, in Israel, but every man did that which was right in his own eyes.' He frequently deposed the Provincial Ministers without cause—his sixth defect, though St Francis had not wished appointments to be held necessarily for life and had rebuked those who regarded office as an honour and resented being removed[3]—and sent them 'from East to West, i.e. from Sicily or Apulia to Spain or England and *vice versa*';[4] a strange complaint for such a wanderer as Salimbene, and contrary to the tradition of the friars, who bound themselves to no fixed home. Then, with complete disregard for consistency, he reversed his standards when he came to deal with Elias' own deposition, and went off into a long digression in support of the maxim 'conservatio religionum est frequens mutatio prelatorum' ![5]

The examples he gave to illustrate his accusations are often inadequate or unsatisfactory. Some have no connection with Elias' Generalate at all. Salimbene may, in his time, have had a lay custodian and several lay guardians, but Elias can hardly have been responsible for all of them, as his rule only lasted the one year of Salimbene's noviciate. The elderly lay brother, who was accustomed to wander through the city without a companion, Salimbene noticed in Siena. He was living in the convent there in 1241–3.[6] As to Elias' treatment of the Provincial Ministers, that is given far too much in terms of general statements. There is only one example of the deposition of a Minister—Albert of

---

[1] B. pp. 141–3, H. pp. 101–2.   [2] B. p. 143, H. p. 102.
[3] Cf. *1 Cel.* 104; *2 Cel.* 145, 188.   [4] B. pp. 146 ff., H. pp. 104 ff.
[5] B. pp. 157–229, H. pp. 112–57.   [6] B. pp. 143; 59, 938; H. pp. 102; 44, ix.

Parma, Minister of Bologna, was absolved and Salimbene's friend
Gerard of Modena, who was to replace him, was ordered to take
him before Elias wearing a probationer's hood—but it ceases to
be relevant because Elias' anger departed, and he reinstated
Albert.[1] Reference to other sources does nothing to confirm the
charge, though it cannot be actually disproved in the absence of
complete statistics. For the provinces whose Ministers are known
for the years 1232–9 there was only one change except in the
case of death. Gregory of Naples was Provincial of France c.
1223–33,[2] John of Piano Carpine of Saxony 1232–9,[3] Richard of
Ingworth of Ireland 1230–9,[4] John of Kethene of Scotland 1233–9,[5]
Agnellus of Pisa of England from 1224 until his death in 1236,
Albert of Pisa of England 1236–9.[6] It will be noticed that among
these examples only two were not already in office when Elias
became General, and only two—Gregory of Naples and John of
Piano Carpine—represent a change, as Scotland was a new Province. Moreover, changes were usual at the beginning of a
Generalate—John Parenti made at least two in 1227[7] and in 1239
almost all the offices were redistributed. The proportion of laymen
to priests cannot be estimated, but some at least, Agnellus of Pisa,
Albert of Pisa, Richard of Ingworth,[8] and one of the two Ministers
who shared the March of Ancona when Salimbene was a novice,[9]
were priests. Similarly it is not known how many of them were
Elias' friends.[10] As a class they were foremost in deposing him,
and some, as John of Piano Carpine, John of Kethene and Albert
of Pisa, were able men to whom several Ministers General gave
authority.[11] Only Gregory of Naples is known to have been punished for supporting Elias, and he had not been promoted by

[1] B. pp. 147–8, H. pp. 105–6. [2] Cf. below, p. 204 n. 2.
[3] Jordan, cc. 61, 68. [4] Eccleston, p. 4 and n.
[5] *Ibid.* pp. 41–2. [6] *Ibid.* pp. 76–9, 85.
[7] See below, p. 128. [8] Eccleston, pp. 78, 69, 4.
[9] B. p. 142, H. p. 101: 'Ministrum nunquam habui laicum.'
[10] B. p. 231, H. p. 158: 'illos fratres faciebat ministros, quos reputabat amicos'.
[11] John of Piano Carpine was a Provincial Minister under John Parenti and
Elias (Jordan, cc. 54, 57, 61), John of Kethene under Elias, Albert of Pisa,
Haymo of Faversham, Crescentius of Jesi and John of Parma (Eccleston, pp.
41–3), and Albert of Pisa under St Francis, John Parenti and Elias (Eccleston,
pp. 78–9; Golubovich, II, 227).

him.[1] John of Piano Carpine was moved from Spain to Saxony, and Albert of Pisa to England probably from Hungary; there are no other examples of sending from East to West, and certainly for those particular men such journeys were quite normal.[2]

But Salimbene saw little need to reinforce his attack, which was vigorous rather than well-supported. 'Brother Elias was a thoroughly bad lot...,' he wrote, 'under him life was very tough.'[3] Yet if he himself found it so very hard to bear for the one year he had experienced it, he must have been very difficult to please. For, in the main body of the Chronicle, when he was describing his own reception, he told how Elias had written to the brothers at Fano commanding that, if Salimbene wished to return to his father, he was to be allowed to go, but if he proved steadfast he was to be cherished—'they were to hold me dear as the apple of their eye'. Furthermore, when Elias heard that the novice 'had played the man and stuck to the Order' he sent him greetings and told him that if he had a preference for a particular province he was to tell him. Salimbene indicated his wish to go to Tuscany, and was sent there.[4] He could scarcely have been treated more kindly; he was even put to study theology without delay.[5]

Yet although Salimbene's complaints were not always warranted, he was never led into a complete disregard for truth. For instance, he had no certain knowledge that Elias dabbled in alchemy, and contented himself with mentioning that it was a possibility:

[1] Eccleston, pp. 28–9. Elias had confirmed him as Minister of France, then removed him, probably to another province, in 1233 (below, p. 204 n.).

[2] Jordan, cc. 57, 61; Golubovich, *loc. cit.* John of Piano Carpine was successively Minister of Germany, Spain and Saxony. Later Innocent IV sent him as a missionary to Tartary, and Salimbene met him on his return near Lyons and later again at Sens (B. pp. 295, 303–4, H. pp. 206, 212–13). Albert of Pisa was Provincial Minister of Tuscany, Ancona, Germany, Spain (?), Bologna, Hungary and England (Eccleston, p. 79 and n.; Golubovich, *loc. cit.*).

[3] B. p. 148, H. p. 106. 'Erat enim frater Helyas pessimus homo....Sub dominio enim suo durissimum erat vivere.'

[4] B. pp. 52–3, 56–7, 59, H. pp. 39, 42, 44.

[5] B. p. 400, H. p. 277: 'Et statim in novitiatu meo in marchia Anconitana, in conventu Fanensi habui doctorem in theologia fratrem Humilem de Mediolano....Et audivi primo anno, quo intravi Ordinem, in scolis theologie Ysaiam et Matheum, sicut frater Humilis legebat ibidem, et non cessavi postea studere et in scolis audire.' Cf. also B. p. 145, H. p. 104.

'Sibi imputetur, viderit ipse!'[1] He was probably ignorant of Elias' deathbed repentance and absolution, for he was living a comparatively quiet and uneventful life at Ferrara from 1249 to 1256.[2] Eccleston came to know of it by some means, but it was not a fact that an Italian should be expected to know automatically. Therefore it would be unjust to accuse him of conscious lying because he wrote: 'Whether he was absolved and whether he ordered well for his soul, he now knows. Let him see to it!... For there are not a few who will not persevere in the good life and who at the end hope to make their peace with God, and are deceived.'[3]

Salimbene's standards were not those of a true friar minor. He never divested himself of an appreciation of worldly comfort or of a respect for secular dignity. He criticised Elias, not because he failed to follow St Francis, but because he failed to transform the Order into a clerical militia organised upon the traditional lines. He was not greatly shocked by his apostasy, which made it all the easier for him to inveigh against him without fear of contradiction. His opinion of what was for the good of the Order is not worthy of serious attention, but his facts, when divested of his interpretation and biased presentation, have generally some truth and may provide helpful indications as to Elias' policy. The 'Liber de Prelato' is not, however, as useful as he believed. His treatment of Elias, though lengthy, is badly proportioned and far from complete. He omits facts, such as Elias' promotion of missionary activities, which might be mentioned in his favour, and even on the side of his demerits, the list of thirteen faults conveys a misleading impression of thoroughness.

[1] B. pp. 233–4, H. p. 160.   [2] B. p. 938.
[3] Eccleston, p. 29; Salimbene, B. p. 237, H. pp. 162–3. Ing. L. Mirri, *art. cit.* p. 233, is over-critical when he writes: 'Salimbene non merita nessuna fede. Più che inesattezze sono bugie quello che egli racconta della nascita di Federico II, il dubbio che affaccia sulla conversione e sull'assoluzione di Elia (e sì che egli avrebbe dovuto, come contemporaneo, non ignorare il relativo processo: se no me lo sapete dire che cosa valga l'autorità dei contemporanei?).'

CHAPTER II

HUGOLINO AND THE
MINISTERS OF ST FRANCIS

TOWARDS the end of 1206 St Francis publicly renounced his earthly father in the Piazza del Vescovato at Assisi, giving back the money and even the clothes he owed to him, and exclaiming: 'From henceforth I wish to say "Our Father Which art in Heaven", and not "my father Peter Bernardone"'.[1] His dramatic action had not the immediate result of drawing others to conversion, but simply secured his own personal freedom to serve God. For a little over two years he lived as a solitary enthusiast, devoting his energies to the care of lepers,[2] and to the rebuilding of neglected churches, in literal obedience to the words he heard at St Damian: 'Go, and repair my house.'[3] Then, on 24 February 1209, the feast of St Matthias, the passage of the Gospel for the day suddenly revealed to him his true vocation, and he went out to preach.[4]

---

[1] 3 Soc. c. 6 (20); 2 Cel. 12. The date of St Francis' conversion is generally given either as 1206 or 1207. There are two indications to assist the reckoning— the number of years he spent in the religious life, and the time at which he was joined by brethren. As to the first, Celano's *Vita Prima* is not internally consistent. St Francis died on the evening of 3 October 1226, and according to *1 Cel.* 88, 109, this was after he had completed twenty years in the service of God (i.e. he began in 1206); according to *1 Cel.* 119, he died in the twentieth year of that service. As to the second, he heard the Gospel in the third year of his conversion (*1 Cel.* 21-2), and his preaching soon won to him disciples (*1 Cel.* 23-5). This can be supplemented by information from the *Vita b. fratris Aegidii* (ed. Lemmens, I, 37-72; ed. W. W. Seton, *Blessed Giles of Assisi* (Manchester, 1918), pp. 52-88), which may well have been written by brother Leo. Giles joined the Order two years after St Francis' conversion (c. 1), and it was in the eighteenth year of Giles' conversion that St Francis died (c. 8). This would date St Francis' conversion to 1206 (or the opening months of 1207). The circumstance that the saint, after he had renounced his father, was thrown into a deep drift of snow by robbers (*1 Cel.* 16) suggests that it was towards midwinter.

[2] Cf. *1 Cel.* 17 and St Francis' *Testament*.

[3] 3 Soc. c. 5 (14); 2 Cel. 10.   [4] 1 Cel. 21-2; 3 Soc. c. 8 (25).

Disciples now joined him quickly. Giles was received on 23 April, the feast of St George, and Bernard of Quintavalle and a certain brother Peter had come before him.[1] Others soon followed their example, and since they, as well as their leader, preached to the people, their numbers increased more and more rapidly, a geo-metrical succeeding an arithmetical progression.[2]

At first St Francis was their sole director. When he had eleven companions he wrote a Rule for them and for any future brethren, aided or influenced by no man, and taking as his pattern not earlier religious legislation but the Gospels themselves.[3] This *Regula Primitiva* enunciated the general principles of their religion: poverty, chastity, obedience, faith, humility—but left the actual details of behaviour largely uncontrolled, so that each might be at liberty to make his service as the Holy Spirit moved him,

[1] *Vita b. fratris Aegidii*, c. 1; *1 Cel.* 24–5; *3 Soc.* cc. 8–9 (27–32). It has been suggested that this brother Peter was Peter Catanii, a doctor of law and canon of S. Rufino, whom St Francis later put in charge of the Order. The identification was first made in the fourteenth century (cf. *24 Gen.*, *A.F.* III, 4; Bartholomew of Pisa, *A.F.* IV, 203), and has been accepted by Golubovich, I, 120–2, in spite of the objections raised by Suyskens, *Acta SS.*, October, II, 581–2. The arguments of the Bollandist Father are, however, convincing. St Francis' second disciple lived but a short time in the Order (*1 Cel.* 25), whereas Peter Catanii did not die until 1221; and the Peter who went to the Church of St Nicholas was, like Bernard, illiterate, and did not know where to find in the Gospel Christ's teaching about renunciation of the world (*3 Soc.* c. 8 (27–9)).

[2] Cf. *1 Cel.* 29. The number of those allowed to preach was later restricted. The *Reg. Prima* allowed brothers to preach if licensed by their Provincial Minister (c. 17); the *Reg. Bullata* only if licensed by the Minister General (c. 9). Similarly the right to admit postulants was later confined to the Ministers (*Reg. Prima*, c. 2, *Reg. Bullata*, c. 2), though at the beginning all the brothers were allowed to do so (*3 Soc.* c. 11 (41)).

The rapid spread of the Order was noted by James of Vitry in a letter written at Damietta in 1220 (printed in part by Lemmens, *Testimonia Minora Saeculi XIII de S. Francisco Assisiensi* (Quaracchi, 1926), p. 80): 'Dominus Reinerus, prior S. Michaelis, tradidit se religioni Minorum Fratrum; quae religio valde multi-plicatur per universum mundum, eo quod expresse imitatur formam primitivae Ecclesiae et per omnia vitam apostolorum....Eidem religioni tradidit se Colinus Anglicus, clericus noster, et alii duo de sociis, scilicet magister Michael et dominus Matthaeus, cui curam ecclesiae s. Crucis commiseram; Cantorem et Heinricium et alios vix retineo.' Cf. also James' *Historia Orientalis, op. cit.* pp. 81–4.

[3] *1 Cel.* 32; *Testament*.

unhampered by formal regulations. None was to have authority over another, but all were to be equally 'friars minor'. And, while the brothers were few and native to Umbria, St Francis' example, teaching and presence sufficed to guide them. But when the movement spread not only throughout Italy but beyond the Alps and beyond the sea he lost something of his ascendancy. The majority were now necessarily without his personal and inspired direction, and felt the need for definite rules of conduct and for some form of regional and hierarchical organisation, analogous to that existing in other societies.[1] The many learned men and clerics who eagerly joined the Order were, perhaps unconsciously, unwilling to have their superior abilities and training pass unnoticed and unutilised, and desired to play a leading part in its activities and in its development. Their leaven worked quickly and thoroughly, and already before St Francis' death the Franciscans were a very different body from what they had been at the beginning.

The contrast arouses questions fundamental to any interpretation of their history. Should the changes that took place be regarded as progress, as retrogression, or simply as evolution? Was St Francis opposed to them to the end, or did he come to accept some or all? Were they the result of a necessity over which men had little or no control, or were they due to the conscious volition of certain individuals? Sabatier and Lempp believed that Hugolino, using Elias as his agent, was responsible for transforming the character of the movement, and represented both men as chief actors in a tragic conflict between St Francis' ideals and the policy of the Curia.[2] Attal considers this view utterly mistaken. He maintains that there was not conflict but harmony— Hugolino understood and respected the saint's ideal, and helped him towards its realisation by persuading him to adopt his eminently sensible and practical advice.[3] A solution to this problem can best be approached through the personalities who exercised

---

[1] Cf. *Verba*, c. 5, ed. Lemmens, I, 103–4.

[2] Sabatier, *Vie de S. François d'Assise*, pp. 228, 276 ff., 313, 323; Lempp, pp. 42, 44–7.

[3] S. Attal, *S. Francesco d'Assisi* (Padua, 1947), pp. 332–3.

most influence upon the Order during the formative years. The Order of Friars Minor was not entirely St Francis' work. He was the architect, and gave the inspiration and the theme, but much of the actual construction was done by others. Did his builders, while expressing their individuality in the execution of detail, yet fulfil his design, in some such way as the masons employed in our medieval churches and cathedrals at times carved the ornament of the capitals independently, but did not extend their diversities to the main structure? Or did they make basic alterations; and if so, did St Francis adopt their suggestions and make them his, or was he obliged to allow an interpretation that was far from his own, because he was not able to prevent it? He put others in charge of the operations. Did they realise, or improve, or undermine his foundation?

I. THE CARDINAL PROTECTOR

The Church at the beginning of the thirteenth century was seriously menaced by heresy. If she was not to continue to lose ground she had need to improve her own example and to engage in active propaganda. The urgent need of the age, as understood by the majority of her enlightened champions, was for a strongly organised body of devoted and learned men under curial control, preaching the Law (Mosaic, Christian, Canon) and the Gospel—in other words, for the Dominicans. Hugolino accepted this standard, and it is greatly to his credit that he did not allow it to interfere with St Francis' work beyond the minimum which he believed necessary for security. Perhaps because he was an elderly lawyer, set in his ways, he had a certain exemption from the dominant current of opinion among younger men. It was *not* Hugolino who converted the Friars Minor into another version of the Friars Preachers.

The close dependence of the Friars Minor upon the Curia was due in the first instance to St Francis' initiative. Of his own accord, and not, as might perhaps have been expected, at the suggestion of the bishop of Assisi, he sought Papal confirmation of his Rule while his followers were still few and only locally known. The bishop, indeed, was unaware of his intention beforehand, and happening to be himself in Rome when the twelve arrived there, he was displeased to see them, imagining that they wished to leave his diocese. Reassured on that point, however, he offered to help them, and it was through his recommendation that they gained the favour of John of St Paul, Cardinal bishop of Sabina.[1] He at first tried hard to persuade them to adopt an established monastic or eremitical Rule, but at length, impressed by their fervour and by their faith, he came to believe that through them Christendom might be reformed. Therefore he spoke on their behalf before the Pope and Cardinals, urging against objections that to deny validity to their way of life as being beyond human strength was to impute impossibility to the teaching of the Gospel. His arguments, and St Francis' holiness, orthodoxy and humble obedience to the Church, together, it may be, with a vision of St John Lateran about to fall and saved by the efforts of a small religious, combined to secure a favourable answer. Innocent III verbally approved their purpose, and promised to allow them more if they showed themselves worthy of greater grace.[2]

This recognition was the determining factor in their future fortunes. It enabled them to grow into a great movement, for without Papal sanction the Franciscans could not have spread widely among the faithful, any more than could the other popular religious fraternities that resembled them in composition, poverty and preaching. That they fared differently from these was due to the wisdom and sympathy of Innocent III, for the granting of their request had been by no means a matter of course. They were not the first to come on such an errand. Peter Waldo had petitioned to be allowed to preach and to live in poverty in 1179, but he had been scorned as ignorant, and his followers, known as the Poor Men of Lyons, were condemned at the Council of Verona in 1184.[3] Not in origin anti-sacerdotal, these men were driven outside the Church less by their own desire than by the

---

[1] 1 Cel. 32; 3 Soc. c. 12 (47–8).
[2] 1 Cel. 33; 3 Soc. c. 12 (49–53); Bonav. c. 3; 2 Cel. 17.
[3] C. J. Hefele–H. Leclercq, *Hist. des Conciles*, v, ii (Paris, 1913), pp. 1119–26; cf. E. Scott Davison, *Forerunners of St Francis* (Boston, 1927), pp. 247 ff.

failure of Alexander III and Lucius III—and the episcopate at large —to conciliate or understand them. They were only one of numerous groups, often heretical or semi-heretical, that were flourishing and multiplying in the late twelfth and early thirteenth centuries, and which constituted a serious problem for the ecclesiastical authorities. How best to deal with them had been one of the main questions on the agenda before the Third Lateran Council, and was again debated at the Fourth.[1] There was little to distinguish the Friars Minor, in their beginnings, from the rest, and had St Francis come before one of Innocent's predecessors he too might well have been denied authority to preach.

The connection with the Papacy that arose through the approbation of the Rule was strengthened and tightened by the appointment of a Cardinal Protector to whose special care the Franciscans were committed. But though the creation of this office—for it was not customary for religious Orders to have such—brought them into unusually close dependence, it should not be considered as an expedient devised by the Curia to keep the movement securely under its control. No cardinal was assigned to the Humiliati, whom Innocent III tactfully won back to obedience, though he might with reason have thought it advisable to put them under some form of surveillance.[2] The Protectorate was not imposed from above, but conceded at St Francis' own request.[3] Once established, however, it assumed a large measure of authority, and the manner of its institution and the nature of its functions present problems and involve issues that must be carefully examined.

An account of how St Francis came to put himself and his brethren into the charge of a Protector is given in the *Vita Prima* and in Jordan of Giano,[4] but the details and the context of their two descriptions make it clear that they do not refer to one and the same episode. They relate to separate stages in the process by which the office was evolved. Before it received official sanction and recognition, there had existed for some time an informal, mainly personal, relationship. John of St Paul had afforded St

---

[1] Mansi, *Concilia*, XXII, coll. 231–3, 986–90.
[2] E. Scott Davison, *op. cit.* pp. 168 ff.
[3] See below, pp. 67–8.   [4] *1 Cel.* 74–5; Jordan, c. 14.

Francis counsel and protection, and had been his advocate;[1] after
his death his place was taken by a nephew of Innocent III's, Hugolino, Cardinal bishop of Ostia, and later Pope Gregory IX. In
his hands these activities took on the attributes of a proper office,
and the Protectorate is usually dated from the time of his first
definite association with the Minors. This began as the result of
a small but important incident, the chance meeting between himself and St Francis in Florence, and many scholars have tried to
determine satisfactorily exactly when this took place.

The circumstances would seem to have been somewhat as
follows:[2] in a year not specified by any of the sources, a Chapter
was held at the Portiuncula from which a number of brothers
were sent off to provinces outside Italy. When they had gone,
St Francis, unwilling that they should endure labours and sufferings in which he had no share, decided that he should go himself
to a distant province, and determined upon France. He took with
him Sylvester, who had been one of the first priests to join the
Order. On their way northwards they came to Arezzo, but did
not immediately enter the city, which was then a prey to noisy
and violent civil discord. It seemed to Francis that devils were
exulting over it, and he told his companion to approach the gate
and command the evil spirits in God's name to be gone. He did
so, and peace was soon restored among the citizens. They then
continued their journey as far as Florence, where they waited
upon Hugolino, who was residing there in his capacity of Papal
Legate to Tuscany. He received them graciously, and indicated
his readiness to become their protector. He did not, however,
approve of their immediate intention, fearing that hostile prelates
might do harm to the young Order if the saint left Italy. Francis
allowed himself to be dissuaded, and returned to the valley of
Spoleto, sending Pacifico to France in his stead.

None of the factual details, though they are numerous and
circumstantial, has yet disclosed conclusive evidence of the precise

[1] 3 *Soc.* cc. 12 (47–8), 15 (61).
[2] This reconstruction is based on a conflation of the notices found in *1 Cel.*
74–5 and MS. Perugia, c. 103 = 79–82 (cf. *Sp. L.* c. 37, *Sp. S.* c. 65, MS. Little,
Coll. Fr. I, 97 ff.).

date of the meeting. A wide variety of years, ranging from *c*. 1213 to 1221, have been suggested,[1] but by assembling all the material that has bearing on the occasion, it is possible to reduce the field. The encounter cannot have taken place earlier than 1217 or later than 1218.[2] To decide between the respective claims of these two years, for each of which a good case can be made out, is a problem that is difficult rather than intrinsically important. While the meeting in Florence does indeed mark a definite development in the relations between St Francis and Hugolino, being both the beginning of their friendship and the first occasion on which the Cardinal's influence was exerted to change the founder's plans, it was only an intermediate stage in the process by which the office of Cardinal Protector was evolved. It did not lead immediately to Hugolino's formal appointment; nor was it necessarily the means by which the two men became acquainted with each other. There are several earlier occasions on which they might have met. Hugolino had been in Rome in 1210, when St Francis came to seek Papal approval of his Rule, and according to Angelo Clareno he had joined with John of St Paul in urging that his petition should be granted.[3] The Fourth Lateran Council, held in 1215, is also a possibility, for, although Celano does not refer to it at all, the Dominican biographer Gerard of Fracheto said that both St Francis and St Dominic were present there, and his information came ultimately from a Friar Minor.[4] Again, in 1216, St Francis and the College of Cardinals were together in Perugia at the time of Innocent III's death.[5] Lastly, in March 1217, Hugolino acted

---

[1] 1213–14, *Acta SS.* October, II, 607; 1217, A. Callebaut, *A.F.H.* XIX (1926), 530–58; H. Boehmer, *Chronica fratris Jordani*, pp. lxxiv–lxxv; 1218, E. Brem, *Papst Gregor IX bis zum Beginn seines Pontifikats* (Heidelberg, 1911), pp. 80, 111 ff.; 1221, R. Davidsohn, *Forschungen zur Geschichte von Florenz*, IV (Berlin, 1908), pp. 68–70.

[2] For a discussion of this question see Appendix I.

[3] Angelo Clareno, *Rendiconti*, pp. 21–2.

[4] Gerard of Fracheto, *Vitae fratrum*, *M.O.P.H.* I, 9–11. St Dominic was in Rome in 1215 and in 1216. The vision quoted by Gerard in this passage is recorded in Henry of Hervord's chronicle under the year 1215 (*op. cit.* p. 9 n.).

[5] Eccleston, p. 95: '…et Innocentium, in cuius obitu fuit praesentialiter sanctus Franciscus'. Innocent III died at Perugia on 16 July 1216 and Honorius III was elected there on 18 July.

as arbitrator in a quarrel between Bishop Guido and the canons of S. Rufino within Assisi itself.[1]

The informal protection that Hugolino offered and St Francis accepted at Florence in 1217 or 1218 was transformed shortly afterwards into a regular and strong control. How this came about was recorded at some length by Jordan, and his account can be supplemented from information contained in *1* and *2 Celano* and the Three Companions. St Francis had set out for the East with twelve companions after the General Chapter of 26 May 1219, leaving behind him as his vicars Matthew of Narni and Gregory of Naples,[2] men who unfortunately did not fully comprehend or appreciate his ideals. They took advantage of his absence to condone and even to introduce far-reaching changes and modifications into the way of life of the brethren. Fixed residences were set up in the towns, the most glaring disregard for the founder's wishes being shown at Bologna. Here Peter of Stachia, the Provincial Minister, set up a 'studium' of fine proportions, thus at once contravening St Francis' teaching on the subjects of learning, the owning of property, and the use of houses not in accordance with the standards of poverty.[3] A Chapter was held, attended by the vicars and some of the senior friars of Italy, at which regular fasts and abstinence from meat were imposed on the brethren, possibly as a gesture of atonement for the modification of the rule of absolute poverty, more probably in conscious imitation of the monastic Orders. A certain brother Philip constituted himself the defender of the Poor Ladies and procured privileges on their behalf providing for the excommunication of their enemies. Another brother, John of Conpello, left the Order and caused scandal to the Fraternity by attempting to found an Order of lepers of both sexes. Such developments were viewed with the utmost anxiety by those who valued and wished to maintain St Francis' conception in its original purity. They so distressed one of the lay brothers that he took a copy of the new constitutions

---

[1] Callebaut, *art. cit.* p. 541 and n.

[2] *24 Gen.*, A.F. III, 22; Jordan, cc. 10–11.

[3] Cf. Angelo Clareno, *Rendiconti*, pp. 106–8; *Actus b. Francisci*, ed. Sabatier, c. 61. The story is substantiated by *2 Cel.* 58.

and sailed in haste and without leave for Syria to inform St Francis of the mischief that was being done, even at the risk of thereby incurring his displeasure. The news caused the saint to embark speedily for Italy, and indeed his presence was urgently needed, for rumours of his death had been spread abroad and the general atmosphere was one of tension and uncertainty. On his arrival he learnt further disquieting details, but instead of seeking out those responsible he addressed himself directly to the Pope. Not presuming, however, to intrude upon Honorius with his troubles, he did not knock for admittance but waited humbly and patiently outside his door until he emerged, and then presented a petition. He realised, he said, that His Holiness was too much occupied to have time to attend personally to the needs of poor and lowly religious whenever they were in difficulties, and therefore begged that his Order might be put into the especial keeping of Cardinal Hugolino, and that he might turn to him for help as to the Pope himself. His request was willingly granted, and Hugolino became the official Protector of the Friars Minor. St Francis explained to him the causes of his distress, and with his assistance the Order was reformed. In particular, the privileges that brother Philip had acquired for the Poor Ladies were annulled, and John of Conpello and his associates were dismissed from the Curia.[1]

It can be deduced that these events took place in the winter of 1220,[2] and Celano and the Legend of the Three Companions

---

[1] Jordan, cc. 11–14.

[2] Francis left Damietta for Syria soon after 2 February 1220 (James of Vitry, quoted Golubovich, I, 6–8, 14), and stayed there until he received news of the Chapter held by his vicars and of the other troubles. This Chapter presumably took place at one of the usual seasons, Whitsun or Michaelmas. Since Francis took Peter Catanii back with him to Italy, and Peter died on 10 March 1221 (below, p. 77 n. 2), it must have been at Whitsun or Michaelmas 1220, or just possibly at Michaelmas 1219. The voyage between Syria and Italy was normally made in March and September (Golubovich, I, 97), rarely later than September or earlier than March. Thus Michaelmas 1220 is too late for the Chapter, and Francis' return was probably made *c*. March or *c*. September 1220. But he went straight to the Pope, who was at Rome (see next note), which dates his arrival to October 1220 at the earliest; and we may therefore presume that the Chapter was held at Whitsun 1220 and that the saint returned in September. This is confirmed by the fact that St Francis' next Chapter (Jordan, cc. 15–16) was held at Whitsun 1221.

explicitly mention that the request was made in Rome.[1] In the
Vita Prima only the manner in which St Francis, 'not having yet
many brethren' put himself and his Order under Hugolino's protection when they met in Florence is described at all fully; but
the saint's later formal request for him to the Pope is also referred
to.[2] In the *Vita Secunda* the account of this later stage is expanded.
St Francis had a vision in which he saw a little black hen surrounded
by more chicks than she was able to gather under her wings,
and interpreted this to signify that his own strength had become
insufficient to protect the growing number of his friars. He therefore went to Rome, and, after he had preached before the Pope
and Cardinals, he asked that Hugolino might be granted to him
as a Protector. Substantially the same story is told, in the same
order, in the Three Companions.[3] The episode is clearly identical
with that related by Jordan, and the gist of the petition is the
same in all three accounts. There is one minor variation—whereas
in Jordan the request is preceded by patient waiting outside the
door of the Pope's chamber, it comes, in *2 Celano* and *3 Soc.*,
after a moving sermon delivered to the whole Papal court. Jordan's
version is probably to be preferred, both because his charming
details bear an impression of truthfulness and because Celano, in
his earlier Life, implied that St Francis preached his sermon after
and not before Hugolino's official appointment—the Cardinal was
anxious that the saint should make a favourable impression 'since
he had been set as a father over his family'.[4] The discrepancy is
not in itself important, but it is an interesting example of the

[1] See below. Sabatier, *Vie de S. François*, p. 278, followed by Boehmer
(Jordan, p. 14 n. 2) and Attal (*S. Francesco d'Assisi*, p. 333), staged the request
in Orvieto. For this there is no early evidence, and it seems to be based on the
assumption that the request was made between June and September 1220, when
the papal Curia was at Orvieto. Moorman, *Sources for the life of St Francis of
Assisi*, p. 69, believed that the relevant part of *3 Soc.* (cc. 15–16 (61–7)) was
written later, by one of the 'conventuals', because it contains enthusiastic praise
of Hugolino. Comparison with the corresponding sections of *2 Cel.* 24–5
shows quite clearly, however, that both are based on a common source. Moorman's theory that *3 Soc.* was written in stages by different scribes has been
confuted convincingly and at length by Father M. Bihl, *A.F.H.* xxxix (1946–8),
3–37, esp. pp. 4 ff.   [2] *1 Cel.* 74–5, 100.
[3] *2 Cel.* 24–5; *3 Soc.* c. 16 (63–7).   [4] *1 Cel.* 73.

way in which two separate incidents could so easily become combined as the stories of St Francis were retold.

There remains the important question of why the request was made. Did St Francis ask spontaneously and of his own free will, or did Hugolino instruct him to do so? A tradition preserved by Wadding relates that, before he repaired to the Curia, St Francis met the Cardinal in Bologna and was taken by him to a hermitage in the Casentino, where they both spent some time in retreat.[1] Sabatier utilised this story in support of his contention that the Curia was responsible for undermining the saint's ideal, and his vivid, imaginative account has impressed certain of his critics in spite of themselves.[2] He described how Hugolino, mingling his avowals of admiration and affection with arguments and reproaches, played upon Francis' humility to urge him to renounce his own will, his own plans and hopes for his Order, and to be guided by the practical wisdom and experience of the Church, till in the end the saint submitted and decided to ask the Pope for an official controller. His interpretation, however, far from being borne out, is refuted by the words of the contemporary sources, which leave little doubt that St Francis did not resign himself to, but positively desired Hugolino's assistance. The request was precipitated by the activities of his vicars during his absence. He turned to Hugolino rather than to any other probably because he remembered that the Cardinal had already, when they met at Florence, declared his readiness to help. Nevertheless he asked for him not just as a temporary expedient to end a crisis but as a permanent governor. The petition to Honorius was in a way the logical outcome of the petition to Innocent III, for it too was derived from Francis' wish that his brothers should be especially subject to the Church. With the rapid expansion and development of the Order he had ceased to be satisfied with the measure of obedience implied by the Papal sanction of the Rule and desired a

---

[1] Wadding, *Annales*, I, 339–40.

[2] Sabatier, *Vie de S. François*, pp. 275 ff. Attal, *S. Francesco d'Assisi*, pp. 330–3, accepts the story of St Francis' and Hugolino's retirement in the Casentino as Sabatier has reconstructed it, and tells it almost in his words, though putting upon it an entirely different interpretation, by which Hugolino fulfilled instead of undermining the saint's ideal.

closer, more immediate tie. The Pope was obviously unable to take a constant active interest in its affairs, and Francis had the wisdom to realise that he would not achieve his object best by bringing all matters to him. The initiative was his. In the words of the *Vita Prima*: 'St Francis had chosen Hugolino to be father and lord over the whole community and Order of Friars Minor, with the assent and goodwill of Pope Honorius.'[1] He ensured that the relationship between the Friars Minor and the Curia, thus instituted, should not lapse by inserting in the *Regula Bullata* a clause requiring his successors to continue the practice of asking the Pope for a Cardinal Protector.[2] In course of time the immediate occasion of the request was forgotten and Philip of Perugia, writing for the Minister General Gonsalvus his *Epistola de cardinalibus protectoribus Ordinis Fratrum Minorum* at the beginning of the fourteenth century, was aware only of the underlying reasons—the difficulty of obtaining access to the Pope, and the need for the brothers to be always and especially subject to the Church—though it must be admitted that he added one new and highly improbable motive, the desire to evade the spirit of absolute poverty by making a cardinal the nominal owner of Franciscan property.[3]

The functions of the Cardinal Protector are not specified in detail in any document. The early chroniclers of the Order refer to him as 'pater', 'dominus', 'benefactor',[4] or echo the words of the *Regula Bullata*: 'gubernator, protector et corrector',[5] which approach closest to a definition. St Francis, in his Testament, called him 'dominus, protector et corrector' and made it clear what was meant by the last of these terms—any brother found to be heretical was to be closely guarded until he could be brought before the Cardinal. The protection was implemented by Hugolino in two ways. He defended the young fraternity against its enemies within the Curia,[6] and he wrote letters to the bishops of distant

[1] *1 Cel.* 99; cf. Jordan, c. 14.   [2] *Reg. Bullata*, c. 12.
[3] Philip of Perugia, 'Epistola de cardinalibus protectoribus', *M.G.H. Scr.* XXXII, 678 ff.
[4] *1 Cel.* 73, 100; Salimbene, B. p. 251, H. p. 174.
[5] *Reg. Bullata*, c. 12; Salimbene, B. p. 48, H. pp. 35–6.
[6] *1 Cel.* 74. In this connection it is perhaps relevant to quote Hugolino's manner of persuading St Francis to abandon his proposed journey to France:

parts guaranteeing the orthodoxy of the friars and asking that they be favourably received.[1] As governor, he assisted St Francis to compose the final version of the Rule that was confirmed by Honorius III on 29 November 1223.[2] But, while his activities in connection with the Minors can be roughly classified under these headings, consideration of his theoretical duties is not the most rewarding method of approach, as theory played little part in the initial building-up of the office, and his relations with St Francis were far more personal than official. His behaviour, therefore, should be examined rather for the light it can throw upon the problems of his attitude to the new movement and his influence upon it, which are of greater interest and greater importance. Was he, fundamentally, at one with St Francis, or with the educated friars? Or was his contribution an independent factor in the interplay of aims and policies?

Of Hugolino's deep affection and reverence for St Francis there can be no doubt. Whatever the saint did or said could not fail to please him, his presence alone had the power to move him profoundly, and in talking to him he found rest from all troubles and sadness. When they met he received him 'devotissime', and would bow down to him and kiss his hands.[3] He showed himself greatly edified by the Franciscan way of life, and extended to the brethren as well as to their leader many public marks of his respect. He made a practice of attending the Whitsun General Chapter, and when the friars came out in procession to meet him, he used to dismount and accompany them back to the Portiuncula on foot.[4] On one such occasion he was struck by the extreme poverty of their sleeping quarters, and wept at the sight of them before all the

'Frater, nolo quod vadas ultra montes, quoniam multi prelati sunt et alii qui libenter impedirent bona tue religionis in curia Romana. Ego autem et alii cardinales qui diligimus tuam religionem libentius protegimus et adiuvamus ipsam, si manseris in circuitu istius provincie', MS. Perugia c. 103 = 82, MS. Little, *Coll. Fr.* I, 99 (cf. above, p. 62).

[1] *3 Soc.* c. 16 (66).

[2] Sbaralea, I, 15–19, no. H3, 14 (I) (*Solet annuere*). *Ibid.*, p. 68, no. G9, 56 (IV) (*Quo elongati*)—'...et in condendo praedictam Regulam ac obtinendo confirmationem ipsius per sedem apostolicam sibi astiterimus, dum adhuc essemus in minori officio constituti'.

[3] *1 Cel.* 99, 101.   [4] *3 Soc.* c. 15 (61).

bystanders.[1] More than this, he was not content merely to express
his admiration; though he was already elderly when he became
St Francis' friend he strove to emulate his example.[2] He is even
said to have once asked St Francis whether it would be better for
him to remain a cardinal or to become a Friar Minor.[3] He would
sometimes cast aside his costly robes and go as one of the friars, in
mean garments and barefooted.[4] After he became Pope he still
put on the grey habit, and thus incognito would visit religious
houses and churches, taking Franciscans with him as his companions. He housed lepers in his palace and ministered to them:
he used also to wash the feet of the poor wearing the same habit,
and Philip of Perugia recounted an amusing story of how some
poor men, not knowing who he was, refused his ministrations,
saying that another of the friars was more efficient![5]

His readiness to acknowledge, and to adopt in his own life,
St Francis' teaching does him the greatest credit, but it must nevertheless be remembered that he did not embrace the ideal fully. His
age, his legal upbringing and his career alike precluded unreserved
acceptance of something so original, so startlingly direct and single
in its purpose. His outlook had been already formed and set. His
regard for St Francis was impulsive and affectionate, founded on
emotion rather than on reason. He believed in him, but doubted
his own judgement. Thus, when the saint preached before the
Curia, he was the whole time in an agony of suspense lest his protégé's simplicity should be despised.[6] They were not spiritually akin,
and though Hugolino was much edified when Francis explained
to him the principles that underlay his actions, he did not antici-
pate the answers to his questions, and was capable of suggesting

---

[1] *2 Cel.* 63. He had, apparently, the gift of tears, which medieval man
regarded as a virtue. Salimbene said of him: 'Erat enim homo multum com-
passivus, habens viscera pietatis', B. p. 122, H. p. 88.

[2] *1 Cel.* 99: 'Conformabat se dominus ille moribus fratrum, et in desiderio
sanctitatis cum simplicibus erat simplex, cum humilibus erat humilis, cum
pauperibus erat pauper. Erat frater inter fratres, inter minores minimus, et
velut unus caeterorum, in quantum licitum erat, in vita et moribus gerere se
studebat.'

[3] Bartholomew of Pisa, *A.F.* IV, 454.   [4] *1 Cel.* 99.

[5] Philip of Perugia, *op. cit.* pp. 680–1; Bonav. *Sermo de S. patre nostro Francisco,*
II, *Opera Omnia,* IX, 577.   [6] *1 Cel.* 73.

that for the good of the Church the Friars Minor should be appointed to bishoprics.[1] He showed the same devotion, the same deficiency in depth of understanding, in his dealings with St Clare. There is a letter that he wrote to her which reveals most eloquently his homage and his humility before her sanctity;[2] yet he obliged her to struggle all her life for permission to follow the essentially Franciscan precepts that she valued. He tried hard to persuade her to abandon the practice of absolute poverty, and imposed upon the Poor Ladies, in place of St Francis' Rule, a Rule based upon the Benedictine, with certain additional constitutions which made it harsh almost beyond endurance.[3]

The essential difference between Francis and Hugolino lay in their sense of values. To Francis there was one thing alone that mattered, the approach of the soul to God, and the way that he had found was through literal obedience to the Gospel. The standards of the world lost their validity for him, and he desired neither property, nor security, nor success. Indeed, he would have preferred his followers to remain few and without influence, finding their greatest joy in suffering, and prizing derision more than honour. While he looked to the spiritual perfecting of individuals, Hugolino saw the potential usefulness of his inspiration in the world as a whole, for the strengthening of faith and the improvement of morals. He was therefore ambitious to increase the num-

---

[1] 2 Cel. 73, 148. [2] A.F. III, 183.

[3] Cf. Cuthbert, Life of St Francis of Assisi (1914 ed.), pp. 291–2. The severity of the Rule caused Hugolino himself later to press the sisters to accept dispensations (e.g. Quia et Apostolus, 10 April 1233), and he is said to have wept as he composed it (Philip of Perugia, p. 680: 'Propter cuius regule artitudinem partim devotione, partim conpassione cardinalis ipse perfundebatur multis lacrimis in scribendo'). His successors criticised its prescriptions publicly—Innocent IV in Quoties a nobis petitur, 23 August 1247: 'Cum igitur nuper regulam vestram, et vivendi formam, ob cuius difficultatem nimiam conscientiae vestrae ambiguitatis scrupulo premebantur, et intollerabile personis dispendium imminebat...'; Clement IV in Ut ordo b. Clarae, 11 December 1265: 'Formula per fel. record. Gregorium papam praedecessorem nostrum edita...graves adeo asperitates, atque importabiles iudicabat, quod vix aut nunquam possent etiam a iunioribus et robustioribus observari' (Sbaralea, I, 101, 488, nos. G9, 98 (105), I 4, 236 (474 n.), III, 63, no. C4, 61 (1250)). (The new theories of Z. Lazzeri about St Clare's Rules, propounded since this was written, are discussed in A.F.H. XLVIII (1955), 151.)

bers, prestige and authority of the movement, and thought it better to work for tangible, practical, quantitative results, even if that involved a lessening of quality. This danger, however, did not at the beginning appear obvious, or serious, or imminent, and he did not realise the ultimate logical consequences of his ideas. It was the promotion of the Order that seemed to him a measure of incontestable wisdom. His instinctive reaction to the news of Francis' abortive missionary ventures was to deplore an unproductive waste of energy and opportunity. He felt from the start that they would not succeed. 'Why', he said to him, 'have you sent your brothers so far, to die of hunger and bear other tribulations?'[1] The sensible course was to acquire letters of introduction and recommendation, and thus ensure a welcome from the clergy; to set up schools of theology to equip the preachers with knowledge and style; to mitigate poverty and allow a measure of security and comfort in the interests of health and efficiency.

This was also the opinion of the Ministers.[2] These men were discouraged by rebuffs, and irked by failures that they felt need not have happened. They lacked trust in the new pathways that they were called upon to tread, and hankered after the tried, traditional methods. They pressed for certain changes, and Hugolino was prepared to support and assist their efforts. He issued bulls on behalf of the friars, instructing the clergy to refrain from persecuting them, and to receive them as true catholics, and when St Francis ordered all friars to leave a house in Bologna because they were spoken of as its owners, he enabled them to return by publicly announcing that the property belonged to him.[3] At one of the Chapter meetings that he attended a deputation came to him asking him to use his influence with St Francis to persuade him to adopt one of the old monastic Rules. He agreed to be their spokesman and admonished the saint to give way. The question was one that was causing the Friars Minor considerable anxiety. The Fourth Lateran Council of 1215 had prohibited the creation of any new

---

[1] MS. Perugia, c. 103 = 82.
[2] I use this term for convenience, to signify the 'fratres sapientes et in scientia docti' from whom the officers of the Order were mostly drawn.
[3] 2 Cel. 58; Sp. S. c. 6.

religious Orders, regarding a multiplicity of Rules as undesirable in view of the prevailing heterodoxy, and St Dominic, who had come to the Council to obtain approval for the Friars Preachers, was told to base his brotherhood upon a Rule already sanctioned. St Francis' Rule had been approved some five years earlier by Innocent III, but only verbally, so that its legal position was dubious. The records of the Council preserve no mention of it, and the only authority for supposing it to have been named at all is a statement in the *Intentio Regulae*.[1] But, while it had not been ratified, it had, equally, not been condemned, and the Pope had said that he allowed it. St Francis, for his part, categorically refused to have any other. Taking the Cardinal by the hand, he led him before the assembled brethren and exclaimed: 'My brothers, my brothers, God has called me by the way of simplicity, and has shown me the way of simplicity; I do not want you to name to me any rule, neither St Augustine's, nor St Benedict's, nor St Bernard's. And God told me that he wished me to be a new kind of simpleton in the world —God did not wish to lead you by any other road but by *this* learning, but by *your* learning and wisdom God will confound you.' Hugolino, respecting his idealism, made no attempt to force him and said no more.[2]

The Cardinal, indeed, in all his dealings with St Francis, was torn between his common sense and his glimpse of the sublime, and was thus prevented from holding or implementing a clear, confident policy. He could offer only an eager and sincere desire to help. When St Francis asked him to do anything definite he complied. He came to the Whitsun General Chapters at his request, and he suppressed the developments that had taken place during Francis' absence in the East in accordance with his instructions.[3]

---

[1] C. 3, ed. Lemmens, I, 85: '...sicut revelatum fuit b. Francisco, ut deberet vocari religio Fratrum Minorum; et ita scribi fecit in prima regula cum portavit eam domino papae Innocentio; et ipse approbavit et concessit et postea in concilio omnibus annuntiavit'. I quote the reading of MS. S. Isidore 1/73, f. 20r-v, as Lemmens' transcription is inaccurate.

[2] *Verba S. Francisci*, c. 5, ed. Lemmens, I, 103-4. In quoting I have again followed the MS. and not Lemmens' edition. For a discussion of the date of this episode, see Appendix I.

[3] *3 Soc.* c. 15 (61); Jordan, cc. 14-15.

He did not instigate the Ministers to oppose St Francis, and there is no evidence to support Lempp's gratuitous assertion that he induced Elias to become his tool and then put him in actual control of the Order.[1] He shared many of their aspirations, and realising that he sympathised with them, they appealed to him. The actual extent of his responsibility for the course that events took is hard to assess. Whatever the standard of judgement, whether what did in fact happen is regarded as a betrayal or as a fulfilment, he does not deserve all the blame or all the credit, for he was not the primary cause or chief agent of change. Nevertheless, his share is properly far greater than that of a private individual, since he had, and did not use, the power to prevent much that occurred. It would be unfair to charge him with having done nothing to preserve St Francis' arrangements while he was in the East, as he had at that time no particular official authority over the brothers, and may not have felt justified in intervening. But later he had not the same excuse, and it cannot be denied that after St Francis' death he allowed the policy of the Ministers to triumph. They appealed to him when he was Pope for an interpretation of the Rule, and, instead of upholding the observance of the saint's clear and emphatically expressed desires, he modified what seemed to him an intransigent, unpractical idealism, and, in the bull *Quo elongati*, declared that the Testament was not legally binding, that only the Gospel precepts actually quoted in the Rule had to be obeyed, and that the brethren might deposit funds with 'spiritual friends' for the purchase of future necessaries.[2] For the acquisition of privileges he again shares responsibility with the Ministers. How it should be divided between them is a delicate problem. He was the more directly concerned with their promulgation, and it would be hard to say how far such phrases as 'devotionis vestrae precibus inclinati'[3] should be taken literally. The Rule itself in its final form may be partly his work, but on what side his influence was exerted is not established—the modifications it sustained were attributed by brother Leo to the Ministers alone.[4] The alleged differences between

[1] Lempp, pp. 41 ff.   [2] Sbaralea, I, 68–70, no. G 9, 56 (IV).
[3] Addressed to St Francis and the Order at large: *ibid.* I, 9, 15, nos. H 3, 10, 14 (10, 1).   [4] *Intentio*, pp. 88, 98–9; cf. p. 83.

the *Regula Prima* and the *Regula Bullata* have been much discussed,[1] and study of the extent to which either represents St Francis' true spirit has suffered from a prejudiced, subjective approach. To contemporaries there was only one Rule. Elias, writing to the convent of Valenciennes, exhorted the brothers to observe the Rule 'approved by Pope Innocent and recently confirmed by the present Pope Honorius',[2] and, in case his words inspire no great confidence, St Francis' own shall be added to them. He replied to a novice who said it would be a great comfort to him to have a psalter: 'whoever wishes to be a Friar Minor ought to have nothing but a tunic, as the rule has allowed him, and breeches, and those who are compelled to can wear shoes', and gave a similar answer to a Minister who wanted to keep the many books that he possessed. The reference is to the *Regula Bullata*, for there is no mention of shoes in the *Regula Prima*.[3]

Contemporary Friars Minor, when they recorded Hugolino's activities on behalf of their Order, represented them as entirely praiseworthy and beneficial. Celano extolled his behaviour, and though allowance must be made for the fact that he wrote the *Vita Prima* at the Cardinal's request, and after he had been elevated to the Papacy, there is no reason to suppose that he was insincere. The criticisms that modern writers have levelled against the Protector are based on a realisation of dangers and tendencies in his policy that were hardly, if at all, apparent at the time. Hugolino's relations with the friars were kindly and well-intentioned. They throw light, indeed, upon what was probably the most attractive side of his character, and, in seeking to understand the man, his capacity as Cardinal Protector should not be considered in isolation, or its importance over-emphasised. He was, first and foremost, a Church politician engaged in a bitter, relentless and pedantic

---

[1] Cf. Moorman, *Sources for the Life of St Francis*, pp. 29–35; Cuthbert, *Life of St Francis*, pp. 311–15, 379–87; Sabatier, *Vie de S. François*, pp. 290 ff.

[2] *M.G.H. Scr.* xxx, i, 295. See also *Solet annuere*, 29 November 1223 (Sbaralea, I, 15, no. H3, 14 (I)): 'Eapropter, dilecti in Domino filii, vestris piis precibus inclinati, ordinis vestri regulam a bonae memoriae Innocentio papa praedecessore nostro approbatam, annotatam praesentibus, auctoritate vobis apostolica confirmamus.'

[3] *Intentio*, pp. 94, 87; *Reg. Prima*, c. 2; *Reg. Bullata*, c. 2.

conflict of principle and politics with the Emperor Frederick II, and a learned canon lawyer, who was responsible for codifying the *Decretals*. Only a little of his time was spent in being a 'friar among the friars'.

2. PETER CATANII

Although St Francis was always, by virtue of his inspiration and his holiness, the foremost of the Friars Minor, and alone of them all could be called simply 'the brother',[1] he was not, in the last years of his life, their official superior. The fact of his abdication is recorded by Celano in the *Vita Secunda*. At a certain Chapter meeting, he wrote, the saint publicly and firmly announced his intention of having no further charge of the Order, and nominated in his stead Peter Catanii, to whom he then and there bowed down and promised obedience.[2] The story is not given in its historical context, but is related as an apt illustration in the section on humility, and it is therefore necessary to discover its chronological setting, its causes and its significance.

The circumstances are generally considered to have been somewhat as follows. The saint alleged his bodily infirmities as the reason for his action; and his most serious illness, the infection of his eyes, was contracted while he was in the East 1219–20.[3] The changes and disturbances within the Order that so distressed him can be dated to that same period, and in the *Intentio Regulae* he is reported as having said that he had ceased to hold office over the brethren because they no longer walked in his way.[4] Both factors may have influenced and discouraged him, and taken together they have suggested the conclusion that he resigned from office on his return to Italy. He is represented as feeling unequal to the task of dealing with the problems that had arisen, through pain, sorrow and a consciousness of his own limitations as a governor. His followers needed to be corrected, and he was averse to punishing them; they needed to be controlled, and he lacked the gifts of an

---

[1] Jordan, c. 17: '(Helyas) ait: Fratres, ita dicit frater—significans b. Franciscum, qui quasi per excellentiam a fratribus frater dicebatur....'
[2] 2 *Cel.* 143.   [3] *Sp. S.* c. 91.
[4] Jordan, cc. 11–15; *Intentio*, c. 13.

administrator; they needed to be guided, and had grown too
numerous for the personal care of a single leader. They were
becoming independent, ambitious and wilful, and at this time of
crisis in their development he relinquished, with grief, his authority
over them. It was to him a bitter sacrifice, the renunciation not of
a burden, but of his own ideal, whose spiritual purity was now
being of necessity modified to a less exalted level within the reach
of the many too frail to grasp perfection. The wrench was made
abruptly and completely in the presence of the assembled brethren,
and the Chapter that witnessed it is stated, almost invariably, as
having been held in September 1220.[1]

   This reconstruction and interpretation are open to several objections. In the first place it allows to Peter, who died on 10 March 1221,[2]
an extremely brief period of office—little more than five months
—and, if that were the case, it is rather surprising that there are so
many stories connected with his tenure. The *Vita Secunda* and the
Speculum Perfectionis relate between them eight distinct episodes,
all of which involve St Francis as well as Peter, in his capacity as
vicar.[3] This makes it more difficult to believe that they should all
be assigned to these few months, since for much of the winter of
1220–1 the saint was away from Assisi (where Peter worked and
died[4]) conferring with Hugolino.[5] One story in particular can

---

[1] Sabatier, *Vie de S. François*, pp. 280 ff.; Attal, *S. Francesco d'Assisi*, 2 ed.
(Padua, 1947), pp. 334–5; Gratien, *Histoire de l'Ordre des Frères Mineurs au XIIIe
siècle*, pp. 16–17; Moorman, *Sources for the Life of St Francis*, pp. 30–1; Lempp,
p. 45 and n. 3. Golubovich, I, 122–3, does not accept this date and says that
the appointment as Minister General must have been made at the Whitsun
Chapter of 1217. I am inclined to agree with his conclusion (see below), but
the reasons he gives for arriving at it—that the Chapter was a General Chapter,
and that General Chapters were held every other year—are not sound. The
sources speak only of 'quodam capitulo' and General Chapters were annual
events (*3 Soc.* c. 14 (57); James of Vitry, *Epistola*, printed by Golubovich,
I, 5–6; *Reg. Prima*, c. 18).
   [2] The date in the inscription carved in the stone of the chapel of the Portiuncula reads 'Anno Domini MCCXXI.VI ID. MARTII'. Cf. Golubovich, I, 125.
   [3] *2 Cel.* 91, 143, 144, 151 = *Sp. S.* cc. 38, 39, 40, 46; *2 Cel.* 67, 182; *Sp. S.*
cc. 8, 61 (for full references, see Moorman, *Sources*, pp. 104 ff.).
   [4] The incidents related in *2 Cel.* 67, and in *Sp. S.* cc. 8, 38, 39, 61, took place
at Assisi. Peter died at Assisi in St Francis' absence (*24 Gen.*, *A.F.* III, 30–1
and nn.).
   [5] Jordan, c. 14.

hardly have reference to this period. At a time when the Portiuncula was crowded with brethren from distant parts, Peter noticed that the alms were insufficient to supply their needs. He asked St Francis to allow him to reserve some of the property of novices in future against such another emergency, but was rebuked for his prudence.[1] The occasion seems clearly to have been a Chapter meeting, as only then did the brethren gather together from the remoter districts, and Chapters were never held more than twice a year, at Whitsun and Michaelmas. Peter died a month before Whitsun 1221, and if he was appointed at Michaelmas 1220 there could have been no Chapter held for him to provide for while he was in office.

The difficulty of fitting the stories of his activities into his supposed period of office is avoided in a modified version of the usual account—while his permanent appointment as Minister General is still dated 29 September 1220, some scholars have held that he had earlier exercised temporarily the functions of a vicar on the many occasions when St Francis was away on missionary journeys.[2] In support of this hypothesis it is possible to quote from Bartholomew of Pisa: 'Brother Peter was first the vicar of St Francis; and then became Minister General when St Francis surrendered the office in the presence of the brethren.'[3] There is also the fact that from the very beginnings of the Order St Francis showed readiness to hand over his authority to another. When the first twelve friars were on their way to Rome to seek Papal confirmation of the Rule, he suggested to his companions that they should elect a leader, and in deference to his wish they chose Bernard of Quintavalle.[4] But the saint was here concerned to make himself subject to obedience and to strengthen his own humility, and it is not until he went to Egypt in 1219 that there is any evidence of his arranging for vicars to take over the business of the Order in his absence.[5] The argument that it would have been impossible for him not to have appointed a deputy whenever he went abroad,[6]

[1] 2 Cel. 67.
[2] Attal, op. cit. p. 335; Gratien, pp. 8, 16–17.
[3] A.F. IV, 203.   [4] 3 Soc. c. 12 (46).   [5] Jordan, c. 11.
[6] Golubovich, I, 122.

though theoretically sensible, loses its force when applied to St Francis, to whom it was a virtue to be improvident and unpractical, taking no thought for the morrow, and joyfully casting all care upon the Lord. Bartholomew of Pisa's statement likewise proves nothing. It was written near the end of the fourteenth century, and is not based upon actual knowledge. It appears rather to be an attempt to rationalise and explain the differences in terminology which the writer found in the earlier sources that he used for his work. The problem of the constitutional significance of the two terms 'vicar' and 'minister general' will be considered in detail later. During St Francis' lifetime both titles referred to the same office. They were not used to distinguish consecutive stages in constitutional evolution, but merely reflected the writer's subjective conception of the proper functions and status of the holder.[1] They are consequently interchangeable. When Celano told the story of how the saint caused Peter to give the only New Testament that they had to a poor woman, he is referred to as vicar; the version of the same story in the *Scripta Leonis* speaks of him as minister general.[2] Thus there are inadequate grounds for presuming that Peter had a temporary official position before his permanent appointment, and the first objection to dating this September 1220 remains unanswered.

The indications as to the time at which the appointment was made, and the length of its duration, which can be gleaned from the sources, provide another very serious objection. The Chapter at which St Francis abdicated was said, by Celano, the *Speculum Perfectionis* and the *Speculum Lemmens*, to have been held 'a few years after his conversion',[3] and his conversion took place in 1206 (or early 1207). Then, after he had handed over his authority to the ministers, he still feared that he was not sufficiently a subject, and therefore, 'a long while before his death', he asked for a guardian whom in especial he was to obey.[4] He died on

---

[1] See below, pp. 106 ff.

[2] MS. Perugia, c. 89=56, *Sp. S.* c. 38; *2 Cel.* 91.

[3] *2 Cel.* 143; *Sp. S.* c. 39; *Sp. L.* c. 14.

[4] *Sp. L.* c. 15; *Sp. S.* c. 46. The story is also told in *2 Cel.* 151, though here the indication of when it occurred is more vague: 'Dixit enim fratri Petro Cathanii, cui pridem obedientiam sanctam promiserat....'

3 October 1226. Also, a notice on Peter Catanii contained in the MS. St Anthony de Urbe says of him: 'after he joined the Order he was for a long time St Francis' vicar',[1] and if a period of five months is thereby intended, reckonings of 'a long time' have altered much. The inference to be drawn from each of these phrases is that 1220 is too late a date.

Finally, the assumption that St Francis and Peter Catanii were present at a Chapter at Michaelmas 1220 rests on no sure foundation. They were both in Syria in the summer of that year, and returned together when news reached them of the troubles that had broken out.[2] Since they probably did not embark before September, they could not have reached Assisi by 29 September.[3] But quite apart from this, Jordan's evidence precludes the possibility that the saint attended that Michaelmas Chapter. He said explicitly that Francis, on his return, went straight to the Pope, without confronting the innovators at Assisi. Then, when Hugolino had helped him to reform the Order, he immediately (*statim*) summoned a General Chapter which met at Whitsun 1221. This was his first public appearance since his journey to the East, and the brethren, many of whom had believed him dead, rejoiced exceedingly to have him among them again.[4]

Thus the contention that St Francis made over his authority to Peter Catanii in the autumn of 1220 not only possesses no concrete support, but is in imperfect accord with the stories told of them after the transfer, hardly reconcilable with the indications of time that are given, and flatly contradictory to Jordan's narrative. It can therefore be confidently eliminated, and it is now necessary to find a more probable alternative. As the scene was staged at a Chapter meeting it can only have taken place at one of two seasons of the year, at Whitsun or at Michaelmas. The years 1219, 1220 and 1221 may be dismissed at once. After the Whitsun Chapter of 1219 St Francis took Peter with him overseas, leaving Matthew of Narni and Gregory of Naples as his vicars; for the rest of 1219 and most of 1220 they were still abroad;[5] and Peter was

---

[1] This is printed by Father L. Oliger, *A.F.H.* XII (1919), 378.
[2] Jordan, cc. 10–14.   [3] See above, p. 65 n.
[4] Jordan, cc. 14–16.   [5] *Ibid.* cc. 3, 10–14.

dead before Whitsun 1221. The only other clue lies in the circumstance that the appointment was not made before the institution of Ministers; and that step is traditionally assigned to the Whitsun Chapter of 1217.[1] Whether Peter's appointment took place then, or slightly later, in September 1217, or in 1218, is uncertain. In favour of the earliest possible date, 14 May 1217, it may be suggested that that agrees best with such statements as 'a few years after his conversion', and that the establishment of a regular ministry may well have prompted St Francis to submit himself to them as to a recognised authority approved by the Gospels.[2]

Against this theory it might be urged that before his mission to the East St Francis would not have been justified in laying down the burden of office on the ground of ill-health. It is indeed undeniable that his greatest bodily sufferings were borne in the last years of his life, but nonetheless there is ample evidence that he underwent much pain and sickness from the time that he was first converted from the world. In his youth he had been delicate, and after he turned away from pleasure he weakened his physique by rigorous abstinence.[3] Accounts of his activities in the early days constantly draw attention to his infirmities: he would help poor people with their burdens, though his own shoulders were weak; he was prevented from reaching Morocco by a threatened illness, and would not lightly have abandoned the project, for he had been so eager to arrive there that he had frequently outstripped his companion in his haste; he once lay grievously sick in a hermitage and was restored to health by a miraculous turning of water into wine.[4] There is no need to multiply examples further, or to question the truth of his own words, recorded by brother Leo in the

[1] Ministers are mentioned in 2 Cel. 143 (the account of Peter Catanii's appointment). Cf. 24 Generals, A.F. III, 9–10.
[2] The name 'minister' derived from the Gospel passage: 'quicumque voluerit inter eos maior fieri sit eorum minister' (Matt. xxiii. 11), which is quoted in the Reg. Prima, c. 5, and which was adopted in preference to any of the normal official titles in token of humility. In the Reg. Prima, c. 6, the friars are expressly forbidden to use the title of 'prior'.
[3] Legenda Vetus, Lemmens, II, 92–3; MS. Perugia, c. 112=92.
[4] 1 Cel. 76, 56, 61.

Intentio Regulae, 'although I have been a sick man since the begin-ning of my conversion'.[1]

Another criticism is more difficult to answer. If St Francis had put Peter Catanii in his place before 1219, why did he take him with him to the East? The most sensible course would, surely, have been to leave him behind in charge of the Order, especially since the saint hoped that his own journey might be crowned with martyrdom. The point is incapable of proof, but in reply it may perhaps be said that, unless the objections that have here been raised against September 1220 as the date of the appointment can be satisfactorily met, there is no choice but to presume it was made earlier. Moreover, it would be highly unrealistic to main-tain that men naturally act in accordance with what others might think wise, and individual actions that cannot be fitted into an intelligible pattern may for that very reason be authentic. On a more concrete level, there is an incident related by Jordan, which illustrates the personal relations of the two men when they were in the East. Each called the other 'Domine' as a sign of their mutual respect: and they treated each other with the same respect in the East as in Italy.[2]

The objections to dating Peter Catanii's appointment to 1217 or 1218 are not strong, and the hypothesis has in its favour the great advantage that it conflicts with none of the positive evidence. The acceptance of the earlier date in place of 1220 is not without consequence; it involves essential changes in the interpretation of the meaning and the causes of St Francis' action. It was not the outcome of insubordination or of attempts of the brethren to refashion the Order after their own desires, for before the saint left Italy for Egypt the tendencies leading to alteration of his work had not yet become articulate. Nor is it at all likely, as Lempp would have us believe, that it was due partly to pressure from the Curia.[3] If it was implemented at the Whitsun Chapter of 1217 it actually preceded Hugolino's association with the Friars Minor,

---

[1] *Intentio*, c. 13: 'licet ab initio mee conversionis ad Christum infirmitius fuerim'. Lemmens, I, 96, gives 'infirmus' but the reading of MS. S. Isidore 1/73, on which it is based, is unmistakable (so also MS. Perugia).

[2] Jordan, c. 12.   [3] Lempp, pp. 44–5.

but even if it were later there are still no grounds for attributing it to the Cardinal's influence. At their meeting in Florence he showed no inclination to remove St Francis from the leadership of his followers. On the contrary, he urged the saint not to leave Italy, where he deemed his presence necessary for the continued existence of the movement he inspired.[1] It would, therefore, be incorrect to explain Francis' resignation in terms of tragedy. Why, then, did he do it? The answer is not complicated or obscure; it was given precisely and explicitly by Celano—St Francis had no wish to command, by virtue of his great humility. His plea of illness, though it was made with truth, was probably made chiefly to convince others, and in his own mind was secondary to his aversion to exercising authority. He appointed Peter Catanii because he did not want, himself, to be a prelate.[2]

3. ELIAS

You ask why St Francis, though he foresaw that brother Elias would prove so useless and dangerous to the Order, nevertheless left him in charge? Ask likewise: why did Christ raise Judas to the pinnacle of Apostleship, though he knew that he would prove a thief, would betray his Lord, would show himself (not by nature, but by imitation) a devil?[3]

When Peter Catanii died St Francis did not resume the charge of the Order himself, and it was again entrusted to another, this time to brother Elias. Why he, of all the saint's followers, should have been singled out for this position is a question that has acquired for many something of a sinister significance by reason of his later history and, still more, of his unenviable posthumous reputation. Even the easy-going Salimbene referred to him as 'a thoroughly bad lot',[4] and he was regarded by the Spirituals, at the turn of the

---

[1] See above p. 62 and n. 2.

[2] *2 Cel.* 143: 'Ad servandam humilitatis sanctae virtutem...praelationis officium resignavit.' Cf. Cod. S. Ant. de Urbe, *A.F.H.* xii, 378: 'Frater Petrus Catanii...fuit diu vicarius b. Francisci. Nam b. Franciscus nihil proprium habere volens, nec ipsam prelationem, voluit eum esse sibi vicarium.'

[3] Note to *Speculum Vitae b. Francisci et sociorum eius*, ed. Spoelberch (Antwerp, 1620), part ii, 99.

[4] Salimbene B. pp. 148, 155, H. pp. 106, 110.

thirteenth century, fighting for an uncompromising interpretation of absolute poverty, as the arch-traitor of the Fraternity. Was he not the leader of those who tormented St Francis in his last years by their behaviour and their demands, and who, after his death, brought tribulation upon his true sons?[1] How came it that he was given power to work such harm: surely the saint, who sensed the inmost thoughts of men and was not normally misled by outward appearances,[2] could not have been deceived as to his true moral character? He must have known him for what he was, and been forced against his reason to cherish him. Elias' appointment was not a misfortune; it was a punishment ordained of God.[3]

Shorn of its most lurid phraseology and its strained biblical comparisons, the denunciation has been revived by some modern writers on Franciscan history. St Francis' affection for Elias appeared to Sabatier as a baffling psychological phenomenon, about which he could only say that 'men of loving hearts seldom have a perfectly clear intelligence', and the latter's nomination to office seemed to him to mark a decisive stage in the movement away from the original ideal: 'almost everything which was done in the Order after 1221 was done either without St Francis' knowledge or against his will.... The last five years of his life were only one incessant effort at protest, both by his example and his words.'[4] Sabatier's disciple, Lempp, was of the same opinion: the men chiefly responsible for introducing modifications in opposition to the founder's intention were the Ministers, and at the head of the Ministers was Elias.[5]

That St Francis was not altogether happy about the future of his Order is shown both by the stories of the *Intentio Regulae*, that were recorded by his close companion brother Leo[6] (to mention but one witness), and by his own pleading with the brethren in the Rules and in the Testament. It is also clear that those who occasioned him most distress were generally Ministers, or prelates,

[1] Cf. Angelo Clareno, *Rendiconti*, pp. 97–131, 221–36.
[2] Cf. 2 *Cel.* 27–9, 31–4.
[3] *Speculum Vitae*, ed. Spoelberch, *ut sup.*, p. 99.
[4] Sabatier, *Vie de S. François*, pp. 277, 316 (English translation by L. S. Houghton (London, 1926), pp. 243, 275–6).
[5] Lempp, pp. 96–8.   [6] *Intentio*, cc. 1, 4–16.

or learned men, and that the main cause of difficulties and friction
was the injunction to observe absolute poverty. This was the chief
external characteristic of the Franciscan way of life. When the
saint had opened the Book of the Gospel in the Church of St
Nicholas to find counsel for his first disciples, Bernard and Peter,
he had come upon the texts: 'If thou wouldst be perfect, go, and
sell all that thou hast, and give to the poor, and thou shalt have
treasure in Heaven'; 'Take nothing with you on your journey';
'He that will come after me let him deny himself'; and he had
taken them to heart in all their directness.[1] The son of a prosperous
merchant who had passed his youth in irresponsible and extravagant gaiety, he was ignorant of the theological commentaries on
the words that might have slurred over their challenge, and he
accepted, impulsively and with joy, their literal, practical application. The friars were to have nothing beyond their necessary
clothing, and were to travel through the world as strangers and
pilgrims. Not only were they to own no private property; they
were to have nothing in common either. The requirement was
unprecedented among established religious Orders, but it was not
so much this that concerned some of his literate followers as the
fact that it was so drastic. St Francis asked of the educated that
they should forsake even their learning, so that, stripped of all
their possessions, they might offer themselves naked to the naked
Christ,[2] but this particular sacrifice was harder than the renunciation of money, or of comfort, and few fulfilled it, though St
Anthony of Padua showed them the way.[3] Many, indeed, saw
no virtue in such a sacrifice, and argued that knowledge was essential to a preacher of the catholic faith, both to enable him to
confute heretics, and to preserve himself from error. Upon one
level of understanding they were justified, and the union of wisdom and holiness, of theology and the Gospel way of life, was an
ideal that naturally exercised a strong attraction for the learned
men who were as eager as the simple and ignorant to put on the
habit of the Friar Minor. St Francis opposed their aspiration, for

---

[1] 3 Soc. c. 8 (28–9).   [2] 2 Cel. 194.
[3] S. Antonii Legenda Prima, ed. L. de Kerval, S. Antonii de Padua Vitae duae,
Collection d'études et de documents, v (Paris, 1904), cc. 7–8.

he was at once more of an idealist and more of a realist. He was fully aware of the value of theology,[1] but recognised that study, for most men, would be pursued to the detriment of poverty, simplicity and humility, which were the essential foundation of the Franciscan calling. Others might serve the Church with their knowledge, but his mission, and the mission of his followers, was not to demonstrate the truth of the Gospel, but to show forth the beauty of the way it revealed in the example of their own lives. Above all things they were to be imitators of the life of Christ, and all their other activities, however good in themselves, manual labour, care of the sick, begging, preaching, were to be subordinate to this.

His prohibitions and exhortations on this subject were swept aside by the current of intellectual enthusiasm that had caught hold of the progressive and thoughtful spirits of the age. The attraction and stimulus exercised by the universities proved too strong to be gainsaid, and the Friars Minor quickly rivalled the Friars Preachers as a student Order. The development was not effected without injury to the Rule. Books, and the expenses and requirements incidental to their keeping, brought with them as an inevitable corollary a mitigation in poverty, an increase in stability, and a distaste for other forms of service. In the interests of study the learned wanted libraries and leisure, and, if they were to read with a good conscience, they had first to alter the obligations of their profession. St Francis' attempts to redraft the Rule in 1221-3, prior to its formal approbation by the Papacy, gave them their opportunity. They conferred with him over its provisions, they argued, criticised, complained, and the saint, unwilling to contend with them, at times gave way. It seems that he was subjected to much well-intentioned pressure, for brother Leo, who was his companion and scribe while he was composing the new Rule, refers to the suggestions and objections put forward by the brothers more than once. But though he deplored their attitude, Leo did not regard it as culpable, observing that the

[1] Cf. *Testament*: 'Et omnes theologos et qui ministrant sanctissima verba divina debemus honorare et venerari sicut qui ministrant nobis spiritum et vitam.'

protests were made in ignorance of future trouble, and the absence of rancour in his stories is in marked contrast to the bitterness displayed by the group that later appealed to his reminiscences.[1]

St Francis was naturally upset by the opposition to principles of life that were the fruit of a very personal and very deep religious experience, and that were enunciated after long prayer and meditation, in the conviction that they were received of Christ. Nevertheless his distress, and the extent of his failure to secure acceptance of his ideal in its entirety, must not be exaggerated. The seeds of discord and disaffection had not yet germinated, and the arguments that occurred over the text of the Rule should not be seen too much in terms of latent or impending tragedy. Discussion was rather the manifestation of a keen desire to do everything possible to ensure its excellence, and revealed a state of mind infinitely preferable to mere acquiescence or indifference. The Ministers are said to have deleted many of the precepts that he wished observed,[2] but the charge is supported with extraordinarily few concrete examples. They prevented the inclusion of an obligation to see that the consecrated Elements were decently kept by the parish priests, as they felt that this was not a fit subject for command; and they likewise refused to be bound to collect all writings that might contain the name of God and to have them safely stored.[3] They tried also to modify the practice of poverty,

---

[1] *Intentio*, cc. 4, 6, 16. The Spirituals, whose writings were controversial and apologetic, needed to establish the authority for their statements, and appealed to brother Leo as the source of their more unplausible stories about St Francis. The first pseudo-Leonine collection under Spiritual influence is the so-called *Verba S. Francisci* (I hope to expound the evidence for this in a separate study).

[2] *Intentio*, rubric (probably not Leonine): '...postea fecit illam, quam Papa Honorius confirmavit cum bulla, de qua regula multa fuerunt ejecta per ministros contra voluntatem b. Francisci'. Cf. the story about Honorius himself in *Legenda Vetus*, *Opuscules*, VI, 90–5, Angelo Clareno, *Rendiconti*, pp. 122–5.

[3] MS. Perugia, c. 103 = 80; *Sp. S.* c. 65; etc. Injunctions on these matters appear in neither the *Reg. Prima* nor the *Reg. Bullata*, and St Francis, who had on one occasion intended to send the brethren throughout the provinces with new pyxes for the better housing of Our Lord's body, and who made a habit of salvaging odd scraps of paper (*ibid.*; *2 Cel.* 201; *1 Cel.* 82) had perforce to be content with exhorting his followers to show these signs of reverence (*Testament, Admon.* I, *Epist.* 2, 5, *De reverentia corporis Domini et de munditia altaris*).

and caused the words 'Take nothing with you on your journey' to be struck out of the final version, but the saint countered this by having it written at the beginning and end of the Rule that the brothers were to observe the Holy Gospel,[1] and it was not until after his death that this was nullified by an appeal to the Pope.[2] On the immediate issue of the spirit and essence of the Rule, that is the full and unreserved acceptance of the life of the Gospel revelation, the saint did in fact prevail, and the danger, which he himself recognised and did his utmost to forestall, lay less in the wording of the Rule than in the interpretations that the artful and unscrupulous might later put upon it, despite the plainness of its meaning.[3]

Those who were with the saint when he rewrote the Rule declared that the brothers, and in particular the prelates, withstood him on many points, and the fact of their opposition remains unaltered by the measure of its efficacy. What part did Elias have in the debates that took place? Was he among those who gave St Francis pain, as his detractors averred? He only enters the story once, at its most dramatic moment, and his role is illuminating. St Francis, so the tradition holds, had retired to Fonte Colombo with brother Leo and brother Bonizo, to whom he dictated the Rule that he received by prayer, fasting and meditation. Some of the Ministers, fearing that in such surroundings and without their restraining influence he might make regulations stricter than they cared to observe, came in a deputation to Elias, and asked him to protest in their name that they would not be holden to it. He replied that he had no desire to incur the saint's displeasure by being the bearer of such a message, but at length he agreed to go, on condition that they came with him. They went in a body, therefore, up the valley of Rieti until they were within calling distance, and then Elias voiced their complaint. Francis, when he heard it, invoked the Deity, and Christ answered audibly that

---

[1] *Intentio*, c. 6.   [2] Sbaralea, I, 68, no. G 9, 56 (IV).

[3] *Testament*: 'Et omnibus fratribus meis clericis et laicis praecipio firmiter per obedientiam, ut non mittant glossas in regula neque in istis verbis dicendo: Ita volunt intelligi; sed sicut dedit mihi Dominus simpliciter et pure dicere et scribere regulam et ista verba, ita simpliciter et pure intelligatis et cum sancta operatione observetis usque in finem.'

the Rule was His and that He wished it kept to the letter and without gloss. Thereupon the saint cried out in triumph, and, more amenable than the witches in Macbeth, offered to play the record again. The Ministers, however, had had their lesson and departed abashed.[1]

It is a remarkable incident, and in this, its developed form, not very plausible. The harshness of tone, the emphasis on the divine nature of the Rule, and the direct intervention of Christ are details that alike proclaim it a characteristic specimen of Spiritual apocalyptic writing, and it was the Spirituals who circulated and popularised the story in the *Verba S. Francisci*, the *Arbor Vitae* (1305), the *Speculum Perfectionis* (1318), the *Historia VII Tribulationum* (*c.* 1314–23), and the *Verba Fratris Conradi* (*c.* 1328). There is not time or necessity here to enter into a full discussion of the problems connected with it, its probable author, or its proper place in the Franciscan tradition, but for the immediate purpose of discovering Elias' contribution to the making (or marring) of the *Regula Bullata* it is profitable and interesting to trace the growth and elaboration of the narrative, which yields information about two categories of fact—the actual events, and how and why they came to be misrepresented.

For all that concerns the writing of the Rule St Francis himself is the ultimate authority, and the earliest, and the only first-hand account is in his Testament. In a passage reminiscent of St Paul's Epistle to the Galatians he describes how no one had shown him what he should do, but the Lord had revealed to him that he should live according to the pattern of the Holy Gospel; and he had caused it to be written down, in few words and simply, and the Pope had confirmed it. Further on he straitly commanded all the brothers on obedience not to put glosses on the Rule, but, as the Lord had granted him to write it 'simpliciter et pure', so it was to be understood. His words imply that he saw no essential difference between the various redactions of the Rule—the first reference quoted is apparently to the *Regula Primitiva*, the second to the *Regula Bullata*—and show that he wished the text to be sacrosanct for the reason that it had been inspired directly by God.

[1] *Verba*, c. 4.

There is also, perhaps, a hint that he remembered complaints against its precepts and feared a fresh outburst, for near the end of the Testament he wrote: 'Let not the brothers say: This is another Rule', as if anticipating that they might murmur even at his dying wishes. But being concerned to bear witness to his own inward, spiritual experience and certainty, he mentioned no concrete instances of human help or opposition, and these can be reconstructed only from the notices vouchsafed by his biographers.

Thomas of Celano saw no useful purpose of edification to be served by recording what happened in the period when the Rule was in preparation and almost entirely ignored it. The *Vita Prima* says nothing of any Rule but the *Regula Primitiva*, and the *Vita Secunda* is little more informative. It does, however, contain one relevant section, an account of a vision that St Francis had while the question of the final confirmation of the Rule was being discussed. He dreamt that he was surrounded by many starving brothers and that he tried to feed them by gathering crumbs of bread from the ground, but the particles were so tiny that they slipped through his fingers. He hesitated, not knowing how to distribute them, and then he heard a voice tell him to make the crumbs into a host, which could be divided and eaten. He obeyed, and, as he gave it to the brothers, such as did not receive it devoutly became infected with leprosy. The meaning of the vision was not immediately revealed to him, but during the day, as he watched in prayer, the voice came to him again, saying: 'Francis, the crumbs of last night are the words of the Gospel, the host is the Rule, and the leprosy wickedness.'[1]

St Bonaventure incorporated the tale into his *Legenda Maior S. Francisci*—written at the request of the General Chapter held at Narbonne in 1260[2]—copying very closely the wording of 2 *Celano*; but he put it into a tangible setting and related it to circumstantial details that he must have learnt from another source. The vision was sent to admonish St Francis, and caused him, led by the Holy Spirit, to retire to a certain mountain with two companions. There, fasting upon bread and water and praying constantly for guidance, he composed the Rule. When it was

[1] *1 Cel.* 32; *2 Cel.* 209.   [2] Bonav., Prologue; cf. *24 Gen., A.F.* III, 328.

written he entrusted it to his vicar, and behold, within a few days
it had been lost through negligence. The saint returned to his
former retreat and drew it up again in the same terms as before,
as though he had received the very words from the mouth of
God, and this time it was taken to the Pope, Honorius III, and
confirmed. He exhorted the brothers fervently to observe it,
affirming that he had included nothing of his own, but had
received all it contained through divine revelation, and that his
claim was true was soon established. The Lord acknowledged his
son by imprinting upon him the five wounds of Christ, the
Stigmata.[1]

St Bonaventure's account, though there is no reason to doubt
that it was founded upon fact, contains the embryo that was to
grow into a full-fledged legend, nourished upon biblical analogies
and topographical and other details imaginatively dramatised. In
the *Legenda Maior* there are echoes of two biblical stories, which,
while they are kept subordinate to the sequence of events, yet
affect the tone of the narrative. There is, first of all, Jeremiah's
description of how the Lord ordered him to write down all his
prophecies in a book, and of how, after he had dictated them to
Baruch the scribe, the book was taken to Jehoiakim, king of Judah,
who cast it into the fire. Then the Lord spoke to Jeremiah again,
and told him to take another roll and to write upon it all that had
been written in the one that was burnt, and he did so. There is
also the story of Moses receiving the commandments of God
upon Mount Sinai.[2] The first parallel was not developed, and the
vicar (Elias) who lost the Rule was never likened to Jehoiakim.
The *Speculum Perfectionis* and its associated texts actually kept
silence about his responsibility in the matter and passed over the
incident with the briefest mention, saying baldly: 'After the
second Rule that St Francis drew up had been lost, he went up
into a mountain with brother Leo of Assisi and brother Bonizo
of Bologna to make another Rule....'[3] The version in MS. Little
implicitly minimised Elias' part: St Francis gave the manuscript
of the Rule not to Elias personally but to the Ministers collectively,

[1] Bonav., c. 4. [2] Jer. xxxvi; Exod. xix–xxxii.
[3] *Sp. S.* c. 1.

and they were careless enough to lose it.[1] The opportunities for defamation of character were not, however, entirely wasted. It seemed inconceivable to some that a document so precious as the Rule could have been lost by mistake, and they were not loath to suggest discreditable motives. Thus Bartholomew of Pisa declared that Elias read the text that the saint handed to him, and, being ill-pleased with it, he destroyed it and made pretence that it was a mishap. This interpretation was accepted and repeated by Wadding.[2] Angelo Clareno preferred an alternative calumny: St Francis did not hand over the Rule to Elias at all, but entrusted it to brother Leo, whereupon Elias with certain of his followers contrived to steal it, hoping so to frustrate the saint's designs.[3]

It seems surprising that the authors of the *Speculum* 'floretta' soft-pedalled the losing of the Rule by Elias. The probable explanation is that they were too preoccupied with the conception of the Rule as God-given and too liable to regard its genesis only in terms of that other biblical parallel, the Mosaic analogy. Fonte Colombo was the Sinai of the Order; God gave the Rule to St Francis as He had given the Law to Moses; the Ministers forced Elias to repudiate it as the Jewish people had forced Aaron to construct the golden calf. What would not fit easily into this context was relegated to the background.[4] The manifestations of divine intervention were increasingly emphasised and became increasingly more sensational. St Francis had testified that the Lord had enabled him to dictate and write the Rule in pure and simple

---

[1] MS. Little, *Coll. Fr.* I, 76: '...et dum fuisset regula ita correcta ab ore Christi, tradidit eam b. Franciscus ministris, et ipsi per cautelam (MS. Ashburnham 326, in Bibl. Laurentiana, f. 29, gives correctly "incautelam") eam perdiderunt'.

[2] Barth., *A.F.* IV, 371; Wadding, *Annales*, II, 62.

[3] Angelo Clareno, *Rendiconti*, p. 120: 'Tumultuant et extuant [i.e. aestuant], dum Deo vacat Moyses iste Franciscus, frater Elyas cum sequacibus suis et quibusdam ministris et qui adversari ei palam non audebant, viro Dei fratri Leoni, qui regulam sibi a Sancto traditam conservabat, furtim seu latenter subtrahunt et abscondunt, putantes tali modo s. Francisci propositum impedire, ne iuxta verbum Christi ad eum celitus factum regulam Summo Pontifici presentaret et eam faceret approbari....'

[4] The Mosaic analogy occurs in MS. Little, *Coll. Fr.* I, 76, c. 144 (rubric); *Verba fratris Conradi, Opuscules*, VI, 373; Angelo Clareno, *loc. cit.*; 24 *Gen., A.F.* III, 29; *Actus in Valle Reatina*, printed in *Sp. S.* (1898), pp. 255 ff.

words; the brethren of the English province petitioned in 1241 that the Rule might be allowed to remain as the saint had made it 'dictante Spiritu Sancto'; St Bonaventure declared that the entire contents of the Rule were revealed by God and that St Francis added nothing himself[1]—already there is a slight but definite progression. The *Verba Fratris Conradi* volunteers the information that St Francis made his cell in a fissure of the rock a little apart from his companions, but that he reported to them whatever was revealed to him in his prayers. This they recorded, brother Bonizo dictating and brother Leo doing the writing.[2] The *Actus Beati Francisci in Valle Reatina* describes the scene more vividly, the saint coming from the cave in haste to impart his inspiration and calling to brother Leo to bring writing materials.[3] The culmination is reached in a version preserved in MSS. Little, Ashburnham and St Anthony de Urbe, according to which each chapter of the Rule was corrected by Christ. As the sections were finished St Francis prayed the Lord to alter them if He wished, and He replied 'in voce audibili'.[4] He likewise answered in a tone that all could hear the saint's appeal to Him against the recalcitrant Ministers, confounding them with the words: 'Francis, the Rule was made by Me, and...there is nothing of thine in it;...and I wish it to be observed to the letter, and without gloss....'[5] The final improvement upon this astounding declaration was the introduction of a threefold repetition—'ad litteram, ad litteram, ad litteram, sine glosa, sine glosa, sine glosa'.[6] The idea may have been suggested to the perpetrators partly by the story of the voice from Heaven that came to St Francis in his dream—the dream being dispensed with for the sake of effect—and partly by the site, whose possible contribution will be familiar to those who have read Professor Burkitt's fascinating article.[7] There is said to be a powerful echo there, and Professor Burkitt argues that a natural explana-

---

[1] Eccleston, pp. 71–2; Bonav., c. 4.
[2] *Verba fratris Conradi, ut sup.,* p. 371.
[3] *Actus in Valle Reatina, ut sup.,* p. 257.   [4] MS. Little, *loc. cit.* pp. 75–6.
[5] Ubertino da Casale, *Arbor Vitae,* lib. v, c. 5, f. E. iii rb.
[6] *Sp. S.* c. 1.
[7] 2 *Cel.* 209; F. C. Burkitt, 'Fonte Colombo and its Traditions', *Franciscan Essays,* II, 41–55.

tion of the voice from Heaven that Leo thought he heard may be found in this topographical fact. It may be so, but when I myself went to the spot to test this theory, and called down into the valley as loudly as I was able, I did not succeed in awakening any echo.

The role of the Deity is, then, the central theme in the evolution of the legend. It was most stressed in the early fourteenth century, when its importance, as a sanction for the *Regula Bullata*, is fully understandable in the light of the controversy waged between the Spirituals and the Conventuals over the strict, literal observance of the Rule. Elias' place is subordinate, but none the less he did not quite escape the strictures of the censorious once the authority of the Rule had ceased to be a burning issue. Bartholomew of Pisa, writing at the end of the century, is again the first to give the story a decided twist. Instead of accepting that the Ministers took the initiative in approaching Elias with their complaints and uneasiness he affirmed that, when St Francis returned to Fonte Colombo to reproduce his work, Elias, who had seen the lost document and was acquainted with its tenor, notified the Ministers of what they might expect, and they consequently asked him to intervene.[1] Wadding's version is even more explicit in ascribing unworthy motives and behaviour: Elias told the Ministers, on the evidence of the Rule that he had lost, that St Francis intended to compel them to adopt a harder way of life, and when they responded to his warning he dissembled, and pretended that they had forced him to complain.[2] The imputation was cunningly contrived. It provided a plausible reason for an otherwise rather mysterious and seemingly pointless losing of the Rule, and therefore obtained wide acceptance in spite of its late arrival into the story.[3]

---

[1] *A.F.* IV, 372.   [2] Wadding, *Annales*, II, 62–3.

[3] It might seem logical to suppose that the loss of the Rule ought to follow the incident of the deputation, since the *Verba* implies that the ministers' anxiety was due to their *ignorance*—not so easily explicable if a first draft had been seen and lost. This sequence is supported by a version of the *Sp. S.* which reads *priusquam* for *postquam* in the crucial passage (a sermon by Jacob of Tresanto, ed. Sbaralea, *Supplementum ad scriptores a Waddingo descriptos* (Rome, 1806), p. 63, no. 392. Sbaralea dates the sermon *c.* 1300, but it quotes its source

How much real truth there was behind the tradition of the Ministers' opposition is difficult to determine. The tale was improved by fine descriptive writing, notably in the *Arbor Vitae* and the *Actus in Valle Reatina*, and the numbers of those implicated tended to increase. The *Verba S. Francisci* spoke of 'ministri quamplures' and the *Verba Fratris Conradi* of all the brothers in Italy. The direct intervention of Christ was not a historical fact, but a device to express the narrator's great admiration for Francis' sanctity and for the worthiness of the Rule. Yet that there was some substance to the story is indicated by the firm belief of the Spirituals that it came originally from brother Leo, who was with St Francis when these things were done. Moreover the Leonine roll known to Ubertino and to brother Conrad and his entourage was possibly known to and used by St Bonaventure. He mentioned no names, but said that the saint went up into a certain mountain with two companions, and later gave the Rule to his vicar. The *Verba S. Francisci* and the rest describe the same circumstances but more exactly: the mountain was called Fonte Colombo or Mons Ranerii; the companions were brother Leo of Assisi and brother Bonizo of Bologna; the vicar was Elias. The loss of the Rule seems indisputable—it was not the type of incident to be recorded if it were not true, for it was neither edifying nor admirable. It may have been an accident; if it was intentional, it was the action of a man not forceful enough to criticise its author openly. In any case, the accounts of the rewriting of the Rule, when shorn of their accretions and spiteful innuendoes, show that Elias played no energetic or influential part in the proceedings. He was not the instigator of unrest, but the unwilling spokesman of the Ministers. He was not properly one of their number, holding a position apart as the saint's personal deputy, and was made their envoy solely by reason of his office.

The making of the *Regula Bullata* was not the only occasion

specifically as the *Speculum Perfectionis*, and clearly derives the story from some version of *Sp. S.*); and also by the *Actus in Valle Reatina*. But the *Actus* is of no authority; the sermon probably contains, or is based on a scribal error; it is in conflict with all the other early versions of the *Verba* (there is an error in Lemmens' text at this point) and the *Speculum*; and to reconstruct such a story on logical principles is foolhardy.

that permitted of aspersions upon Elias' character. The growth of
falsehood can be traced in other stories also, an especially fine
example of the process being provided by the events of St Francis'
last days. Argument as to whom he intended to honour with his
dying blessing has led to so much misunderstanding and confusion
that it seems desirable to preface an exposure of fictitious developments by a straightforward narrative of what he did. The saint,
whose final illness was protracted, blessed his brothers not once but
many times.[1] Four separate occasions can be distinguished in the
sources, which quite probably omit many obtained by individuals.
The first of which there is record was given six months before he
died, at Siena, whither he had gone for the treatment of his eyes.
He was suffering acutely from weakness of the stomach, and lost
so much blood through sickness that his companions, believing
him dying, begged for a last blessing. He accordingly blessed all
who had joined and all who would join him and added a short
exhortation. At his request his words were written down by a
priest, brother Benedict of Prato.[2] Elias, meanwhile, had heard
of his serious condition and hastened to him. When he was a little
better he brought him to Celle de Cortona and thence to Assisi.[3]
Here, while he lay in the Bishop's palace, St Francis desired certain
of his brothers to come to him. By this time he was blind, and,
having crossed his arms, he asked to make sure on whom his right
hand rested. Satisfied that it was Elias, he blessed him, and the
other brethren in him, but granting to Elias alone a moving,
personal and abundant benediction. Then he warned them all of
tribulation to come.[4] Soon afterwards he was moved to the Portiuncula, and there, a few days before his death, he was visited by
the lady Jacoba de Settesoli. He tasted the marzipan she brought
him, and remembering brother Bernard's fondness for good food,

[1] This reconstruction is based upon the combination of information derived
from (a) Thomas of Celano—Vita Prima, Julian, Legenda Neapolitana (cf. above,
pp. 18–19); (b) St Francis' companions—MS. Perugia, Sp. L., MS. S. Antonii
de Urbe, Sp. S.
[2] 1 Cel. 105, Leg. Nap. lectio 2 (Abate), 4 (Bihl); MS. Perugia, c. 52=17,
Sp. L. c. 30, Sp. S. c. 87, MS. S. Antonii, ff. 53 v–54 r (cf. A.F.H. XII (1919),
338).
[3] 1 Cel. 105.   [4] 1 Cel. 108, Julian, c. 68, Leg. Nap. lectio 2 (A), 5–6 (B).

wanted him to share it. Bernard was immediately fetched from
Assisi, and before he left the bedside he asked for a blessing. St
Francis stretched out his hand and put it upon the head of brother
Giles. Feeling his mistake he transferred it to Bernard, whom he
blessed as his first friar, enjoining all the others to respect and love
him.[1] Finally, on the day of his death, he commanded Angelo and
Leo to sing to him the Praises of the creatures, and himself sang
part of Psalm 141 (142). Then Elias obtained from him a blessing
and a pardon for all the brothers, absent as well as present, which
it was left to him to proclaim. The Gospel codex was brought in,
and a passage from St John read aloud. The brothers gathered
round him as he died.[2]

The especial blessing that St Francis bestowed upon Elias in the
Bishop's palace at Assisi was recorded by Celano in the *Vita Prima*,
and this account, which there is no good reason to disbelieve, is
the source from which all subsequent versions diverge, and the
standard against which they must be weighed. The first stage in
evolution was also achieved by Celano, in his next biography, the
Vita Secunda. How he mixed his ingredients has already been fully
demonstrated in the section on Celano's reliability.[3] This garbled
version succeeded in ousting his former statements and received
wide acceptance. It was repeated in its main features in St Bonaventure's *Legenda Maior S. Francisci*, in both redactions of the
Speculum Perfectionis, and in the *Speculum Vitae*.[4] Its significance is
that it represents the facts after they had been censored, and all
favourable emphasis on Elias suppressed.

The next stage was the confusion of persons. Elias was altogether
denied a blessing. St Francis blessed, not his vicar, but his first
disciple, Bernard of Quintavalle. Thus Angelo Clareno began his

[1] Celano, *Tractatus de Miraculis*, cc. 37 ff., *1 Cel.* 108, *Sp. L.* c. 17 (= *Sp. S.*
c. 107), *Actus b. Francisci*, c. 18.

[2] *1 Cel.* 109–10, Julian, c. 69, *Leg. Nap.* lectio 3 (A), 6–7 (B). See also
Elias' letter to the Provincial Ministers (Lempp, pp. 70–1).

[3] See above, pp. 17–18.

[4] Bonav., c. 14; *Sp. S.* c. 88; *Sp. L.* c. 34; MS. Perugia, c. 21 (pp. 36–7)=117;
Spec. Vitae, ed. Spoelberch, part 1, p. 171. The Perugia and *Speculum* versions have
suppressed the mention of the vicar, and are almost certainly derived from
Celano, not *vice versa*; but the relations of these stories does not affect my
argument.

narration of the second tribulation of the Friars Minor with a description of the saint blessing his brothers upon his deathbed that is derived from 2 *Celano*, but instead of putting his right hand upon Elias' head, Francis called for brother Bernard.[1] The substitution was not effected without further complications in the story. Bernard was now credited with two blessings, and the details of each became entangled, a state of affairs for which the prevailing aptitude for discovering biblical parallels was probably responsible. St Francis had been likened to the patriarch Jacob in the very first account of his blessing that was written—Elias' letter to the Provincial Ministers—and the analogy persisted. The resemblance was chiefly that Jacob's eyes were dim with age so that he could not see, and Francis' were blinded by sickness; but it did not pass unnoticed that the Jewish blessing had a special regard for the first-born, and therefore a particular application to brother Bernard. Then the coincidence that, in the blessing Bernard really did receive, St Francis had first of all touched brother Giles in mistake for him suggested a more familiar parallel, and an unacknowledged transition was made from Jacob's blessing of Manasseh and Ephraim, the sons of Joseph, to Isaac's blessing of Esau and Jacob. The result was a charming story. St Francis called for brother Bernard to come close to him, but he in his humility whispered to Elias that he should go up to the saint's right side and receive a blessing in his stead. He accordingly approached, but Francis, touching him, knew at once that he was not Bernard. The latter therefore came and stood at his left side and Francis, crossing his arms so that his right hand rested on brother Bernard, gave him, as his first friar, a particular blessing. The saint is still likened to Jacob, but the phraseology is borrowed from Isaac's blessing: his words are given as 'Where is my firstborn son? Come near to me that my soul may bless thee before I die'; and in the actual blessing appears: 'Be thou lord over thy brethren.'[2] Actually neither Isaac's blessing nor Jacob's was really suitable to the legend that was being elaborated, and Bernard's claims could not satisfactorily be preferred to those of Elias. In the first place, Isaac had mistaken

[1] Angelo Clareno, *Rendiconti*, pp. 221–3.
[2] *24 Gen.*, A.F. III, 42–3; Gen., xxvii. 4, 19, 29.

Jacob for Esau because of the hairiness of his hands, but Francis was not made to mistake Elias for Bernard. Indeed in reality he had blessed the man he intended in both cases, on one occasion touching Elias and asking to make sure that it was he, and on the other momentarily touching Giles but quickly rectifying his error. In the second place, the first-born were not the favoured sons in either of the biblical instances recalled—Jacob stole Esau's blessing, and Ephraim was preferred above Manasseh. The friars would have been more faithful to the sources had they allowed to Bernard only the marzipan, as Esau received pottage for his birthright!

St Francis, besides blessing his brethren before he died, also blessed bread and distributed it in memory of the Last Supper, and this action gave rise to another fabrication. The incident was first recorded in *2 Celano*, where it is told in its shortest form. The saint ordered bread to be brought to him; then he blessed it and broke it and handed a morsel to each of the friars.[1] The *Legenda Neapolitana*, which appears to have been compiled from very early sources, adds a most interesting detail not generally known. The brothers ate the consecrated bread with great devotion, all except Elias, who, weeping at the thought of Francis' imminent death, was unable to eat it. He held his portion reverently in his hand until brother Leo begged it from him. Leo preserved it carefully, and by its merits many sick persons were healed.[2] Since Elias' great affection for St Francis is amply proved by the indications given in the *Vita Prima* the fact should not be dismissed as unplausible on the ground either that Elias had no praiseworthy feelings or that Leo was always hostile to him—both of them entirely unwarranted assumptions.[3] It was not, however, permitted to remain in the story. The relevant chapter of the *Speculum Perfectionis* says merely that one of the brothers kept back a morsel that subsequently healed many

[1] *2 Cel.* 217.

[2] P. G. Abate, *La Leggenda Napolitana di S. Francesco*, p. 35 (cf. above, p. 19 and n.).

[3] There are signs of hostility to Elias in anecdotes attributed to Leo, but not in his genuine writings. The story of Leo breaking the collecting vase that Elias had put by the Basilica (*A.F.* III, 33–4, 72; *Spec. Vitae*, ed. Lempp, p. 163), is of more than doubtful authenticity (see below, p. 150).

sufferers.[1] But the reticence of the early fourteenth-century compilers concerning Elias' part in the scene is purely negative, and
pales into insignificance beside the positive distortion introduced
by Bartholomew of Pisa. He was aware that the only brother
who did not eat a morsel of bread was Elias, and coolly alleged
that he left it through contempt, deeming St Francis' action silly.
Leo, seeing it scorned, asked for it; Elias gave it away because he
did not value it, and in Leo's possession it worked miracles.[2]

The perversion of Elias' genuine acts was but one of the ways in
which the conception of his personality became falsified. Another
way was to invent anecdotes, which, while they were in harmony
with the failings and characteristics he displayed in later life, were
not typical of his behaviour during St Francis' lifetime. To this
category belong the sections in the *Arbor Vitae* and the *Speculum
Vitae* which tell that Elias at one time provided himself with an
unnecessarily ample tunic. St Francis saw it, and asked him, in the
presence of a number of the brethren, if he might borrow it. When
he had put it on he assumed a proud stance, and strutted up and
down, saluting the bystanders in lordly wise. Then he cast the
garment from him in great indignation, and publicly rebuked
Elias for not being content with a mean and meagre habit.[3] A
similar incident is given in the *Fioretti*, where, among the examples
illustrating St Francis' power to penetrate into the hearts of men
and to divine their inmost thoughts, Elias is mentioned as having
been frequently chidden for the sin of pride.[4] Such tales deserve
no credence. They spring from a familiarity with later history—
it was well known in the fourteenth century that Elias, when he
was General, had become addicted to pomp and splendour, had
dressed richly and become haughty in his bearing—and were
designed to glorify the virtue of foreknowledge that Francis,
as a saint, was presumed to possess. Elias' excommunication
and banishment from the Order, and his deathbed penitence and
reconciliation provided an opportunity that was likewise exploited.

[1] *Sp. S.* c. 88 (also in MS. Perugia—cf. above, p. 97 n. 4).
[2] *A.F.* v, 355.
[3] Ubertino da Casale, *Arbor Vitae*, lib. v, c. 7, f. E.v rb; *Spec. Vitae*, ed.
Spoelberch, part II, p. 98.   [4] *Fioretti*, c. 31.

According to the *Fioretti* it was revealed to St Francis that Elias would leave the Order and find his place among the damned. Knowing this he avoided him and would not speak with him. Elias eventually persuaded him to explain why he so shunned his company, and hearing of his doom, he besought the saint with tears to pray for him and to lighten his sentence by his merits. Francis complied, and succeeded in gaining part of his petition: Elias would forsake the Order and be disgraced, but he would not at the last be damned.[1] This story certainly exalted the saint's prophetic gifts and the efficacy of his prayers, but it was hardly complimentary to his charity or his good sense. It gave an utterly false impression of the relationship between the two men and is exposed and contradicted by the loving blessing Francis gave Elias when he was dying.

The misdemeanours and shameful motives that were invented for Elias for the period while St Francis was alive did not always have even a connection with some fact of his career. There is an unattractive story in the *Arbor Vitae* and the *Speculum Vitae* purporting to be an illustration of how St Francis treated Elias. One day, after a meal at which the latter had provided especially tasty food, Francis instructed him to do still better for the morrow. When the tables were set the holy father called all the humble, simple and despised brothers to sit by him, and said to those who considered themselves important: 'The rest of you go and sit where you like', those being the words that Elias had used the day before to the lowly. Later Elias criticised him for snubbing the influential brethren, and the saint exclaimed: 'Elias, Elias, your presumption, pride and hypocrisy will bring my Order to nought, and undermine the observance of the Gospel. Terrible is the will of God, who foreknows I must leave the Order in your hands.' This is not merely untrue; it is blasphemous.[2] But to demonstrate its untruth, it is only necessary to call to mind Salimbene's com-

---

[1] *Fioretti*, c. 38.

[2] Ubertino da Casale, *Arbor Vitae*, *loc. cit.*; *Spec. Vitae*, ed. Spoelberch, part II, p. 99. A marginal note 'Blasphemia' has been written against this passage in the Codex of the *Arbor Vitae* kept in the Sacro Convento at Assisi. Cf. B. Marinangeli, 'Frate Elia—Fondatore della Provincia di Terra Santa', *Misc. Fr.* XXXIV (1934), 7.

plaint that Elias admitted and promoted to office men of no account.[1] Among his faults was not that of drawing invidious distinctions between persons.

Another unfounded charge assigned to him the responsibility for promulgating a decree forbidding the brothers to eat meat. At one time, the *Fioretti* tells us, St Francis, brother Elias, brother Masseo and certain other friars lived together in a secluded place in the Valley of Spoleto, and St Francis used to retire to a wood to be undisturbed in his prayers. Once while he was so engaged a youth arrived at the friary and knocked loudly at the door. Brother Masseo answered him and taught him how he should have knocked. Then he went to fetch Elias, because the youth wished to ask him a question, but Elias took offence and would not come. The youth, realising this, sent Masseo to St Francis, who straightway ordered Elias on obedience to listen to the question. He complied in angry humour and asked the youth rudely what he wanted. He was asked: 'Is it lawful for observers of the Gospel to eat whatever is set before them, as Christ bade his disciples, and has any man the right to command aught contrary to the Gospel?' To which he replied proudly: 'I know the answer well, but I will not tell it; begone with you', and slammed the door. Then he bethought him that the question was directed against himself and the decree he had made (for he was vicar of the Order) prohibiting the eating of flesh, and his conscience troubled him. He went back and opened the door, hoping the youth would expound the answer to his own question, but he had already departed, and (being an angel) was that same hour many miles away recounting the incident to brother Bernard.[2] The date given to this marvellous tale in the *Fioretti* is manifestly absurd. It is supposed to have taken place a little more than a year after St Francis' pilgrimage to Spain (i.e. *c.* 1214),[3] and Elias did not become vicar until 1221. In the *Chronicle of the 24 Generals*[4] the decree is ascribed to *c.* 1224, but this is also wrong, as is proved by Jordan of Giano's reliable account of what really happened. The decree ordering the brothers to abstain from meat was not

[1] Salimbene, B. pp. 139–42, H. pp. 99–102.   [2] *Fioretti*, c. 4.
[3] Cf. *1 Cel.* 56, and Golubovich, I, 86.   [4] *A.F.* III, 31.

itself an invention, but its association with Elias was wholly imaginary. It was imposed while St Francis was in the East, probably in May 1220, and was the act of the vicars he had left in charge, Matthew of Narni and Gregory of Naples. Elias was not even present at the Chapter that agreed to it, for he was in Syria at the time.[1]

This example provides a good opportunity for stressing the fact that Elias had no share whatever in initiating the policy that transformed the Order. His personal responsibility for any undesirable developments has been too easily assumed, his later conduct rendering him liable to automatic condemnation. The troubles were begun in his absence. Their originators were the educated men and the Ministers, whose conception of the proper aims and methods for the fraternity accorded imperfectly with St Francis' exceptional ideal. Nor did he make their cause his own when he returned to Italy. He did not put himself at their head, or become an energetic promoter of their plans, as is sufficiently shown by his far from enthusiastic attitude towards their complaints on the subject of the second Rule.

Now that the stories attributing unworthy behaviour to Elias during St Francis' lifetime have been exposed as uncharitable falsifications and inventions, the representation of him as wholly vicious can be rejected as libellous.[2] Of the two contradictory descriptions of the man as he was when Francis knew him, only that provided in the *Vita Prima* and in Jordan approximates to the truth.[3] This conclusion removes the chief obstacle to the understanding of why he was given the charge of the Order when Peter Catanii died. Labouring under the delusion that Elias was fundamentally wicked, many writers have invested the problem with an artificial urgency because it seemed to reflect upon the judgement of a saint. They have assumed that Francis could not conceivably have made any but a proper choice of persons and

[1] Jordan, cc. 9, 11–14.

[2] That the uncomplimentary stories told about Elias in these years were fables was recognised by Affò, *Frate Elia* (Parma, 1783), pp. 27–35, and his eminently sensible remarks have not received the attention they deserve from many more modern scholars.

[3] See above, ch. 1, secs. 2 and 3.

have therefore been compelled to seek hidden reasons for Elias' preferment in order to free the saint from an aspersion of their own devising. Their dilemma has caused the formulation of even such wild theories as a divine command overriding man's common sense,[1] and on a more rational level has led to the suggestion that Hugolino was really responsible for the appointment.[2] This is pure guess-work, as there is nothing in the sources to imply that such was the case. Indeed, the known facts render it unlikely. Hugolino did not offer his protection to the Friars Minor earlier than the summer of 1217, and Elias had probably departed for Syria immediately after the Whitsun Chapter of that year. He remained in the East until 1220, returning to Italy with St Francis in the autumn. He succeeded Peter Catanii in the spring of 1221, and so the Cardinal cannot have been more than slightly acquainted with him at the time that he was made Minister. There is, moreover, no good reason to assume that Hugolino wanted to nominate anybody with the intention of using him as a tool to fashion the Order according to his own taste. Those who believe that he interfered for the sake of a policy different from St Francis' misjudge him. He was actuated chiefly by a desire to assist, not to control. There is no need to pursue the point further, since the attempt to substitute Hugolino for St Francis as the man to whom Elias owed his promotion is not based on historical evidence, but upon prejudices and preconceptions concerning the attributes of sanctity, the schemes of Hugolino and the villainy of Elias.

The reliable sources show quite clearly that St Francis had a great respect and affection for Elias, and create a strong presumption in favour of his having appointed him voluntarily. It was Francis, after all, who had started Elias on his official career, by entrusting to him the leadership of the first permanent mission to the Near East.[3] This in itself is a striking proof of his regard. The saint esteemed the Holy Land the most important of all provinces, both because it was the birthplace of our Lord, and because it offered to the Christian preacher the possibility of winning the

[1] Cf. above, pp. 83–4, 101.
[2] Sabatier, *Speculum Perfectionis* (Paris, 1898), p. ciii; Lempp, pp. 44–6.
[3] Jordan, c. 9.

crown of martyrdom, for which he longed.[1] Little is known of
Elias' activities as Provincial Minister, but it would seem that he
did well, for he left an established province to his successor.[2] St
Francis joined him in the East in 1219–20, and so had an opportunity to inspect his achievement and test his abilities. He evidently
found no cause to repent that he had selected him, for, when
news reached him of what had happened in Italy through his
absence, he chose Elias to be among the companions he took
back with him to deal with the emergency.[3] A few months later
Elias was put in charge of the brethren, and his appointment may,
indeed, almost be regarded as one of the measures that were taken
to counteract the subversive tendencies. There was no immediate
connection as St Francis had abdicated prior to his journey to
Egypt, but when Peter died the need to replace him with someone
competent to grapple with the situation must have been in his
mind. Leaders other than St Francis were never demanded by the
Ministers; it was entirely the saint's idea that he should resign, and
the brothers had been sincerely grieved.[4] Peter and Elias were
his agents and representatives. Their appointment was in no way
a concession to the innovators. There is thus no reason to doubt
Celano's words in the *Vita Prima* to the effect that the saint made
Elias the father of the brethren.[5]

Nor was St Francis' choice of an officer so foolish and misguided
as later Spirituals believed. Elias won the confidence and affection
not only of St Francis but of several other of the chief personalities
of the time, and his friends included St Clare, Gregory IX and
Frederick II.[6] A worthless man could not have inspired such widespread commendation, and even his enemies admitted that he was
able.[7]

---

[1] *1 Cel.* 55–7.
[2] Cf. Attal, *Frate Elia*, pp. 28–9, 34–5; Golubovich, I, 107, 109; Marinangeli,
art. cit. pp. 10–11.
[3] Jordan, c. 14.   [4] *2 Cel.* 143, etc.   [5] *1 Cel.* 98.
[6] Salimbene, B. p. 134, H. p. 96. See above, p. 14 and nn.
[7] Eccleston, p. 29; Bernard of Bessa, *Catalogus*, *A.F.* III, 695.

4. THE CONSTITUTIONAL POSITION, 1217-27

It is recorded by Celano in the *Vita Secunda* that at a Chapter meeting (held in 1217 or 1218), St Francis dramatically renounced all control over the Friars Minor and himself promised obedience to Peter Catanii, whom he had nominated in his stead.[1] From then until his death nearly ten years later his position was anomalous. He held no office, and claimed no power; yet he remained in a very real sense the head of his Order and exercised great spiritual authority. Unlike his Spanish contemporary, St Dominic, he was not gifted as a legislator, and he never defined his relationship to the officers he had chosen. Were Peter Catanii and his successor Elias St Francis' vicars, exercising only a delegated authority, or were they all-powerful Ministers General? Uncertainty on this point resulted in conflicting interpretations when the Franciscans came to systematise their history. Some writers called them one, some the other, and some again used the two terms indiscriminately.[2]

St Francis saw no problem. His intention, revealed in his own writings and in certain sayings preserved in other sources, is quite clear. In a letter that he wrote towards the end of his life to all the brethren assembled in General Chapter he explicitly addressed Elias as Minister General,[3] and in the *Regula Prima* there is mention of a minister of the whole Order.[4] There is a story also that when a brother asked him why he did not correct the excesses of the Order he replied that such matters did not pertain to his office, for he had renounced the office of prelacy; yet if the brothers had walked in his way they should have had no minister but himself until his death.[5] It was characteristic of him that he did not delegate powers to a vicar, but appointed a minister to serve the brethren. He interpreted all questions of authority in the light of Christ's teaching in the Gospel, and saw office as a matter not

---

[1] *2 Cel.* 143. See above, pp. 76 ff.

[2] '...quidam frater novitius qui sciebat legere psalterium...obtinuit a generali ministro *id est vicario b. Francisci* licentiam habendi ipsum' (*Sp. S.* c. 4, and n. 5 for the words I have italicised).

[3] *Epistola* 2.   [4] *Reg. Prima,* c. 18.

[5] *Intentio,* c. 13, *Sp. S.* c. 71.

of rights but of duties. The appointment of a vicar, powerful but dependent, would not have been consistent with humility. His renunciation was complete, emphasised by word and practised in deed, even to the extent of having a warden whom in particular he was to obey.[1]

Nevertheless the matter would not allow of so simple a solution. It was not in St Francis' power wholly to relinquish authority over his followers. Both his own vocation and external circumstances prevented him. He loved men too well for the words 'from henceforth I am dead to you' to be literally fulfilled. He never fled from the world like the hermits of the Egyptian desert in the first centuries of Christianity. He handed over the rule of the Order to the Lord and to the Ministers because he was not minded to become an executioner, punishing and flogging the brothers, like the magistrates of the world; but by preaching, admonition and example he sought always to correct and lead them.[2] He wrote at least three letters of exhortation and instruction after 1217, addressed to the General Chapter, to a certain minister, and to all the custodians. To this period also probably belongs the short rule *De religiosa habitatione in eremis*. Above all, in these years the saint wrote three drafts of the Rule which was finally accepted and confirmed by Papal bull in 1223. Two of these have survived and both the *Regula Prima* and the *Regula Bullata* bear the stamp of his personality, although he yielded to outside pressure on some points. Here he was acting as undisputed head of the Order.

The paradox is strikingly apparent in the Testament: 'My firm will is to obey the Minister General of this brotherhood', and yet 'I firmly command all the brothers, on obedience', and even 'the Minister General and all the other Ministers and Custodians are held on obedience not to add or subtract anything from these words'. While himself obedient to the Minister General, and even to a novice of an hour's standing, regarding the conduct of his own life,[3] he still remembered and remained faithful to the decision and choice made in the early days with the help (according

---

[1] *2 Cel.* 151.   [2] *Intentio*, c. 13, *Sp. S.* c. 71.
[3] *2 Cel.* 151.

to the *Fioretti*) of Sylvester and St Clare between the contemplative life and the salvation of others.[1] Until his death he tried, with all the means of which he allowed himself the use, to draw all men, and especially his Order, nearer to the life of the Gospel. He even seems to have considered preaching as the chief duty of the controller of the Order: 'Suppose that, being set over the brethren, I go to the Chapter and preach to them and admonish them, and at the end they speak against me, saying: "An unlettered and contemptible man will not do for us, therefore we will not have thee to reign over us...."'[2] Hence it is arguable that, while he undoubtedly called Peter Catanii and Elias Ministers General, they were in reality only administrative officials, charged with the business involved in running any large community, summoning Chapter, organising the distribution of food, and so forth. At most they were Ministers General 'saving always St Francis' spiritual authority and leadership'.

This argument is reinforced by the attitude of the many who would neither accept nor admit the reality of his renunciation. The Papacy always considered him the head of the fraternity. The introduction to the *Regula Prima* expressed the Papal view of the situation—it was copied most probably from the *Regula Primitiva* and the wording in the *Regula Bullata* was substantially the same: in all it is St Francis who promises obedience to the Holy See, and the brothers are to obey him and his successors. This interpretation was upheld by Gregory IX. In the bull *Quo elongati* he argued that the Testament was not binding, not because St Francis was no longer in authority when he wrote it, but because one Minister General could not bind another.[3]

The brethren themselves wished to recognise no one but St Francis. Already there were signs that the great and growing numbers of his followers were not of one mind regarding the fulfilment of their calling. What measure of unity there was depended largely on their common loyalty and devotion to Francis, and on the inspiration of his example. Many, like the

---

[1] *Fioretti*, c. 16.   [2] *2 Cel.* 145.
[3] Sbaralea, I, 68, no. G9, 56 (IV): '...nec successorem suum quomodolibet obligavit, cum non habeat imperium par in parem'.

brother whose question is recorded in the *Intentio Regulae*,[1] could not understand why he made no attempt to enforce the observance of his ideals. They wished to have no minister but him. So Wadding wrote, concerning the appointment of Peter Catanii: 'The brothers took it hardly and sorrowfully, nor would they, while the saint still lived, that any should be called their minister, but only vicar.'[2]

Evidence of this unwillingness is abundantly provided in early and generally reliable accounts. Thomas of Celano's *Vita Secunda* contains five references to the saint's vicar.[3] It also includes a description of the ideal Minister General, introduced into the narrative by a brother asking St Francis if he knew of anyone fit to succeed him. 'Father, thou wilt pass away, and the family which has followed thee will be left in the vale of tears. Point out someone, if thou knowest of any in the Order, on whom thy spirit may rest, and on whom the burden of the office of Minister General may safely be laid.'[4] There is, besides, the mention of a passage that St Francis wished to insert in the Rule after the Papal confirmation, the phraseology of which Celano can hardly have invented: 'With God', he said, 'there is no respect of persons, and the Holy Spirit, Minister General of the religious Order, rests equally upon the poor and simple.'[5] Had Elias been the only man referred to as vicar it would be permissible to discount this evidence, as Celano has already been convicted of purposely belittling his importance in his second Life, but three, or possibly four, of the references concern Peter Catanii.[6] Even so, the use of the term 'vicar' is not a decisive argument in favour of the acceptance of its constitutional implications, especially as Celano on two occasions seems to imply a state of affairs rather different from that presumed by his general presentation. He wrote in one place that St Francis renounced the office of General, and in another that the saint was once asked why he had so cast all the brethren out

[1] C. 13; *Sp. S.* c. 71.   [2] Wadding, *Annales*, I, 345.
[3] *2 Cel.* 67, 91, 144, 182, 216.   [4] *Ibid.* 184-5.
[5] *Ibid.* 193.
[6] *Ibid.* 67, 91, 182 and possibly 144. (144 ultimately derives from *Sp. L.* c. 16, which for *vicarius* reads *minister generalis*. *Sp. S.*, c. 40, has *vicarius*.)

of his own keeping and given them over to strange hands, as though they in no wise belonged to him.[1]

Jordan of Giano referred both indirectly and directly to Elias as St Francis' vicar. He said that it was St Francis who held a General Chapter at the Portiuncula at Whitsun 1221, and he considered John Parenti, elected in the Chapter of 1227, as the first Minister General. When speaking of the letter Elias sent to the Provincial Ministers to inform them of St Francis' death he explicitly called him vicar.[2] It is probable, however, that on this point Jordan should not be considered as an independent source. Celano's *Vita Secunda* was known to him, and he may well have taken the term from there.[3]

Eccleston, notwithstanding a certain superficial appearance to the contrary, also seems to have considered Elias as vicar from 1221–6, and although he did not finish writing until *c.* 1258, there is no clear indication, either of style or subject-matter, to show that he was acquainted with *2 Celano*. He apparently believed that St Francis remained in active control of the Order to the end of his life. For instance, he wrote that Agnellus of Pisa was designated Provincial Minister of England by St Francis at the General Chapter of 1224, and mentioned that the first ordinance that the saint made after the confirmation of the Rule—in November 1223 —forbade the brothers to eat more than three morsels of meat when dining with laymen.[4] He did indeed say that Elias was the first Minister General after St Francis, but the mention is so brief as to suggest that by this he meant only for the short time that elapsed between St Francis' death and the election of John Parenti.[5]

Lists of the Ministers General, either compiled as such or implicit in the Chronicles, fall into two categories. Eccleston, Salimbene and Peregrinus of Bologna give the order thus: St Francis, Elias, John Parenti, Elias.[6] Jordan and the *Chronicle of the 24 Generals* consider John Parenti as the first Minister General after St Francis.[7]

---

[1] *2 Cel.* 151, 188.   [2] Jordan, cc. 16, 50, 51.   [3] Cf. Jordan, c. 19.
[4] Eccleston, pp. 3–4, 25.   [5] *Ibid.* p. 65.
[6] Eccleston, pp. 65–7; Salimbene, B. pp. 135, 143, H. pp. 96, 102; Peregrinus of Bologna, *Chronicon abbreviatum de successione Ministrorum Generalium*, ap. Eccleston, 1 ed. (1909), Appendix II, p. 142.
[7] Jordan, c. 51; *A.F.* III, 210, 216.

It is surprising that the first group does not assign second place to Peter Catanii, since his position and Elias' were analogous. The omission may be due to Peter's comparative insignificance, or, as has been suggested, to a belief that Elias' first generalate was limited to the interim period, 4 October 1226–31 May 1227.

The main body of the friars adopted the Celanese attitude, and later compilers, like Arnold of Sarano, considered Peter and Elias as vicars.[1] But the group which preserved in Umbria and the Marches the spirit of the first companions retained St Francis' terminology, though with a few lapses. Brother Leo and his associates generally referred to them as Ministers General.[2]

Examination of the use of the two terms thus points to the conclusion that St Francis and 'those who were with him' called both Peter and Elias Ministers General, whereas others, particularly the Papacy and the greater part of the Order, called them vicars. But the use of a name either by the Pope, or by an official historiographer like Celano, or by St Francis, though it may throw light on the situation and explain the element of confusion that has arisen, is not after all the deciding factor in assessing the actual constitutional position, especially since the early Franciscan society lacked, to a degree unusual among religious bodies, definitive institutions of government. In order to determine this it is necessary to find out, as far as is possible from the incidental mention of their activities in the sources, whether or not either exercised the functions of a Minister General.

[1] Elias does not seem to have been referred to generally as vicar until after the appearance of Celano's *Vita Secunda*—cf. Delorme, 'La Legenda Antiqua s. Francisci', *A.F.H.* xv (1922), 322.

[2] The following have *minister generalis*: MS. Perugia, cc. 57=22, 74=39, 81=46, 89=56 (*Sp. S.* cc. 58, 61, 115, 38); *Sp. L.* cc. 15-16 (*Sp. S.* cc. 46, 40—the latter has *vicarius*); *Intentio*, cc. 7, 10 (*Sp. S.* c. 4); *Sp. S.* c. 39 (rubric). *Verba*, c. 4 (*Sp. S.* c. 1) has *vicarius*. Cf. Wadding, *Annales*, IV, 277, quoting from Francis of Fabriano, who knew brother Leo: 'de supradicto fratre Petro Cathanii, quod fuerit Generalis Minister, habetur ex dictis fratris Leonis...'. He is referred to as Minister General in the First Life of St Anthony of Padua, c. 7. According to L. de Kerval, *S. Antonii de Padua vitae duae*, pp. 2–5, the *Legenda Prima* was written before 1245, and probably soon after 1232.

In the first place St Francis' conception of authority as service, so frequently and clearly expressed, made it unlikely that anyone, whether officially vicar or Minister General, would act autocratically during his lifetime. But there are two circumstances which indicate that even a vicar would have exercised considerable powers in these years. St Francis was reluctant to override the will of others, even when provoked. This is well illustrated by his treatment of Matthew of Narni and Gregory of Naples. These two, whom he had left as his vicars when he went to the East in 1219, took advantage of his absence to reduce the liberty of the friars by imposing new regulations over and above the Rule. When news of this was brought to him he asked his companion, Peter Catanii, what he ought to do, and was answered: 'Why, my lord Francis, what you will, for it is you who hold power.' Nevertheless he did not annul the decrees of the vicars on his own authority, but persuaded the Papacy to take action through Hugolino.[1] Also, St Francis was an increasingly sick man, and his plea of illness was not only a pretext for resignation, but a genuine disability. At the same time mystical experiences caused him to withdraw more and more within himself and to lose contact with the world.[2] Consequently he interfered but little with those he had left in charge, and refused to listen to entreaties to resume office, though occasionally he could not conceal his anxiety and grief at the course events were taking.[3]

Some light is thrown on the constitutional position by the form of their appointment. Celano described the nomination of Peter Catanii,[4] but nowhere are there any details concerning that of Elias. All that is known definitely is that Peter died at Assisi on 10 March 1221, while St Francis was away; that Elias succeeded him; and that the latter was already in office when the General Chapter met at the Portiuncula on May 30.[5] The probability is that Francis appointed Elias before the Chapter met, without any dramatic scene or public declaration—anything memorable would have been unlikely to escape record—and that his position was

---

[1] Jordan, cc. 11–15.   [2] Cf. 2 Cel. 94, 95, 98.
[3] Cf. ibid. 188.   [4] Ibid. 143.
[5] Golubovich, I, 125; 24 Gen., A.F. III, 30–1; Jordan, c. 17.

essentially the same as his predecessor's.[1] In spite of the scantiness of the evidence two significant facts emerge. Neither Peter nor Elias was elected, and they did not owe their position to the wishes of the friars. Both were imposed upon the brethren from above, by the saint acting as head of the Order. Therefore their status differed from that of all subsequent Ministers General, elected by Chapter in accordance with the provisions of the *Regula Bullata*[2]— a possible legal argument for denying them that title. Furthermore there seem to have been no stated reservations or limitation of their powers, as might be expected on the appointment of a vicar. Their sphere of action was not restricted or defined— in 1219 St Francis had established Matthew of Narni at the Portiuncula to receive postulants and had sent Gregory of Naples throughout Italy to visit the brethren[3]—nor were they required to report to the saint or to consult him on any point. On the contrary, Francis had promised absolute submission to Peter Catanii.[4]

Their functions seem to have been predominantly administrative. They were responsible for all the arrangements connected with the holding of the General Chapter. They decided whether or not it should meet; they had to see that the brethren were adequately fed while it lasted.[5] Elias also presided at the actual gathering, addressed the brothers himself, and announced any wishes of St Francis. In addition he settled any difficulties that arose out of its proceedings. For instance, in 1221, when the brethren were being assigned to the various provinces, two groups wished Jordan of Giano to go with them, and the matter was referred to Elias for decision.[6] After 1223 no brother could obtain a licence to preach without first having been examined and approved by him.[7] The correction of the brothers was also in

---

[1] Lempp, pp. 56-7, and Attal, *Frate Elia*, p. 68, assert that in the last two or three years of St Francis' lifetime Elias' position was different from Peter's, as he rose from being vicar to being Minister General. Attal even fixes the time of his promotion, which he places at the General Chapter of 1224. There is no evidence whatever to support this supposition.

[2] *Reg. Bullata*, c. 8.   [3] Jordan, c. 11.
[4] *2 Cel.* 143.   [5] *Reg. Prima*, c. 18; *2 Cel.* 67.
[6] Jordan, cc. 17-18.   [7] *Reg. Bullata*, c. 9.

their hands. On this question the saint wrote a letter urging merciful treatment even of those offenders who did not ask it.[1] On another occasion he demanded the severe punishment of slanderers.[2] All these powers could have been legitimately exercised by a vicar. As to those two prerogatives that pre-eminently pertained to the office of Minister General up till 1239—the appointment and deposition of Provincial Ministers, and the promulgation of constitutions supplementary to the Rule[3]—there is unfortunately no clear evidence either way. They were not explicitly stated as outside their competence, but it cannot be proved that they exercised them. Elias may have appointed Caesar of Speyer Provincial Minister of Germany in 1221, and he may have replaced him by Albert of Pisa in 1223, but it is also possible that St Francis was responsible for one or both.[4] If Elias made any constitutions in these years they have not survived.[5]

It seems almost as if St Francis divided the office of Minister General to meet the practical necessities caused by his own illness and the growth of the Order. He himself continued to preach and admonish, and retained the power to make adjustments to the Rule, while Peter and later Elias saw to the day-to-day arrangements, a task which involved not only routine matters, but also decisions of policy. St Francis took the part of Mary, Peter and Elias that of Martha. The saint's affection for both men made it unnecessary for their respective spheres to be legally defined. At least—and this is important for determining their constitutional position—there does not seem to have been a recognised right of appeal to St Francis, as to a higher authority. Brothers did on occasion appeal direct to him, but this was neither encouraged nor successful.[6] Jordan, afraid of the ferocity of the Germans, was

---

[1] *Epistola* 3.   [2] *2 Cel.* 182.

[3] Cf. Eccleston, p. 70; *24 Gen.*, A.F. III, 217, 246.

[4] Cf. Jordan, cc. 18, 31.

[5] Elias was later accused of promulgating a decree forbidding the brothers to eat meat (*Fioretti*, c. 4), but Matthew of Narni and Gregory of Naples, not he, were responsible for this (Jordan, c. 11; see above, pp. 102–3). Eccleston (p. 25) states that Francis made at least one constitution after November 1223, and curiously enough the one he mentions was concerned with reducing the amount of flesh the brethren might eat.

[6] Cf. *Intentio*, c. 13.

taken to Elias as to the final judge of whether he should go, although St Francis was present at the Chapter.[1] The case of the novice who desired to have a psalter stands apart. He went to St Francis, not because he thought the General's permission necessarily insufficient, but because his conscience was uneasy, and he wished to make assurance doubly sure by obtaining the permission of the Order's spiritual leader also. The point was one on which the saint felt deeply, because of the repercussions of learning upon the ideal of absolute poverty, simplicity and humility. He contradicted the licence, yet not as if condemning the action of a subordinate, but by quoting the Rule: 'Whoever wishes to be a Friar Minor ought to have nothing but a tunic, as the Rule has allowed him, and breeches, and those who are compelled to can wear shoes.'[2]

The vague terminology of Celano's *Vita Prima* perhaps describes the actual relationship better than any more precise term—St Francis chose Elias to be, so to say, his own mother, and made him the father of the other brethren.[3] Peter and Elias, unhampered by precedent or legal restrictions, were free to make much or little of the office assigned to them, and the extent of their powers depended largely on their characters. Peter was always extremely deferential to St Francis. He addressed him as 'domine',[4] and never presumed to gainsay his wishes. He allowed himself to be no more that the saint's titular superior, and Francis' object in offering him obedience and reverence was largely nullified by this failure of his to act as if he were master. The nearest approach to subjection that Francis achieved was in telling Peter to command him to do something that he already had a mind to do. With these directions Peter complied, even when the action contemplated was obviously detrimental to the saint's health. One winter Francis preached to the people of Assisi when he had barely recovered from a fever, and after the sermon, in spite of the intense cold and his own frailty, he divested himself of his tunic and caused Peter to drag him through the streets so that he might proclaim to those who had heard his preaching that he was a sinner

[1] Jordan, cc. 17-18.   [2] *Intentio*, cc. 10-12.
[3] *1 Cel.* 98.   [4] Jordan, c. 12.

who had eaten flesh while he was ill. Peter wept from compassion
in the performance of this ceremony, but had not tried to dissuade
him from it, humbly replying to the saint's demand for his co-
operation: 'Brother, I neither can nor ought to will anything
except what you choose for me and for yourself.'[1] Another time
Francis feared that he had embarrassed a leper and asked Peter to
confirm the penance that he wished to impose upon himself. He
was told to do as he thought good, and proceeded to eat out of
the same bowl as the leper. Peter was greatly distressed, but did
not dare to contradict his mood.[2] The relationship between Elias
and St Francis was different. Elias had not the same fear and awe
of the founder, though he deeply and sincerely admired and loved
him. He was able to treat him not as a living saint but as a human
being, and was thus proved worthy to become his friend. He did
not blindly accept that Francis' behaviour and attitude were bound
to be right, but would offer criticism and counsel. When he saw
that the saint was aggravating his illness by neglect, instead of
acquiescing he argued with him, and succeeded in persuading him
to consult doctors and to follow their prescriptions.[3] His ability
to disapprove may have been one of the reasons why Francis so
respected him.

Peter had not the courage to assume responsibility, and behaved
simply as a vicar. When in doubt he turned to St Francis for
guidance, and once, when the Portiuncula was crowded with
brethren, he went to him to ask permission to be allowed to put
by some of the goods of postulants in case food grew seriously
short.[4] He gives the impression of a man worried as to how to
reconcile the task of running a large Order efficiently with the
Gospel precept of taking no thought for the morrow. Elias acted
much more as if he were in full control. One small incident may
be taken as an instance of his way of dealing. In 1219 the brothers
at Valenciennes, with St Francis' consent, had moved from their

---

[1] MS. Perugia, c. 74=39; *Sp. S.* c. 61.
[2] MS. Perugia, c. 57 = 22 (*Sp. S.* c. 58): 'Nam frater Petrus tantum venera-
batur et timebat b. Franciscum et tantum erat ei obediens, quod non praesumebat
mutare obedientiam eius, licet tunc et multoties interius et exterius inde
affligeretur.'
[3] *1 Cel.* 98.   [4] *2 Cel.* 67.

first very uncomfortable and inconvenient site to the hospital of St Bartholomew, which was also situated outside the gate. In 1225 the Countess Joanna and her husband, Ferrand of Portugal, then the prisoner of Louis VIII, granted to the Franciscans their town palace, popularly known as 'Le Dongeon'. They firmly refused to move to such a worldly place, so Joanna wrote to the Pope, St Francis, the bishop of Cambrai, and, according to his letter, Elias, begging them to use their influence. The Pope sent a bull, and Elias wrote telling the friars to move 'to this suitable place within the town walls'. His letter was dated in the tenth year of Honorius' pontificate (1225–6). The heading ran: 'The *obedience* which brother Elias the Minister General sent to the brothers of St Bartholomew at Valenciennes'; St Francis was not mentioned.[1] Had Peter been still alive he would probably have suggested to the saint the advisability of accepting the Countess' gift, and would have been rebuked for his prudence. Elias appreciated the advantages of the offer, and was prepared to act in the matter on his own authority.

It was impossible that, while the saint lived, anyone else should exercise complete control. But when this is said, it remains that Peter and Elias were Ministers General in name during these years, and that Elias was also to a large extent in fact. The limitations on his powers were the saint's great personal authority, and the attitude of the many brethren who wished to minimise his importance. His position was described as accurately as is possible in constitutional language by Bernard of Bessa: 'After the death of brother Peter, St Francis put brother Elias of Assisi in control... who, although he was called minister by the saint and by many of the brethren, was neither elected General nor accepted as such by the Order while Francis was alive.'[2]

The medieval saint tended to find himself either in the position of the Old Testament prophet, denouncing sin, especially sin in high places, like St Bernard; or of the patriarch, the father of his

[1] Jacobus de Guisia, *Annales Hanoniae*, M.G.H. Scr. xxx, part I, 282–97. Cf. also S. Le Boucq, *Histoire ecclésiastique de Valentienne* (1650) (Valenciennes, 1844), pp. 99–113.
[2] A.F. III, 31.

family, like St Benedict or St Francis.[1] As patriarch of his Order
St Francis could never delegate his authority entirely to another.
His position was something akin to that of the legislator in Plato's
Republic, whose sphere necessarily overlapped with that of the
guardians whom he educated and set up. Such overlapping is
logically a confusion, but is in human societies inevitable.

In view of the fact that Elias attempted to retain his office by
intimidation in 1239, so loath was he to relinquish the exercise of
power, it would have caused little surprise to his enemies if he
had held on to the reins of government after St Francis' death.
All the sources agree that he was actually in control of the Order
for the period October 1226–May 1227. Indeed he was the obvious
interim ruler. The constitutional problem remains: was he Minister General by virtue of St Francis' earlier appointment, or was
he a vicar exercising full powers during a vacancy?

The question admits of a definite answer, for it appears that at
this juncture Elias deliberately chose to play the part of vicar.
When St Francis died he dispatched 'litteras consolatorias' to the
provinces without delay, to inform them of the sad news and to
proclaim the hitherto unheard-of miracle of the stigmata. The
copy sent to Gregory of Naples, Provincial Minister of France, is
extant.[2] To this letter, according to Jordan of Giano, was attached
a note summoning all the Provincial Ministers and Custodians to
a Chapter for the purpose of electing a Minister General.[3] There
is no reason to doubt the truth of this. The summons has not
survived, but there was no incentive to preserve an administrative
order of this kind. Jordan was a reliable chronicler and his description of the contents of the letter itself is accurate. We may
presume that a General Chapter did meet at the Portiuncula at
Pentecost 1227, and that it proceeded to an election.[4]

In sending this summons Elias acted in what can only be described
as an irreproachably constitutional manner. The lay brothers who
later supported him were not invited to attend. The promptness

---

[1] St Francis seems consciously to have played the part of a patriarch—the
blessing that he gave his brothers on his deathbed was recognisably patriarchal
(above, p. 98).   [2] Printed by Lempp, pp. 70–1.
[3] Jordan, c. 50.   [4] Cf. A.F. III, 34 and n.

with which it was sent is also significant. Had Elias continued to rule the Order, taking his authority for granted, he could have made out a strong case in defence of his title. He did not try the experiment, or wait to see whether the reactions of the brothers made it unnecessary to hold a Chapter. Such consideration for the wishes of the Order seems at variance with his later conduct, which showed little respect for the Rule. Why then was he so scrupulous in 1226?

One suggested reason is that he did not wish to continue in office, preferring to be free to concentrate on his designs for the Basilica.[1] Such an hypothesis is not convincing. Elias was an ambitious and a very able man. He is unlikely to have felt that the building, however magnificent its conception, would occupy all his energies. When he became Minister General in 1232 the Church was far from completed, and he energetically promoted its construction and embellishment simultaneously with attending to the duties of office.[2] That he wished simply to return to private life would be a supposition entirely at variance with what is known of his character.

Common prudence and a shrewd understanding of the practical situation, its difficulties and dangers, probably determined his action. He was aware of the element of uncertainty as to his status, and of the flaws in his title to office. Though he had received a special blessing from St Francis, only his active partisans interpreted it as a clear designation.[3] Celano, perhaps prophesying after the event, by implication denies that St Francis nominated his successor. According to his story, when a brother asked him if he knew of anyone worthy to succeed him, the saint did not reply that, though none possessed all the requirements, Elias would do, but described the perfect Minister General in terms which read, in the light of later developments, like a detailed criticism of Elias.[4] Elias' own reference to his position in the letter to the

[1] Cf. H. E. Goad, *Franciscan Italy* (London, 1926), p. 145; Moorman, *Sources for the Life of St Francis*, p. 59; F. Tocco, *Studii Francescani*, pp. 108–9; Attal, *Frate Elia*, p. 94.
[2] Jordan, c. 61.
[3] *1 Cel.* 108; *24 Gen.*, A.F. III, 215; cf. *Spec. Vitae*, ed. Lempp, p. 163.
[4] *2 Cel.* 184–5.

Provincial Ministers is probably intentionally vague. He wrote
of St Francis' death: 'A loss to all, but to me a particular peril,
since he has left me in the shadow of night, in the midst of many
cares and weighed down by all manner of anxiety.'[1] He recognised that from now on he would have to take more account of
the attitude of the brothers than he had done in the past. During
St Francis' lifetime his authority had been upheld by the saint,
who refused to listen to entreaties that he should interfere, and
he had been sheltered by his friendship. But it was clear that there
were many in the Order who disapproved of him. Another version of St Francis' deathbed blessing indicates that possibly the
zealots intended to set up Bernard of Quintavalle as a rival claimant
to the succession.[2] By setting in motion constitutional machinery
Elias forestalled any such independent movement to overthrow
him. For it must be remembered that the Chapter he summoned
was composed not of all the friars nor of the early companions,
but of the official element in the Order only, the Provincial
Ministers and Custodians. Another consideration that may have
influenced him was that a Chapter was due in any case—the last
had met in 1224—and much discontent was to be expected if he
did not arrange for one.[3] When one did meet the question of the
succession was bound to be raised, since Elias was not universally
acceptable and had never been elected. It was wiser to obviate
possible grounds of complaint.

Altogether it is reasonable to suppose that Elias did not feel justified in attempting to govern the Order without a further mandate.
He was prepared to try constitutional means in order to reinforce
his authority, and may have been encouraged to adopt this course
by calculations as to the probability of his election. The odds were
in his favour. He was St Francis' friend, chosen by him to office;
he was experienced; and he was in possession. The ministers as a
body were likely to prefer him to one of the zealots, and there
was no obviously dangerous rival among their number. However,

---

[1] Printed by Lempp, p. 70.   [2] Cf. Angelo Clareno, *Rendiconti*, pp. 221–3.
[3] *Reg. Bullata*, c. 8. When Elias was Minister General in 1232–9 he held no
General Chapters (see below, p. 156 n. 2), as a result, perhaps, of the lesson
he learnt in 1227!

as it happened, he was not confirmed in his tenure, and his place was taken by John Parenti, the Provincial Minister of Spain.

Why Elias failed to secure the votes of the electors is a question that cannot be answered with confidence. No record of the proceedings of the Chapter has survived, and nothing can be deduced from the little information that there is concerning Elias' activities during the short period of the 'interregnum'. The only thing that he is known to have done is to have licensed seven of the brethren to undertake a mission to the heathen in Morocco,[1] an action to which exception can hardly have been taken. All seven were martyred at Ceuta on 10 October 1227, and the circumstances of their death formed the subject of a letter written by brother Mariano of Genoa on 27 October.[2] John Parenti was then Minister General, but news of his election had not yet reached Morocco. The letter is addressed: 'Venerabili in Christo Patri Aelie, Vicario Generali Pauperum Minorum. . . .'

An explanation of his defeat has been put forward by Sabatier and Lempp,[3] based on the evidence of the *Speculum Vitae* and the Mazarin MS. of the *Speculum Perfectionis*, but it is not well-grounded. They contend that Elias began his preparations for a magnificent church in Francis' honour immediately after his death, and thus offended all who valued the primitive ideals, and who felt that the saint's wish to be buried humbly at the Portiuncula should have been respected. He particularly shocked the sensitive disciples by putting a marble vase in front of the building to collect the offerings of the faithful. Brother Leo broke this in righteous indignation: Elias had him flogged and driven from Assisi, thereby greatly increasing his own unpopularity. Leo retaliated by writing the *Speculum Perfectionis*, a document which exposed Elias as no true Friar Minor, and which appeared at the beginning of May 1227, a little less than a month before the Chapter was held. If this reconstruction were correct, there would be amply sufficient data to account for the outcome of the meeting. It is, however,

[1] Cf. *A.F.* III, 32.

[2] *Acta SS.*, October, VI, 384 ff. Cf. F. Russo, 'Le Fonti della Passione dei SS. Martiri di Ceuta', *Misc. Fr.* XXXIV (1934), 113.

[3] *Sp. S.* (1898), pp. li–lvi; Lempp, pp. 74–7.

untenable. The *Speculum Vitae* was wrong in alleging the Basilica as a source of grievances contributing to John Parenti's election, since the site was not acquired until March 1228 and consequently no building was in progress in 1226–7.[1] The dating of the *Speculum Perfectionis* to May 1227 was due to an unfortunate scribal error, and it is now fully established that that work was completed on 11 May 1318.

As Elias' conduct offers no clue to the problem, it is necessary to approach it from the alternative angle of the positive deserts and qualifications of his supplanter, and these will be considered in the next chapter. There is just one possible independent factor that may be mentioned here. The early Franciscans generally were anxious to prevent the rise of permanent officers. Thus Peregrinus of Bologna said that 'because the brothers of that time did not want their Ministers to be permanent, nor for life, Elias and they agreed that he should resign'.[2] The Ministers may well have thought a change would be advantageous. It is to be doubted that Elias was equally convinced of the desirability of short tenures, but he had need to conceal his chagrin at the time, having then no means of influencing their free choice.

[1] Cf. Lempp, pp. 170–1.
[2] Peregrinus of Bologna, *ap.* Eccleston, 1 ed. (1909), p. 142.

CHAPTER III

THE CHARACTER AND SIGNIFICANCE OF JOHN PARENTI

JOHN PARENTI's period of office was brief, and the sources tell us very little about him. Consequently he has suffered from neglect and superficial treatment at the hands of some modern historians, who considered him a nonentity and awarded the responsibility for the developments which occurred in his Generalate to Elias. Yet he was Minister of the Order at a most crucial moment in its history and might have exercised a far-reaching influence by virtue of his office. The death of St Francis left the Friars Minor troubled and divided, in a state perhaps inevitable when a body of men of widely differing upbringing attempt to realise an ideal. St Francis himself had been unable entirely to stem the flood of good intentions which threatened to quench his purer flame. The tide was rising strongly, and, were it not quickly and vigorously fought, might prove irresistible. The future depended upon the attitude and abilities of those in control immediately after the inspiration of the saint had been removed. Were the Franciscans to be as a light, revealing the Gospel truth, or were they to be as water, which cleanses but at the cost of sullying its own purity? We know how this question was answered, but the reasons for that answer are not so easy to determine. In seeking these the part played by John Parenti must not be left out of account. Simply because he was the first Minister General to be elected, he was, whether positively or negatively, in some degree responsible for what happened. An appreciation of him as a man and as a Minister lessens the surprise often expressed at his election, and makes it possible to deduce, rather than simply assume,[1] his attitude towards the problems confronting the Order and the extent to which he was able to make his will effective.

---

[1] Cf. Lempp, pp. 76–8; Gratien, p. 139.

Modern historians have been at once kind and slighting to his memory. They have agreed in representing him as a fervent religious, imbued with the Franciscan spirit, whose sympathies were with the group later known as the Spirituals.[1] But the most striking fact about him to be gathered from their accounts is his insignificance. He is allowed to be Minister General only in name, the development of the Order being taken to prove that Elias' influence remained predominant.[2]

This is not the only possible explanation of the known facts, and need be accepted neither wholly nor in part. The important stages in the transformation of the Order that were reached between 1227 and 1232 may be taken as proof that John Parenti's authority was ineffective only if he did indeed favour the primitive observance. Such an assumption, though plausible, is hardly justified. It is the result of an interest in the Generalate directed primarily towards its bearing on the career of Elias, and involves an over-simplification of the possibilities. In order to bring this one figure into clear relief it creates an artificial contrast and postulates too rigid a party alignment. Moreover the evidence cited in support of this interpretation has been selected from works open to the same criticism, and is used not as a foundation on which to build conclusions but as a prop for a prefabricated argument. It consists of the statement in the *Chronicle of the 24 Generals*: 'He was a General with a pre-eminent gift of tears, who visited a great part of the Order barefoot', taken in conjunction with the extremely confused account of these years in the *Speculum Vitae*, particular stress being laid on Elias' boastful claim to have obtained numerous Papal privileges, and on the circumstances of John Parenti's resignation.[3] These accounts reflect the attitude of

---

[1] Cf. e.g. Mandonnet in *Opuscules*, IV, 196.

[2] Cf. Sabatier, *Spec. Perfectionis* (ed. 1898), p. cxiii: 'Le parti de l'étroite observance régnait encore en la personne de Jean Parenti, mais...déjà il ne gouvernait plus. Frère Elie, tout puissant dans Assise, agissait sans tenir aucun compte du général installé à la Portioncule.' Cf. also Lempp, p. 92; F. Tocco in *Studii Francescani*, p. 109.

[3] *A.F.* III, 211; *Spec. Vitae*, pp. 163-5. It was suggested by d'Alençon that John Parenti was the author of the *Sacrum Commercium* (ed. E. d'Alençon, Rome, 1900; cf. also Canon Rawnsley's ed., with introd. by Sabatier and

the friars several generations later, after the conflict between the Spirituals and the Conventuals had become bitter and sharply defined. Their eagerness to vilify Elias led them to 'spiritualise' John Parenti.

An examination of all the scraps of information concerning him, scattered through many chronicles of varying reliability, produces a likeness which does not fit into the generally accepted pattern. He was probably born in Civita Castellana,[1] about thirty miles from Rome, and enjoyed the privilege of Roman citizenship. He was a doctor of law with a grown-up son when he joined the Franciscans. The circumstances of his conversion are worth quoting—they might have been cited by Caesarius of Heisterbach as an example of those impelled by fear. The *Chronicle of the 24 Generals* speaks as follows: 'He entered the Order in this wise. When he was a lawyer and judge in Civita Castellana, he once looked out of a window and saw a swineherd, who was unable to shut in his pigs, instructed by his companion, cast a spell over them with these words: "Pigs, pigs, go down to your sty, as lawyers and judges go down to hell." At once the whole herd of pigs went in without a grunt. And, struck on this account with the fear of the Lord, he went into the Order of Friars Minor with his son.'[2] In 1219 he was sent to succeed Bernard of Quintavalle as Provincial Minister of Spain, and under his guidance the friars in the peninsula flourished exceedingly. The number of 'places' multiplied, and St Francis was delighted with reports of the holiness

English trans. (London, 1904); and English trans. by M. Carmichael (London, 1901)). If he were the author of this charming allegory, it would give him a more plausible claim to be considered one of the *zelanti*. But the sole evidence is an uncertain tradition that it was written by a Minister General, and the colophon of d'Alençon's MS., which dates it to July 1227, when John Parenti was General. The value of the tradition can be judged from the fact that in one MS. it was attributed to Crescentius of Jesi, and by the *Chron. 24 Gen.* (*A.F.* III, 283) to John of Parma (this is inconsistent with the date 1227—John of Parma entered the Order in 1232-3). There is little chance of identifying the author, and it seems best to accept the statement of Ubertino of Casale that it was written by a certain doctor, 'sancte paupertatis professor et zelator strenuus' (cited Carmichael, *op. cit.* pp. xxxvii, xli).

[1] Jordan, c. 51. Eccleston, p. 65, calls him 'Johannes Parens de Florentia' (cf. also *Spec. Vitae*, p. 164).

[2] *A.F.* III, 210.

of the Spanish brethren.[1] Gonzaga preserves several stories illustrating John's success in persuading princes and bishops of Aragon and Castile to favour the Minors. His method was to produce Honorius III's letters of recommendation rather than to rely on that example of life which so frequently caused the Franciscans to be suspected of heresy in the early days.[2]

While he cannot be said to have possessed a forceful personality, there is little reason to accuse him of weakness—the gift of tears was comparatively common in the Middle Ages, and was taken as a sign of grace. The impression is rather of a strict disciplinarian in whom legal training had imbedded a firm respect for the letter of the law. Eccleston described him as 'vir sapiens et religiosus et summi rigoris', and Bernard of Bessa as 'vir sanctus et iustus, et spiritualis parentis officio vere pollens'.[3] 'Rigor' is best translated as severity, 'pollens' as strong or powerful. The fact that the phrase in the *Catalogus* contains a stylistic play on his name need not necessarily detract from its truth. His reputation as a martinet, however, does not rest upon verbal criticism alone, being substantiated by two recorded incidents. Peregrinus of Bologna, writing to the Minister General Gonsalvus in 1305, found John Parenti memorable for one action only: 'He had a son in the Order, who did wrong, and he punished him severely—in nothing sparing himself.'[4] Eccleston remarks that those responsible for the disturbances in 1230 were sent throughout the provinces to do penance, presumably by the Minister General.[5]

In the early sources he is represented as devout, but not specifically as being fervently attached to the spirit of St Francis. Nevertheless his sympathies can be deduced more accurately from a study of his behaviour than by reliance upon descriptions and opinions personal to the chroniclers. Affinity with the upholders of the primitive observance is noticeable only in his attitude towards the Rule. We learn, indirectly on the authority of St

---

[1] 2 Cel. 178.

[2] Gonzaga, *De origine seraphicae religionis Franciscanae* (Rome, 1587), pars III, 605–6, 699–700; cf. Jordan, cc. 4–5, 3 Soc. c. 16 (62, 66).

[3] Eccleston, p. 65; A.F. III, 694.

[4] *Ap.* Eccleston, 1 ed. (1909), p. 142.   [5] Eccleston (1951), pp. 65–6.

Bonaventure, that when, in 1230, the Rule was criticised as being obscure and too hard to be observed, John Parenti declared that its meaning was clear and that it was binding on all 'ad litteram'. When he found that its provisions were to be relaxed he resigned his office.[1] His own constitutions, decreeing that no friar might be called 'master', and enjoining due respect for the Blessed Sacrament, are in the true Franciscan tradition.[2] But it is important to remember, when trying to discover his standpoint, that a desire to observe the Rule was not peculiar to those friars who might be called 'spirituals'. The position he took up was not extreme or intransigent—he eventually led the deputation sent to Gregory IX to request an elucidation of difficult points[3]—and it is sufficiently explained by a respect for law, inherited from his secular life, and by loyalty to his predecessor.

In other matters John Parenti's policy lacked much that had been characteristic of the saint. His own education and outlook prevented him from rejecting learning as a legitimate means of action for the Franciscans. Because of his encouragement of studies he may be held not a little responsible for the decline in simplicity that so rapidly transformed the Order. In 1228, hearing that Germany had no Reader in theology, he appointed Simon the Englishman, 'virum scholasticum et magnum theologum', to that office, and, after Simon's death in 1230, he sent Bartholomew, also an Englishman, to Saxony.[4] He did not need to take an active part in promoting learning in those two other provinces, England and France, about which information exists. At Oxford brother Agnellus had a school built in the precincts, and Robert Grosseteste, the first chancellor of the University, began to lecture there c. 1229.[5] At Paris studies flourished, thanks to the Provincial Minister, Gregory of Naples, and to the favour of such men as the bishop William of Auvergne and the chancellor Eudes of Châteauroux.[6] In view of what Jordan says[7] it is probable that

---

[1] *A.F.* III, 213–14.   [2] Bernard of Bessa, *Catalogus, ibid.* pp. 694–5.

[3] Eccleston, p. 66; cf. Sbaralea, I, 68, no. G9, 56 (IV) (*Quo elongati*).

[4] Jordan, cc. 52, 54, 58.   [5] Eccleston, p. 48 and n. b.

[6] Cf. Callebaut, *A.F.H.* x (1917), 305–7; Gratien, p. 127.

[7] Jordan, c. 54, 'audiens quod Theutonia lectorem in theologia non haberet ...', suggests that other provinces were already equipped with Readers.

learning was promoted generally throughout the provinces, either directly by John Parenti, or through the Provincial Ministers. All these, as far as we can discover, seem to have been learned men. Agnellus of Pisa and Gregory of Naples were in office before his election and remained so during his Generalate.[1] In Germany he appointed successively Simon the Englishman, afterwards made the first Reader in theology, John of Piano Carpine, who later went as a missionary to Tartary, bringing back valuable geographical and ethnographical information to Innocent IV,[2] Otto, a Lombard learned in the law, and John the Englishman (or John of Reading), whom Innocent IV later sent as Papal collector to England.[3]   He made Richard of Ingworth, a priest and the first Franciscan to preach publicly north of the Alps, first Provincial Minister of Ireland.[4] It is also probable that he appointed St Anthony of Padua (now venerated as a Doctor of the Church) Provincial of Bologna 1227–30,[5] and Albert of Pisa, a priest and a man of very wide practical experience, Provincial of Spain c. 1227–30 and of Bologna c. 1230–2.[6] The fact that John Parenti ordered all the provinces to be supplied with breviaries and antiphonaries is an additional indication of his activity: St Francis had thrown ashes on his head at the very thought of possessing a breviary.[7] Elias but followed in the footsteps of his predecessor in promoting the study of theology.[8] The Papal bull *Quo elongati*, of 28 September 1230, may be cited as independent evidence of

---

[1] Agnellus (Provincial of England 1224–36) was a priest, and had been Custodian of Paris (cf. Eccleston, pp. 3–4, 76–8). Of Gregory of Naples (Provincial of France, c. 1223–33) Eccleston wrote (p. 29) 'Quis enim Gregorio in praedicatione vel praelatione in universitate Parisius vel clero totius Franciae comparabilis?'

[2] Jordan, cc. 52, 54; Salimbene, B. pp. 295–8, 300–1, 303–4, H. pp. 206–8, 210, 212–13.

[3] Jordan, cc. 57–8, 61; Eccleston, p. 18 n; for his activities as Papal collector, see W. E. Lunt, *Financial Relations of the Papacy with England to 1327* (Cambridge, Mass., 1939), pp. 220–3, 613, etc.

[4] Eccleston, p. 4.

[5] *Vitae duae*, ed. L. de Kerval (Paris, 1904), p. 217 (cf. pp. 43–4); below, p. 158 and n. 4.

[6] Cf. Golubovich, II, 227; *A.F.H.* XVII (1924), 576.

[7] Jordan, c. 57; *Intentio regulae*, c. 11.

[8] Cf. Salimbene, B. p. 145, H. p. 104.

the speed with which the Franciscans developed into a student Order. In answer to questions Gregory IX declared that theologians might preach without special permission from the Minister General, and he particularly mentioned books among the articles which the friars were allowed to use.[1]

The constitutional changes he introduced are likewise significant. The evidence is not conclusive, but it seems probable that it was John Parenti who took those measures to organise an efficient provincial administration that are generally regarded as the work of the 1239 General Chapter. The number of provinces, which at the time of St Francis' death had been thirteen,[2] and which Elias had attempted to raise to seventy-two, was in that year limited by statute to thirty-two.[3] The problem is to discover at what date were established the additional nineteen that were then confirmed. The 1239 Chapter itself probably reorganised the administration of eastern Europe and was responsible for two new provinces, Dacia and Bohemia–Poland. The rest were in existence earlier, as is proved by incidental mention in chronicles and Papal documents.[4] Of these the majority almost certainly did not owe their foundation to Elias. The provinces he created were small and were reassembled into their former units in 1239—so much can be deduced from the fate of those concerning which we have any definite knowledge. Eccleston relates that Elias made Scotland into a separate province, Salimbene that Ancona had been divided into two and Tuscany into three before 1239—most probably by Elias. In 1239 there was a return to the *status quo ante*. Haymo of Faversham was appointed Minister 'totius Angliae' and Salimbene found many lay brothers in Tuscany 'which had been made one province instead of three'. He had been a novice in the March of

[1] Sbaralea, I, 68–70, no. G9, 56 (IV).
[2] Tuscany, the March of Ancona, Lombardy, Naples, Apulia, Calabria, Germany, France, Provence, Spain, Syria, Aquitaine and England.
[3] Eccleston, pp. 41, 43.
[4] For a detailed discussion of the whole question, see Golubovich, II, 214 ff.; and cf. H. Lippens, *A.F.H.* XLVIII (1955), 217–24, who shows that the division of the Rhine province did not take place as early as 1239, as Golubovich supposed. This leaves one of the thirty-two provinces of 1239 unaccounted for, but it is possible that the symmetrical pattern of sixteen provinces either side of the Alps planned in 1239 was not immediately achieved.

Ancona at the time when it was under two Provincial Ministers.[1] Elias' only permanent addition to the number of provinces was in central Europe, where Austria, Hungary and Slavonia cannot be traced back as autonomous divisions beyond 1232. That leaves thirteen or fourteen provinces still to be accounted for. In the absence of any evidence to the contrary it is reasonable to assume that these were created it the 1230 General Chapter. It is certain that Ireland and Saxony became independent then, and that Castile, Aragon and Venice were separated from their 'province madri' during John Parenti's Generalate.[2] In all these cases the subdivision was the result of the original provinces having become unwieldy through size or prosperity. But other provinces were equally unwieldy; they are known to have been divided during the 1230's; and in 1239 the wisdom of their division was acknowledged. John Parenti is known to have created nine provinces out of four. The probability is that he reorganised all the provinces systematically at the 1230 General Chapter, creating twenty-six out of thirteen, thus doubling their number. Only in central Europe was his division inadequate and only there did Elias and the 1239 General Chapter improve upon his work.

If this hypothesis is correct it becomes easier to understand the reasons behind the constitution, promulgated in the 1230 Chapter and approved later in the year by Gregory IX in *Quo elongati*, to the effect that only one Custodian from each province should come as a representative to the General Chapter.[3] The *Regula Bullata* had provided that all the Provincial Ministers and Custodians should be present for the election of the Minister General, so that the Chapter which elected John Parenti in 1227 may have consisted of about sixty-five members, though it is unlikely that all the Custodians actually attended. If the number of the provinces were increased to twenty-six it would be necessary to convoke some hundred and thirty officials, which involved obvious incon-

---

[1] Eccleston, pp. 41, 69; Salimbene, B. pp. 144–5, H. pp. 102–4.
[2] Cf. Eccleston, p. 4 (Ireland); Jordan, c. 57 (Saxony); Golubovich, II, 225, and *idem, A.F.H.* I (1908), 6 (Castile, Aragon); Sbaralea, I, 77–8, no. G9, 68 (79) (Venice).
[3] *Ibid.* I, 70, no. G9, 56 (IV); cf. Appendix II.

venience. In 1230 the custodies averaged roughly four to a province, so that 'omnium Custodum multitudo' aptly described the new conditions.[1] Membership was limited not only to save journeys and expense, but also to facilitate business at the meetings. The phrase 'ut omnia cum majori tranquillitate tractentur' may have been a feeling comment on the experience of the 1230 General Chapter itself.

The composition of the General Chapter was a burning constitutional issue. Though the *Regula Bullata* enumerated the officials who were obliged to attend, it was silent on the question of whether ordinary brothers might participate if they wished. In the early days all had gathered together at the Portiuncula, professed and novices alike,[2] but the spread of the Order and the growth of the official element had combined to end this custom. In 1230, when many brothers were coming to Assisi for the translation, Elias took it upon himself to say that they might all go to the Chapter meeting, but John Parenti countermanded this invitation.[3] Elias' motives may not have been disinterested, but his action was more in keeping with the early Franciscan freedom than was the General's prohibition. The latter desired the Order to be ruled on aristocratic rather than on democratic lines. It was to this end that he successfully restricted the membership of the Chapter to officials only and showed favour to the Provincial Ministers on whom, as a class, he relied. He appointed men of learning and outstanding ability, who were generally, if not always, priests; he increased their powers—no one might now hear confessions without their licence;[4] and, most important of all, he consulted them on important matters, instead of acting independently on his own private judgement. For instance, he released Albert of Pisa from the administration of Germany and appointed Simon, Custodian of Normandy, in his place on the

---

[1] *Ibid.* In England there were four custodies at first, soon increased to six or seven (Eccleston, pp. xxix, 34–6, 89); in Germany five before the division of the province (Jordan, c. 32, cf. c. 47); in France, four (cf. Callebaut, *A.F.H.* x, 295). But some of the new provinces cannot have had so many custodies at first, so that the figure of *c.* 130 would only be potential in 1230.

[2] Jordan, c. 16; *3 Soc.* c. 14 (57).   [3] Eccleston, pp. 65–6.

[4] Cf. Bernard of Bessa, *A.F.* III, 695.

advice of Gregory of Naples, Provincial Minister of France. In 1230 he granted Jordan of Giano's request that John the Englishman might be sent as Minister to Saxony.[1] He probably appointed Richard of Ingworth Provincial of Ireland on the recommendation of Agnellus of Pisa, who had left him as vicar in England when he went to the 1230 General Chapter.[2]

Finally, in John Parenti's Generalate the Friars Minor acquired a new status. They had been from their foundation highly favoured by the Papacy, and even while St Francis was alive they had accepted some privileges, in spite of the saint's objection.[3] Now they allowed themselves to become an undeniably privileged Order. Gregory IX had renewed certain of the privileges granted by Honorius III at the beginning of his Pontificate, and about two months after John Parenti's election he gave them two more —ostensibly at their request—authorising them to bury their own members freely in their convents, and releasing them from the burden of being cited in the Church courts save in exceptional cases. In 1228 and 1230 he lavished extensive privileges upon the Basilica. In 1230, also, he was asked by the brothers whether they were bound to obey the precepts contained in the Testament— a question clearly expecting a negative answer—and he replied, as they desired, that they were not.[4] One result of his decision was that St Francis' strict injunction to the friars not to seek for Papal privileges of any kind, even when these could assist their preaching or spare them from persecution, was deprived of legal force, and the brethren were not slow to take advantage of their dispensation. They made representations to the Curia, complaining that some of the bishops were hindering them in their work and keeping them in irksome dependence. They said that they were often forbidden to have a private chapel, bell or cemetery, and were obliged to attend the parish church for all services and sacraments; that tithes and other taxes were levied on their houses

---

[1] Jordan, cc. 52, 58.   [2] Eccleston, p. 4.
[3] Sbaralea, I, pp. 9–10, 19–26 (between 1222 and 1226). St Francis' attitude to privileges is clearly and emphatically stated in the *Testament*.
[4] Sbaralea, I, 27–8, nos. G9, 1, 2, 4 (27–8, 30), cf. 3 (29); I, 31, nos. G9, 8–9 (32–3); I, 40–1, 46, 60–2, nos. G9, 21, 29, 49 (43, 50, 68); I, 68, no. G9, 56 (IV).

and gardens; that it was difficult for them to establish new convents because obstacles were put in their way; that an oath of obedience was exacted from them. Their sense of grievance does them no credit. It betrays their inability to persevere wholeheartedly in the path of humility, and their inclination to seek material more than spiritual improvement. But from a purely practical standpoint their attitude was justified and reasonable, and Gregory, appreciating the good that they might do for the Church if they were freed from such annoyances, responded by according to them two very important and significant privileges in August 1231. The bulls *Nimis iniqua* and *Nimis prava* affirmed that the Friars Minor were to enjoy almost complete exemption from episcopal jurisdiction; the bishops were severely reprimanded for molesting them; and all appeal against their liberty of action was forbidden. Furthermore, prelates known to be friends of the Minors were officially instructed to make themselves responsible for seeing that their rights were not violated.[1]

By obtaining the bulls *Quo elongati* and *Nimis iniqua* the brothers who were directing the development of the Order consciously repudiated much of their loyalty to the distinctive and original qualities that had characterised their institute. While John Parenti was Minister the grey friars became less humble and less poor, and their way of life tended towards imitation of that of the monks. Many left wandering preaching for a settled life of study within the convent walls, where they were freed from urgent care about material things by the 'nuncii' and 'spirituales amici' mentioned in *Quo elongati*. The Chapter meetings of Ministers and Custodians in some degree resembled the Cistercian Chapters, composed of the abbots of dependent houses. Also the Third Order was in his time made to conform more to the traditional practices of the religious life. The 1228 additions to the *Memoriale*, besides strengthening the control of the Minors over the Penitents, made monthly confession obligatory and instituted a Chapter of faults. By thus enforcing a close association between the Third Order and the ecclesiastical hierarchy the Minister hoped to free the Penitents

[1] *Ibid.* I, 74 ff., nos. G9, 63–6 (v and n.).

from all suspicion of heresy, which might ultimately reflect upon the friars themselves.[1]

It is now possible to suggest the reasons for John Parenti's election. The essential fact to be remembered is that he was the choice of the Provincial Ministers and Custodians. The first companions might have chosen Bernard of Quintavalle; the Italian lay brothers might have acclaimed Elias; the officials chose one of their own number. John Parenti commended himself to them by his learning and by the proofs of organising ability and powers of persuasion that he had displayed during the eight years when he was Provincial Minister of Spain. Their good opinion was largely justified. As General he encouraged learning and organised the administration with a view to obtaining the maximum degree of efficiency. His abilities were recognised by Gregory IX, who on two occasions chose him as his agent on political missions. In the spring of 1228 the Pope was driven from Rome by a popular revolt, the direct result of his excommunication of Frederick II, and was forced to take refuge in Perugia, where he remained throughout 1229 with no prospect of an early return. In this plight he sent John Parenti, himself a Roman citizen, to attempt to bring the Romans back to peace and obedience. The General was unsuccessful, but was credited with prophesying the terrible pestilence and famine which ravaged the city early in 1230, when the Tiber flooded, a calamity which led to Gregory's triumphant return to a penitent people.[2] Again, in December 1230, the Pope addressed a bull to the Podestà and people of Florence informing them that he was sending John Parenti, whose worth he praised, to establish peace among them.[3]

John Parenti's Generalate was not insignificant, and the Order

---

[1] Cf. Mandonnet, 'Les règles et le gouvernement de l'Ordo de Poenitentia au XIIIe siècle', *Opuscules*, IV, esp. pp. 197–205. He believes, however, that the traditional religious practices were introduced by the Pope against John Parenti's wish.

[2] *A.F.* III, 211; cf. Gregorovius, *History of...Rome in the Middle Ages* (English trans. 2 ed.), v, i (1906), 147–55.

[3] Sbaralea, I, 70–1, no. G9, 57 (74): '...virum utique religiosum, providum et maturum, de cuius discretione ac sinceritate indubitatam fiduciam obtinemus'.

travelled far along a new road in his short period of office. Was he himself responsible for this, or was it the work of another, carried on in spite of him? The three main developments to be considered are the advancement of learning, the changes in government, and the acquisition of privileges. The first two present no difficulty. Jordan's evidence is sufficient to prove that it was John who encouraged study in these years.[1] The provinces were divided at the Chapter of 1230 in which Elias was temporarily confounded, and the membership of the Chapter was restricted in direct opposition to Elias' will, his attempt to include ordinary brothers being defeated. The General was the victor in that violent and dramatic encounter.[2] The third is at first sight more disputable as, according to the *Speculum Vitae*, Elias claimed the credit for obtaining many Papal privileges, especially those allowing the indirect acceptance of money.[3] Examination of the bulls addressed to the Franciscans, however, exposes this claim as the invention of a late, confused and untrustworthy source. The two new privileges granted in 1227 were both explicitly directed to John Parenti, and even those bulls relating to the Basilica (which is considered essentially the work of Elias), were addressed to the General, into whose hands the translation was entrusted.[4] There is no evidence of any privilege about the receiving of money through interposed persons before *Quo elongati*, which was issued four months after Elias' claim was supposed to have been made. This bull was acquired at the instance of the Ministers; John had not wanted to ask for it, but he acquiesced in their demands.[5] Since he was their leader he must be held responsible for it. The same is true of *Nimis iniqua* and *Nimis prava*. One or perhaps both of these may have been due to the initiative of the Provincial Minister of England, Agnellus of Pisa,[6] but as they closely concerned the whole Order they can hardly have been granted without, at least, the General's consent. This was recognised by Lempp, but he failed to draw the neces-

---

[1] Jordan, cc. 52–4, 57–8.
[2] Eccleston, pp. 65–6; cf. below, pp. 141–3, and Appendix II.
[3] *Spec. Vitae*, p. 165.
[4] Sbaralea, I, 31, 46, 60–2, 64–5, nos. G9, 8, 9, 29, 49, 52 (32–3, 50, 68, 71); cf. I, 66, no. G9, 54 (72).
[5] *A.F.* III, 213; Eccleston, p. 66.   [6] Cf. Eccleston, p. 62 and n.

sary conclusion that John was technically and logically accountable for the privileges sought while he was Minister.[1]

Jordan, writing about Elias' Generalate, 1232–9, remarked: 'He had the whole Order in his power, as St Francis and John Parenti had had before him.'[2] It would seem that John Parenti was Minister General in fact as well as in name, and that he pursued a clear and decided policy, aimed at making the Order learned, efficiently governed, and free from tiresome dependence on the ecclesiastical authorities. Later tradition interpreted him as a Spiritual so that he might serve as a contrast to Elias, and thus presumed his weakness and insignificance.

[1] Lempp, p. 15.   [2] Jordan, c. 61.

CHAPTER IV

ELIAS' GENERALATE, 1232-9

Erat enim frater Helias pessimus homo....Sub dominio enim suo durissimum erat vivere.[1]

WHEN Elias had been absolved from office at the Whitsun Chapter of 1227 he was given employment by Hugolino, who had earlier that year been elevated to the Papacy as Gregory IX. The new Pope was eager to express his veneration for Francis, and was pleased to decide that a special church should be built in his honour. The important and enviable task of superintending the operations was entrusted to Elias. The project was enthusiastically supported by the people of Assisi. Already they looked upon Francis as a saint.[2] A succession of miracles occurred at his resting-place; and had not many of them seen the wondrous sign of grace, the Stigmata, on his dead body?[3] One citizen, Simon Puzarelli, gave a piece of land to be the site of the new edifice in March 1228, and another, Monaldus Leonardi, ceded an adjoining plot in July 1229 as this did not prove sufficient.[4] Local labour was forthcoming for the construction. The whole work was performed under Papal auspices. Elias received the first gift of land on behalf of Gregory IX, and a month later the Pope informed all Christians in the bull *Recolentes qualiter* that Francis deserved to be glorified in this way. An indulgence of forty days was promised to those who contributed towards the expenses.[5] He came in person to Assisi with the Cardinals for the official ceremony of canonisation, held at

---

[1] Salimbene, B. p. 148, H. p. 106.

[2] In a document dated 29 March 1228 a gift of land was recorded 'pro beatissimo corpore sancti Francisci', although the canonisation did not take place until 16 July. The document is preserved in the archives of the Sacro Convento at Assisi, and has been printed by Lempp, pp. 170-1.

[3] Cf. *1 Cel.* 121, 125, 127-50; *Tract. de miraculis*, c. 5.

[4] H. Thode, *Franz von Assisi und die Anfänge der Kunst der Renaissance in Italien* (Berlin, 1885), p. 201.

[5] Sbaralea, I, 40-1, no. G9, 21 (43).

the Church of St George on 16 July, and the day after he repaired to the *Collis Inferni*, now renamed *Collis Paradisi*, to lay the foundation stone.[1] In October he declared that the estate and buildings were Church property and were to be subject to no lesser jurisdiction than that of the Holy See. In April 1230 he confirmed this privilege, and further laid it down that the Basilica was to be considered 'caput et mater'of the Order.[2]

Rapid progress was made with the construction, and the Lower Church was ready to receive the saint's body early in 1230. It was arranged for the translation to take place on 25 May. The Pope was unable to attend, as the negotiations with Frederick II, preliminary to the peace terms ratified at San Germano on 23 July, kept him in Rome. He thus missed witnessing some extraordinarily unedifying behaviour. The translation, instead of being an occasion for rejoicing and religious enthusiasm, was profaned by angry rioting, and the General Chapter meeting that was held afterwards was the scene of a violent demonstration. In both these untoward disturbances Elias was implicated. The details of what happened are rather obscure. Some writers, as St Bonaventure, Bernard of Bessa and the compiler of the *Legend of the Three Companions*, record a magnificent and stately procession, with no hint of any regrettable incidents whatsoever.[3] But Gregory IX, in a bull issued little more than a fortnight after the event, accused the Podestà and people of Assisi of usurping the functions he had entrusted to the Minister General by seizing the body and daring to move it without authority, thereby preventing the friars from expressing the veneration due to the saint. Eccleston said that Elias translated the body three days earlier than the time appointed, and before the brothers had gathered together for the ceremony.[4] The apparent contradiction has led modern historians of widely different views into rejecting a portion of the evidence. Lempp and Sabatier took the bull *Speravimus hactenus* as the basis of their reconstruction, and interpreted it in conjunction with the accounts

---

[1] *1 Cel.* 123–6; Sbaralea, I, 66, no. G9, 54 (72).
[2] *Ibid.* I, 46, 60–2, nos. G9, 29 (50), 49 (68).
[3] Bonav., c. 15; Bernard of Bessa, *A.F.* III, 688, 694; *3 Soc.* c. 18 (72).
[4] Sbaralea, I, 66, no. G9, 54 (72) (*Speravimus hactenus*); Eccleston, p. 65.

of a premature translation.[1] They dismissed the descriptions of a spectacle on 25 May as fictitious. Gratien, Goad and Attal also started from the information contained in the bull, but they combined it with the reports of a splendid celebration. According to their version the translation took place on the proper day— Eccleston's story being quite erroneous—but was not accomplished peacefully, possibly because of the excitement of the crowd. The city armed guard, that Elias had by in readiness, took control of the situation, hastened the coffin into the Church, and shut the doors.[2]

Of the two presentations the latter is the less well-founded, as it involves an imaginative elaboration of the wording of *Speravimus hactenus* that is hardly warranted. Neither, however, makes adequate use of the available material. The difficulty of interpreting the sources has lain partly in the fact that modern scholars have given the place of honour to the Papal bull, which has been accepted as authoritative, both because it is an official document and because it was drawn up so promptly. Yet, since it is not an eyewitness account, its almost contemporary appearance is not necessarily an advantage. A news bulletin issued the next day is likely to be less, not more, reliable and well-proportioned than a report written up later when all the relevant information has been assembled. The Pope at that time may have heard only one version of what had happened. It is possible that the legates reported to him at once, and that the deputation of eminent friars set out for Rome, with their questions about the Rule and their charges against Elias, soon after the Chapter ended,[3] but the one person who had a motive for hurrying to get his story in quickly was Elias. It is significant that the bull attaches no blame to him, and this strengthens the supposition that it was based on his testimony. It provides no straightforward narrative of the facts, and though the few details it gives may be true, they are certainly not

---

[1] Lempp, pp. 84–6; Sabatier, *Opuscules*, XI, 173 ff.

[2] Gratien, pp. 23–4; H. Goad, *Franciscan Italy*, pp. 152–3, and in *Franciscan Essays*, II, 72–3; Attal, *Frate Elia*, p. 100. Cf. also A. Fortini, *Assisi nel Medio Evo*, pp. 111–15.

[3] Cf. Eccleston, pp. 65–6.

the whole truth. It should therefore be used rather as one of several imperfect and biased sources than as the foundation itself.

The evidence for an early translation is incontrovertible. It has been shown in an earlier Chapter that Eccleston was accurately informed, and the Papal pronouncement does at least prove that the official plans were upset. Together they indicate that the civil authorities took St Francis' body secretly to the Basilica three days before the ceremony was due, and that they did so not of their own initiative but at the bidding of Elias. Gregory attached the chief blame to the friars. Though the people were threatened with an interdict if they did not make satisfaction, the main penalties were imposed on the Basilica.[1] There is also good reason to presume that there was a ceremony. St Bonaventure and some later writers state that the translation was performed on 25 May.[2] Celano, too, confirms the fact in the *Tractatus de Miraculis*. James of Yseo, who later joined the Franciscans, told him that he had been present at the translation when he was a boy, and had rejoiced with the rest of the crowd.[3] It would be an unduly harsh judgement on the integrity of the friars to regard all this as a concerted attempt to substitute a bogus account of what should have happened for what did. Moreover the probability of a celebration was inherent in the situation. The Italians delight in holidays, and a great many people had come to Assisi expecting music, pomp, and ceremony. The Pope had sent Cardinals to represent him for the occasion, and their dignity demanded a suitable reception. For the Minister General to have to say that the body could

---

[1] Sbaralea, I, 66–7, no. G9, 54 (72). The privileges earlier granted to the Basilica were revoked; it was again subjected to episcopal jurisdiction, and the convent was put under an interdict. No brothers were to live there, and no General Chapter might be held there.

[2] Attal, *Frate Elia*, pp. 123–4, quotes a passage describing the formal translation never before observed in any medieval source, and gives as reference the Register of Gregory IX. In fact, the passage is a quotation from Wadding (*Annales*, II, 234–5), and the reference, also from Wadding (though slightly mutilated by Attal), was to *Speravimus hactenus* (as was realised by Suyskens, who quoted the passage from Wadding at length in *Acta SS.*, October, II, 682–3). Attal omits the second half of Wadding's account, which is a very close paraphrase of the relevant part of *Speravimus hactenus*.

[3] *Tract. de miraculis*, c. 109; cf. Salimbene, B. p. 95, H. p. 68.

not be found would have been humiliating, and it is reasonable to suppose that the arrangements for the day were carried out as planned, except for the exposure of the saint for veneration, which Elias had made impossible. This is the answer that the fourteenth-century compiler Arnold of Sarano deduced from the sources, and though he lacked the assistance of scientific critical apparatus in his investigations he possessed one advantage over modern scholars in that he was nearer to the events he studied, and had access to documents that have since perished.[1]

As to the commotion that occurred in the Chapter meeting, there is no need to discuss the problems presented by the sources here, since it has already been proved that the best account is in Eccleston and not in the *Speculum Vitae*.[2] What seems to have happened is this: during a session of the Ministers in Chapter a number of the ordinary brothers who had been excluded from the meeting tried by unconstitutional means to make Elias General. They fetched him out from his cell and carried him to the door of the Chapter-house. They then made a violent entry, wishing to put him in John Parenti's place, and uproar ensued. John Parenti divested himself of his habit and eventually managed to restore order. Elias, his reputation now doubly damaged, retired to a hermitage to do penance.[3]

Both episodes require explanation. Eccleston said that Elias effected the translation in a clandestine manner because he bore a grudge against John Parenti, who was officially in charge of the ceremony. But whether vindictiveness in fact prompted him, or not, he had at his disposal more than one acceptable and cogent reason to put forward in defence of his action. The surreptitious removal and burial of the body could be claimed as necessary protective measures. The *Speculum Vitae* said that he acted under the stress of fear, and the *Chronicle of the 24 Generals* that it was because he wished only a few to know exactly where the saint lay.[4] It has been suggested by sceptics that his eagerness for concealment was due to a guilty knowledge that the marks of the Stigmata would not bear inspection, but even if the phenomenon

[1] *A.F.* III, 212.   [2] Cf. above, pp. 34 ff.
[3] Eccleston, pp. 65–6.   [4] *Spec. Vitae*, p. 165; *A.F.* III, 212.

is approached on a strictly historical level, the consensus of independent, contemporary witness to the wounds precludes the possibility of fraud.[1] The majority of modern scholars, including hostile biographers like Lempp, have favoured a much more plausible interpretation, and have condoned secrecy as a precaution necessitated by the medieval attitude to relics. There was a real danger of mutilation and even of total theft, as the possession of miracle-working bones was coveted by many. At her translation in 1236 the breasts of St Elizabeth were cut by the faithful in their enthusiasm, and in 1232 the citizens of Padua literally fought over the body of St Anthony. The relics of Elisha were pillaged in the same century. St Bonaventure with difficulty obtained a tooth, and later Salimbene secured the whole body for the Franciscan convent at Parma, except the head, which the Austin Friars had purloined![2] As it was, St Francis did not quite escape the depredations of devotion. It is said that St Clare asked for a finger nail, and a few months after the translation Celano gave Jordan some relics to take back to Germany.[3] When the Perugians sacked Assisi in 1442 they tried to appropriate his body, thus vindicating Elias' wisdom in hiding the coffin and putting it in a Church that was also a strategically placed fortress.[4] It is interesting to note in passing that the practice of concealing the remains of saints for greater security was not unusual. The resting-place of St Rufinus in the cathedral of Assisi was known only to one custodian, whose duty it was to guard it safely and to pass on the secret of its whereabouts to his successor before his death.[5] So it is probable that Elias prevailed upon the civil authorities to assist him by using some such arguments as the likelihood of the body being damaged or seized.

For the eruption of his supporters into the Chapter meeting Elias does not seem to have been primarily responsible. He was

[1] Cf. J. E. Renan, 'François d'Assise', *Nouvelles Études d'histoire religieuse* (Paris, 1884), pp. 345–8; Thode, *op. cit.* p. 202; W. W. Seton, *Hibbert Journal*, XXIII (1924–5), 633–43, and Coulton's reply, *ibid.* XXIV (1926–7), 292–302.
[2] Salimbene, B. p. 575, H. p. 400 and n.   [3] Jordan, c. 59.
[4] Attal, *Frate Elia*, pp. 125–6 n. 35; Fortini, *Assisi nel Medio Evo*, pp. 451–76. For an earlier episode cf. *ibid.* pp. 277–81. Cf. Goad, *Franciscan Essays*, II, 70–1.
[5] Cf. Fortini, *op. cit.* p. 66.

reputed a wise man, and he would have been foolish indeed had he instigated a rising in his favour at such an unpropitious moment, when Assisi was thronged with friars whom he had deliberately cheated of their expectation of seeing St Francis. Eccleston relates the incident as if the initiative was with his partisans, and he perhaps indirectly provides the motive for their action. Elias had extended an invitation to all those who came to Assisi for the translation to attend the Chapter. John Parenti refused to admit them, and Elias took this as a personal affront. Possibly some of those debarred the meeting also felt slighted, and used this means to express their indignation against the Minister General. Elias allowed himself to be swept away by their enthusiasm. His acquiescence was blameworthy, and he acknowledged his fault by visible penitence. For the next two years he lived in retirement at Celle de Cortona, and did not shave the hairs of his head and beard.[1]

By so doing he regained the favour of Gregory IX, which he had temporarily forfeited, and became reconciled to the brethren. So completely was he forgiven that only two years after his offence he was restored to office. The circumstances are difficult to establish, as the evidence is sparse and not wholly consistent. According to Jordan he supplanted John Parenti at a Chapter held at Rome; Eccleston said it was at Rieti; and the *Speculum Vitae* implied that it was at Assisi.[2] Assisi has the weakest claim, both because it is not directly named and because the authority of the *Speculum Vitae* is not sufficient to challenge either of the others. Both Jordan and Eccleston are generally reliable, and neither can be preferred on grounds of intrinsic excellence. The mention, however, of an insignificant place as opposed to the Papal city carries with it a presumption of accuracy, and therefore it seems more probable that the Chapter took place at Rieti.[3] Its date fortunately presents

---

[1] Eccleston's evidence (p. 66) to this effect is confirmed by a document (cited by Thode, pp. 202–3) which shows that Elias was not superintending the work on the Basilica in these years. It records that John Parenti appointed one Picardus Morico administrator of the funds destined for the church, on condition that he shared his functions with Philip of Campello.

[2] Jordan, c. 61; Eccleston, pp. 66–7; *Spec. Vitae*, p. 164.

[3] Eccleston, pp. 66–7; 'Rome' in Jordan may be a copyist's error (cf. Boehmer's note *ad loc.*).

no problem. Jordan is the only source that provides one—1232—
and there is no reason to suspect that the figures are in error as
he confirms it by saying that Elias remained in power for seven
years, and his deposition was certainly in 1239.[1] The proceedings
of the Chapter are a mystery. We are told that Elias was not
canonically elected, and it is usually believed that he owed his
appointment either to violence, or to direct Papal intervention,
or to a combination of both.[2] The imputation that he succeeded
by means of force has already been examined in detail and discredited.[3] The case for Papal interference is equally unsound in
its developed form. According to the *Speculum Vitae* Gregory IX
admitted when he was called upon to depose Elias that he had
made him General; in the corresponding passage in Eccleston he
merely says that he had believed that he was acceptable to the
brethren.[4] Eccleston is the better text, and the *Speculum* rendering
is an elaboration that unduly magnifies the Pope's share. The part
assigned to him in Eccleston, and indeed in one portion of the
Speculum narrative, is passive: he confirmed the choice of Elias
by a section of the brothers when appeal was made to him.[5] Why
there was an appeal is a question that admits of only a tentative
explanation, but perhaps the answer may be found in the nature
of the Chapter. A General Chapter was not due until Whitsun
1233, and therefore the Chapter at Rieti may well have been only
a Provincial or semi-general Cismontane Chapter. If this was
the case, ordinary brothers as well as Ministers and Custodians
would have been present, and could have made their wishes known.
John Parenti was ready to resign, and the brethren, knowing that
an election was imminent, may have pressed there and then for
the candidate they desired, instead of leaving the matter entirely to
the Ministers and Custodians as the Rule prescribed. Elias was
popular with the rank and file. Whether from artfulness, conviction, or as a matter of form, he protested his unworthiness, and

[1] Jordan, cc. 61, 65-6; Salimbene, B. p. 239, H. p. 164.
[2] Cf. *Chron. anonym.*, A.F. I, 289, Lempp, pp. 92-5, Sabatier, *Opuscules*, XI,
192-3.
[3] Above, pp. 37-8.   [4] *Spec. Vitae*, p. 167; Eccleston, p. 68.
[5] Eccleston, pp. 66-7; *Spec. Vitae*, p. 164.

PLATE II. The Basilica of St Francis at Assisi

his supporters cried that they would rather he was dispensed from observing the Rule than have another leader.[1] The Ministers and the majority of the Italian friars being thus divided, the matter was referred to Gregory, who decided for the brethren. His approval suggests that, but for the incidents of 1230, Elias' conduct had been more or less exemplary, as had his actions been frequently reprehensible the Pope would have been unlikely to waive the requirements of the Rule concerning election.

As General, Elias actively fostered the material development of the Order. His chief concern was with the Basilica, a dazzling tribute to St Francis that is essentially his work. Experts on the architecture of the Church are agreed that the conception was his, although he received help from a professional architect, Philip of Campello.[2] The idea may have come to him from the fortress-sepulchres cut out of the living rock that he had seen in Syria. Its realisation was also due to him. The Church, begun in 1228, was practically completed in 1239.[3] This is a remarkable achievement. Large medieval churches usually took a century or more in the building, and many Italian cathedrals of the period were never finished. That the head of a mendicant Order with no resources of its own succeeded in amassing the requisite money, materials and labour for such an enterprise is convincing proof of exceptional organising ability and perseverance. The Church, moreover, was of an unusual magnificence. To understand the impression that it must have made upon contemporaries it is only necessary to contrast it with the other churches of Assisi, and particularly with the new cathedral of St Rufinus. This cathedral was the tangible expression of the victory of the commune over the bishop, and was the pride of the townspeople. It contained the relics of the martyr, who, we are told by St Peter Damian, had refused to be translated to the old cathedral, Santa Maria Maggiore.[4] It was only finished at the beginning of the thirteenth century, and the altar was consecrated by Gregory IX in July 1228.[5]

---

[1] Eccleston, p. 67; *Spec. Vitae*, p. 164.   [2] Cf. Thode, pp. 202-3.
[3] *A.F.* III, 228.
[4] Sermo xxxvi, 'de S. Ruffino martyre', *P.L.* CXLIV, coll. 693 ff., esp. col. 695.
[5] Fortini, *op. cit.* p. 97.

It is much larger than the old cathedral, and has a fine façade, but it is not comparable to the Basilica.

Elias' accession was also marked by a great increase in missionary activity, which was enthusiastically supported by the Pope. The scale of the undertaking can be inferred from the Papal records. In 1233 no less than five bulls were addressed to the Friars Minor who were setting out for countries held by the Saracens and other unbelievers, and letters were also sent to the Sultan of Damascus, the Caliph of Baghdad and the Miramolin of Morocco courteously requesting that the missionaries might be given a hearing. The king of Georgia received a letter asking him to help the friars who wished to use his territories as a base for heathen missions.[1] In 1235 the friars were established in Tunis, and in 1238 at Aleppo.[2] It has been suggested by those who look automatically for a wrong motive behind all his actions that Elias' interest in this field was not sincere, but sprang from a desire to rid Italy of fervent and respected brethren who would be likely to oppose his policy.[3] Such insinuations are as incapable of refutation as they are of proof. Not even the names of those who went are known, except in a very few cases.[4] It is more charitable, and probably nearer the truth, to suppose that his keen encouragement derived from his own experience in Syria in 1217-20.

In Christendom the Order continued to increase in numbers and in influence. It was regarded with very great favour and respect, and its ranks included many distinguished men. The Minors, and also the Poor Ladies and the Third Order, were patronised by royalty.[5] Offerings for the Basilica were sent by many secular princes, including John of Brienne and Baldwin II, Latin Emperors of Constantinople, Wenceslas, King of Bohemia, and the Emperor

[1] Cf. Sbaralea, I, 100-3, nos. G9, 95, 97, 100-2; I, 93-6, 102, 105-7, nos. G9, 87, 99, 106 (Eubel, Epitome, nos. 102, 104, 107 and nn.; 95, 106, 111-12).

[2] Ibid. I, 155-6, 245, nos. G9, 164 (163), 266 (246).

[3] Cf. Sabatier, Opuscules, XI, 191.

[4] A brother James of Russano led the mission to Georgia in 1233 (cf. Sbaralea, I, 102, no. G9, 99 (106), Golubovich, I, 162-3), and a brother John was Minister of the Friars Minor in Tunis in 1235 (cf. Sbaralea, I, 155-6, no. G9, 164 (163), Golubovich, I, 170).

[5] The royal patrons are listed by Attal, Frate Elia, p. 110.

Frederick II. Many convents were enlarged, or moved to better, more central sites in populated areas. Expansion was particularly noticeable in university towns. Hardly any positive evidence of Elias' share in this exists, as after his disgrace the Franciscans were loath to recognise any contribution that might redound to his credit. But since even in St Francis' lifetime he had urged the friars to move to more convenient and valuable sites when these were offered them, the development may be presumed to have had his support.[1] That he encouraged the study of theology his detractors themselves did not deny.[2]

Elias personally enjoyed very high prestige. He was the friend of both Pope and Emperor. His correspondence included many letters from the great, which his secretary, brother Illuminato, copied into a book.[3] This, unfortunately, has not survived, but a fraction of its contents is known independently. Frederick II wrote to him on at least two occasions. In the first he described the miracles of St Elizabeth of Hungary, and ended by asking the brothers to pray for him; in the second he told Elias to return brother Salimbene to his father if he valued his regard.[4] Grosseteste also wrote him two letters. In both he solicited favours. He wanted the Minister General to assign to him two or four brothers who were to be permanently attached to his household; and he wanted him to instruct the Friars Minor at the Curia to further some business that he had there. He clearly believed that Elias had considerable influence and that his friendship was worth cultivating.[5] Elias indeed was an important person, and his good offices were much in demand. In 1233 he was chosen as arbiter in a dispute between the communes of Spoleto and Cerreto; and

[1] Cf. above, p. 117 and n.   [2] Cf. Salimbene, B. p. 145, H. p. 104.
[3] Ibid. B. pp. 134, 53, H. pp. 96, 39.
[4] E. Winkelmann, Acta imperii inedita, I (Innsbruck, 1880), pp. 299–300; Salimbene, B. p. 52, H. p. 39.
[5] Grosseteste, Epistolae, ed. H. R. Luard, nos. XXXI, XLI. These two letters were evidently written to Elias c. 1236–7, before the movement to overthrow him became organised (and cf. S. H. Thomson, The Writings of Robert Grosseteste (Cambridge, 1940), pp. 199–200). The 1237–8 visitation caused him to change his opinion, and he actively supported the brethren in their complaints, writing two more letters (nos. LVIII, LIX)—this time to the Pope and the Cardinal Protector—urging that the complaints be heard (i.e. that Elias be deposed).

in 1238 he was charged by Gregory IX with the delicate mission of acting as mediator between the Empire and the Papacy.[1] Such was his reputation that Eccleston was able to write after his fall: 'Who in the whole of Christendom had a greater or a fairer fame than Elias?'[2]

But though he helped the Order to win material expansion, prosperity, popularity and esteem his brothers were not grateful to him or content with his leadership. On the contrary they disliked him, and rejoiced openly when he was deposed. The sources describe at length how, in spite of his achievements, he managed in seven years to antagonise so many, and no surprise can be felt at his fall. There is no lack of information about his demerits and his misdeeds. Not all the complaints that were made against him were serious, however, as it became fashionable to abuse him, and it is worth while to analyse the charges and to isolate the operative causes of his downfall. He could be judged by two standards: by his fidelity to St Francis' ideal, or by the extent to which he promoted the aims of the 'progressives'. The kinds of behaviour that were felt as grievances indicate by contrast what type of man the Friars Minor desired to have as their Minister General.

It might be assumed *a priori* that the activities to which most exception was taken were those which could be classified as grievances of principle. It would be a simple and satisfying juxtaposition of cause and effect if the brothers repudiated Elias because he disobeyed the Rule, and because in particular he disregarded the injunction to observe absolute poverty. The main reasons for his fall could then be easily found: they would be connected directly and indirectly with the Basilica.[3] This Church insulted everything that the true Franciscan held dear. It was large and splendid; it was privileged; it was paid for with money.

Though superficially sound, there is a serious flaw in this argument. It takes the attitude of the *zelanti* for granted, and from a modern standpoint. Even Sabatier felt compelled to admire the Church, and his hesitation in applauding it came from the fact

---

[1] Lempp, pp. 171-2; Salimbene, B. p. 134, H. p. 96.
[2] Eccleston, p. 29.   [3] Cf. Gratien, p. 142.

that it epitomised for him the modifications of poverty, simplicity and humility that he deplored.[1] But did the friars who had known and loved St Francis regard it in that light? Was it nothing to them but a worldly rival to the Portiuncula as a centre for the Order? Was it not rather, as Dr Goad has suggested,[2] a form of homage to the saint in which all shared? Noble churches were not raised to display material wealth and magnificence for their own sake, or to exalt the builder; they were designed to the glory of God and his saints. They could never therefore be excessive in their splendour. Medieval religious were not as a rule aware of any contradiction or inconsistency when, having vowed themselves to live in dire poverty, they spent large sums upon their churches.[3] A convenient example may be taken from the life of the blessed Benedetta, St Clare's immediate successor as abbess of the Poor Ladies at St Damian. She was venerated after her death c. 1260, and worked miracles, but in some respects her career resembled that of brother Elias. She showed a like desire to have the founder of her Order glorified, and expressed it in the same way, by promoting the building of a large church, modelled upon the Upper Church of the Franciscan Basilica, and designed by the same architect, Philip of Campello. At the same time she and her sisters kept their vow of poverty, and refused endowments.[4]

There is no contemporary evidence that the first companions had any conscientious objection to the Basilica. Bernard, Masseo, Angelo, Rufino and Leo all chose to be buried there, and Leo bequeathed to it his most treasured possession—the blessing that St Francis had written for him on La Verna. The first criticisms of its size and adornment were made in the fourteenth century. They were, however, made to appear earlier to give them greater weight, and, in particular, two anecdotes were circulated implying hostility between Elias and the zealots, one associated with Giles, one with Leo. In the first, Giles, when he had been shown

---

[1] Sabatier, *Vie de S. François*, p. 399.

[2] *Franciscan Essays*, II, 71–4.

[3] There are, however, such notable exceptions to this general statement as St Bernard of Clairvaux and St Francis himself.

[4] Cf. G. Abate, 'La Casa paterna di S. Chiara', *Bollettino della R. Deputazione di Storia Patria per l'Umbria*, XLI (1944), 118 ff.

over the convent with its sumptuous buildings, in which the brothers took obvious pride, said to them: 'Now you have need of nothing except wives', and, seeing their shocked faces, explained that it was as wrong to break the vow of poverty as of chastity.[1] In the other, Leo, distressed at the building of a large and sumptuous church and at the collecting of money towards its cost, publicly protested by breaking the vase that had been put out to receive offerings. Elias ordered him to be flogged and driven from Assisi.[2] Both stories are of more than doubtful authenticity. The former does not occur in brother Leo's *Life of brother Giles*, but in the longer *Life* incorporated into the *Chronicle of the 24 Generals*. This is a later work, and though many of its added details may be true, it gives perhaps, as Professor Burkitt has pointed out, an exaggerated impression of the element of sarcasm in Giles' conversation.[3] The latter incident could not have occurred at the date of which it is told;[4] and the likelihood of its ever having happened is slender, since it owes its 'preservation' to late, inaccurate and prejudiced sources. Yet even if they are allowed as evidence, the opposition they reflect can be applied to the Basilica only by a confusion. Giles scorned the lavishness not of the Church but of the adjoining convent: Leo attacked not the fabric but the alms-box. Leo's action, indeed, whether he really did it or not, typifies very well the attitude of the brothers towards the Basilica. In so far as they murmured against it at all, they said, not that it was improper, but that it was expensive. One gets the impression that if it could have been paid for entirely with voluntary gifts from the great, without their co-operation, they would have been content. What troubled and annoyed them was that they were required to assist in raising funds. Elias, by exacting money from the provinces, both broke the Rule himself and forced the brethren to break it, and his levies were regarded as a legitimate grievance.[5] They constituted, moreover, a serious drain on the friars' resources, which were never ample. Taxation is always resented, and taxes on alms must be particularly burdensome. However,

[1] *A.F.* iii, 90.   [2] *Spec. Vitae*, p. 163.
[3] *Franciscan Essays*, ii, 58–60.   [4] Cf. above, pp. 121–2.
[5] *Reg. Bullata*, c. 4; cf. Jordan, c. 61, Eccleston, p. 68.

since the object for which the money was needed met with their approval, they could not in fairness be too indignant with him on that score, and, had there been no other grounds for complaint, they would in all probability have pardoned him his financial demands.

More serious exception was taken to his personal conduct. He did not set a good example to the brethren, but behaved in a way that ill befitted a Friar Minor. The most vivid description of his mode of life was penned by Salimbene, and the main essentials of his account are confirmed by statements and details in independent sources. He developed a taste for luxury and comfort, and acted as if he were a prince. He avoided travelling whenever possible, preferring to divide his time between his two favourite residences, at Assisi and at Celle de Cortona, both of them places of great natural beauty. When he did have to make a journey he went on horseback, even if the distance were only half a mile. He employed a private cook to serve him with tasty dishes. He kept a retinue of servants, clad in many-coloured livery. He was not seen of seculars humbly seated on the ground, but reclining upon a couch with a good fire before him. He was proud, aloof, and on his dignity as well as self-indulgent. He seldom dined with the brothers, but ate his meals apart.[1] Brother Bernard indicated his disapproval of this practice by rising once from the refectory table in great fervour of spirit and intruding himself upon Elias, who had grudgingly to share his food with this uninvited guest.[2] In public, also, he was ungracious. He gave but a churlish reception to the Podestà of Parma, who paid him the honour of visiting him when he was on his way to the Emperor as the Pope's ambassador. Elias did not deign to rise when his visitor entered, and his lack of courtesy was observed and censured by the bystanders.[3]

When he was defending himself before the Pope Elias pleaded that the charges made against his behaviour were unfair. He admitted that he had not observed the Rule strictly in this matter, but claimed that his indulgence had been dictated by his poor

[1] Salimbene, B. pp. 134, 145–6, 229–30, H. pp. 96, 104, 157–8.
[2] A.F. III, 229.   [3] Salimbene, B. pp. 134, 137, H. pp. 96, 98.

health. Further, he said, the brothers had been under no mis-
apprehension as to the consequences of his infirmities. He had
expressly drawn their attention to the impossibility of his setting
them an example in bodily austerities when they clamoured for
his appointment, and they had undertaken then to excuse him.
Now they turned on him and cried 'shame'.[1] This plea was not
an adequate answer to the indictment, as Haymo of Faversham
was able to point out. The question at issue was one of degree,
and of the spirit in which mitigations were made. The Franciscans
were not intolerant or exacting. They did not expect exceptional
abstinence of their Ministers. They were sincerely willing for the
weak and the sick to have all the comfort and attention that their
need required. It is probable that Elias was delicate—his enemies
do not comment that his excuse was a lie—and the details of his
behaviour are explicable in terms of some chronic illness. He led
a sedentary life: he avoided long journeys; he went short distances
on horseback; he reclined on a couch in his apartments, and failed
to rise even when common politeness demanded that he should.
All these suggest that he suffered from a disease of the legs or
feet—possibly some form of gout—which obliged him to rest, and,
it would seem, to diet. The brothers probably did assure him of
their readiness to allow him invalid food and a horse. The best
of precedents sanctioned such dispensation. St Francis in his last
years had been driven by illness to eat cooked foods and to ride
upon an ass. But whereas St Francis had had to be persuaded to
take a little care of his body, and had agreed to do so only when
in dire distress,[2] Elias took excessive care of his. He was reluctant
to forgo the amenities that accompanied indisposition, and by
continuing and adding to them unnecessarily he lapsed into self-
indulgence. He was allowed a horse; he took a palfrey. The
brothers were not hoodwinked. When Bernard saw the type of
steed he rode, he ran after him, panting: 'This animal is too big
and too fat; this is not as the Rule allows.'[3] And for his haughti-
ness there was no excuse.

His worldliness and pride were unworthy of any religious; they

[1] Cf. Eccleston, p. 67.   [2] Cf. *1 Cel.* 98, *2 Cel.* 131, 210–11.
[3] Eccleston, pp. 67–8; *A.F.* III, 44, 229.

were especially reprehensible in a man of his position. The conduct of one in authority is more noticed than that of a private individual, and therefore Elias had the greater obligation to refrain from offending. He should have been aware of his public responsibility, but he seems to have been dazzled and intoxicated by the knowledge of his own importance, and by the eminence and brilliance of the society in which, as the leader of a popular and influential Order, he was able to move. He was fascinated by the spectacular court of the gifted and eccentric Frederick II, and he was flattered by the Emperor's regard. This was unfortunate. Frederick II's interests, his experiments, his conversation, his alert, inquiring and sceptical mind, disconcerted and scandalised the conventional. His faith was suspect, and his power menaced the political independence of the Church. There was actual war between Empire and Papacy during much of his reign, and even when, ostensibly, there was peace, the embers of conflict did not die, but smouldered until they could again be fanned into a blaze. By associating with the Emperor Elias jeopardised his standing at the Curia. The Minors were stalwart and valued supporters of the Papacy,[1] and it was dangerous for their Minister to lay himself open to the charge of entertaining Ghibelline sympathies.[2] Men questioned his loyalty, and looked askance at his pursuits—the rumour that he dabbled in alchemy may well have been due to his acquaintance with the astrologers and magicians who accompanied Frederick.[3]

[1] Cf. Matthew Paris, *Chronica maiora*, IV, 256, V, 66.

[2] Some modern Italian writers, determined to vindicate Elias' conduct as General, have put forward the suggestion that his friendship with the Emperor was the cause of his deposition (cf. Attal, *Frate Elia*, pp. 116, 144–8, Fortini, *Assisi nel Medio Evo*, pp. 135, 139, C. L. Sagui, *Frate Elia e la lotta fra la Chiesa e l'Impero nel tredicesimo secolo*). This is clearly to exaggerate.

[3] Salimbene, B. pp. 233–4, H. p. 160. Certain alchemical treatises and *sonetti* bear his name, but it has been much disputed whether he in fact wrote them. I have not been able to study the MSS., and am not competent to decide the question of authorship. For the arguments, see *Vita di Frate Elia da Cortona, Ministro Generale dell'Ordine di San Francesco, scritta da un anonimo Cortonese; composte da un anonimo Pisano,...*(Livorno, 1763), pp. 32–3 n., 69–70; Golubovich, I, 116–17; M. Mazzone, *Sonetti alchemici-eremitici di Frate Elia e Cecco d'Ascoli* (San Gimignano, 1930). Cf. also L. Thorndike, *Hist. of Magic and Experimental Science*, II (London, 1923), pp. 308, 334–5; C. H. Haskins, *Studies in...mediaeval science* (Cambridge, Mass., 1924), pp. 259–60, 281.

In short, Elias belied the promise of his early career, and turned out to be a person thoroughly unsuitable to be a successor of St Francis. His unedifying behaviour provided just grounds for dissatisfaction and complaint, and was a development that all devout and conscientious Franciscans, not only the 'zelanti', must have deplored. It was one of the main counts brought against him at his 'trial', and has been a theme much harped upon by later writers. It is not, however, sufficient to account for the widespread movement to procure his overthrow, being a grievance more weighty in retrospect than at the time. Most of the brothers knew of his short-comings only by hearsay. News of his worldly doings may have caused them to shake their heads sadly, but his misdemeanours were known directly to comparatively few. Such determined hostility as they bore towards him is unlikely to have been caused completely or even primarily by considerations that were remote and outside their personal experience. They provided additional reasons that could be alleged, with great effect, in justification of an opposition that was actually based on other grounds.

Elias came into contact with the brethren as a whole in one sphere only, that of government. And it is in his methods of government and in his policy for the Order that the cogent reasons for his general and positive unpopularity are to be found.

Here again Salimbene is the most informative of the chroniclers. His details cover a wide range of activities, but they can nearly all of them be grouped together as criticisms bearing on Elias' relations with his Provincial Ministers. They are worth enumerating, even though some are unjust. Elias appointed unsuitable men to office, actually giving authority to laymen, which, said Salimbene, was patently absurd. His criterion when selecting them was the measure of their friendliness towards himself. It was less important that they should be qualified than that they should be compliant and subservient. For he required them to be tools, not collaborators. He treated them as inferiors, and excluded them from any responsible share in the direction of the Order. He did not want to hear discussion of his policy, or advice, let alone criticism from them, and therefore gave them no opportunity to express their views. During the whole of his ministry he never held a General Chapter.[1] Even within the provinces he undermined and interfered with their authority. He curtailed the area which each controlled by extensive subdivision of the units of administration. He sent out visitors who remained inordinately long in the places they visited, and who usurped the functions of their hosts. They behaved as if it was they who were the Ministers, and were capricious in the exercise of their powers, so that they would alter or annul whatever the Ministers ordained if they felt inclined. Finally, he did his utmost to prevent the growth of a corporate spirit among them, realising that united they would be stronger than he. He did not allow them to build up a body of supporters in a given locality, but before they had had time to establish themselves anywhere he moved them to other provinces, as distant from the first as he could arrange. He made it clear to them that their tenure was precarious and entirely dependent on his good pleasure. To make them amenable he employed a calculated severity. He punished them when they were not at fault and deposed them arbitrarily. He lent a ready ear to complaints made against them by the despised lay brothers. As a result of their treatment many of the Ministers, especially in Italy where Elias' power was most felt, were cowed and browbeaten into submission; many resorted to bribery as a means of retaining their positions. The others bided their time.[2]

The list is certainly not lacking in quantity. Even Salimbene grew tired of writing down the items: 'It would take far too long if I tried to relate all the horrid abuses I have seen. Perchance I should run out of time and paper and my listeners would be bored rather than edified.'[3]

The precision of much of Salimbene's tirade creates an impression of factual accuracy, but his examples are not always appropriate, or exact. It is fortunate that his statements can to some extent be checked by comparison with other evidence, which

[1] Salimbene, B. pp. 142, 231, H. pp. 101, 158; cf. Jordan, c. 61, and below, p. 156 n.

[2] Salimbene, B. pp. 146-50, H. pp. 104-7; cf. Eccleston, p. 41.

[3] Salimbene, B. p. 144, H. p. 103.

serves to cast doubt upon some of the individual charges, while it confirms some, and supplements others. Many are not as straightforward as they appear. It has already been shown that such statistics as there are quite fail to bear out the assertions that Elias appointed many Ministers who were laymen, or his friends; that he transferred them from east to west; and that he frequently deposed them.[1] His alleged sins of omission also present difficulties. Salimbene tells us that, following a precedent set by St Francis and John Parenti, he made no general constitutions for the Order.[2] Constitutions were made by all three. Eccleston implies that St

---

[1] Cf. above, pp. 52-4.

[2] Salimbene, B. p. 143, H. p. 102. Very difficult to check is Salimbene's statement (B. p. 231, H. p. 158) that Elias held no General Chapters, a charge confirmed by Jordan (c. 61). But a Papal bull addressed to the Minister General and the other Ministers gathered at General Chapter is dated 6 July 1233 (Sbaralea, I, 113-14, no. G9, 114 (120)). Furthermore, we are told by Eccleston that the Scottish province objected to their visitor in 1238 because a General Chapter had appointed the Minister of Ireland to visit them. Since the Scottish province was set up after Elias became General (probably in 1233 or 1234, since the first Minister had been in office about twenty years when he was absolved in 1254: Eccleston, pp. 41, 43), this Chapter was presumably held later than 1232. That Elias was deposed in 1239 may be a coincidence, but it is suggestive that it falls exactly six years from 1233, nine years from 1230, which certainly fits a full sequence of triennial chapters from 1221 (1221, 1224, 1227, 1230, (1232), 1233, (?)1236, 1239). It is possible that Chapters were held, but that they were irregular—perhaps, as Salimbene indicates, because only the Italian Ministers took part, perhaps also because Elias threw the meetings open to ordinary brethren (cf. B. pp. 143-4, 231, H. pp. 102, 158, and Eccleston, pp. 65, 66).

But on closer inspection, the sequence of Chapters really depends on an inference from a slight remark in Eccleston, and on the bull of 1233. Unfortunately, it is doubtful if the bull can be used as evidence. Eubel (*Epitome*, no. 120 n.) observed that bulls were addressed on the same day to the General Chapters of the Dominicans and the Cistercians, and it would be a strange coincidence if all three Orders were holding General Chapters at this time—both Orders of friars normally held their Chapters at Whitsun, which fell on 22 May in 1233. It is likely, either that the Papal chancery made a slip, or more probably, that it was simply intended that the bull be read out at the next General Chapter, whenever held. There is thus no clear evidence that a Chapter was held in 1233 (still less that it was held at Soria in Castile, as asserted by Wadding and Sbaralea: cf. Wadding, *Annales*, 3 ed. II (Quaracchi, 1931), p. 352). The whole question remains obscure. Probably Elias held some kind of meetings, which were regarded as inconsistent with the letter of the *Reg. Bullata*.

Francis made several, and mentions the first, to the effect that the friars were not to eat more than three morsels of meat when dining with laymen.[1] John Parenti made five.[2] Elias ordered that the brothers were to wash their breeches themselves.[3] Apparently Salimbene did not recognise any of these as constitutions; the regulations he thought worthy of that name were those aimed at introducing uniformity into the Order, or at reducing the numbers and importance of the lay brethren. The enactments promulgated at the 1239 General Chapter were of the type that he approved.

The charge of cruelty raises allied problems. It is made against Elias by almost all the sources. Eccleston said that it was because of his worldliness and his cruelty that the brethren were driven to rebellion; Jordan that he dealt summarily with his opponents; Salimbene that he kept among his companions a certain brother John, who was strong and brutal, and who used to flog the brothers unmercifully at Elias' command. Angelo Clareno went into considerable detail in describing the torments that were inflicted on the righteous, and he listed the names of those who suffered.[4] Yet in spite of the consensus of testimony not one of Elias' accusers is capable of furnishing satisfactory concrete proof. Every single instance that they provide turns out on examination to be either wrongly attributed or seriously inaccurate. The untimely death of Caesar of Speyer is laid at his door by Angelo Clareno. He tells us that Elias had caused this brother, whom Jordan praised for his learning and his sanctity,[5] to be kept in the strictest confinement, and that he had appointed as his gaoler a savage lay brother who detested him, and who contrived to kill him. One unlucky day Caesar found the door of his cell had been left open, and went out to take some exercise; his gaoler, thinking he intended flight, struck him heavily, and as a result of this blow he died. This accident could have been only indirectly Elias' fault, as the gaoler's superior, but in fact he may not even to that extent have

---

[1] Eccleston, p. 25.   [2] See below, Appendix II.   [3] Eccleston, p. 42.
[4] Eccleston, p. 67; Jordan, c. 61; Salimbene, B. p. 230, H. p. 158; Angelo Clareno, *Rendiconti*, pp. 225–33.
[5] Jordan, c. 9.

been to blame. According to Wadding's account Caesar was killed in 1240, and at that date Elias was no longer General.[1] Then it is said that he imprisoned the blessed Andrea of Spello, together with certain other of St Francis' companions, and that they were liberated by Gregory IX at the request of St Anthony of Padua. But since these brethren were imprisoned in 1231, John Parenti and not Elias must have sentenced them.[2] Finally, Elias is accused of having maltreated St Anthony of Padua himself. According to Angelo Clareno, St Anthony, coming from Sicily to venerate the body of St Francis, was seized by Elias' minions and beaten till he bled. This is palpably untrue. It is not found in the early biographies, and its details are not in accord with the known facts of his life. It would appear from its context in the *Tribulations* that Elias persecuted St Anthony shortly before his deposition, in 1239, and the saint died in 1231![3] Nor can this be explained away as a mere mistake in chronology. No plausible time can be found for the incident. After John Parenti was made Minister in May 1227 Elias had not the authority to punish a pilgrim, and in the few months between St Francis' death and the General Chapter meeting he would hardly have jeopardised his chances of election by such a flagrant act of unprovoked aggression. And if he had, it would surely have been remembered by more than one of his accusers. The story is pure invention, even to the reference to Sicily—from c. June 1226 until c. May 1227 St Anthony was Custodian of Limoges; from c. May 1227 until May 1230 he was Provincial Minister of Bologna; and from then until his death he seems to have spent his time in Northern and Central Italy, chiefly in Padua.[4] It is but another example of the arbitrary representation of St Anthony as one of Elias' chief opponents, a legend which was so little founded upon fact that its

---

[1] Angelo Clareno, *Rendiconti*, pp. 229–31; for the date, cf. Wadding, III, 19–21. Neither account is of much authority.

[2] *Acta SS.*, June, I, 357. It cannot be later as St Anthony would not have been alive.

[3] Angelo Clareno, pp. 232–3 (the date intended is not entirely clear since Clareno's chronology is very shaky).

[4] Cf. G. Benvenuti, 'Cronologia della vita di S. Antonio di Padova', *Misc. Fr.* XXXI (1931), 49–57.

best product—St Anthony's speech for the prosecution in 1239—
required the resurrection of his ghost![1]

The lack of satisfactory examples is strange and annoying, the
more so as there seems to be no reason for it. Destructive criticism
only serves to expose many details of the complaints as false,
inaccurate, or misleading, and yet the charges themselves cannot
be dismissed. They seem to be true in spite of the ineffectiveness
of particular instances given in their support. The Provincial Ministers may not have been badly treated in quite the way that
Salimbene suggests, but nevertheless the fact remains that Elias
offended them and made them his enemies. Twelve years after
his deposition he still feared their vengeance.[2]

Behind the individual annoyances they complained about were
certain general objections that acted as a constant irritant. Elias
utterly failed to show the humility that was required of a Friar
Minor when he was in office, and acted as a secular master rather
than as a religious leader. He was not the servant but the ruler of
his brethren. For this he could be justly censured by all the followers of St Francis. The Ministers resented it deeply. However, their
indignation did not entirely spring from respect for the saint's
teaching and example. They, too, tended to regard office and
authority as an honour, and coveted what they had been exhorted
to shun.[3] They felt that they had a right to share in the direction
of the Order, and the strength of their hostility to Elias was due
rather to their sense of their own importance than to considerations of principle. The relationship in which the Provincials stood
to their Minister General had not yet been constitutionally defined,
and depended largely on his personality. John Parenti had consulted them on important matters, and had behaved consistently
as 'primus inter pares'. With Elias it was far otherwise. He liked
to deal with everything himself, and hated any attempt to influence
his decisions. Thus he broke the Provincial seal of England in a
burst of anger because the brethren had presumed to request that
he appoint their Minister from a 'short list' of candidates whom
they thought suitable.[4] The learned men in the Order, who were

---

[1] *Spec. Vitae*, pp. 165–7 (cf. above, p. 43).   [2] Salimbene, B. p. 236, H. p. 162.
[3] Cf. *2 Cel.* 145.   [4] Eccleston, pp. 76, 78–9.

accustomed to have their ideas and proposals treated with respect, found him too arrogant and too independent to be borne.

His refusal to govern with their consent might not have been so serious if the Ministers had approved whole-heartedly of the policy that he pursued. But although he was active in promoting learning and missionary work, and although the brethren multiplied and prospered under his charge, there were several matters that they thought should be tackled differently. The most noticeable disagreement was over the question of the position and treatment of the lay brothers. Elias was himself a layman, and he made no distinction between them and the clerics when he was admitting postulants or choosing officers. His impartiality was theoretically admirable—St Francis had done likewise—but the clerics thought that the time for such equality as had existed in the early days was past. They despised the laity because they were ignorant of Latin and because they could not administer the sacraments. They were, in their judgement, useless persons, who could bring no profit to the Order.[1] St Francis had not thought them useless. He said to the learned who congratulated themselves on the good that they did by their preaching: 'Why do you boast of men converted, when it is my simple brethren that have converted them by their prayers?'[2] He had hoped that the learned and the simple among his sons would respect each other, living together in unity, and enriching each other with their several gifts. He saw one as the complement of the other. He wanted them to understand their opportunities for mutual edification, and illustrated his meaning by a parable. He imagined a Chapter meeting of all the brethren, at which two men were chosen to preach, one learned and one simple. The learned man, realising that before this audience it would be unfitting to parade his knowledge, delivered a short and simple exhortation, and so moved his hearers that they reverenced him as a saint. The simple man, not wishing to repeat what his brother had done so well, proposed some verses of a Psalm as his theme, and, inspired by the Holy Spirit, he discoursed upon them most eloquently and profoundly.[3]

[1] Salimbene, B. pp. 139–43, H. pp. 99–102; cf. below, pp. 243–5.
[2] 2 Cel. 164.   [3] 2 Cel. 191.

But the Ministers did not appreciate this aspect of St Francis' teaching, and wanted it to be superseded in the interests of propriety and efficiency. They probably deplored the large percentage of lay brethren as a characteristic that was shared by the numerous popular heretical movements. The older Orders were predominantly clerical in composition, and the Friars Minor should be the same. They had hankered after traditional methods even in St Francis' lifetime, and they had been withstood, but not converted from their views. The practices of existing institutions attracted them irresistibly, and they were determined to introduce the features they admired as soon as possible. Elias would not let them have their way, and they considered that he was obstructing essential progress.

In one other important matter, that of privileges, Elias was backward in promoting the Order's interests. In the fourteenth century he was accused of gaining numerous privileges, which included dispensations from the vow of poverty, but this is contrary to the surviving evidence. According to the collection of Papal bulls, the reverse seems to have been true. He did not accelerate the progress away from St Francis' ideal by obtaining many additional privileges. Only two new ones were acquired during the whole of his Generalate, and they were neither of them of much significance.[1] In the opinion of the Ministers, who did not share the saint's aversion to privileges and the like, this was not praiseworthy but remiss. In the two years immediately following his deposition they remedied this 'defect' by acquiring fourteen.[2]

This examination and analysis of the complaints that were made of Elias show that there was amply sufficient justification for reproaching and disliking him. They further show that his transgressions against the Rule were less instrumental in provoking determined resistance to his authority than were his 'reactionary' tendencies. It was not the *zelanti* who successfully combined against him, but the learned. The stages of the process by which these

---

[1] Sbaralea, I, 167, 184–5, nos. G9, 174, 190 (171, 186) (*Cum iam per Eius* and *Quieti vestrae*).

[2] *Ibid.* I, pp. 277–300.

achieved their object can be reconstructed in some detail from the accounts provided by Jordan and Eccleston. The first step was taken by a group of distinguished ultramontane brethren, led by Alexander of Hales, John of La Rochelle and Haymo of Faversham, who came together, without permission, to discuss proposals for reform. It seems that their meeting was at Paris, and it was probably held some time in 1236.[1] It was not of any great importance, though the recommendations there put forward may have been the starting-point of the subsequent discussions and legislation. It might have had no sequel had not Elias aggravated the exasperation of the brothers by instituting a visitation of the provinces in 1237. This was the final grievance, and was taken by the Ministers as a challenge to battle. Almost everything about the visitors was objectionable—they informed Elias of all that they learned in the course of their inquiry; they punished those who had dared to criticise him; they were armed with powers of excommunication; they exacted yet further contributions for the Basilica. Everywhere they were greeted with a storm

---

[1] Jordan, c. 61, Eccleston, p. 67. Both mention a single ultramontane meeting, and almost certainly intend to refer to the same one, though the details of their notices do not quite tally. Both imply that it was held at Paris, but whereas Eccleston places it just before the 1239 General Chapter, Jordan seems to imply that it was prior to the visitation sent out in 1237. Jordan's account is the more detailed. He clearly distinguishes this meeting from that held in Rome in 1238, which ended with Gregory telling the friars to return to their provinces and elect a committee (Jordan, c. 64); and it is probable that Eccleston has confused the two. Elias may have held a cismontane Chapter in 1236, and it is likely enough that the excluded ultramontane brethren held this meeting by way of protest. Against so early a date is the suggestion made by J. C. Russell (Dictionary of Writers of Thirteenth Century England (London, 1936), pp. 13-14) that Alexander of Hales may not have joined the Order until 1238. But the evidence he cites only proves that Alexander was still a secular and archdeacon of Coventry on 25 August 1235 (Cal. Patent Rolls, 1232-47, p. 116). In addition to the preferments noted by Russell, Alexander held a prebend at St Paul's, where he had been succeeded by 1237 (according to the prebendal catalogue—for which see C. N. L. Brooke, Camb. Hist. Journal, x, ii (1951), 113 ff.—his successor was William of Welbourn, who occurs as canon in 1237; M. Gibbs, Early Charters of the Cathedral Church of St Paul, London, Camden 3rd series, LVIII (1939), no. 100). It is clear that the date usually given for his conversion, c. 1231 (cf. Denifle, Chartularium Univ. Parisiensis, I (Paris, 1889), p. 135) is too early; but if he entered 1235-6, his intervention c. 1236, though surprising, is not impossible, in view of his eminence in the learned world.

of protest. There was still, however, no concerted action on the part of Elias' opponents, who were not as yet fully organised. In some at least of the provinces the brothers held Chapters and drew up their complaints.[1] The brothers of Saxony sent representatives to Elias in the hope of obtaining redress, but were wholly unsuccessful. They therefore felt compelled to appeal to the Pope, and Jordan of Giano was given the delicate task of persuading Gregory to listen to their petition. He has left us a description of the interview. The Pope tried to cut the audience short, but Jordan was blandly impervious to rebuffs, and his cheerful impudence was so amusing that he was at length allowed to speak. He stated the case for the brethren well, and managed to convince Gregory that their demands could not properly be ignored.[2]

At Rome Jordan found deputations from other provinces who had come on the same errand. They all congregated at the Curia, and after long consultation agreed that the removal of the Minister General was the only remedy likely to be effective. They therefore collected all the information they could against Elias, and laid their accusation before the Pope. He, punctilious lawyer that he was, told them to arrange the material in the form of a logical argument, and when they had drawn up a balanced indictment he studied it, and decided that his personal intervention was necessary. The next General Chapter would have to be held in his presence. He sent the brethren back to their respective provinces with instructions to elect a committee of twenty learned and respected brethren, who were to come to Rome a month before the meeting to prepare measures of reform for its approval.[3]

Elias, faced with this growing threat, acted ill-advisedly. Had he made timely concessions he might perhaps have mollified his critics, but he made not the slightest effort to conciliate his outraged subordinates. Instead, he turned a deaf ear to their complaints, and trusted to his influence with the Pope, and to intimidation, to save him. At first he hoped simply to stifle the movement by denying it expression. He thought that he could prevent appeals against himself from ever being heard by prejudicing Gregory in his

---

[1] Jordan, c. 62; Eccleston, pp. 38–9.   [2] Jordan, c. 63.
[3] *Ibid.* cc. 63–4; Eccleston, p. 67.

favour. So he hastened to forestall the deputations from the provinces by warning the Pope that he might be pestered by certain brethren with a grievance, who, he assured him, were quite irresponsible and unworthy of consideration. They represented nothing more than an insubordinate and seditious faction in the Order. Gregory's judgement seems to have been swayed by this stratagem, for the brethren found it hard to interest him in their cause, but the preconceptions he had cunningly instilled were not proof against Jordan's good-humoured insistence. It is possible that Elias also tried to capture some of the appellants on their way to Rome, but brother Arnulf, the Papal penitentiary, insisted on their release.[1]

Since he could not silence his accusers, he defied them. It was beyond his power to stop the General Chapter from meeting, but he planned to reduce it to impotence by 'packing' it with his supporters. He sent out a command to all the able-bodied Italian lay brothers, on whom he could rely, telling them to attend the Chapter in force, for he believed that they would be ready to defend him, even with their cudgels if need be. But this scheme too was frustrated, again by brother Arnulf. When his intention was discovered, the orders he had given were quashed, and it was announced that the membership of the Chapter was to be confined to the officials specified in the Rule, and to 'suitable and prudent' companions.[2]

Lastly Elias tried the weapon of spiritual exhortation, but since he showed no sign of mending his ways this availed him little. He told the brethren that he wished them to recite Psalm 79 (80): 'Qui regis Israel intende...' every day in Chapter, and they obeyed. The psalm was said regularly, at least at the convent where Salimbene was residing, for a whole month before the General Chapter opened. Its twenty verses were commonly understood to have an especial significance for the Friars Minor, and perhaps Elias hoped that the verse: 'Fiat manus tua super virum dexterae tuae: et super filium hominis, quem confirmasti tibi', would be applied to him. Then if they said it daily they might cease to agitate

---

[1] *Spec. Vitae*, p. 165; cf. above, p. 42.
[2] Salimbene, B. pp. 230–1, 157, H. pp. 158, 112.

against him. It was an uncertain hope. Salimbene found a different verse appropriate: 'The wild boar out of the wood hath rooted it up: and the wild beast of the field devoured it.'[1]

Even when the Chapter met, and in spite of his uncompromising obstinacy and his blustering, Elias' fall was not a foregone conclusion. The Pope was still predisposed in his favour, and was prepared to give him the benefit of the doubt. He was allowed to justify his conduct without any formal charge being made, and, as he was an able speaker,[2] he probably exploited his advantage to the full. Gregory was satisfied that he had been unjustly accused, and saw no reason for listening to any more speeches. The case for the prosecution would have been defeated unheard had not Cardinal Robert of Somercote intervened at this critical moment, and persuaded the Pope to wait at least for the reply of Haymo of Faversham, who, he said, deserved consideration on account of his age, and who, he was sure, would be brief. At this stage Elias felt confident of his acquittal, but he had underestimated his opponent. A little disconcerted by his unfavourable reception, Haymo had begun rather hesitantly, but he too was an excellent speaker, and the evidence that he brought forward in support of his attack was unanswerable. When he pointed out that although the brethren had said they were prepared for Elias to spend gold they had not said they wished him to have a treasure, and although they had said they wished him to have a horse they had not said they wished him to have a palfrey or a charger, Elias was goaded into losing his self-control. He interrupted, protesting that Haymo lied. His supporters echoed the insult[3] and his enemies replied in kind; but the Pope's sharp rebuke put an end to the exchange. While they sat in shamed and anxious silence the Cardinal Protector suggested to Elias that he should offer to

[1] *Ibid.* B. pp. 231–2, H. p. 159.

[2] Cf. Jordan, c. 9; Salimbene, B. pp. 138–9, H. p. 99; Matthew Paris, *Chronica maiora*, III, 628.

[3] Apparently Elias had other supporters apart from the lay brethren who were excluded from the Chapter. He was never entirely without friends— cf. Salimbene, B. p. 230, H. pp. 157–8. Even at the moment of his deposition, when the majority were overjoyed at having got rid of him, the Pope was asked whether it would be legal to re-elect him (Eccleston, p. 101).

resign, but he bluntly refused. Then, after he had considered the matter for some time, Gregory announced that he had had a great respect for Elias, and had believed him a suitable Minister, both because he had seemed popular with the brethren and because he had been St Francis' friend, but as it was obvious that his rule was not approved of, he declared him deposed. His decision was acclaimed with undisguised delight.[1]

Ironically enough Elias was deposed not so much because he failed to follow St Francis as because he failed to adopt the 'enlightened' opinions of the Ministers. It is true to say that he thoroughly deserved to be deposed, but it was not moral indignation that actually determined his overthrow. He exasperated his opponents less by his personal life than by his administration.[2] The actions to which strong exception was taken were not always contraventions of St Francis' will. His treatment of the lay brothers, for instance, was a survival from the early days. Owing to the natural tendency of the educated men to assume the leadership of the rest, their equality of status was becoming an anachronism, but Elias' attempt to preserve the balance of the Order was 'Franciscan' even if it was not disinterested. It was more commendable than the pride and exclusiveness of the clerics. He was formally in the right when he appointed Provincial Ministers on his own unaided authority. But it is not necessary for a thing to be a legitimate grievance for it to be deeply resented. The Franciscans did not excel in showing meek resignation in the face of discomfort and injustice, but early displayed a certain promptitude to feel aggrieved and to complain of their superiors. The proceedings of the visitatorial Chapters held in England in 1238 were embittered by mutual recriminations.[3] Elias was violently attacked for his, admittedly numerous, imperfections. Nor was he by any means the only Minister General to arouse discontent. The lay brethren demon-

---

[1] Eccleston, pp. 67-8.

[2] Cf. Richard of San Germano, *M.G.H. Scr.* XIX, 379: 'Quidam frater Helyas ...pro eo, quod apud Gregorium papam delatus a fratribus quod male amministrasset, eum ipse papa ab amministratione removit.'

[3] Cf. Eccleston, p. 39 and n.

strated against John Parenti, and Haymo of Faversham was cited before the Cardinal Protector to answer his accusers.[1] Elias' policy was not sufficiently in harmony with the progressive tendencies to content the Ministers, and because in the conduct of his own life he flagrantly disobeyed the Rule, these were enabled to enlist the support of the fervent brethren, and were provided with an excellent excuse for attacking him.

[1] *Ibid.* pp. 65, 71.

CHAPTER V

EPILOGUE

Some fell upon stony places, where they had not much earth: and
forthwith they sprung up, because they had no deepness of earth.
And when the sun was up, they were scorched; and because they
had no root, they withered away (Matt. xiii. 5–6).[1]

WHY was Elias a failure as Minister General? He should have
been in many ways an ideal choice, for he possessed many of the
qualities that were needed by the brethren at that moment. The
Order was passing through a critical phase in its evolution. It
was composed of very diverse elements which had not fully
merged their identity into an integral whole. St Francis had,
though with some difficulty, held the ingredients together, but
after his death they showed a tendency to separate. There was
friction between the learned and the simple, between the clerics
and the lay brethren. There were serious differences of opinion
as to what was the right future, and the proper mission, of the
Order. One group, led by Italians from Umbria and the Marches,
accepted St Francis' teaching as perfect and final, and insisted
that it should be obeyed strictly and literally; another, to which
belonged the masters from the northern universities and the Ministers, believed that it was capable of improvement, and wished
it to be modified and supplemented to include features whose
worth had been proved by experience in other religious fraternities. The centrifugal forces that were destined later to disrupt the
Order were already present in a rudimentary form, but they might
have been checked by wise handling, and the sharp division that
there was between the Spirituals and the Conventuals in the fourteenth century was not an inevitable sequel.

It was naturally more difficult for the saint's immediate successors to retain the spontaneous allegiance of all the Friars Minor
than it had been for Francis. His was so rare a personality that,

[1] The parable is quoted in *Reg. Prima*, c. 22.

whatever their gifts, they were bound to be something of an anticlimax. Their policy would probably meet with the approval only of a section, and, as has been shown, John Parenti shared the mentality of the Ministers, and did as they thought best. Elias, however, was more widely acceptable. His friendship with St Francis, and with St Clare, recommended him to the first companions; and, though he was a layman, his learning, his abilities, his work for the Basilica, and the esteem in which he was held by the Pope, made him respected by the clerics. He might perhaps, by a judicious blending of the primitive standards and the aspirations of the progressives, have helped to weld the two together, but he did not grasp his opportunity. Instead he pleased neither: he went his own way without regard for the feelings of any. Thus, with the exception of the Italian lay brothers, he made enemies without making friends. He antagonised the Ministers by governing without consent, and he scandalised the fervent by his life. He played a lone hand, and the result of his over-great independence was a victory for the clerics, who procured his downfall and succeeded in establishing themselves as the dominant party in the Order.

Elias' behaviour after he became General calls for explanation. If he had indeed been loved and trusted by St Francis, his subsequent conduct was, to say the least, surprising. Celano at one time praised him; the majority of Franciscan writers disparaged him. The contradiction has disconcerted many who have studied his career. These have thought it necessary to choose between the sources, and have either condemned him absolutely, or exonerated him with equal thoroughness. The portraits provided by both schools are far too simple to be lifelike. The sources are not essentially inconsistent. That they are different is merely the reflection of the fact that in the course of his life Elias' character underwent considerable modification. His behaviour was not determined by certain fixed principles that never changed; nor did it mark a steady development in one particular direction. He showed much early promise; and then suddenly and radically degenerated. Men's opinion of him was in consequence revised, and the attitude towards him displayed in the various sources is dependent on the date at which they were written. The *Vita Prima* described the man that St Francis knew; Jordan, Eccleston and Salimbene found fault with the Minister General; the Spirituals heaped opprobrium upon the renegade.

The underlying reason for Elias' moral collapse was that he joined the Friars Minor without having a true vocation. According to tradition he was received by St Francis, and the power of the saint's words to move his hearers has been vouched for by more than one contemporary observer.[1] Elias probably took the decisive step of renouncing the world in an access of enthusiasm, and his profession put the seal not on a calm and carefully considered decision but on a transitory emotional impulse. His initial progress was chiefly due, whether consciously or unconsciously, to his desire to emulate and to please St Francis, for whom he had the deepest admiration. When Francis died, he lost the *raison d'être* of his endeavours. Deprived of what had been for him a necessary stimulus, he had not the strength of purpose to persevere. The discipline of the religious life, unless it is the outward expression of a loving, willing, and humble service offered to God, is a hard and an exacting one. Elias made no complete and joyful self-surrender; he was not actuated by a deep conviction of the need for spiritual perfection and for grace; and therefore he experienced a reaction. The precepts of the Rule did not inspire him, they constrained him. They exercised no compelling hold on his obedience.

As the foundation of his religious life was so insecure, adverse external circumstances soon served to undermine it. First there was his illness, which made some relaxation of the rigours of abstinence permissible. The extra comforts which were originally intended merely to alleviate actual suffering insidiously overcame his self-control. They acted like a drug upon his senses, and he succumbed to the temptation. The bare minimum needed for relief did not long content him, and he acquired and gratified a taste for them for their own sake. Then there was his elevation to the Generalate, which was also disastrous in its effect upon his character. He considered that it made him, not responsible, but

[1] Cf. Wadding, *Annales*, I, 108 (see below); *2 Cel.* 107; Thomas of Spalato, *Hist. Salonitanorum, ap.* Lemmens, *Testimonia Minora saeculi XIII*, p. 10.

privileged, and he therefore misused his position, separating himself from the brethren, and putting himself above the Rule. No one in the Order could command or forbid him anything, and, as he was not self-disciplined, he did as he pleased. His own conscience did not hold him answerable for his vows, and he thought he could evade his obligations with impunity. When challenged, he resorted to casuistry, saying that he had never formally sworn obedience to the *Regula Bullata*, and therefore was not bound by it.[1] He conceived an exaggerated idea of his own importance, and nourished his growing conceit by frequenting the Curia and the court of Frederick II. His dignity, however, was not innate but acquired, and he behaved with the aggressive arrogance of the parvenu. He needed to assert his superiority, and did so in ways that were sometimes childish. He is supposed to have wanted to have seventy-two Provincial Ministers under him in memory of the seventy-two disciples, because the Master General of the Friars Preachers had twelve, in memory of the apostles.[2] His sense of duty was not strong. Some things he did achieve: he built the Basilica; he sent out missions; he encouraged learning. But he pursued no well thought-out and energetic policy calculated to benefit his brethren. He was not deeply concerned about their welfare, or very eager to be of service to them. His ambition was not to unite, inspire and lead them, but to experience the personal satisfaction of being a ruler. His attitude to office was thoroughly selfish and irresponsible. He valued it not because it enabled him to promote the good of his Order, but because it gave him power and freedom. Consequently he clung to it, unwilling to lose the material advantages he derived from it, and unable to bear the humiliation of being 'reduced to the ranks'. After his deposition pride prevented him from acknowledging his faults and his mistakes, and rather than submit to discipline, he deserted.[3] St Francis' admonitions were, in his case, unavailing. 'Woe to that religious, who is set on high by others, and will not of his own free will climb down.'[4]

The conclusion seems to be that Elias was, essentially, a weak

---

[1] Eccleston, pp. 68–9. [2] *Ibid.* p. 41.
[3] *Ibid.* p. 69. [4] *Admonitio* 20.

man. He had no staying power. He was one of those mentioned in the parable of the sower, who receive the Word with joy, and endure for a while, but in time of tribulation or temptation fall away. He could not master his desire for bodily comfort, or bear responsibility, or subdue his pride. He lacked physical courage. When, late in 1239, he set out for the Curia, with a safe conduct, to negotiate peace terms for the Emperor and to explain why he himself had joined Frederick, he never accomplished his mission, but turned back at Viterbo, because he heard that his enemies planned to capture him; and when, in 1251, Gerard of Modena urged him to return to his Order and reconcile himself with his brethren, he replied that he dared not, as he feared that the Ministers would cast him into prison, and feed him on bread and water.[1] He was afraid of pain and hardship, and it was not until he lay on his deathbed that he declared himself ready to make submission and to do penance.[2] He was a domineering and an obstinate Minister and neither of these qualities is the mark of a strong character. They are rather the resort of the weak, who pretend to a confidence in themselves that they do not possess. The modern psychologist would probably deny that Elias had a commanding or effective personality, and would find in his unwillingness to admit himself in the wrong, or to adopt the suggestions of others, evidence of an inferiority complex. He made but a feeble resistance to the Ministers who attacked him, and was easily deposed, the only real difficulty that his adversaries encountered being the Pope's partiality for him.

His character was not 'black', or 'white', or even any single consistent shade of grey, but, as it were, 'piebald'. His failings have already received sufficient attention, and there is no need to dwell upon them further here, but his better qualities, which are more liable to be forgotten, should perhaps be recalled. He was a complex individual, and his nature included traits that pulled him in opposite directions. He enjoyed living in luxury, and yet he had in him a leaning towards asceticism. At times he preferred the hermit's cell to the comfortable apartments of

---

[1] Cf. above, p. 40; Salimbene, B. p. 236, H. p. 162.

[2] For his deathbed repentance and reconciliation, see above, p. 39.

the great. There is a tradition at Celle de Cortona that he spent the first six years after his profession in a tiny cell beside the gorge that the Capuchin friars still point out to the visitor.[1] It is made of mud and stones, and is near to one that St Francis himself occupied. It was to this cell that Elias retired in 1230, when he was in disgrace; it was one of the few places that he visited while he was General; and after his deposition he was often there.[2] St Francis understood how much he was attracted to the solitary life, and, in a letter that he wrote to him, urging him to be more kindly in his dealings with the brethren, he exhorted him to value charity more than a hermitage.[3] Elias needed this counsel, for he was inclined to be autocratic and haughty towards others, and he acquired a reputation for harshness, but he was not always overbearing and unsympathetic. The way in which he protected Salimbene from the violence of his father was irreproachable, and Jordan of Giano found him a considerate superior. This brother, as a result of his inquisitiveness, was numbered among the volunteers for a dangerous mission to Germany, and his friends were anxious to save him from this fate. His case was brought to Elias, who, far from coercing him or assigning him arbitrarily to a province, told him to make up his own mind where he wished to go. Nor are these isolated

---

[1] According to Wadding, *Annales*, I, 108-9, Elias was received into the Order at Cortona in 1211, but this is probably a guess based on Marianus of Florence (*A.F.H.* I (1908), 105-6), whose arrangement of his material at this point does not seem to be based on any sound chronological information.

[2] Cf. Salimbene, B. pp. 229, 230, 236, H. pp. 157, 158, 162; Eccleston, p. 69; and the record of the trial of Ghibelline conspirators in 1245, discovered in the Perugia archives and printed by D. M. Faloci-Pulignani in *Misc. Fr.* XXIX (1929), 129-33.

[3] *Epistola* 3: 'Et dilige eos qui ista [the various injuries outlined in the first sentence of the letter] faciunt tibi, et non velis aliud de eis, nisi quantum Dominus dederit tibi, et in hoc dilige eos, ut non velis, quod sint meliores Christiani. Et istud sit tibi plus quam eremitorium.' There seems no reason to doubt the reading 'ministro generali' in the address in some of the MSS., and the probability is strong that it is Elias not Peter Catanii who is addressed. The Quaracchi editors, against the weight of the MS. tradition, read 'ut velis' for 'ut non velis'. This is obviously an easier reading than 'ut non velis', but it misses the characteristic Franciscan irony—and the even more characteristic concentration on the *person* addressed. Every argument to St Francis was an *argumentum ad hominem*.

examples. He was gentle and understanding to women. He remembered St Clare when Francis died, and had the body taken round by St Damian's—though the convent was not on the direct route from the Portiuncula to Assisi—so that she might see him for the last time.[1] Both Clare and her sister thought well of him, and Agnes, lonely in her convent at Florence, begged that he might come often to comfort her in the Lord.[2] To Jacoba de Settesoli, also, he showed charity. After Francis' death he came up to her as she stood weeping, and laid the body of the saint in her arms, saying: 'You loved him while he lived; hold him now that he is dead.'[3]

Elias could behave courteously and commendably, and there were some who appreciated his good qualities. It is said that a man's worth may be judged by the type of his friends, and his included people of great virtue and of high intelligence—St Francis, St Clare, Gregory IX, Frederick II. In spite of his faults he had a real capacity for friendship. None of the members of his household deserted him when he was deposed, or even when he was excommunicated and expelled from his Order,[4] and that he was able to keep their loyalty in such circumstances shows that he never lost his graciousness or his power to inspire confidence.

He had great abilities; he was a renowned preacher, an imaginative architect, and a skilled diplomat.[5] Frederick II, who expected a very high standard of efficiency and resourcefulness from his servants, was glad to employ him. He had the makings of greatness, but instead of developing his talents in the service of God, to which he was vowed, he wasted them. The end of his life was without real purpose, and he derived little success or satisfaction from the worldly, political undertakings to which he turned. He became a staunch adherent of the Emperor, and thereby incurred the ban of the Church. He accompanied him on his campaigns; he built fortresses for him in Sicily; he went as his envoy to

---

[1] 1 *Cel.* 116; cf. U. Cosmo 'La tragedia di Frate Elia', in *Bollettino della Società Internazionale di Studi Francescani in Assisi* (1927).

[2] *A.F.* III, 175–7.　　　　　　　[3] Celano, *Tract. de miraculis*, c. 39.

[4] Salimbene, B. p. 230, H. pp. 157–8.

[5] Cf. e.g. Matthew Paris, *Chronica maiora*, ed. H. R. Luard, III, 628; Marianus of Florence, *loc. cit.*, and *A.F.H.* II, 107, *Tractatus provinciae Tusciae*, f. 95; Salimbene, B. p. 134, H. p. 96.

Constantinople to arrange an alliance; he even promoted an abortive plot to hand Assisi over to the Ghibellines, and his cell at
Celle de Cortona became the meeting-place of conspirators.[1] He
sacrificed his spiritual welfare to empty ambition and fear, and
brought shame upon himself and his brethren, whose habit he
continued to wear. He made himself notorious, and children used
to taunt the grey friars, singing after them:

> Hor atorno fratt Helya
> Ke pres' ha la mala via[2]

St Francis regarded the Order as his, and was bitterly distressed
if it did not develop as he wanted; and his sanctity has hypnotised
us into thinking likewise. We tend to exaggerate his personal
importance in the same way as he did. Even during his lifetime
many joined the Order not through any especial feeling for him,
its founder, but as a way of life. As much is admitted, with
delightful candour, by Jordan. He had not been particularly
impressed by Francis, whom he had seen and regarded as an
ordinary human being; and it was only after the brethren of
Thuringia welcomed Jordan into the church at Eisenach with a
solemn procession and joyful chant 'hic est fratrum amator'—a
welcome which startled him into recalling that he had with him
relics of the saint which he had forgotten about—that he began
to hold Francis in special respect.[3] To us Francis is more alive
and more interesting than all his followers; his contemporaries
may be forgiven for having a more normal sense of proportion.
And there is a further danger in seeing its early history through
his eyes. We may share his self-confidence but not his humility,
and so come to regard him as always, and inevitably, in the right.
The friendship of Francis and Elias was no mere unhappy accident,
nor simply due to blindness on Francis' part. They had much in
common. Francis could be inconsistent; he could be arbitrary;
and he could make life very difficult for others. But his arbitrari-

---

[1] Marianus of Florence, *locc. cit.*; *Spec. Vitae*, p. 168; cf. D. M. Faloci-Pulignani,
'Aneddoto sconosciuto di Frate Elia', in *Misc. Fr.* xxix (1929), 129–33.
[2] Salimbene, B. pp. 233, 235, H. pp. 159–60, 161. Perhaps the opening of
a ballad.   [3] Jordan, c. 59.

ness was in part at least the outcome of his sensitivity; like his Master, he solved, not abstract problems, but personal predicaments. Government in his tradition but without his grace was doomed. The sources try to fasten on Elias during Francis' lifetime the one fault Francis would not have tolerated, that of autocracy. But Elias had other faults, some of them, ironically, Francis' own. When he was Minister no one knew what he was going to do next, and the uncertainty and insecurity were deeply resented. Elias' rule was unpopular largely because he insisted on letting the morrow take care of itself. This is no defence of his failings, which by the end of his Generalate were scandalous; but it does help to explain the confidence St Francis placed in him. Partly it was, so it seems to me, that Francis saw in Elias a mirror of his own wayward nature; and partly that he did not wish his Order to be ruled by a comfortable administrator. Francis failed to perceive the flaws in Elias' character, but not so completely as has sometimes been supposed. In the long run, Francis himself must take some of the blame for Elias' rule. It was a harsh image of a genuine part of the Franciscan ideal. But his victims could hardly be expected to see it in this light.

By his wilful disobedience Elias ruined his reputation, and became an object for scorn and hatred. Therefore, when the divisions that had begun to trouble the Order even in his time gave place to a sharp and bitter conflict between Spirituals and Conventuals, and men looked about for someone who could be blamed for this misfortune, he was seized upon as a convenient scapegoat. He became a legendary figure, a caricature. All merit was denied him, and his misdeeds were emphasised, elaborated, multiplied.

In their eagerness to vilify and condemn him later writers not only intensified his wickedness, they exaggerated his importance. He was made responsible for all the developments that the Spirituals deplored: he was the prototype of their adversaries, the Judas who betrayed St Francis' ideal. Their prejudiced and crude interpretation has been accepted in its main essentials by some modern scholars, notably by Sabatier and Lempp. Others, chiefly Italians, have realised that he has been much maligned, but in their attempts to do him justice they have allowed themselves to be carried to the other extreme. It is far too superficial to blame the decline of the Order on him; it is preposterous to suggest that but for him it might not have survived at all. Elias left no very deep imprint, except in legend. His Generalate was not nearly so significant as that of Haymo of Faversham or St Bonaventure. His personal life and posthumous notoriety have obscured the issue. No one man, however wicked or however powerful, could seriously or permanently corrupt a body of fervent and upright religious.

The modifications in the Rule were not due to Elias' behaviour, his pride, his self-indulgence, or his apostasy, but to the Ministers. Though this term is convenient it is misleading, as it suggests a coherent party. There was as yet no party within the Order in any organised sense: there were a number of 'elder statesmen', who had not a coherent voice—if they had had Elias would never have been elected in 1232—but who would naturally come to the fore in time of crisis, and did so in fact in 1239. Elias was not properly one of their number, and had little share in their achievements. They introduced the first changes in 1220, while he was in Syria; when he returned to Italy he did not join them, and that he succeeded Peter Catanii was Francis' wish, not theirs. In 1227 they elected John Parenti rather than confirm Elias in office; in 1230 and 1232 it was not they, but the ordinary brothers, who desired his reappointment; when he was General they disliked his policy and his methods, and it was they and their learned associates who brought about his overthrow. The constitutions that they then proceeded to promulgate were not the culmination or fulfilment of his government, but rather its negation. His Generalate was, in fact, nothing more than an interlude. He resisted the progressive tendencies—he did not acquire many privileges, and he did not allow the clerics to assume control—but as he had no following apart from the lay brethren he was not strong enough to withstand them for long. After his fall the thread was taken up where it had been left by John Parenti. The new pattern was worked out by Haymo of Faversham, and fixed by St Bonaventure.

Et hec de fratre Helya dicta sufficiant.[1]

---

[1] Salimbene, B. p. 238, H. p. 163.

BOOK II
THE DECISIVE YEARS: 1239-1260

CHAPTER VI

PROLOGUE

Quia enim intentionis nostre fuit loqui de generalibus ministris ordinis beati Francisci, cum tempus occurreret oportunum, et Helias, qui fuit unus ex illis...grandem materiam historie continebat, ideo me prius volui expedire de ipso, ut eius deposita sarcina facilius historiam prosequerer inchoatam.[1]

AN *élite* of intellectuals and administrators had succeeded in drawing from Gregory IX the reluctant admission that Elias was unfit to rule the Friars Minor. His deposition gave them a great opportunity and also a great responsibility. The immediate problem was a practical one. They must choose a General worthy of the trust imposed upon him, able to unite and lead the brethren in St Francis' footsteps. At the same time they must insure against the risk of mistake: should an unsuitable man be elected in the future the consequences for the Order must be minimised. They therefore initiated legislation aimed at limiting the powers of the executive, correcting the tendencies fostered by Elias of which they disapproved, and generally at overhauling and reforming the organisation and regulation of the brotherhood. The years 1239–42 are of crucial significance in the history of the Order. The changes made were the most rapid and sweeping since St Francis' death and they had a vitality that won for them a permanent place in the Order's constitution. These years cannot, however, be studied fruitfully in isolation, and so this study is continued up to the time of St Bonaventure, partly in order to put them into a wider context, partly because the enactments that made them important do not survive independently and can only be studied with the help of the Constitutions of Narbonne, promulgated in 1260. The ministry of St Bonaventure provides a convenient term, both because St Bonaventure was himself a great constructive reformer who consolidated and completed the characteristic

[1] Salimbene, B. p. 238, H. p. 163.

achievement of his predecessors, and because his Generalate was the last before the period of conflict and schism between Conventuals and Spirituals opened. The period 1239–60 was marked by great expansion and success among the people and by a lively zeal for improvement within the Order. The Ministers General were all, with one exception, able, distinguished and fervent. However much the forces of decay may have developed in this period, there was little indication that they would get the upper hand, still less that schism was on the way. But our problem is not to judge the Order, but to understand the processes of change.

CHAPTER VII

ALBERT OF PISA

ELIAS' election had been irregular, and Gregory IX, not unnaturally, took personal care to see that the requirements of the Rule were not waived a second time. He summoned the Ministers and Custodians to attend him in a cell apart and made each in turn declare his vote orally before allowing any of them to be written down. Thus supervised they chose as their General brother Albert of Pisa, then Provincial of England. He had, however, but little opportunity to justify their hopes of him, as he died only a few months after his election.[1] Little space has consequently been allotted to Albert in histories of the Order, both medieval and modern; and yet something of general importance may be gained from a study of him. Simply by electing him, the leading spirits of the Order have provided us with a positive clue to their aspirations. Although no subsequent General was permitted to exercise such uncontrolled authority as Elias had enjoyed, his competence coming to be defined and curtailed by Chapter, he was by no means reduced to a mere figurehead, and certainly not at this juncture. Flushed with their victory, the Ministers and Custodians were called upon to make an immediate election, before any constitutional safeguards had been passed. At that moment they could have had no assurance that their victory was likely to be permanent, and they can hardly have failed to believe that the ultimate success or failure of their ideals might well depend upon their present choice. Albert's appointment is therefore of great interest. It is evidence that his character, his abilities and, more especially, his interpretation of the Franciscan way of life had won the approval of at least a majority of his colleagues; and an understanding of his personality and policy, as revealed by his previous career of service in the Order, is consequently of more than purely biographical value.

[1] Eccleston, pp. 68–70.

According to tradition Agnellus of Pisa and Albert of Pisa were received into the Order together by St Francis himself in 1211.[1] Both were rapidly advanced to positions of responsibility. Albert was probably Provincial Minister of Tuscany from 1217 to 1221, and of the March of Ancona from 1221 to 1223; certainly Provincial Minister of Germany from 1223 to 1227 and possibly of Spain, 1227–30; probably Provincial of Bologna, *c.* 1230–2, of Hungary, *c.* 1232–6, and certainly of England, 1236–9, in which year he was elected General—there can scarcely have been a more experienced official in the Order![2] It is fortunate that Germany and England were numbered among his administrations. In the one he came into contact with Jordan of Giano, in the other with Eccleston, and both have left record of him in their chronicles. Thus we possess two independent, reliable, first-hand accounts of a man who, but for them, would have come down to us as little more than a name, in spite of his long and varied ministry. As it is we can become acquainted not only with some of his public activities, but also with more intimate aspects of his personality, for neither Jordan nor Eccleston were content to write down a bald catalogue of facts; each enlivened his narrative with personal anecdotes and even recorded snatches of actual conversation.

Albert was sent to Germany in 1223. Here the Franciscans had encountered a certain amount of initial difficulty in establishing a province. The first Italian friars who attempted to penetrate the region had found the language unintelligible, the climate cold and the people ferocious. The story of their sufferings had so impressed their brethren that brother Jordan habitually included in his prayers a petition that the Lord might graciously preserve him from the heresies of the Lombards, and from the fury of the Germans; and those who volunteered for the second expedition believed that they stood in some danger of martyrdom. This mission, however, prospered and within two years Caesar of Speyer,

---

[1] Wadding, *Annales*, I, 115. This is probably based on Marianus (*A.F.H.* I (1908), 106), who seems to have put them together for no better reason than that they both came from Pisa.

[2] Cf. Golubovich, II, 227; Bihl, in *A.F.H.* XVII (1924), 576.

the first Provincial, had built up a nucleus of eight houses and had erected one custody.[1] When Albert arrived to take his place the worst difficulties were already over, but the province was still in the pioneer stage, and there was need for consolidation and further expansion. He was a foreigner and a newcomer, and in order to make himself familiar with the nature of his task and its problems, he summoned the senior friars to attend a Chapter which was held in the leper-house outside the walls of Speyer. Here all solemnly discussed what course they could best pursue. The province was now divided into four custodies: two, Bavaria and Saxony, were entrusted to Angelus of Worms and John of Piano Carpine, who were already members of the province; and two, Franconia and Alsace, to Mark of Milan and James of Treviso, learned brothers whom Albert had brought with him.[2] Another Provincial Chapter was held at Würzburg the next year but to this only the custodians, guardians, and preachers were summoned. John of Piano Carpine, who had even in this short time settled friars in five cities, was replaced as Custodian of Saxony by James of Treviso, Custodian of Alsace. James was a gracious, gentle, modest and pious man, and there were sent with him several senior brethren, both clerk and lay, who by their conduct and humility soon won the favour of the Saxons. Albert was quick to turn this good beginning to further advantage. Now was the time to close the gap between Franconia and Saxony. He sent Jordan himself with seven companions to set up houses at suitable places in Thuringia. Success attended this venture likewise, and within a year Thuringia had been raised to the status of a custody.[3]

Jordan now relates an episode which gives us a valuable glimpse of Albert's appreciation and treatment of other men. In 1225 Albert sent him, for his consolation and support, brother Nicholas, nicknamed 'the Humble'. Jordan assigned him to the house at Erfurt and determined to make him its guardian. He notified him of this by letter instead of in person, and put off visiting Erfurt for six weeks, so overcome was he by Nicholas' humility.

---

[1] Jordan, cc. 5, 17–18, 23–4, 30.   [2] *Ibid.* cc. 32–3.
[3] *Ibid.* cc. 36–8, 47.

By his mere presence, he informs us, Nicholas could maintain better discipline than others could achieve by reproaches and commands. Shortly afterwards James of Treviso died and Albert chose Nicholas to succeed him as custodian of Saxony. Knowing it would not be easy to induce so humble a man to take the office, he decided he would have to approach him personally. Accordingly he came to Erfurt and explained to Jordan his hopes of talking Nicholas into accepting. The two engaged the guardian in informal conversation, but when Albert tentatively raised the subject, Nicholas humbly excused himself, saying that he was in every way unfitted to be a lord or prelate—why, he could not even count. Albert saw his opportunity. Simulating indignation he exclaimed: 'So you don't know how to be a lord. Are we lords who hold office in the Order? Confess your fault, brother, quickly, since you have presumed our offices, which should rather be held as burdens and servitudes, to be lordships and prelacies.' Nicholas humbly acknowledged his mistake and Albert imposed the custodianship of Saxony upon him as a penance! The appointment was well made, and very popular with the friars. Authority did not wean Nicholas from humility. He was still foremost in washing the dishes and the brothers' feet, and if for any fault he had to correct a brother, he would undergo the same punishment with him. But to the persistently disobedient he was stern and severe, and could hardly bring himself to restore such to favour even when they repented, so high a value did he set upon obedience.[1] He became vicar of the province when Albert left Germany to attend the General Chapter of 1227[2] and later was for many years the Provincial Minister first of Hungary and then of Dalmatia. The close of his life he spent as an ordinary friar in the convent at Bologna. Salimbene met him there, and has left a portrait of him in his chronicle which admirably confirms and amplifies Jordan's narrative.

His humility was greater than that of any other man I have ever come across [wrote Salimbene]. His humility indeed was such that anyone coming with the intention of showing him reverence was likely to be forestalled—Nicholas would hasten to prostrate himself upon the

---

[1] Jordan, cc. 47–9.   [2] *Ibid.* c. 51.

ground and kiss his feet! He...judged all others superior to himself, believing this to be really true. When the refectory bell was rung for meals he was the first to pour water into the basin for the brothers to wash their hands. When visiting friars arrived he was the first to go to wash their feet. And although he was, as far as appearance went, little fitted for such services, being old and stout, yet charity, humility, holiness, courtesy, generosity and alacrity rendered him apt, suitable and acceptable.[1]

In 1236 Albert was sent to England by brother Elias. Here as in Germany he was the second to hold the office of Provincial, but the two countries presented for him rather different administrative problems. The German province when entrusted to him had been only two years old; the English that he now entered was already twelve. It was well-organised and flourishing, and numbered at that date at least twenty-five houses.[2] He established a few more in some of the important centres which still lacked Franciscan friaries, but was mainly concerned with the running of existing foundations and the maintenance of standards.

He arrived in this country in December 1236 and two months later held a Provincial Chapter at Oxford. Far from making any attempt to ingratiate himself with his new charges, he immediately made it quite clear that he intended to govern the brethren strictly. He preached from the text: 'Look unto the rock whence ye are hewn, and to the hole of the pit whence ye are digged.' He used them according to his pleasure, in a multitude of ways making trial of their humility, docility, simplicity, zeal, charity and patience. Little escaped his keen eye. He noticed that the brethren of the Oxford convent made bundles to serve as pillows for their heads, and rebuked them before all for unseemly indulgence. He warned them to expect no softening or improvement in his behaviour towards them, but in fact, says Eccleston, the English brethren so won his heart that from that day forward he showed himself entirely changed, wisely offering the salt of the Gospel in every

---

[1] Salimbene, B. pp. 798–9, H. pp. 556–7. Boehmer's identification of the Nicholas of Montefeltro described by Salimbene with the Nicholas known to Jordan (Jordan, p. 41 n.) seems fully justified by the evidence.

[2] F.P. pp. 217–21.

sacrifice more than he had been accustomed. He found them ever eager to tread any path to perfection, ready to go with him into prison or exile for the sake of reform.[1]

With their concurrence he passed a decree requiring that silence be observed during meals in the guest-house, unless Dominicans or Minors from other provinces were being entertained. He also desired them to wear old tunics over their new ones, both for the sake of shabbiness and to make them last longer. He travelled through the country visiting the friaries, commending those who kept the Rule strictly, correcting those who infringed it. At Southampton he found a stone cloister which offended against poverty and simplicity, and insisted that it be destroyed, in spite of the opposition of the townsfolk. At Reading he learnt of an even more serious departure from St Francis' precepts. The brethren had encountered opposition from the abbot of the Benedictine house there and had notwithstanding established themselves on a site near the bridge on the Caversham road. But they did not feel secure and applied to the king for protection, with the result that Henry III compelled the abbot to grant a charter guaranteeing the friars in their holding. If the abbot tried to turn them out through no fault of theirs, then the land was automatically to revert to the Crown, that the friars might continue to hold of the king what they had formerly held of the abbot. They had got what they wanted, but it left an unfortunate impression. It accorded ill with a profession of obedience to the Gospel, as monastic contemporaries did not fail to observe. Royal favour was not confined to providing security alone. Henry III showed himself a generous benefactor and contributed largely to the expenses of the buildings that could now be confidently raised. Albert was greatly concerned and did what he could to bring the house into conformity with Franciscan standards and principles. He most zealously returned the offending charter to the monks and expressed himself ready to remove the brethren at once if they so desired. He would have liked to reduce the chapel to modest proportions, and when he found that he was powerless to restrain the royal

---

[1] Eccleston, pp. 34–5, 79; for 'sal evangelicum in omni sacrificio...offerens', cf. Mark ix. 48; Lev. ii. 13 (quoted in 2 Cel. 22).

bounty he hoped darkly that the heavens might destroy it. But he received no co-operation from that quarter, and during as well as after his Provincialate Henry III continued to promote the extension and enrichment of the buildings. In 1238 he gave three oaks for making stalls in the choir, and in August 1239, perhaps encouraged by Albert's recent departure for Italy, he not only arranged for the stalls to be completed but ordered and paid for two altars, an altar-board painted with gold stars, and the construction of a dormitory and Chapter-house on an upper floor. A little later he added a private chamber, and then a refectory. In 1244 he instructed that the walls of the latter should be heightened and three large permanent windows put in, in addition to the one already made, that a suitable pulpit should be placed in the centre, and that the whole should be well roofed with shingles.[1] With Cambridge Albert was better pleased. This custody was famed for its rejection of money, and he noticed with approval that the brethren within its boundaries had no cloaks to wear.[2]

Agnellus of Pisa, Albert's predecessor, had been an admirable Minister: he had both fostered the expansion and development of the province, and imbued it with his own zeal for poverty and strict observance. There was comparatively little for Albert to correct. Indeed at some places he found it necessary, in view of the popularity of the Order and the ever-increasing number of its adherents, to authorise the erection of more and larger buildings, the acquisition of further plots of land, or even a transfer to a more commodious position altogether.[3]

It was the duty of the Ministers to visit, instruct and correct with charity the brethren committed to their charge.[4] Positive spiritual instruction was as essential to a useful visitation as was correction, and its value was well understood by the friars. When Albert came to Leicester John of Kethene humbly begged him to expound the Rule to the brothers.[5] He was an experienced and gifted preacher, who modelled his style upon the Gospels

---

[1] *Ibid.* pp. 79, 80 and nn.; the charter is printed in Eccleston, 1 ed. pp. 171–2; cf. pp. 173 ff.
[2] Eccleston, p. 35.
[3] *Ibid.* p. 44.
[4] *Reg. Bullata*, c. 10.
[5] Eccleston, pp. 41–2.

and made brilliant use of homely parables. He did not regard the function of a sermon as primarily censorious, and rebuked for his vainglory a young friar who, in preaching to the Chapter at Oxford, boldly condemned superfluity in buildings and abundance of food. It is only too easy to criticise and he preferred to stress the importance of obedience and respect. Eccleston has recorded two of his homilies. Both are directed against youthful presumption. They are delightful examples of early Franciscan preaching and deserve to be quoted.

A countryman [he once told his companions as they rested after a blood-letting], hearing of the wonderful repose and many delights of Paradise, set out to seek where it was, in case he might perhaps by some means enter in. At length he came to the gate, where he found St Peter, and asked to be admitted. Peter asked whether he was able and prepared to keep the laws of Paradise, and he replied, certainly, if he would be so good as to tell him what they were. Peter said that the only thing required of him would be to refrain from speaking. This he willingly promised and was let in. When he had gone a little way he saw a man ploughing with two oxen, one lean and one fat; the fat one he allowed to go at its own pace and the lean one he was constantly goading. Automatically he hastened to him to expostulate. St Peter at once came up and wished to turn him out; however this time he spared him, and warned him to be more careful. Going further he saw a man carrying a long beam, who was trying to enter a house but could not because he held the beam crosswise to the door, and the countryman hurried over to show him that he should advance one end of the beam. Immediately up came St Peter intending at all events to eject him now; however he spared him this time also. A third time he went forward and saw another man cutting timber in a wood, and he spared all the old, gnarled trunks, and felled and chopped up the straight and young and fairest saplings. He went to rebuke him and again St Peter appeared, and this time he did turn him out.

Those under authority, concluded Albert, should always hold their superiors in reverence. Heaven forbid that familiarity should breed contempt. The second tale is also of the countryside.

A young bull used daily to wander as he listed through the meadows and cornfields. Once, about the hour of Prime or Terce, he turned aside towards the plough and saw the older oxen plodding along at a snail's pace. He chided them because they had ploughed so little, and boasted that he could have done that much at one charge. They asked him to help them, and when he was yoked he rushed off in fine style; but half-way up the furrow he tired, began to pant and looking back, exclaimed: 'What! Is it not all done yet?' The older beasts replied: 'Not yet', mocking him as it were. The bull confessed that he could go no farther. They then explained to him that they went thus soberly because they had to work all the time, not just occasionally.[1]

The picture that emerges is far from being that of the traditional 'Minister' of spiritual polemic. Indeed Albert was, in many ways, a friar after St Francis' own heart. The saint's teaching had made a deep and lasting impression on him. He is said to have become a Minor in response to St Francis' preaching, and he certainly spent some time in his company. He recalled how once, when they were both staying together in a hospital, Francis had compelled him to eat twice as much food each day as he had been accustomed to take. So he in his turn obliged Eustace de Merc to eat fish contrary to his wont, saying that the Order lost many good men through their indiscretion.[2] In character he was unlike St Francis, and yet he so modelled his life upon his example as to achieve his likeness. His was a strong personality, a trifle eccentric, somewhat formidable. St Francis could compel endeavour as much by the power of charm and holiness as by direct command. Men shunned Albert's displeasure, and it was chiefly by his force of character that he led them. But though not a delightful, he was undoubtedly an attractive person. He had not the faculty for inspiring spontaneous friendship, but when his brethren came to know him well they held him in great affection. In their company he was always merry and agreeable, generous and compassionate. He reproved the guardian and procurator of one convent for not providing better fare for the brethren after their extra labours on a festival. When a brother became infirm he sent him on obedience to visit his native place, and allowed him to travel from place to place throughout the custody if he wished, offering to provide for his maintenance himself if it became a burden on the brethren. He was exceedingly devout, and throughout the

---

[1] *Ibid.* pp. 83–4.   [2] *Ibid.* p. 85; cf. 2 *Cel.* 22.

Divine Office kept his eyes closed, to prevent his thoughts from wandering.[1] But the most supremely Franciscan (and Christian) thing about him was his intuitive approach to the problems of the religious life. He was not tied by the letter of the law, but used and adapted it in terms of individual human need, thus in his moral counsel following the methods of Francis and of a greater than Francis.

Albert was early entrusted with authority, and as a Minister he capably and sincerely tried to apply St Francis' personal message and ideal in practice to a rapidly expanding and diverse community. He valued and upheld the essential and distinguishing characteristics of the Minors. He said that there were three things that in particular exalted the Order: bare feet, shabby clothing and rejection of money. The little that we know about his attitude towards the Dominicans is instructive in view of the later approximation of the two institutes. He was appreciative but detached. He tried, as a Franciscan should, to encourage friendly feeling between the two, but he was far from regarding the Dominicans as a model that the Minors would do well to copy. 'We ought', he said, 'greatly to love the Friars Preachers, because in many ways they benefit our Order and on occasion have taught us to guard against future dangers.'[2] They were a warning as well as an example. His own sermons were homely and vivid, and his regard for simplicity and humility is also reflected in his choice of his lieutenants, among whom were such men as Nicholas the Humble and Jordan of Giano.[3]

Albert's conduct in office offers a fine commentary on the impact of St Francis' call upon a priest and an administrator. In his case at any rate there seems to have been remarkably little tension between the claims of efficiency, prudence and his vocation. But he does not seem to have shared the saint's marked unwillingness to encourage learning. One of his first acts on coming to England was to appoint lectors to the convents of London and Canterbury.[4] That he did so is significant. The transformation of the Minors, in origin a predominantly lay and simple

[1] Eccleston, pp. 83, 85.   [2] *Ibid.* p. 82.
[3] See above, pp. 185-7, 24-5.   [4] Eccleston, p. 49.

brotherhood, into an Order predominantly learned and clerical, was, in fact, facilitated by some of its best spirits. For all his many excellent Franciscan qualities Albert was not untouched by the academic enthusiasm characteristic of many of the higher clergy of his day.

In 1237 Wygerius, a distinguished lawyer, was sent to England by Elias to conduct a visitation. The proceedings he instituted provoked consternation throughout the province. Meetings held in London, Southampton, Gloucester and Oxford were turbulent and unseemly, and once the visitation was over a Provincial Chapter held at Oxford preferred a unanimous appeal against Elias. Albert fully shared the indignation of his flock and was eager to take active measures to secure reform. He put himself at the head of the English resistance movement and personally led a deputation to Italy.[1] Here they found brethren from other provinces bent upon the same errand. As a result of the representations they all made to the Pope a General Chapter was held in 1239. Elias was overthrown and Albert was chosen in his stead.

Information about his Generalate is fragmentary and haphazard, as is to be expected. The eight months of his tenure afforded him neither the time, nor probably the health, to impose a clear pattern upon his activities. Reform of the Order was the key-note of policy.[2] At the General Chapter itself the absolute and binding authority of the Rule was solemnly affirmed. Elias had soiled his hands with money, excusing himself on the ground that he had never professed obedience to the *Regula Bullata* and therefore was not bound by it. Not only was he now made to swear to observe it, but likewise every member of the Chapter without exception, on their own behalf and also on behalf of the provinces they represented, that thus the entire Order might renew its allegiance. There is a certain irony in such a public acknowledgement at this moment when the Rule St Francis had given was about to be overlaid with a mass of capitular legislation that wounded its spirit. There were signs already for the weather-wise that the wind was going to back against the sun. Albert was a priest, the first priest to hold the office of Minister General, a fact to which

---

[1] Eccleston, pp. 38-40, 85, and cf. p. 79.   [2] See below, pp. 231-5.

he himself drew attention when he celebrated Mass after his election.

Albert began to undo Elias' work in Italy, where, says Eccleston, the havoc done had been greatest, but we have no details. The ex-Minister occasioned him much embarrassment. He resented his dismissal and felt it humiliating to be under obedience. He retired to Cortona, and there paid a visit to the Clares, which no friar was allowed to do without licence, under pain of excommunication. Albert required him to come to seek absolution, or at least to meet him half-way. Elias scorned his overtures, and when the Pope told him that he must obey the Minister General like any other friar he found his position intolerable. He joined Frederick II, whom the Pope had excommunicated in March, and was therefore publicly excommunicated himself.[1] This caused serious scandal and Albert exerted his influence to try to effect a reconciliation. Elias, afraid to approach Gregory in person, lest he be punished for what he had done, wrote a letter explaining and excusing his conduct. He entrusted it to Albert, but the Minister was prevented by death from fulfilling this mission of charity. It was found upon his body, and, it seems, destroyed.[2] Albert died at Rome on 23 January 1240. On his deathbed, so Eccleston proudly records, he praised the English above all other nations for their zeal for the Order.[3]

[1] Eccleston, pp. 68–9, and n. x.

[2] Angelo Clareno, in *Rendiconti*, p. 228; cf. J.-L.-A. Huillard-Bréholles, *Historia diplomatica Friderici II*, v, i (Paris, 1857), pp. 346 ff.

[3] Jordan, c. 70; Salimbene, B. p. 240, H. p. 165; Eccleston, pp. 69–70, 85; for other evidence, *ibid.* pp. 69–70, n. z.

CHAPTER VIII

HAYMO OF FAVERSHAM

ALBERT's death decided Gregory IX to intervene once more in the constitutional affairs of the Order. The next General Chapter was apparently not due to meet before Whitsun 1241,[1] but the Pope felt that it would be unwise to allow the Minors to remain so long without a leader. He instructed the electors to meet in Rome on 1 November 1240 and here, in his presence, they chose as their new Minister brother Haymo of Faversham.[2] His appointment seems to have been due, in part at any rate, to a desire to secure a certain continuity of policy. Haymo, wrote Eccleston, was most diligent in pressing forward what Albert had begun.[3] The two men had much in common, and indeed tended to be associated together in men's minds and considered as alternative candidates. In 1236 Agnellus of Pisa on his deathbed had advised the English brethren to send Hugh of Wells to Elias, the Minister General, to request that it might please him to assign them as Provincial Albert of Pisa, or Haymo, or Ralph of Rheims.[4] Both Albert and Haymo were priests and noted preachers; both were active opponents of Elias' misgovernment. Haymo was an Englishman, and Albert praised the English for their zeal for the Order. Haymo followed him as Provincial of England and as General. But it is seldom that two able men when given the opportunity will follow an identical policy, even though they belong to the same 'party'—in this case Elias' adversaries. For all their shared labours, and although others bracketed them as administrators, as individuals they differed markedly. Albert was not so much replaced as superseded.

Why was it Albert who was elected in 1239? He was not the

[1] Cf. *Reg. Bullata*, c. 8; *Narb.* c. IX, 7, 8.
[2] *A.F.* III, 234 (the Curia was in Rome at this date).
[3] Eccleston, p. 70.
[4] *Ibid.* p. 76.

most obvious candidate: a member, even an influential member, but not the ringleader of the opposition. It is possible that at this moment of crisis the electors felt the need for caution and moderation. At any rate they did not attempt to make a controversial appointment. They needed a gifted Minister to repair the effects of Elias' malpractices, and they chose the most experienced of all their administrators. They also needed one who would be welcomed and supported by the main body of ordinary friars, one therefore who was not too closely linked with any extremist group. They chose a man who was generally respected and acceptable, of blameless life, no longer young, who had known St Francis, and who was not noted for advanced views. When he died Haymo, who had been the ringleader and spokesman of the opposition in 1239, came into his own.

Haymo was austere, eloquent, a trifle impatient of human weakness. While still a secular he had worn a hair shirt down to his knees and had so mortified his flesh with penances that he had permanently undermined his health. He overdid it and his now frail body needed gentle treatment and warm, soft clothing. In spite of this, when he felt called to join St Francis' followers, he did violence to his fears, forcing himself to go without shoes and other clothing than the rough habit, cord and breeches that the Rule allowed, and was rewarded when, contrary to his expectations, his health improved. Entrusted with office in the Order he continued to set others an example of abstinence and humility. At a Provincial Chapter held while he was Minister of England he appeared in a very poor and tattered habit and at meals sat down upon the ground at the lowest end of the refectory. His zeal for poverty made him oppose the desire evinced by many friaries to acquire their own private altars and cemeteries: for once ground had been consecrated it could not subsequently revert to secular uses, and by such dedications the friars made themselves virtual possessors of sites that had properly only been lent to them.[1] But for all this Haymo does not leave the impression of ever having fully entered into the Franciscan spirit.

He joined the Order when it was already well-established, popu-

[1] Eccleston, pp. 27, 86.

lar, esteemed. Unlike Albert of Pisa he never experienced the struggles of the earliest days in Italy, the joyous, unpractical but compelling idealism; he never knew St Francis. His profession was a carefully considered, deliberate act, not the impulsive response of an imagination fired with a sudden enthusiasm. The manner of his conversion is characteristically medieval.[1] He had a vision, in which it seemed to him that he was praying in the church at Faversham, and behold, a cord was let down from the skies and he grasped it and was drawn up into heaven. Later when he chanced to notice some Friars Minor in Paris, the sight of the cord they wore revived the memory of this vision and gave it significance. Feeling that he needed counsel in the face of so disturbing a challenge, he sought out his friend Master Simon of Sandwich and two other distinguished masters, and prevailed upon them to beseech the Lord for guidance while he himself celebrated Mass. With one accord they pronounced that the Franciscan way of life was best pleasing to God, but for greater assurance they went to call on Jordan of Saxony, Master General of the Dominicans, and charged him on his own soul to give them his advice without partiality or favour. Jordan would undoubtedly have been delighted to welcome such eminent and learned men into his own ranks—they were just the type of recruit that he most desired—but he generously and unfeignedly applauded their suggestion of joining the other Order.[2] All four consequently repaired to Gregory of Naples, Provincial of the Minors, and made profession at Saint-Denis on Good Friday, after Haymo had preached his last sermon as a secular, taking as his text: 'When the Lord turned again the captivity of Sion we were made like unto the comforted.' And already on the third day he preached his first sermon as a friar. He was attending divine service in the parish church along with the other brethren and a great crowd of folk and he was filled with anxiety lest some of these were

---

[1] For what follows, see Eccleston, pp. 27–8.

[2] Jordan's delight when his unflagging efforts to secure university men for his Order met with success finds expression time and again in his letters to Diana d'Andalo. Jordan of Saxony, *Epp.* XIV, XXVI, XXXII, XL, XLIX, L, ed. B. Altaner, 'Die Briefe Jordans von Sachsen', *Quellen und Forschungen zur Geschichte des Dominikanerordens in Deutschland*, XX (Leipzig, 1925).

about to take their Easter communion while in mortal sin. He therefore begged leave from the custodian, a layman named Bene-ventus, to speak to them, and so moving was his exhortation that many delayed their communion until they had confessed to him. For three whole days he had to remain at the church, hearing confessions and comforting the people.

The course of Haymo's career is not as adequately signposted as we could wish. He probably joined the Order in 1226.[1] Eccles-ton's account of his progress is rather muddled. In one place he says that Haymo came to England with the first brethren, in another that he came over with William de Colevile.[2] The second may well be correct as the detail is precise; the first is in any case clearly wrong. At the beginning of his book Eccleston gives a complete list of the first brethren to reach England, a list in which Haymo's name does not appear, and, more conclusive still, in 1224 Haymo had not yet joined the Order. He goes on to inform us that Haymo's skill in preaching and disputation proved so useful to his brethren that he was appointed, first, Custodian of Paris, and afterwards lector at Tours, Bologna and Padua. This can hardly represent the true chronological sequence. Haymo was active in France in the years immediately preceding Elias' deposition and was presumably either Custodian of Paris or lector

---

[1] Haymo joined the Order when Jordan of Saxony, Master General of the Dominicans, was in Paris. The Dominican General Chapter, which was held at Whitsun, took place at Paris every other year. Since Haymo was professed on Good Friday, it seems likely that he met Jordan in one of the years when the Chapter was at Paris; particularly as Jordan was in the habit of spending Lent in the place where the Chapter was held (*M.O.P.H.* I, 108–9: he was certainly in northern Italy in the spring of 1227 and 1229—cf. the chronology in Altaner, *op. cit.* pp. 116–18). Other evidence confirms that Jordan was in Paris in Lent in 1224, 1226 and 1228 (*ibid.*). Eccleston says that Beneventus was Custodian of Paris when Haymo was received, and Agnellus of Pisa held that office up to Whitsun 1224 (Eccleston, pp. 28, 3–4); by 1230 Haymo's position in the Order was well-established. His meeting with Jordan could therefore only have taken place in 1226 or 1228 (or 1225, if, as seems unlikely, Jordan was in Paris that year before going to Bologna). Of the two, 1226 is the more likely, since the number of his known activities suggests that he had already worn the habit for some time before 1230, and a recent recruit would probably not have been chosen to join the Minister General on the embassy to the Pope which secured *Quo elongati*.

[2] Eccleston, pp. 28, 29.

at Tours then. Eccleston's 'primo' and 'postea' are unambiguous, so we are probably safe in assuming that he was first made Custodian and later lecturer. Such a transfer from an administrative to an academic post, though it may seem to us a little surprising, was not unknown within the Order. John Parenti actually released from office a Provincial Minister of Germany (Simon the Englishman) in order to appoint him reader in theology to that same province.[1]

When Haymo joined the Order he was already in middle life and of established reputation. This ensured his speedy promotion and he was soon appointed custodian of Paris. He returned to England *c.* 1229 in the company of William de Colevile the elder, who had been commissioned by John Parenti to conduct a visitation of the province.[2] In 1230 he was in Italy. Whether he took part in the General Chapter of that year in an official capacity, or whether he came to Assisi like many others to attend St Francis' translation is not clear. But it is certain that after the Chapter was over he, together with other spokesmen, set out for the Curia to petition the Pope for an elucidation of problems raised by the Rule. The fruit of their eloquence was the bull *Quo elongati*, issued by Gregory IX on 28 September 1230. The delegation was led by the Minister General John Parenti and numbered besides Haymo, St Anthony of Padua, Gerard Rusinol, a Papal penitentiary, Peter of Brescia, Leo of Milan and Gerard of Modena.[3] All these others were either Italian or at this time working in Italy[4]—which perhaps lends a kind of support to a suggestion that Haymo was now beginning his own sojourn in Italy. It may well be that at the General Chapter of 1230 he was assigned as lector to the convent at either Bologna or Padua. Bologna is perhaps to be preferred, as brother Humilis of Milan, who

---

[1] Jordan, c. 54. [2] Eccleston, pp. 29, 37 and n.
[3] Eccleston, p. 66.
[4] St Anthony, Provincial Minister of Lombardy 1227–30, spent the remaining two years of his life principally in Padua (cf. above, p. 158 and n. 4); Leo of Milan played an active part in the religious life of that city before becoming archbishop there in 1241 (cf. Salimbene, B. pp. 103–4, 851, H. pp. 74–5, 595); and Gerard of Modena's known activities were also in Italy (*ibid.* B. pp. 105, 107, H. pp. 75–7, on the Alleluia of 1233).

studied under Haymo at Bologna, was by 1238 himself a doctor
of theology and lector to the convent at Fano, where Salimbene
attended his lectures on Isaiah and St Matthew.[1] In April 1232
there is an isolated English reference to Haymo. Letters Patent
of Henry III exempting William the Cutler of Holland, an Oxford
merchant, from all tallages for life contain a note to the effect
that brother Haymo of Faversham had petitioned for this concession on the ground that William was procurator to the Franciscans
at Oxford.[2]

In 1233 the normal tenor of Haymo's work in the Order was
interrupted by his employment on a Papal mission to the Eastern
Church. The capture of Constantinople by the Crusaders in 1204
had inaugurated a new phase in the relations between the two
Churches. The proximity of Latin and Greek both stimulated
Western hopes for reunion and further alienated and embittered
the oppressed Greeks. Correspondence and conversations between
the two communions were fairly frequent throughout the thirteenth century and in 1274 the military embarrassments of the
Greek Emperor Michael Palaeologus so befriended the negotiations that a momentary reunion was actually achieved. Among
the earlier, less favoured, series of discussions was one with which
the Franciscans were particularly associated. In 1232 five brothers
Minor, after having suffered imprisonment at the hands of the
Turks, came to Nicaea and were hospitably entertained by the
Greek patriarch, Germanus II. They talked of the differences that
divided their Churches and the patriarch was persuaded to send
an envoy to the Curia. Gregory IX replied with the letter *Frater-
nitatis tuae* of 26 July 1232 and promised to send him 'religious
men of proved and estimable worth' to talk things over further.
Accordingly the next year he dispatched four delegates, Peter
and Hugh, both Frenchmen, of the Order of Friars Preachers,
and Haymo of Faversham and Ralph of Rheims of the Minors,
all four 'distinguished for their excellent character and knowledge
of Holy Writ'. They set out about the middle of 1233 and arrived
at Nicaea on 15 January 1234. They kept a careful record of the
proceedings and of their own experiences and reactions, so that it

---

[1] Salimbene, B. p. 400, H. p. 277.   [2] Eccleston, p. 37 n.

is possible to follow the course of the negotiations in some detail.[1] The first session opened in Nicaea on 17 January in the presence of the Patriarch Germanus and the Emperor Vatatzes and continued for ten days. The Papal delegates wished to hear why the Eastern Church persisted in disobedience to the Roman See, but the Greeks were determined to discuss articles of faith. Interminable disputations on the procession of the Holy Spirit consequently succeeded in monopolising their energies, the Greeks maintaining that the Holy Spirit proceeded from the Father alone, and not from the Father and the Son, as the Latins believed. The departure of the Emperor on 27 January mercifully put an end to discussion of this particular topic and the Papal embassy returned to Constantinople. After Easter talks were resumed, this time at Nymphaeum in Lydia and in a Council at which not only the Emperor and the Greek Patriarch were present but also the Patriarchs of Jerusalem, Alexandria and Antioch. Dispute now turned mainly on the Sacrament of the altar, the Greeks denying that the use of unleavened bread was legitimate. The atmosphere of this debate was not cordial. The friars were exasperated by the delays that had already detained them in the East much longer than they had anticipated and by the, to them, frivolous equivocations and subterfuges of the Greeks. On 26 April they walked out of the Council, having first relieved their feelings by telling the assembled prelates and people, without mincing their language, just what they thought of them. Vatatzes persuaded them to return but relations were scarcely improved. Finally on 4 May, believing that any further discussion must be profitless since the Greeks had obviously not the slightest intention of retracting their opinions, and also suspecting that the Patriarch was about to incite the populace against them, they took advantage of a silence to recapitulate the Greek tenets and concluded: 'Because we find you heretics and excommunicate as such we leave you.' A shout came after them: 'Nay rather it is you who are heretics!' Thus their mission ended on a note of insult and recrimination. On the first stages of their homeward journey they suffered much annoyance and discomfort, being pestered by Imperial and Church

[1] Golubovich, *A.F.H.* XII (1919), 428–65.

officials to hand back a document given to them by the Patriarchs and containing their signed declaration of faith. Their baggage was searched, their books examined. How they eventually succeeded in overcoming the last obstacles to their return remains unknown as their own narrative stops abruptly at this point. They presumably reached Italy towards the end of the year. Internal evidence suggests that the account of their stewardship that the delegates presented for Papal inspection was composed by one of the two Franciscan members, probably by Ralph of Rheims.[1] It reveals Haymo and his colleagues as extremely competent conventional theologians with a wealth of authorities, biblical and patristic, at their command and, by their own account at least, more incisive and more scholarly than their opponents.

On his return to Italy Haymo resumed his duties as lector to the brethren. He probably taught for about a year at Padua and was then transferred to the French province as lector to Tours. Here he immediately associated himself with other Paris Masters, notably Alexander of Hales and his pupil and successor John of La Rochelle, who *c.* 1236 were encouraging and organising resistance to Elias. When it was decided that the best means of securing a remedy was to appeal to the Pope, Haymo of Faversham and Richard Rufus, another Englishman, were the two lectors chosen to proceed to the Curia to represent France.[2] Haymo's eloquence, popularity and zeal for the cause made him pre-eminent among the appellants and marked him out as the man best fitted to hold the honourable but delicate brief for the prosecution.[3] When Elias had been deposed Albert of Pisa was elected Minister General. His place as Provincial of England was taken by Haymo. Within eighteen months England lost this Minister also to the Order as a whole.

Unlike Albert, who was an administrator of very long and wide experience, Haymo held as many academic as he did administrative posts. He was a priest and a theologian before he was a friar and neither was a profession he could renounce on becoming

[1] Golubovich, *Biblioteca*, 1 (1906), p. 165 n.; revised by *idem, A.F.H.* XII (1919), 425 (mispr. 435)–6.
[2] Eccleston, pp. 29, 30, 67; Jordan, c. 61.   [3] See above, p. 165.

a minor. Both fundamentally conditioned his outlook and his approach to the Franciscan way of life. He would have made an ideal Dominican, possessing just those qualities of mind and heart that best equipped the Friar Preacher for his dogmatic task. And in his heart of hearts he knew this. Intellectually he preferred Dominican methods, Dominican organisation; yet he joined the Franciscans deliberately, sincerely convinced that his destiny lay with them. Despite himself, or rather precisely because he was himself, he bestowed upon his chosen brothers mixed blessings, helping to blur the lines that kept the two Orders distinct. His priest's orders, useful indirectly as well as directly, enabled him to smooth away causes of friction between the seculars and the brethren. He had experienced and therefore could the better appreciate the seculars' point of view. His brothers were not unmindful of such services. Eccleston paid him the tribute of saying that his coming to England was of great benefit to the first friars in their simplicity, both in preaching and in disputation, but more especially in the favour shown to him by prelates.[1] But simplicity itself was a virtue. Laymen, albeit they could neither celebrate Mass nor hear confessions, were not thereby debarred from serving and indeed enriching a religious movement, were not necessarily useless persons 'who did nothing but eat and sleep'.[2] St Francis had emphasised that the prayers of simple laymen might save more souls than the sermons of the learned,[3] but Haymo, like Salimbene, thought the Order had little need of them. Poverty, humility, simplicity were all very edifying, but their worth should not be exaggerated, or pursued to the exclusion of other useful means to conversion. Haymo's nature recoiled from mendicancy. He approved when the brethren increased the acreage of ground on which their convents stood, saying that he would prefer them to have gardens where they could grow their own food than to go out begging for it.[4] Advantage should be taken of rights granted by the Papacy and the bishops should be prevented from interfering in the internal affairs of convents. The number of highly educated priests should be increased.

[1] Eccleston, p. 28.   [2] Salimbene, B. pp. 143-4, H. p. 102.
[3] 2 Cel. 164.   [4] Eccleston, pp. 44-5.

Haymo was an extremely active and productive General, and the excellence and range of his achievement is enviable, especially when set against the difficulties and the disabilities under which he laboured. His body was old, much weakened by ill-health, with only a little over three more years to live, but he drove it as he drove his mind, with undaunted energy and determination. He had attacked another man for his personal conduct and public administration: he was therefore in honour bound to set a high standard and to put right what he thought was amiss.

Elias did not fall quite alone. The majority of his supporters were probably reconciled to the new regime quietly enough; about a dozen followed him faithfully in his disgrace;[1] some at least of his more prominent adherents were punished for their collaboration. The sources are reticent about the punitive measures that were taken but the hints they afford suggest that reprisals were not considered unworthy of a brother. Gregory of Naples was among those to suffer. It was he who received Haymo into the Order but that did not prevent the latter from ruining him. It would seem that Gregory had obeyed Elias' injunctions to imprison his critics and when they got the upper hand in 1239 Haymo persuaded the Chapter and the new General not only to release these 'political' prisoners but also to degrade Gregory from the office of Provincial Minister and to cast him into prison for the rest of his life.[2]

As a further disciplinary measure, and also to mark his difference from Elias, Haymo conscientiously travelled across Europe visit-

---

[1] Salimbene, B. p. 230, H. pp. 157-8.

[2] Eccleston, pp. 28-9. Gregory of Naples was believed to have held the office of Provincial Minister of France from 1223 until his deposition by Haymo (A. Callebaut, *A.F.H.* x (1917), 295 ff.), but in an article entitled 'Bulla inedita Gregorii IX contra fr. Gregorium Neapolitanum' (*A.F.H.* xxvi (1933), 3–28), A. de Sérent established that Gregory had in fact ceased to be Provincial of France before 28 June 1233. On the basis of this he argues that either Gregory held that office twice (p. 5), or he was disgraced in 1233, Haymo being only indirectly responsible (pp. 21–2). Neither of his alternatives is very plausible, and both unnecessarily strain the sense of Eccleston, who says that Gregory, formerly Minister of France, was degraded by Haymo. He does *not* say that Gregory was Minister of France at the time of his fall, but only that he was still a Minister, he may well not have known of what province.

ing the provinces.[1] He visited England and also Germany, where
he held a Provincial Chapter at Altenburg on 29 September 1242
and absolved from office the Provincial Minister, Marquardus the
Short, on account of the fatal illness he had contracted while
promoting resistance to Elias. The Chapter waived its right of
election and asked Haymo to nominate the new Provincial. He
did not make an immediate choice but left Jordan of Giano to
act temporarily as vicar and later appointed Gotfrid, 'a man most
temperate in eating and drinking, a friend to the common life
and a stern enemy of singularities', who assumed his charge in
1243.[2] Haymo himself did not escape censure. Pandora's box
had been opened and carping and recriminations were for long
to plague and hurt the Order. In midwinter he was summoned
by the Protector and other Cardinals to appear before them and
had to cross the Alps to answer the charges preferred against him.
He succeeded in defending himself so skilfully that he was honour-
ably acquitted and won much favour.[3]

Again in contrast to Elias, Haymo consulted the Order over
matters of government, encouraged constitutional experiment
and issued general constitutions to supplement the Rule. During
his Generalate a Chapter of diffinitors met at Montpellier, but
this innovation was not a great success and was allowed to lapse.
Interest in constitutional redefinition and reform was keenly
aroused. The Chapter of diffinitors instructed each province to
nominate a committee of learned brethren with powers to examine
the Rule critically and draw up a report to be submitted to the
Minister General. The response of the French province, known
as the 'Exposition of the Four Masters', is extant. The English
brethren sent in an unsealed parchment with only a few notes,
beseeching the General by the blood that Christ had shed to allow
the Rule to remain untouched, as St Francis had fashioned it under
the guidance of the Holy Spirit.[4] Such sentiments were honoured
but overridden. Haymo himself moved that the authority and
competence of the Minister General and his subordinate officials

[1] Peregrinus of Bologna, *ap.* Eccleston, I ed. p. 142.
[2] Salimbene, B. p. 433, H. p. 298; Jordan, cc. 69, 71–2.
[3] Eccleston, p. 71.   [4] *Ibid.*

should be curtailed and controlled by the Chapters. He also debarred laymen from holding offices in the Order and discouraged their recruitment, a further conscious and deliberate repudiation of Elias' policy. The whole subject of the constitutional changes that were introduced at this time is so complex and important that both the measures themselves and the extent of Haymo's responsibility for them will be considered in detail in the next chapter.

Haymo's attitude to privileges can be only imperfectly known. In his case the number of bulls obtained during his Generalate, usually a good enough basis for a rough estimate, may by no means even approximately represent what he desired. In November his accession was marked as was usual by a number of reissues of earlier privileges. Then in the seven months from December 1240 to June 1241 he received no less than nine bulls on a variety of topics. The right to examine and licence preachers, hitherto confined to the Minister General, might now be exercised by the Provincial Minister in Provincial Chapter; the Ministers might absolve brethren, and likewise postulants, who had incurred excommunication for assault; the Minister of Umbria and the Custodian of the Sacro Convento might appoint a procurator responsible for the funds of the Basilica; no one but the Franciscans might wear a habit identical with or resembling the Franciscan; prelates must not require the friars to kiss their hands in token of obedience; the Ministers, with the consent of discreet and learned brethren, might absolve the friars from excommunication for all but very grave offences, whether committed before or after they joined the Order; brothers who attended others' celebration of the Divine Office were not bound to say their own Office as well; the Ministers might delegate to suitable brethren the right to admit postulants in their absence, provided they were such as would be useful to the Order; the brothers might live and pass freely through lands belonging to the excommunicate[1]—a necessary liberty as excommunicates were legion.

[1] Sbaralea, I, pp. 285, 287–91, 295–6, 298–9 (no. G9, 342 (309), p. 296—on attendance at office—is not entirely clear. The interpretation in the text seems to be the meaning intended).

On 22 August 1241 Gregory IX died. The political situation was critical. Frederick II was advancing on Rome like the 'Libyan Hannibal'. The College of Cardinals was divided, some bent on carrying on the implacable war against the Emperor, others ready for peace. Matthew Orsini, the Senator of Rome, had been warned by the dying Pope that the safety of the city and of the Church depended on the quick election of a properly disposed candidate. His guards rounded up the cardinals, dragged them to the Septizonium of Septimius Severus on the Palatine and imprisoned them there. For two months in the height of a Roman summer ten cardinals, none of whom was young, were forced to live in one room of a building falling into ruin, without shelter from the rain, without sanitation or medical attention, their miseries intensified by the brutality and indecency of the soldiers. In these appalling conditions nearly all of them became seriously ill and Robert of Somercote, the English cardinal to whom Haymo had owed his chance to defeat Elias, died miserably. It says much for the cardinals that they endured it as long as they did, but at last, on 25 October, when the exasperated Senator had fetched Gregory IX's corpse and put it in their midst to speed them on their way, they agreed to elect Godfrey of Sabina, who took the name of Celestine IV. And, as they deserved, the victory really lay with them. Celestine was old and the rigours of the conclave had been too much for him. He died on 10 November. But by then four of the cardinals were safely lodged in Anagni and nothing would induce them to return. For a year and a half the deadlock persisted and the Church lacked a head, till on 25 June 1243 Sinibaldo Fieschi was elected as Innocent IV. By then Haymo himself was ill, too ill perhaps to labour for further franchises. From 26 September to 25 December Innocent IV issued a series of twelve bulls to the Order, but they contain nothing new. All are confirmations of existing privileges, part of the routine of a new Pontificate. So Haymo's score is comparatively modest, though judging from the number he acquired from Gregory IX in the space of a few months, his total might have been much greater had there been a Pope throughout the central years of his Generalate.

In addition to visiting many provinces on foot, drafting intricate constitutional amendments in an atmosphere of controversy, attending to the day-to-day administration of a great community, Haymo found time to undertake a scholarly revision of the liturgy. The Minors were bound by their Rule to celebrate Divine Service according to the rite of the Roman Church, and they used a breviary and a missal based upon the Ordinal drawn up at the Curia *c.* 1220. This Ordinal was not well-suited to their requirements. It provided a complete choral Ordo for the liturgical year, giving for each day both the Office and the Mass. The style of the whole was prolix and imprecise. It was not always easy to distinguish clearly between the rubrics of the Office and those of the Mass. General rubrics were cheek by jowl with rubrics for particular days. Papal feasts and prayers of purely local application were included. Only the *incipits* of liturgical texts were given so that it was necessary to refer to other books, such as the antiphoner. The early Franciscan breviaries, including St Francis' own copy, derived from this Ordinal only too faithfully, contained some inappropriate and lacked some essential rubrics, and many of the less educated brethren were unable to follow them. The missal at first presented fewer problems but it too raised considerable difficulties when the number of priests in the Order rose steeply. Haymo, though he intended to correct the breviary and the missal, first set himself to remove the root of the trouble by providing the Minors with an Ordinal proper to their needs. His achievement was so outstanding that it became a model for all subsequent liturgical works not only within his own Order but in the Church at large. He separated what concerned the missal from what concerned the breviary, and made in fact two distinct Ordinals, one for each. The general rubrics he collected and arranged in order, eleven for the missal, twenty-nine for the breviary. He suppressed specifically Papal feasts and added those that the Franciscans especially celebrated: St Francis' Nativity and Translation, St Anthony of Padua, St Elizabeth of Hungary; also St Dominic and St Catherine of Alexandria. The last was the patroness of philosophy, students and Paris university. Her cult originated in the East and it was perhaps because Haymo, himself a Master of Paris, had been on an embassy to the Greek Church that he commended her to his Order. He drastically revised the style throughout, making it at once much clearer and much shorter. His wording was concise, straightforward, almost legal in tone. Finally he made his work self-sufficient. Each text was cited in full the first time it appeared and a back reference given when it was wanted subsequently. The advantages of all this were particularly applicable to the friars. The new Ordinals were small. Therefore they were less expensive to produce, more quickly copied, more convenient to carry. The instructions were comprehensible, the matter relevant. They were adopted immediately and the new breviary and missal arranged on the same plan, which Haymo had no time to do himself, were completed in a way he would have approved by 1260.[1] He died in the early months of 1244.[2]

---

[1] S. A. van Dijk, 'Il carattere della correzione liturgica di fra Aimone da Faversham, O.F.M. (1243-4)', *Ephemerides liturgicae*, LIX (1945), 177–223, LX (1946), 309–67.

[2] Eccleston (pp. 71–2) records that he died at Anagni and that Innocent IV visited him while he lay ill. Since Innocent was in Anagni from June to October 1243 and not again until 1254, it has been supposed that he died during these months (Marianus asserts that he died in the Curia at Anagni, but he is not an independent witness: *A.F.H.* II (1909), 305); but there is no reason why he should not have lived for some months after the Pope's departure. Both Jordan (c. 73) and Salimbene (B. p. 253, H. p. 176) state that he died in 1244, and Jordan also says that Crescentius was elected in 1244. Since there is reason to believe that Crescentius was elected in the early summer, before 17 June (below, p. 248), and Jordan (see cc. 51, 70; but cf. c. 30) and Salimbene seem to have reckoned the year from Christmas, Haymo's death must have taken place between 25 December 1243 and May 1244.

CHAPTER IX

THE CONSTITUTIONS OF 1239-60

In 1892 Ehrle published the results of his researches into early Franciscan constitutional history.[1] He had collected evidence from the chronicles and histories of the Order, the decisions and decrees of Ministers General and of General Chapters, and from Papal documents, and from these sources he was able to reconstruct a narrative of the Order's constitutional evolution and to analyse the nature of its organisation at the various stages of its development. The treatment accorded to each aspect and period was necessarily conditioned by the quality and quantity of the available material, and at some points was much fuller and more complete than at others. The work of the General Chapter of Narbonne in 1260 was illuminated by the publication of a full text of the constitutions then promulgated; but on the work of the 1239 Chapter his findings were meagre. He noted decisions to reduce the powers of the Ministers and increase those of the General and Provincial Chapters, to hold an experimental Chapter of diffinitors, and to fix the number of provinces at thirty-two; and concluded: 'That is all that I can discover of the "great multitude of constitutions" which according to Salimbene should already have been promulgated at the one single General Chapter meeting at Rome in 1239.'[2] Since the appearance of his article our knowledge of those earlier constitutions has increased very little. When Father Bihl re-edited the Constitutions of Narbonne in 1941 he contented himself with remarking that very few of the constitutions prior to 1260 had survived, and that Ehrle's study of them was by far the best.[3] Father Oliger, writing in 1950, observed that Ehrle's

---

[1] 'Die ältesten Redactionen der Generalconstitutionen des Franziskanerordens', *A.L.K.G.* VI, 1–138. [2] *Ibid.* p. 29.

[3] M. Bihl, 'Statuta generalia Ordinis edita in capitulis generalibus celebratis Narbonae an. 1260, Assisii an. 1279 atque Parisiis an. 1292', *A.F.H.* XXXIV, 338–9 and n.

attempt at reconstruction could be supplemented, but himself only contributed one additional constitution, defining 'money', to the known total for 1239.[1]

The scantiness of our information and the difficulty of obtaining it are due to the deliberate policy of the friars themselves. They were averse from allowing their private concerns to become matter of public knowledge. The sessions of their Chapters were held in private, and no unauthorised person, no secular and no member of another Order was permitted to attend.[2] Severe penalties were imposed on any brother who wittingly disclosed information about what had taken place at a Chapter to an outsider.[3] Every brother was to be well-acquainted with the constitutions which affected him, lest he offend through ignorance, and to this end the guardian of each convent was to be provided with a copy of the constitutions and was to see that they were read out to his community once a month. But at the same time he was to be held personally responsible for the safe keeping of his copy and was to take care that its contents were in no circumstances communicated to non-members. This last provision headed the list of *diffinitiones*, or supplementary instructions, issued by the General Chapter of 1260 in conjunction with the new official edition of the constitutions, and ended with a curt and unambiguous order to the guardians to destroy all the old constitutions as soon as the new ones were proclaimed.[4] To assist them to carry out this part of the order thoroughly and without scruple, another 'diffinition' stated categorically that the Minister General had formally revoked without exception all the edicts and commands of all his predecessors, however issued.[5] This reassurance seems to have had the desired effect and the guardians carried out their orders, from our point of view, only too well. No copy of the 1239 constitutions as

---

[1] L. Oliger, 'Expositio Quatuor Magistrorum super Regulam Fratrum Minorum', *Storia e Letteratura*, xxx, 25–6 and n. (*4 Masters*). I have not seen E. Wagner, *Historia Constitutionum Generalium O.F.M.* (Rome, 1954: cf. *A.F.H.* xLVIII (1955), 433–4).

[2] *Narb.* c. XI, 24.   [3] *Narb.* c. VII, 12.

[4] *A.F.H.* III (1911), 502 (for the other editions of these *diffinitiones*, cf. *A.F.H.* XXXIV, 32).

[5] *Ibid.* pp. 503–4.

such, or of those of the intervening years before 1260, escaped their vigilance. Six years later the same policy was applied to the *Lives* of St Francis. St Bonaventure's *Life* was to supersede all earlier *Lives* just as his Constitutions had superseded all earlier statutes. The brethren were instructed to destroy all the copies of other *Lives* that they could lay their hands on. But this time the attack was less successful. The older *Lives* managed to survive, though some of them only just survived: effectively, only two manuscripts of Thomas of Celano's *Vita Secunda* escaped destruction. The different fate of the two types of document is not surprising. There was less incentive to preserve out of date regulations at the cost of disobedience. The friars who treasured forbidden memories of St Francis would have had little affection for constitutions. Also copies of the constitutions were only required in limited numbers and were jealously guarded within the Order, whereas copies of the *Lives* of the saint had been distributed more widely and many belonged to his devoted admirers in Christendom at large. Neglect would in any case probably have accounted for the loss of most copies of the constitutions— the early Dominican constitutions survived in fewer manuscripts than did the condemned *Lives* of St Francis, and the Constitutions of Narbonne in a single manuscript—but the total disappearance of the early Franciscan constitutions can perhaps be ascribed to the policy of extermination in a favourable environment.

But although we have no copy of the 1239 constitutions to satisfy our curiosity easily, we can find out quite a lot about them. Many independent sources have, directly or indirectly, some bearing on the constitutions, their content, their enforcement or their implications. The Constitutions of Narbonne, the Expositions of the Rule, the Papal bulls to the Order, the Dominican constitutions, all can contribute something towards a fuller understanding of these early Franciscan statutes. The chronicles too can yield more than they have hitherto done. Their descriptions of what led up to the 1239 Chapter, its proceedings, and its immediate results, and their occasional direct references to particular constitutions are well known, and of great value; but besides these there are others, less obviously relevant. A narrative account of a local happening or dispute may explain and date a statute; a mention that such or such was the custom of the brethren may show incidentally that there was, or it may be was not, a constitution governing this practice in force at that time.

The combined total of what can be recovered from diverse hiding-places somewhat resembles the box of pieces of a much used jigsaw puzzle. Some pieces are missing, so that the whole picture cannot be fitted together, and some pieces from other jigsaws have got into the box by mistake and have to be identified and removed. The edition of the Constitutions published at Narbonne includes a great many of the early statutes, but not all. It also contains statutes first promulgated in the 1240's and 1250's and in 1260 itself. When such of these as can be dated are isolated there remains a residue of early statutes, with some unidentified accretions, and a certain number of precepts which simply repeat the Rule and might be of any date. The picture that emerges is unfinished; but its incompleteness is not all that serious. The statutes that St Bonaventure sifted and co-ordinated were created within the space of twenty years, and this short period marks a distinct phase in the history of the constitutions.

The *Lives* of St Francis throw little light on the constitutions of the next generation. The most that Thomas of Celano does in his *Vita Secunda* is to throw out an occasional lament on present disregard for St Francis' wishes and on the increase of laxity and ambition. The works of brother Leo tell us nothing. The chronicles are more helpful. Eccleston's *De Adventu Fratrum Minorum in Angliam* in particular contains a number of suggestive details. It ends in 1258, a date most opportune for our purpose as it means that all the constitutional arrangements it refers to are prior to Narbonne. There are two passages especially, not hitherto used in this connection, which seem to me to throw considerable light on the early statutes. The first occurs at the end of chapter 1, which relates the coming of the friars to England. It reads: 'Until the time of the formation of the Order the brethren were accustomed to take a collation every day and those that wished used to drink in common, and every day they held a Chapter. Nor were they restricted in receiving offerings of food and wine, though in many houses gifts of such "pittances" were only accepted on three days in the week.'[1] The phrase 'usque ad tempus formationis ordinis' is obscure. A footnote to Little's edition suggests that it may perhaps refer to the period before 1223, when the sealing of the *Regula Bullata* marked the full official recognition of the Order, but this hypothesis cannot be maintained. The Friars Minor did not set foot in England until September 1224, and the customs Eccleston is describing were those practised in actual English houses, not by certain missionary brethren in the years before they came to England. When he speaks therefore of the 'formation of the Order' he must be thinking of a reorganisation that took place between 1224 and 1258. What year within these limits could qualify for such a designation, other than 1239? And if he intended the title to apply to the legislation of 1239 he must have attached great significance to that legislation and must have taken it for granted that his readers would understand his reference. Words derived from the same root occur when he is dealing directly with the events of 1239. The brethren provided for the Order's 'reformationem', and Albert of Pisa, who was then elected Minister General, worked hard to correct the excesses of his predecessor in Italy, where the 'deformatio' of the Order had been greatest.[2] It would seem likely then that the constitutions found in Narbonne relating to pittances and to the chapter of faults date back to 1239. Salimbene affirmed that the 1239 constitutions were for the most part incorporated into the Constitutions of Narbonne without change,[3] so that when we find mention of an early statute on a particular subject and there is such a one in Narbonne we may presume that the two are substantially the same unless there is evidence to the contrary. Eccleston says that until 1239 the only restrictions on the brethren's receipt of pittances were self-imposed. The constitution runs: 'Against superfluities of foods we have decreed that the brothers, both in the General and in the Provincial Chapter, and also in the convent, whether in the refectory or in the hospital or the

[1] Eccleston, p. 8.
[2] Eccleston, pp. 67, 69, cf. also p. 79. It is conceivable that 'formatio' is an error for 'reformatio'.   [3] B. p. 231, H. pp. 158–9.

infirmary, are to be content with just one dish for a pittance.'[1] They used to hold a Chapter of faults every day, and the constitution only requires the guardian or his vicar to hold a Chapter at least once a week.[2] There would also seem to have been another regulation, decreed in 1239 but not incorporated into the Constitutions of Narbonne, discouraging the brethren from refreshing themselves with an evening collation at which they drank sociably together.[3]

The other passage occurs in chapter 5, on the purity of the brethren in the early days. Eccleston relates that in those days the brothers did not serve God by observing man-made constitutions, but served Him freely through the devotion of their hearts. They were content with the Rule and with a very few additional statutes which were promulgated later in the same year that the Rule was confirmed. They used to observe silence until Terce and were so assiduous in prayer that there was scarcely an hour throughout the whole night in which one would not find some brothers praying in the oratory. On major festivals they sang so fervently that it was not unusual for Vigils to last the whole night—there was after all an occasional resemblance between the early Franciscans and the Cluniacs—and even when there were only three or four of them, or six at most, they chanted with full solemnity.[4] The tone of the passage suggests that Eccleston was not personally in favour of multiplying statutes and that he preferred voluntary silence till Terce to a compulsory one till Prime.[5] The implied contrast between the 'paucissima statuta' and voluntary devotions and mortifications of the early days and the present (1258 or earlier), when obligations and observance had been fixed by statute, lends support to Salimbene's estimate 'maximae multitudinis constitutionum'. It would seem too that the Franciscans were tending to follow the Dominican lead in getting through the Office as quickly as possible though there is no explicit instruction to hurry or to omit musical elaboration

---

[1] *Narb.* c. IV, 7.   [2] *Narb.* c. VII, 20.
[3] There is nothing about a collation in *Narb.* although some form of social recreation seems to have been permitted in 1260 (cf. c. IV, 18).
[4] Eccleston, p. 25.   [5] *Narb.* c. IV, 10.

in the surviving constitutions.[1] His direct references to individual constitutions and his account of the proceedings of 1239 itself need no discussion here and will be considered later.[2] Jordan of Giano's *Chronicle* also contains some valuable material, which will be used for reconstructing the constitutions, but it again need not be considered in detail here. After he had reached the year 1239 Jordan practically ceased to reminisce and the evidence he gives is fairly straightforward; little extra can be gleaned from it.

Salimbene's garrulous narrative is more promising, and patient search can recover a few more grains of wheat from among the chaff. He tells his niece, a secluded nun, about the people he knows, their doings, their violent deaths and their relations, about important events and the time of their occurrence, and about his own personal experiences; occasionally his behaviour, or the comments made upon it, throws an interesting sidelight on the constitutions and their effectiveness. As a young friar he was an inveterate rover. In 1249 John of Parma caught up with him at Parma and mildly rebuked him. 'You run about too much my son', he said, 'at one moment you are in France, the next in Burgundy, then in Provence, then in the convent at Genoa, and now here you are in Parma.' Salimbene excused himself, saying that he had always had an 'obedience'.[3] Were the constitutions already then in force which attempted to check unnecessary journeys and forbade the brothers to travel any distance without 'litteris obedientialibus'?[4] They may well have been, for Salimbene, aware that some at least of his excursions amounted to misdemeanours, admitted that the Minister General accepted his excuse because he was fond of him. Obediences could perhaps be too easily secured if one knew the right people. Salimbene managed to collect a good assortment, and used whichever suited his inclination, playing off one authority against another. In 1247, when Frederick II was besieging Parma, Rufino, Provincial Minister of Bologna, sent him to study at Paris, and to Paris he had gone, though not as speedily as he might have done. Once arrived he spent eight days in the city 'and saw much

[1] Cf. *A.L.K.G.* i, 197.   [2] Cf. below, pp. 231 ff.
[3] B. pp. 482–3, H. p. 333.   [4] *Narb.* c. v, 3, 10.

which pleased him'.[1] Then he visited other places in France, and Provence, with the authority of the French Provincial Minister, and then the Minister General sent him to Genoa. Here Rufino found him, and was considerably annoyed. 'I sent you to France to study for my province', he exclaimed. 'Why have you come to stay in Genoa? Understand that I take it very ill.'[2] His annoyance was understandable; was it heightened by a realisation that this charming young student's instability rendered him, as his Minister, liable to punishment? Was it already laid down in the constitutions that the students sent to Paris were to be carefully selected for their promise, application and general suitability? If any proved unworthy and failed to take advantage of the opportunity afforded him, the Minister responsible for sending him was to fast three days on bread and water.[3] However, while he can have learnt little in Paris, Salimbene did pursue his studies sufficiently to qualify for the office of preacher. According to the Rule no friar might preach until he had been examined by the Minister General, who alone had authority to confer the office. In 1240 Gregory IX relaxed this regulation and allowed the Provincial Ministers and diffinitors to pass applicants in Provincial Chapter.[4] But Salimbene actually received his aureole from Innocent IV as part of his reward for bringing the Pope tidings of beleaguered Parma. He seems to have valued the honour more than the opportunity for edifying the people and preached rarely if at all. A year later his companion was still unaware that he had a right to preach and asked John of Parma to give them both the necessary authorisation. He misjudged his man for John of Parma was not one to take advantage of his position to promote men he favoured. 'Even if you were both my blood brothers', he said, 'you should not have it in any way except by examination.' Nor would he compromise by allowing them to be examined by Hugh of Digne, who was their friend, and summoned an impartial lector to test them properly.[5] In that same year, 1248, John of Parma gave further

---

[1] B. pp. 303, 483, H. pp. 212, 333 (cf. p. XI).
[2] B. p. 466, H. p. 322.   [3] *Narb.* c. VI, 12–16.
[4] *Reg. Bullata*, c. 9; *Prohibente regula vestra* (Sbaralea, I, 287, no. G9, 325 (295)).
[5] B. pp. 256–7, 431, 450–1, H. pp. 178, 297, 311.

proof of his intention to respect and maintain strict law and discipline. He was not prepared to waive the requirements of the law on the grounds of convenience or friendship, nor to connive at the evasions of his subordinates. He was staying in the convent at Sens at the time when the Provincial Chapter was due to be held there. The king of France, Louis IX, had also announced his intention of being present, so the brethren were doubtless especially anxious that everything should go well. Forty brothers had turned up as candidates for the preacher's office and the French Provincial and the diffinitors had examined them and granted them their licences and sent them away before the Chapter opened so as not to have to be bothered with them later. They came and told John of Parma what they had done, and he told them straight out that they had acted wrongly and unwisely, as Provincials and diffinitors had only been conceded these powers in the General's absence. Not content with rebuking them, he ordered them to fetch back all the candidates from the various houses to which they had scattered, so that they might receive their office from him as the Rule enjoined.[1] While thus insisting on his own prerogatives he was careful not to trespass in matters within the Provincial's normal competence. It would seem that already in his time the power to license brethren to take orders belonged to the Provincials.[2] He did not license Salimbene himself, but when he sent him to Genoa he wrote to the Minister recommending that he should be ordained priest.[3] Two Tuscan brothers once approached him through his secretary, brother Mark, with the request that he would give them licence to preach and to assume the priesthood. John refused, saying they ought to go to their own Ministers, who knew them and could give them what they asked of him. Mark was hurt, not liking to have to own to the two young friars that he had no influence, even in such a little matter. He was perhaps partly to blame, for his intervention was peculiarly badly timed—he had interrupted the General when he was in the middle of Compline—but in any case John disapproved of the brethren asking for favours. 'The brethren do ill', he had told Mark, 'in shamelessly seeking such

[1] B. p. 316, H. p. 221.   [2] Narb. c. vi, 9.   [3] B. p. 453, H. p. 312.

things though the Apostle says: "No man taketh an honour unto himself." [1] Perhaps it was John who first issued the constitution forbidding the brothers to solicit office—anyone who procured his own promotion to office in the Order was to be repulsed from all office as unworthy.[2]

The *Expositions* of the Rule touch both directly and indirectly on the constitutions. The *Expositions* of the four Masters and of Hugh of Digne are especially helpful because of their early date. The *Exposition of the Four Masters* was written very shortly after the promulgation of the 1239 constitutions, in the six months before Whitsun 1242, and so belongs to the period in which the new legislation was being tested and developed. It serves very conveniently to confirm the chronicle evidence as to the quantity of the statutes and their main preoccupation. Commenting on the passage of the Rule instructing the Ministers not to give any orders that are contrary to the Rule, the four Masters express the opinion that the phrase 'contra regulam' should be understood to mean not only what is against the precepts of the Rule but also whatever is contrary to the statutes of the Order, which have been designed to assist the observance of the Rule in all its purity, thus indicating that there were already in existence statutes in sufficient number to warrant separate mention.[3] Both Jordan and Eccleston, writing some twenty years later, connected the 1239 Chapter mainly with legislation on the holding of Chapters and on elections, and the four Masters' précis of that Chapter's achievement singles out the same points.[4] So it seems clear that a redistribution of power and a change in governmental machinery were, and were generally understood to be, the most significant acts of 1239. The four Masters note that the question is being asked whether or not measures decreed by the brethren and the Minister General and the other Ministers in General Chapter concerning the limitation of the General's power and the ordering of the form of Chapters and elections can be changed or revoked by the Minister General on his sole authority. They reply that they cannot,

---

[1] Heb. v. 4 (B. pp. 451–2, H. pp. 311–12).   [2] *Narb.* c. VI, 18.
[3] *Reg. Bullata*, c. 10; 4 *Masters*, p. 165.
[4] Jordan, c. 65, Eccleston, p. 70, 4 *Masters*, pp. 160–1.

because if the Chapter limits the power of the General or Provincial Ministers and ordains some other wholesome regulations to be observed generally among the friars on the authority of the Rule (which endorses the authority of the General Chapter), then they cannot be annulled by the Minister General. Further, what has been generally ordained by the common consent of the inferiors and superiors of the Order in General Chapter, and approved by the Pontiff of the Holy See, cannot be in any way changed by other superiors or inferiors alone, especially in such matters as the ordering and limiting of power. The mention of the Pope is additional evidence that the enactments referred to are those passed in 1239, for Gregory IX took an active part in the proceedings of the Chapter and the proposals there put forward had his approval. In addition to these general statements on the constitutions the four Masters quote from one constitution verbally. Discussing the distinction between money and coin they say that the constitution interprets money as meaning whatever is received in order to be sold.[1] The constitutions in due course returned the compliment by quoting from the learned Masters. The four Masters had said that the Rule meant by 'worthless clothing' clothing that could be valued neither for its price nor for its colour. Their phrase 'vilitas attenditur in pretio pariter et colore' was incorporated into a constitution 'on the quality of the habit'.[2] Their elucidation of the problem of borrowing furnished the substance of a constitution on the contracting of debts— the friars might not undertake to repay their debts because they could own nothing, but they could promise to do their best to persuade benefactors to defray them for them.[3] In both these cases the four Masters, who normally acknowledged their sources, including the constitutions, are not quoting, but giving their own personal views on questions still unsettled. The two constitutions

---

[1] *4 Masters*, p. 141, cf. p. 26: in the early printed texts of the *Exposition*, the reading was 'constitutio antiqua', and so it was supposed that the quotation was from Roman Law, but Father Oliger has established that the correct reading is 'dicit constitutio pecuniam esse, quidquid recipitur ut vendatur', and that 'antiqua' was an interpolation. The constitution is therefore Franciscan and should almost certainly be dated to 1239.

[2] *4 Masters*, p. 136, *Narb.* c. II, 1.   [3] *4 Masters*, pp. 154–5, *Narb.* c. III, 11.

are therefore later than the *Exposition*. The four Masters addressed their work to Haymo and the diffinitors of the General Chapter which met at Bologna in 1242, and it may well be that constitutions making use of their suggestions were framed at that very Chapter, which did so much to revise the Order's statutes.[1]

Hugh of Digne's *Exposition* was written shortly after this Chapter met, probably between the summers of 1242 and 1243.[2] Hugh makes considerable use of the *Exposition* of the four Masters and on one point he interpolates a passage he has taken from them in a way which suggests that a constitution has intervened between their commentary and his. The four Masters discuss the proper definition of 'shoes' and distinguish between shoes and sandals. Hugh quotes this and adds: 'in the constitutions it is laid down that those celebrating Mass are to be shod with shoes and not with sandals, which are not properly speaking shoes'. A constitution of Narbonne enjoins the wearing of shoes for the celebration of Mass and it would seem likely that this regulation was actually passed by the General Chapter of 1242.[3] Other early statutes are also mentioned. When discussing the reception of postulants Hugh recommends that the clauses of the Rule and the statutes governing the conditions of reception should be diligently and strictly applied. For example, inquiry into the orthodoxy of a postulant should be particularly stringent if any suspicion attached to him personally or to the place he came from.[4] He deplores the tendency of superiors themselves to offend against the statutes and to regard

[1] *Narb.* c. III, 4, may also have been suggested by the *4 Masters*, who gloss *Quo elongati* on the use of earmarked funds (pp. 144–5).

[2] Hugh of Digne was a native of Provence, where he spent most of his life. He was an influential figure in the Order, and was later supposed to be a forerunner of the Spirituals. The date in the text is earlier than that usually given, but there is an indication that the *Exposition* was written in the long vacancy of the Holy See which ended in 1243; in any case Hugh was certainly dead by 1257. I hope to publish elsewhere a study of his career and writings, which will include a detailed account of the evidence for these dates. I quote the *Expositio* from the edition in *Firmamenta trium ordinum* (Paris, 1512), part IV, ff. 34va–54rb. It was first printed in the 1506 edition of the *Monumenta Ordinis Minorum*, and was also included in N. Morin's *Speculum Minorum* (Rouen, 1509) and in other editions of the *Monumenta* and *Firmamenta*.

[3] *4 Masters*, pp. 134–6, Hugh of Digne, *Firmamenta*, f. 38rb, *Narb.* c. II, 9.

[4] Ff. 35vb–36ra (Hugh lived in the Midi).

too leniently the offences of others—'nothing so fundamentally weakens the Order's discipline in the matter of silence and the other constitutions. The early brethren used to pray continually, not only in chapel and at the times allotted to prayer, but in their cells and in their beds and at all hours of the day and night. Many used customarily to observe silence till Terce. Nowadays nothing can restrain their loquacity, no silence regulation, no persuasion of a superior, no discipline, no reason for quiet'. The passage is strikingly similar to the one in Eccleston. The two make the same comparison, and confirm each other's evidence. Eccleston's evidence suggests that the statute is pre-1260; Hugh's establishes that it dates at latest from 1242.[1] In another passage extolling the virtues of the early friars Hugh relates that a brother who had belonged to the Order for a great many years used to tell how he had once begged for money as well as wine, and how, although he had not been given so much as a penny, he had been sent to his Minister for absolution. This raises an interesting possibility. The passage occurs in a section contrasting the present unfavourably with the past, so the implication is that nowadays the consciences of the brethren are not so tender about money as they used to be. In the Constitutions of Narbonne there is a statute forbidding the brethren, when in need of bread or wine, to accept money with which to buy these articles. Anyone who deliberately did so was to fast for one day on bread and water.[2] It looks as though there had originally been great strictness on this point, in conformity with the Rule, but that by the time Hugh wrote many had ceased to take it so seriously, and there was no statute dealing with the problem. Later a statute was passed reintroducing the old custom, and assigning a statutory penalty. His comment on the clause of the Rule forbidding the brethren to ride likewise suggests that in his time there was as yet no statute extending this prohibition explicitly to carts. Hugh writes:

Riding is commonly taken to mean the use for purposes of conveyance of any animal whatsoever. There are those however who maintain that strictly speaking to ride is to sit upon an animal belonging to the equine species. Perhaps the letter of the Rule forbids to a less extent

---

[1] F. 44rb, Eccleston, p. 25.   [2] F. 43ra, Narb. c. III, 6.

the use of other animals and of decent vehicles drawn by horses, though it is more blessed, safer and more honest (unless there is an urgent necessity), for us to shun them, and on our journeys to fatigue ourselves on foot with our Lord Jesus Christ. 'Some put their trust in chariots and some in horses; but we will call upon the name of the Lord our God.'[1]

By 1260 a constitution was in force, again upholding the stricter interpretation, imposing the same penance on those who travelled in a cart as was required of those who rode.[2]

Papal bulls to the Order occasionally mention constitutions. On 6 October 1255 Alexander IV assured the friars that a new Minister General was vested with the full authority of his office from the moment of his appointment—immediately on his election according to the Rule and statutes of the Order he received an undisputed title, and full responsibility for the welfare of his brethren.[3] This is an additional, and official, piece of evidence that constitutions governing elections supplementary to the Rule were in operation before 1260. On 28 March 1257 a bull addressed to the Minister General and the Provincials stated that all friars whom they had assigned to convents as lectors in accordance with the constitutions of the Order were thereby entitled to lecture and teach freely in their houses without any other licence whatsoever, except in places boasting a *studium generale*.[4] It is not quite clear whether at this time appointment 'according to the constitutions' meant anything very specific. In the Constitutions of Narbonne the conditions under which lectors were to be appointed were left vague. All that is said is that brothers sent to Paris are to study there for at least four years unless their progress is such that they are judged worthy to proceed to the office of lector.[5] It is possible that more detailed regulations had been applied, and that St Bonaventure omitted them from his edition, or it may be that the phrase is little more than a formula and refers only to this rather general statute. In 1260 itself, just after the General

---

[1] Psalm xix (xx). 8 (Hugh of Digne, f. 39vb).
[2] *Narb.* c. v, 18–19.
[3] Sbaralea, II, 76–7, no. A4, 109 (814: for date see Eubel, *loc. cit.*).
[4] *Ibid.* II, 208, no. A4, 317 (937).   [5] *Narb.* c. VI, 12–13.

Chapter of Narbonne had approved the new edition of the Constitutions, the brethren living at La Verna, one of the most sacred of Franciscan sites, being the place where St Francis received the imprint of the stigmata, applied to the Pope for a dispensation. A bull of 28 August allowed them to use silken vestments for the celebration of the Divine Office, notwithstanding the constitution of the General Chapter to the contrary.[1] An earlier bull of Alexander's Pontificate is interesting because it violates more fundamentally the principles of the Order's foundation. A Venetian, Mark Ziani, son of the doge Peter Ziani, wished to found a new convent for the Franciscans in Venice and to endow it with revenues sufficient to support six brethren and two servants in food and clothing, and thus relieve them of all necessity to beg. The Provincial Minister very properly refused the bequest as incompatible with the vow of absolute poverty and, a bull of 14 May 1255 having failed to move him, a further bull was dispatched on 19 September ordering him without more ado to accept the legacy, 'notwithstanding the statutes of the Order to the contrary'.[2] The Constitutions of Narbonne make no specific reference to perpetual revenues. It may be that in this instance 'statuta' refers not to any supplementary constitutions, but to the Rule itself. The word is occasionally used in this sense by Hugh of Digne.[3] On 25 November 1247 the Pope, then Innocent IV, ordered the Provincial Minister of Burgundy to give licence to William de Roy O.F.M. to accompany Rainald, lord of Bavay, who had taken the Cross. William, who was his confessor and adviser, was to be allowed to ride. Three years later the friars whom Henry III of England wished to take with him overseas were similarly to be permitted to ride, in spite of the rule to the contrary.[4] This again may refer to the constitution to be found in Narbonne, or to the Rule itself.[5] The jealous concern felt by the Order for the safety of its books is reflected

---

[1] Eubel, *Epitome*, no. 1089; cf. *Narb.* c. III, 19.
[2] Sbaralea, II, 47-8, 75, nos. A4, 59, 107 (781 and n.).
[3] Cf. ff. 37va, 50vb (statuta, statutum regule).
[4] Sbaralea, I, 497-8, 542-3, nos. 14, 250 (488), 325 (555).
[5] *Reg. Bullata*, c. 3, *Narb.* c. v, 18.

in the tenor of two bulls. On 21 November 1251 a Friar Minor who, after spending fifteen years in the Order, had transferred himself and his books to the Humiliati without the licence of his superior, is excommunicated until he and his books return. On 5 December 1255 the Minister General and the Provincials are asked to allow brothers who are promoted to the episcopate or to other ecclesiastical dignities to retain the use of the books assigned to them, although these were not their property but pertained to the Order.[1] In the Constitutions of Narbonne it is explicitly stated that books are only assigned to the brethren for their use. They are always to be considered as totally within the Order's power and the Ministers can freely give them out or take them away. If a brother is permanently transferred from one province to another he may take his books with him, but a list of them must be made and on his death they are to be returned. The brethren were forbidden to accept an archbishopric or bishopric without the licence of the Minister General, unless compelled by an obedience, such as a peremptory Papal command, which it would be a mortal sin to disregard. Any who rashly accepted such an appointment was thereby deprived of the books, prayers, society and benefits of the Order both in life and in death.[2]

A number of constitutions can be dated and interpreted by comparison with the early statutes of the Friars Preachers. Of these, not only are important early collections extant, but we have also the proceedings or 'acta' of nearly all the General Chapter meetings of the period, so that it is possible to trace in detail from year to year how the actual process of adjustment took place, and to reconstruct the text of the two official editions which were made, the first at the *Generalissimum* Chapter of 1228, the second revised by Raymond of Peñaforte and accepted in 1239–41.[3] From this wealth of evidence the question of whether, or to what extent, the Franciscans copied the Dominicans can

---

[1] Sbaralea, I, 578, no. 14, 375 (588), II, 91–2, no. A4, 130 (832).
[2] *Narb.* c. VI, 25–7, 8.
[3] For full references to Dominican constitutions and *Acta* connected with Franciscan statutes, see Appendix III.

be decided. A detailed comparison reveals three degrees of affinity. In a number of statutes there is a distinct connection of ideas, the two being the same in substance though independent in wording; in a number more this connection of ideas is reinforced by a slight verbal connection; and in some there is a close verbal connection. In no case is a Dominican constitution lifted bodily by the Franciscans without any change at all. In 1260 the proportion can be fairly accurately assessed. The Constitutions of Narbonne are divided, in Father Bihl's edition, into 255 sections. Of these thirteen show a close verbal connection, and some twenty more a slight verbal connection. In all a total of seventy-four have some kind of connection either of word or thought with the Dominican constitutions. This result is not perhaps quite what we might have expected. The extent of Dominican influence is not particularly impressive. Certainly by the time of St Bonaventure the Franciscan constitutions were not preponderantly of Dominican inspiration. In 1239 the proportion may have been higher. We know for example that an attempt was then made to introduce a Chapter of diffinitors such as the Dominicans employed and that the project was subsequently dropped. Other experiments may have suffered the same fate; though against these losses, certain and uncertain, must be set the fact that by no means all the known surviving cases of relationship go back as early as this. Some relate to Dominican constitutions that were first introduced in that Order in the 1240's and 1250's. There is enough evidence to establish the conclusion that the Franciscans did not turn to the Dominicans just once for guidance in exceptional circumstances, and thereafter remain aloof and allow the concentrated dose taken in 1239 to become more and more diluted over the years. It seems rather that the two Orders kept fairly constantly in touch and from time to time took note of each other's legislation.[1]

---

[1] There is a verbal connection between some Franciscan statutes and Dominican *Acta* which never became constitutions; e.g. the regulation forbidding the wearing of gold-fringed or silken vestments is connected with Dominican *inchoaciones* of 1239 and 1240, and that excluding lay serving boys from the infirmary and kitchen with one of 1249 (*Narb.* c. III, 19; VI, 2; *M.O.P.H.* III, 11, 15; 45, 50).

The great majority of borrowings occur in the chapters on government. Eighteen of the twenty-eight sections of chapter XI, on the General Chapter, are related to the Dominican constitutions;[1] fourteen of the twenty-three sections of chapter IX, on elections; and eight out of the twenty-seven in chapter X, on the Provincial Chapter. The rest are distributed fairly evenly among seven of the remaining chapters.[2]

Individual Dominican constitutions can usually be accurately dated but only rarely do the verbal relations between the two texts establish the date of the Franciscan version. Even when it is certain that the Franciscans were the borrowers, the general identity of wording in the two Dominican recensions often makes it impossible to be sure which of the two the Franciscans were using. Occasionally the context or a slight variation in wording or word order provides the necessary criterion. For example, in the section forbidding the friars to divulge the private concerns of the Order to outsiders or to foment discord among themselves, the Franciscan version is definitely closer to 1228;[3] in the section on the election of the General it is closer to 1241.[4] It is only in the few instances when they adhere to the earlier version and not the later that we can be confident that they are incurring the debt,

[1] Nevertheless, there were fundamental differences between the General Chapters of the two Orders, most notably in the size of the two bodies. In the Franciscan Chapter Ministers and diffinitors (see below, p. 237 n. 1) met together, to a total, after 1239, of up to either ninety-six, or if the Minister's companion (see *Narb.* c. XI, 3) counted as a full member of Chapter, 128; even the working committees contained sixty-four members (*Narb.* c. XI, 12). The Dominican Chapter contained only twelve members, on a three-year rota—first the priors, then two different groups of *diffinitores*; the Franciscan arrangement more resembled the Dominican *Generalissimum* Chapter, but even this body (which only met twice) only had thirty-six members.

[2] None are discernible in c. II, on the quality of the habit, and scarcely any in c. III, on the observance of poverty. Among all the provisions regulating the internal running of the convents only one—on shaving—shows a close verbal connection (*Narb.* c. IV, 20–1; cf. 1228, I, 20, A.L.K.G. I, 205) and only two, both on silence rules, a slight verbal connection (c. IV, 11, 13; cf. 1228, I, 17 and addition to 1241, I, 12, A.L.K.G. I, 203, V, 541).

[3] Both have 'ac' and 'aliquomodo' whereas the 1241 reading is 'et' and 'aliquomodo' is omitted (*Narb.* c. VII, 13; A.L.K.G. I, 217 (dist. II, c. 14), V, 557 (dist. II, c. 8)).

[4] *Narb.* c. IX, 2, 4, A.L.K.G. I, 216 (II, 11), V, 552 (II, 4).

and incurring it precisely in the years 1239 to 1241.[1] For it was not until 1239 that they made an effective start to their own constitution-making, and until they had done so there was no body of Franciscan regulations on which the Dominicans could have drawn.

In some cases we have broader grounds for deciding which Order was the inventor, which the borrower. The value of the principle of absolute poverty was learnt by St Dominic from St Francis; and the Minors were the first to bear the title of friars. The value of a fitting education for preachers was impressed upon the Minors by the Dominican example. They often faced much the same problems in their internal development and dealt with them in a similar way. Thus both attempted to restrain display and extravagance in building by legislation, to exclude ignorant laymen from their fellowship, and to disqualify their members for ecclesiastical preferment.[2] They also shared the burden of external embarrassments, the jealousy and hostility of sections of the secular clergy, and of the universities. In times of crisis the two instinctively drew together and presented a united front.[3]

Now and then the Franciscans can establish a claim to priority;[4] sometimes too the Franciscans took over a Dominican provision, improved upon it, and then the Dominicans considered copying it back. Thus the Dominican regulation concerning the tonsure, itself part of the conventual routine derived by them from the *Institutes* of Prémontré, was adopted by the Franciscans c. 1239.[5] They added regulations to the effect that on the days on which

---

[1] It is possible, but hardly likely, that the Franciscans continued to use the earlier Dominican recension after 1241. When it can be shown that the Franciscans have derived a text from the 1241 recension, we are only provided with a *terminus ante quem non*; we cannot tell how quickly they incurred the debt.

[2] *Narb.* c. III, 15–18, *A.L.K.G.* I, 225 (II, 35), V, 549 (II, 1); *Narb.* c. I, 3–4, *M.O.P.H.* III, 17; *Narb.* c. VI, 8, *A.L.K.G.* V, 562 (II, 13).

[3] See below, pp. 267–9.

[4] At the General Chapter of 1230 John Parenti decreed that no friar should be called master or lord, but that all alike should be styled brothers (*A.F.* III, 211). Among the Dominican admonitions of 1256 (*M.O.P.H.* III, 81) is one directing that their lectors be addressed by their names, not by the title of master or doctor, which may be inspired by the Minors' example.

[5] *Narb.* c. IV, 20–1, *A.L.K.G.* I, 205 (I, 20), V, 541 (I, 11).

they were shaved the brethren were to communicate and were to attend a sermon. In 1249 the Dominicans initiated a constitution requiring the brethren to communicate on shaving days, and approved it in 1250, but they failed to confirm it the following year, so that it was not enforced. An admonition of 1254 instructed the priors to see that a sermon in the vernacular was provided for the 'conversi' on the days they received communion.[1] But when this is said it remains true that the cases in which Franciscan influence on the Dominicans is certain or probable are isolated instances. In the great majority of cases where there is a relationship the Dominicans have furnished the original idea. Their greatest contribution was in the sphere of government. Here the type of their organisation was far in advance of anything that had gone before, and here the Franciscans, in their early days, were notably backward. The events of the 1230's, culminating in the General Chapter of 1239, enabled the more conventionally minded to insist successfully that it was high time formality and order were introduced. The Dominican arrangements provided a splendid model of which they availed themselves as and how convenient, importing some principles and some details virtually unchanged, elaborating others or adjusting them to meet their own special requirements and traditions.

The two Orders were compared to Esau and Jacob,[2] and they were not, and never tried to be identical twins. They could and did influence each other profoundly, as members of a family must, but while learning and profiting from each other, each retained its own distinct individuality and independence. The Minors were ready pupils, but they were critical and selective. St Francis had rejected monastic and canonical rules, and his followers remained to this extent faithful that they ignored almost entirely that part of the Dominican constitutions which was derived from the *Institutes* of Prémontré. They never regulated the activities of the day in comparable detail. The Dominican second distinction, dealing with constitutional and educational machinery, was much

[1] *Narb.* c. IV, 22; *M.O.P.H.* III, 44, 49; 70.
[2] Salimbene, B. pp. 418–19, H. pp. 288–9; cf. Knowles, *Religious Orders in England*, I, 146 and n.

more to their taste, but even here what they took they often transmuted and made peculiarly their own. Parallels between constitutions are more in evidence at some dates than at others, and these dates corroborate in an interesting way what we know of the personal relations between the leaders. Mutual rivalry, at times degenerating into fierce competition for alms or recruits, or into a public bandying of insults and recriminations, too often marred the encounters between the rank and file; but relations never seem to have been unfriendly at the highest level. Sometimes co-operation went no further than official discouragement of overt hostilities,[1] but there were some who attempted much more than this, who kept in close contact with their opposite numbers and who had friends in the other Order. Haymo of Faversham and John of Parma were both on the best of terms with the Dominicans. Haymo actually turned to Jordan of Saxony for advice as to whether or not he should join the Minors, and Jordan generously refrained from trying to persuade him to favour the Preachers instead.[2] Jordan's successor Raymond of Peñaforte shared Haymo's views on the comparative uselessness of laymen in religious Orders, and the two introduced similar measures to discourage the recruitment of unlettered youths.[3] Haymo was probably familiar with the legislative achievement of both Masters. John of Parma and Humbert of Romans maintained if anything even closer ties. In 1254 they took identical measures to cope with the crisis in Paris; in 1255 they issued a joint letter to their brethren, exhorting them to peace and concord.[4] It is perhaps

---

[1] In 1234 it was suggested by the Dominican General Chapter that in each province the Dominicans should elect a Franciscan and the Franciscans a Dominican to judge all offences by members of one Order against the other; but there is no evidence that anything came of the suggestion. In 1236 the Dominicans found it necessary to remind their brothers at length of their duty to live at peace with the Minors (*M.O.P.H.* III, 5, 9). In the constitutions of both Orders the friars are reminded in very similar terms that they are brothers and must treat each other as such (*Narb.* c. IV, 19, *A.L.K.G.* I, 225 (II, 34), V, 562 (II, 13)).

[2] See above, p. 197.   [3] *A.F.* III, 251, *M.O.P.H.* III, 17.

[4] Below, p. 269; *M.O.P.H.* V, 25–31. Another letter of Humbert's (*ibid.* p. 23) included the provision that if a bishop should grant a licence to the Preachers to preach on a certain day but withhold it from the Minors, then the Preachers were not to avail themselves of the permission.

significant that it was Haymo of Faversham and John of Parma who ordered prayers to be said throughout the Order for the soul of the Dominican friar Romeo, 'on account of his outstanding merits',[1] and it is in their Generalates, in the early 1240's and in the 1250's, that most of the parallels between the Franciscan and Dominican constitutions introduced after 1239 occur.

Such are the materials, taken together with what is already familiar, from which the picture of what took place in the years immediately succeeding Elias' deposition must be built up.

1. 1239–44

When the General Chapter met in Rome in 1239 in the presence of the Pope and seven cardinals its chief purpose had already been determined in advance. Its members came together with the avowed intention of procuring Elias' deposition and effecting a radical reform in the Order and its government. Both objects were achieved. The Pope declared Elias deposed amid scenes of general rejoicing, and an impressive number of statutes, destined to become the permanent basis of the Order's constitution, were passed with his approval. The second and constructive part of this programme could hardly have been carried so speedily and successfully had its proposals been first mooted and considered at the Chapter itself. Intrigues and negotiations had been proceeding for two or three years before a definite appeal was made to Gregory IX. On his instructions a body of twenty hand-picked men, drawn principally from the provinces which had shown themselves most anxious for reform, met in Rome a month before the Chapter opened. It was the draft of proposed legislation submitted by these men that furnished the bulk of the new statutes. No doubt some of their suggestions were rejected or amended, and some further ones put forward at the Chapter itself, but the additional motions of individual members would have come up for consideration after the official text, under the category of 'any other business'. The main discussions were conducted on the basis of a preconcerted plan. Some such genesis for the Franciscan

[1] *Diff. Narb.* no. 24 (p. 504).

constitutions is inherently likely in view of the quantity and quality of the achievement, and both Jordan and Eccleston declare that the statutes were actually drafted in this way by a select committee.[1]

The inspiration of the new statutes was twofold. The immediate occasion for all the constitutional changes was provided by Elias' misgovernment. Some measures had the general object of preventing a repetition of his practices, some were a direct reply to particular abuses. But the scope of the new legislation was not confined to such remedies. The evident need for some changes opened the way for a thoroughgoing revision of the constitutions and made it possible for brethren to put forward their own theories and schemes for the Order's improvement, not all of which were at all directly concerned with anything done by Elias.

The deed that had finally exasperated his brethren beyond endurance had been Elias' sending out of visitors armed with unprecedented and exceedingly unpopular powers. It is not surprising therefore that grievances connected with visitation figured prominently in the appeal and that a detailed constitution of visitors resulted.[2] Another feature of his government that had aroused criticism was the number of new provinces he had created. In 1239 it was arranged to redivide the Order into thirty-two provinces, sixteen north and sixteen south of the Alps, and it is possible that it was then decided that no further alteration might be made in future without the consent of a two-thirds majority of the General Chapter.[3] One reason given for reducing the numbers was that as all Provincial Ministers had a vote in the election of the Minister General it was imperative to restrict the size of the Chapter to more manageable proportions. Elias had consistently favoured a wide suffrage (though his attempts to throw open the meetings had met with strong opposition and little success) and other measures to restrict participation in Chapters and to prevent a multitude of comers were probably undertaken at the same time.[4]

[1] Jordan, cc. 64–5, Eccleston, p. 67.
[2] Eccleston, pp. 38–9, *Narb.* c. VIII.
[3] Eccleston, p. 43, *Narb.* c. XI, 14.   [4] E.g. *Narb.* c. X, 2.

Elias' lax personal conduct while General had caused much scandal. Statutes against some of his more glaring offences, his extravagances in food, clothing and horses, may have been enacted as additional safeguards. The statute against riding, for example, or that debarring from office brethren unable to follow the common life, may well have been due to his excesses.[1] Those defining money and prohibiting its acceptance and use were certainly made in 1239 and were in part at least provoked by him.[2] It is indeed likely that many of the statutes whose content does no more than reaffirm the Rule (for example *Narb.* c. II, 5, 6) were passed in 1239 since, as a precaution, all the members of the Chapter, and consequently the whole Order, were made to renew their profession of obedience then.

More significant, because they were innovations and experiments hitherto untested in the Order, were the measures adopted to prevent a repetition of the kind of government Elias stood for. The wide powers enjoyed by the first Ministers General were now curtailed, in particular by regulations covering the holding and composition of Chapters, and the appointment of officials.[3] We do not know much about the detail of these measures as many of them were harshly criticised and were subsequently altered, a speedy nemesis overtaking a number of experiments. It was decided, for example, to institute a Chapter of diffinitors, and one such Chapter accordingly met at Montpellier in 1241, but the deportment of its members was regarded by the Ministers as so insolent that the whole scheme was abandoned forthwith.[4] We have no evidence therefore as to how frequently it was supposed to meet, nor about its competence, its size, or the qualifications and method of selection of its members, though its name suggests that the idea came from the Dominicans. It would seem that a somewhat similar experiment was tried in the provinces. Jordan states that one decree provided for the holding in each province of one Chapter by the Minister and two by the rank and file. This arrangement again was not to prove permanent.[5] The appointment of officials was taken out of the control of the

---

[1] *Narb.* c. V, 18; IX, 23.   [2] *Narb.* c. III, 1, 2.   [3] *4 Masters,* p. 160.
[4] Eccleston, p. 70.   [5] Jordan, c. 65.

General, who had hitherto had power to nominate, and made subject to election. Here too some of the first directions were not long allowed to stand, the original ordinances governing the elections of custodians and guardians being repealed at the same Chapter that abolished the Chapter of diffinitors.[1] Those covering the election of the Provincial Minister found greater favour and have survived. Incorporated into the Constitutions of Narbonne, in c. IX, 10–15, they are closely connected with the Dominican arrangements, and as they follow the order of the Dominican 1228 redaction and not Raymond's they must have been adopted in 1239.[2]

The high opinion entertained by some Friars Minor of the institutions and legislation of the Preachers caused the Minors to turn to them for guidance on a number of matters and to import certain of their regulations. Besides the form of the Provincial's election and the idea of holding a Chapter of diffinitors, other rules that they can be shown to have taken over in 1239 range from the correct cut of the tonsure (*Narb.* c. IV, 21), to the information to be contained in all written accusations sent in to the Provincial Chapter (*Narb.* c. X, 8). They include the statute forbidding the brethren to disclose the private disagreements or shortcomings discussed in Chapter meetings, such as the reasons for a Minister's deposition or the acrimony of a debate, and that forbidding them intentionally to promote or foster schism within the Order (*Narb.* c. VII, 12–13). Some of the other measures that reflect Dominican influence may have been introduced along with these but the date of admission cannot in their case be definitely established.

Other regulations that can reasonably be assigned to 1239 are those in which Albert of Pisa had an especial interest, this being the only Chapter of his short Generalate, and thus his one opportunity to initiate laws. When he was Provincial of England he ordered the brethren to keep silence at mealtimes, unless their guests were Dominicans or friars from other provinces, and he disapproved of such small indulgences as the using of pillows. It is possible that the detailed silence regulations and the rule for-

[1] Eccleston, p. 70.   [2] See above, pp. 227–8, and below, Appendix III.

bidding the use of feather pillows and mattresses by the fit may have been passed at his instigation.[1] We know for certain that he issued a general order prohibiting the friars from visiting the Clares without licence.[2] To these can be added the substitution of a weekly for a daily Chapter of faults (*Narb*. c. VII, 20) and a restriction on the number of pittances the brethren might receive (*Narb*. c. IV, 7). The friars seem always to have been ready to impose new and stringent fasting regulations, and in addition to this last they made others, discouraging the practice of holding a daily collation and restricting the acceptance of gifts of wine.[3] These were, however, subsequently dropped, and the Constitutions of Narbonne contain a new series of constitutions on the subject.[4]

On 23 January 1240 Albert of Pisa died. In November of the same year a Chapter specially summoned to Rome for the purpose by Gregory IX elected Haymo of Faversham to succeed him. In 1241, in accordance with the arrangements made at the 1239 Chapter, the first and as it turned out the only Chapter of diffinitors met at Montpellier; in 1242 Haymo held a General Chapter at Bologna. After the dearth of Chapters in Elias' days the Order had now held four Chapters in as many years.

The Chapter at Bologna in 1242 is of very great importance. Though the third Chapter of Haymo's Generalate it is, properly speaking, his first General Chapter—that of 1240 had been an electoral Chapter only—and it followed the 1239 General Chapter at the correct three-yearly interval. Its place in the history of Franciscan constitutional development has not hitherto been recognised, the general histories of the Order making no special mention of it. This is perhaps partly Salimbene's fault. He draws attention to the legislative achievement of 1239 but says nothing at all of 1242, though this Chapter is entitled to at least an equal share of the credit. The truth is that at this time Salimbene had little interest to spare for the private affairs of the Order, his whole attention being focused on the exciting business of the Church

---

[1] *Narb*. c. IV, 10–14; II, 11; Eccleston, pp. 79, 34.
[2] Eccleston, p. 69.   [3] Cf. *ibid*. p. 8; see above, pp. 213–15.
[4] Cf. *Exp. Narb*. 31 (*A.F.H.* XVIII (1925), 519–20).

during the long Papal vacancy. From 1241 to 1243 there was
no Pope, he writes, because the cardinals were at variance and
dispersed, and Frederick II closed the roads so effectively that
a number of people were captured. 'I myself was captured many
times, and it was then that I learnt and contrived many cunning
devices for writing letters in cypher.'[1] While he carried messages
tinged with the spice of danger his superiors were recasting the
constitutions. It fell to the 1242 General Chapter to review the
situation created by its predecessors. Some of the arrangements
introduced in 1239 were not proving satisfactory—a most con-
spicuous instance being the intolerable behaviour of the diffinitors
the year before. Also the need for further definitions on matters
not previously covered and for clarification of some existing ones
was now fully apparent. The chapter had to consider the commentaries on the Rule sent in from the provinces by order of the
diffinitors and these sufficiently indicated the variety and extent
of the difficulties and inadequacies still outstanding.[2] In addition
all the statutes implementing Haymo's constitutional policy were
probably enacted at this Chapter and his personal contribution
to the Order's legislation was considerable. 1242 was the only
General Chapter over which Haymo presided. He was presumably present at the Chapter of 1240: the Provincial Ministers and
one Custodian from each province would have been duly summoned for the election and he was at that time Provincial of
England. But it is unlikely that the Chapter legislated. The electors
probably had no further mandate and may well have lacked the
authority to alter or countermand the decisions of so solemn and
full a meeting as that of the previous year, and in any case it was then
really too early to assess the effect of the recent measures. There
is no record of any legislation being passed by the 1241 Chapter
at Montpellier, and if any was it was effected without Haymo's
intervention or consent as the diffinitors successfully excluded
him and the other Ministers from their meetings.[3] He died early
in 1244, so the Chapter of 1242 was the last of his Generalate.

The Chapter of 1242 was more conservative and sober in its

---

[1] B. p. 251, H. p. 174.   [2] Eccleston, p. 71; 4 *Masters*, pp. 123 ff.
[3] Eccleston, p. 70.

attitude than that of 1239 had been. Then feeling had run high and although the legislative proposals put forward at the Chapter had been carefully prepared they had been conceived in an atmosphere of tension and controversy. The brethren were ready to accept radical changes. Hatred of Elias' autocratic bearing and methods inclined them to favour the opposite and so they reversed the balance of power, taking to themselves power to elect their officers and instituting a new type of Chapter, composed entirely of subject friars. Three years later these measures seemed too hasty and extreme and there was a swing back towards a more moderate settlement and a more equal distribution of influence. The Chapter of diffinitors was abolished and a compromise solution was reached by which the composition of the General Chapter was adapted to include both official and representative elements. The Provincial Ministers were to come, and one Custodian from each province, and also one ordinary friar, elected by the Provincial Chapter as its representative. The Provincial Chapter further had the choice of deciding whether to have the Custodian or this other friar as its diffinitor.[1]

Another consequence of the insolence of the much maligned rank and file in their moment of authority was the repeal of the measure allowing them to elect the guardians and Custodians.[2]

---

[1] *Narb.* c. XI, 3, 12. There is an ambiguity in the word 'diffinitor' which has caused some confusion. The Dominicans used it both for the members of the select committee that managed the business of the Provincial Chapter and for the members of the General Chapter in the years when these were elected. The Franciscans applied it to the members of the committees of both their General and Provincial Chapters as well as to all the members of the Chapter known as the Chapter of diffinitors. The *Exposition of the Four Masters* is addressed to Haymo, Minister General, and the other diffinitors assembled in Chapter (*4 Masters*, pp. 123–4), and the Chapter of 1242 has therefore been classed as a Chapter of diffinitors (*A.F.* III, 247). But probably the Four Masters were using the term to refer to the committee which they anticipated would consider their report, and so there is no reason to doubt Eccleston's explicit statement (p. 70) that the 1241 Chapter of diffinitors was the only one of its kind ever to be held in the Order.

[2] Eccleston, p. 70 ('eligendis canonice' probably means that Guardians were to be elected by their convents and Custodians by the friars of their custody. In the Dominican Order election of conventual priors 'secundum formam canonicam' meant election by their convents (*A.L.K.G.* v, 550)).

The initiative in these appointments was now given back to the officers, who had exercised the right of nomination up to 1239.[1] If a Custodian was absolved or translated in Provincial Chapter his successor was to be provided by the Provincial Minister. To prevent arbitrary selection or favouritism however he was now required to act with the advice and assent of the diffinitors and to consult those members of the custody who were present at the Chapter. Should a Custodian be needed at a time when the Chapter was not in session the Provincial Minister was to appoint, after consulting at least six responsible brethren of the custody. Guardians of convents of thirteen friars and over were to be chosen by him in Provincial Chapter with the advice and assent of the diffinitors, after he had consulted the Custodian and some of the brethren. If any died during the year or was for some reason removed he was to come to the convent if he conveniently could and appoint another after consultation with some of its more influential members. Guardians of smaller houses were to be appointed by the Custodian, who was to consult some of the residents. He was also to secure the consent of the Provincial Minister if he happened to be in the custody at the time, and might not remove a guardian without the Minister's leave.[2] These regulations represent a successful reaction on the part of the Order's officials. They were not passed without difficulty. To begin with the debate was not even confined to the immediate question of how either Custodians or guardians should be appointed, a serious attack being made on the very existence of the offices themselves. There were some who said that the subdivision of the provinces into custodies created superfluous authorities, and advocated their abolition. They may have called attention to the fact that such intermediate districts between province and convent were not found necessary among the Dominicans, whose provincial units were actually larger than the Franciscans'. Others had noticed

---

[1] *A.F.* III, 217.

[2] *Narb.* c. IX, 18–22. The *24 Gen.* telescopes the decisions of 1239 and 1242 (*A.F.* III, 246). It was in 1239 that the custodians lost the power to institute and depose guardians; under Haymo it was given back to them, only with reservations.

that the word 'guardian' occurs nowhere in the Rule and argued
that they were therefore not bound to obey these officers. Among
the suggestions considered in answer to this objection was one
sent up by the four Masters, who pointed out that the legal difficulty would be overcome if the name were changed from
guardian to custodian or minister of the house.[1] A more radical
section proposed to solve both at once by abolishing the custody;
then the name guardian could be dispensed with and the heads
of houses be called simply custodians. The majority however
opposed this, and their point of view is reflected in the arguments
used by Hugh of Digne. The Custodian derives his authority from
the Rule, which assigns him a definite territorial jurisdiction. Like
the Provincial Minister he has a right to full membership of the
General Chapter and, like the Provincial Minister, he may, after
the General Chapter has met, hold one Chapter of his own. This
title therefore, which in the Rule has the widest possible significance, being used on occasion of a Minister or even of the Minister
General himself, cannot properly be relegated to convey the
more lowly functions of a convent guardian.[2] Their conservatism
and the tenor of the Rule caused them to vote in favour of the
retention of the office and of the old familiar names. The upshot
of it all was the reintroduction of what was more or less the
old system. The offices and their titles were allowed to stand
unchanged and appointments to both were once more vested in
the hands of the government, though subject now to certain
safeguards.

In both these important matters, in their repudiation of all
arrangements for a Chapter of diffinitors and for the canonical
election of local officials, the members of the General Chapter
of 1242 were undoing the work of 1239. But it would be misleading to consider them as hostile to the work of that Chapter
as a whole or even to such part of it as was directly influenced by

[1] Eccleston, pp. 70–1; 4 *Masters*, pp. 161–2. It has been suggested that
Eccleston's account may be inaccurate (*ibid.* p. 71 n.) and only the guardians
were discussed. But it is clear in any case that his account and the 4 *Masters*
refer to different aspects of the discussion, and there is no reason to doubt
that both offices were impugned.

[2] Hugh of Digne, *Expositio*, f. 50 rb, va.

Dominican practice. Chapters of diffinitors and canonical elections did figure prominently in the Dominican constitutional system and these particular two were given a brief trial by the Franciscans and then abandoned; but their rejection was not the result of any reaction against Dominican influence as such. They were discarded quite simply because they had not grafted well. The more authoritarian Franciscan tradition did not take kindly to dictation from below. But though they failed to please, other Dominican institutions were not involved in their unpopularity. Much of the Dominican inspired legislation of 1239 was retained,[1] and the Minors were still willing to profit by the Preachers' experience. Even in the matter of Chapter meetings and elections, where they might have been expected to be chary of further indebtedness, they actually turned to the Dominicans anew. Statutes governing the election of their General show a closer verbal connection with the 1241 version than with the 1228 *Constitutiones*, and the detailed regulation of Chapter procedure (*Narb.* c. XI) is likewise taken from Raymond's edition.[2]

The temper of the 1242 Chapter, revealed both by its constructive activity and its restraint, was perhaps in part due to Haymo's controlling influence. Haymo was deeply committed to the reform programme. He felt a personal responsibility for ensuring that the measures initiated in 1239 were not discredited as a whole because a few proved unpopular or unworkable, and he did his utmost to establish the new constitution on a sound and secure basis. He was an excellent leader at this moment, when a set-back could all too easily have begun. He wanted the statutes to be as good as they could be made; he was prepared to accept criticisms and suggestions; and he remained unshaken in his belief in the

[1] See above, p. 234 and Appendix III.

[2] See below, p. 294 (*Narb.* cc. IX, 2, 4, (?)7–8; XI, 21, 28). The adoption of the Dominican practice of electing disquisitors to take the votes of the electors and write them down did not in practice ensure the voters' independence. Salimbene candidly relates that brother Anselm Rabuinus 'heard the votes of the Lombard Ministers and Custodians at Lyons and procured and brought it about that brother John of Parma should be Minister General' (B. pp. 792–3, H. p. 552). So the tellers seem to have been assigned geographical districts and to have been able, at least on occasion, to influence the voters during the election.

value to his Order of the Dominican example. Thus he was able to hold reaction within safe limits and to harness dissatisfaction to the service of further reform.

In the work of revising and completing the statutes he was assisted by the commentaries and notes on doubtful points sent in to him at the Chapter in response to the request of the diffinitors the year before. These proved extremely helpful, reflecting the state of opinion in the provinces and indicating where definition and adjustment were most needed. Their contributors were chosen from amongst the most learned and distinguished brethren of the Order and Haymo was glad on more than one difficult or technical point to adopt solutions they put forward. The extent of his debt to them cannot be fully known as only one—the *Exposition of the Four Masters*—has survived. From this he incorporated a definition of 'worthless clothing' and a statement on how the brethren might legitimately conduct business with their creditors.[1] Other details and particular constitutions may in fact be quotations from the notes from other provinces that have not been preserved.

But though he was sent a lot of good advice and given useful co-operation and assistance, Haymo can fairly claim the chief credit for the constitutions promulgated in 1242. He himself took the initiative in fixing limits to the powers of the executive. It is recorded that 'he commanded and wished that his own power and likewise that of the Provincial Ministers and Custodians be limited by the General Chapter',[2] and the truth of this seems to be borne out by the constitutions. The quotation from the Rule that opens c. XI, requiring that a General Chapter should be held 'wherever and whenever' the Minister General should ordain, is straitened by the clause 'we decree, *at the wish of the Minister General*, that it shall not be deferred beyond three years, unless the Minister General and the General Chapter in the General

---

[1] *Narb.* c. II, 1, III, 11, and perhaps also III, 4 (see above, p. 220). The substance of *Narb.* c. III, 11 was told to Eccleston by William of Nottingham (Eccleston, p. 101)—presumably, from the context, after 1241. The Four Masters were Alexander of Hales, John of La Rochelle, Robert of La Bassée and Eudes Rigaud, later archbishop of Rouen (Oliger, *4 Masters*, pp. 17–24).

[2] *A.F.* III, 696, 246.

Chapter immediately preceding are led through manifest necessity to prolong the interval'. Haymo's hand is also probably behind the clause: 'We ordain that the Minister General is to make no general statute, except in General Chapter with the assent of the diffinitors' (*Narb.* c. VII, 25). His determination to recognise in the most public and official manner the subordination of the Ministers to the Chapter was of great value to the Order at a critical moment. The General Chapter of 1239 had, it is true, passed laws intended to control the Minister General, but its competence to attempt such control was open to dispute. Some argued that if the Minister General chose to annul decisions made in Chapter he must be obeyed since the Rule enjoined complete obedience on the brethren. The Four Masters denied this. In their opinion the Rule intended the General Chapter to govern superiors and inferiors alike;[1] but their opinion carried no legal weight. Had Haymo wished to emancipate himself from the control of the Chapter he could almost certainly have done so. It is not uncommon for men to advocate stringent control of the executive when in opposition and to change their minds when they are themselves in office. Haymo's consistency was fortunate for the reformers. It enabled them to consolidate their victory and make it permanent. The supremacy of the Chapter was recognised by St Bonaventure as an accomplished fact. In his Prologue to the *Constitutions of Narbonne* he stated explicitly that the highest authority in the Order was vested in the General Chapter.

It would be mistaken, however, to read into Haymo's constitutional policy hostility towards the official element in the Order, or championship of the ordinary friars. Indeed it looks rather as though he insisted that the officers must be accountable to the Chapter because their powers were so extensive; and the simple and ignorant brethren found little favour with him. The very number of the new constitutions of itself increased the work and with it the influence of the administration. Moreover under Haymo the Ministers recovered many of the prerogatives they had lost in 1239—a circumstance that has been sometimes over-

[1] *4 Masters*, pp. 160-1.

looked in assessments of Haymo's position. In 1242 he restored to them the chief say in the appointment of Custodians and guardians and the right to take part in all General Chapter meetings. At the same time he imposed an entirely new regulation disqualifying laymen from holding office.[1] The combination was characteristic of his outlook. If he could ensure that the Ministers would all be clerics he was prepared to entrust wide powers and responsibilities to them.

A constitution of Narbonne (c. 1, 3) states that because the Friars Minor are called not only for their own salvation but for the edification of others, no one is to be admitted to the Order unless he is a clerk already competently instructed in grammar and logic or else someone, be he cleric or layman, whose admission would be 'mightily edifying' to clergy and people. Few changes in the constitution of the Order have had such momentous consequences, and it is therefore vital to come as near as we can to giving it an author and a date. It is certain that some statutes on this or related topics were made not later than 1242: Hugh of Digne, writing shortly after the Chapter in that year, mentions statutes on the conditions for receiving new brothers.[2] The constitution in question, however, is unlikely to be earlier than 1242. The *Exposition of the Four Masters* does not suggest that the Rule had been glossed on this subject. The duty of the Ministers to examine diligently the faith and circumstances of postulants raises an element of uncertainty—the Pope must determine whether this is commanded or merely recommended—but otherwise the Four Masters have no comment to make on the requirements listed in the Rule. These are dismissed as plain and straightforward, as needing no gloss.[3] On 19 June 1241 Haymo obtained from the Pope a bull permitting the Provincial Ministers to authorise suitable brethren to admit postulants in their absence, provided that 'only those be received who would be useful to the Order, and the example of whose conversion would be edifying to

---

[1] Peregrinus of Bologna, *ap.* Eccleston, 1 ed., p. 142; *A.F.* III, 251.
[2] *Expositio,* f. 35 vb: 'In hoc secundum regulam et statuta circa recipiendorum conditiones multa est diligentia et inquisitio adhibenda.' Cf. above, p. 221 and n.
[3] *4 Masters,* pp. 128–31.

others'.[1] This is in itself an illustration of Haymo's methods: more people may undertake administrative duties, but less is left to their discretion. But it is also closely connected with the constitution. It is worded more weakly than the constitution, which must therefore be later in date; but it looks very much as if the constitution was the next stage beyond the bull in the evolution of the regulations on admission. The constitution cannot be certainly dated, but in view of this connection, and of Haymo's known opinions, it seems highly likely that we should ascribe it to the Chapter of 1242.

Coherent with this conclusion are the indications that other statutes on admission—perhaps the major part of the collection that appears in *Narbonne* under the chapter heading 'De religionis ingressu'—were passed on the same occasion. St Bonaventure in 1257 referred to a 'constitutio de receptione', which might as well indicate a collection of regulations as a single statute,[2] and Hugh of Digne's reference was to 'statuta'. Those dealing with the novitiate (*Narb.* c. I, 7–11) have much in common with the Dominican constitutions—one of them, which details the lessons to be inculcated by the novice master, is derivative verbally; the statute listing the questions to be asked of the postulant is identical in substance.[3] These importations are likely to be earlier rather than later: Haymo, personally acquainted with Jordan of Saxony and kindred in spirit to Raymond of Peñaforte can reasonably be suspected of introducing them. The measure directed against laymen was so drastic, and involved so fundamental a change in the Order's composition, that it can hardly be explained simply as a reprisal, due to jealousy at the favour shown to laymen by Elias. It sprang rather from Haymo's conception of what the Order should be like, which he was now in a position to implement, and would still have been introduced even if Elias had not numbered a kindness for laymen among his sins. So momen-

---

[1] *Gloriantibus vobis* (Sbaralea, I, 298, no. G9, 344 (311)): '...non obstante praefato statuto Regulae super receptione talium, aliquibus ex fratribus ad hoc idoneis vices suas committere valeant; vobis auctoritate praesentium concedimus facultatem. Ita tamen, ut non passim admittantur converti volentes; sed illi soli, qui et Ordini utiles, et alii⟨s⟩ aedificari valeant suae conversionis exemplo.'

[2] Bonav. VIII, 469.   [3] *Narb.* c. I, 8, 6 (see Appendix III).

tous an innovation would be launched more naturally as part of a thorough overhaul of the principles and practices controlling entry than alone. It achieved its object. Recruitment of laymen into the Order practically ceased and those that were admitted were relegated to the background, to perform menial tasks as servants of the other brethren. Even the number of these was restricted (*Narb.* c. I, 4), and most of the rough work came to be done by outside labour. Servants who worked for the friars without being themselves members of the Order are mentioned in two bulls of 1248 and 1255,[1] so their numbers must already then have been considerable. Therefore this statute also probably dates from 1242.

It was in this same Chapter at Bologna in 1242 that Haymo issued a new Ordinal for the use of the priests of his Order.[2] This contained in a corrected and convenient form the rubrics for the Mass and was part of Haymo's wider plan to revise all the liturgical books the friars needed. He took pains to have the divine service fittingly, correctly and reverently performed.[3] It was he who decided that the priests, when celebrating Mass, were to wear shoes. This constitution, again, dates from 1242.[4] Other measures which reflect his especial interests and sympathies can also be assigned with some confidence to this Chapter, which was the only one over which he presided and therefore the one which gave him his best opportunity to promote his own legislative proposals. One of the qualities about him which most struck Eccleston was his gift for smoothing away the differences and friction that too often characterised relations between the friars and the secular clergy,[5] and some at least of the constitutions designed to remove the causes of contention may be due to him. One such measure was that forbidding brethren who were present when wills were made to procure any legacies or gifts for themselves or their relations (*Narb.* c. III, 7). That the statute is early

---

[1] Sbaralea, I, 523, no. 14, 290 (521); II, 52, no. A4, 70 (790).

[2] *A.F.* III, 247.

[3] Peregrinus of Bologna, *ap.* Eccleston, I ed. p. 142: 'Hic habuit magnam curam de divino officio celebrando.' See above, pp. 208–9.

[4] *Narb.* c. II, 9: see above, p. 221.   [5] Eccleston, p. 28.

is suggested by Bonaventure's reference, in a letter written in 1257, to 'a constitution concerning wills made some time ago'.[1] Another is that instructing the brethren not to dwell in any convent to which a parish cemetery or baptistry is attached if this involves them in the burial or baptism of parishioners.[2] This is followed by one forbidding them to meddle with any properties that may be attached to their houses or to accept revenues from them (*Narb.* c. III, 21). Both may have been issued in answer to the point made by the Four Masters that the brethren might legitimately feel that they could not observe the Rule spiritually if they had to live in places that carried with them properties or the cure of souls;[3] and these same appurtenances as well as being a source of embarrassment and misgiving to the conscientious brethren were a crucial source of income to the secular clergy. Two further statutes may derive from another matter on which Haymo felt keenly, namely the importance of the sacraments of confession and communion. His first public act after he had joined the Order had been to preach a sermon urgently exhorting the congregation to prepare for their Easter communion by confession.[4] In the Constitutions of Narbonne, the brethren are required, on those fifteen days in the year on which their tonsure is renewed, to make their Communion and to attend a sermon (*Narb.* c. IV, 22); and the guardians are charged to provide confessors, who should hear the confessions of their penitents at least twice a week, and to see that all brethren in their charge are spiritually refreshed by frequent recourse to both sacraments (*Narb.* c. IV, 23). His scruples about begging were reflected in a statute, not included in the Constitutions of Narbonne, urging the friars to keep their demands moderate lest they deprive other poor of necessary assistance.[5]

[1] Bonav. VIII, 469.

[2] *Narb.* c. III, 20 (Haymo disapproved of the brethren dedicating altars and cemeteries in their convents (Eccleston, p. 86)).

[3] *4 Masters*, pp. 165-6.   [4] Eccleston, p. 28.

[5] *Chronologia historico-legalis*, quoted by Ehrle in *A.L.K.G.* VI, 29 n.; cf. Eccleston, pp. 44-5.

2. 1244–60: CRESCENTIUS OF JESI, JOHN OF PARMA AND ST BONAVENTURE

From 1244 until 1260 the General Chapters were much less active in legislation than their immediate predecessors. It is difficult even to determine the times and places at which the Chapters were held in this period, and they left few statutes.[1] The lack of evidence probably reflects a genuine falling off in the volume of legislation. The General Chapters of 1239 and 1242 had been exceptionally productive and together had created a comprehensive and work-able code of law appropriate to the Order. Continuance of effort at the same pitch of intensity was unnecessary, and from this time forward the growth of the constitution could and did follow a normal pattern of development, in which a living body of law is gradually overlaid by an accumulation of *addenda* and *corrigenda* until it becomes inconvenient to manage, bulky and confused and needs to be thoroughly revised; this revision in time becomes outdated and overlaid, as the laws are never perfect, and the work of revising and codifying must be done again. In this sequence the undistinguished but essential link between the legal code and the revision of it was provided by the enactments of 1244–60. Haymo had left the constitutions in the best condition he could, and by 1260 they needed re-editing. In the intervening years minor adjustments to particular statutes were constantly under discussion and new problems had to be dealt with as they arose; and the piecemeal additions, improvements and second thoughts brought a confusion that St Bonaventure found intolerable into a collection that had probably never been fully logical in its arrangement.[2]

After Haymo's death a General Chapter met at Genoa and elected Crescentius of Jesi to succeed him. The choice was not inspired. Crescentius, who had joined the Order late in life, was an educated man, qualified both in canon law and in medicine,

---

[1] Cf. *A.L.K.G.* VI, 29–30.

[2] The state of things that the Dominicans called 'disorder' in their first redac-tion must make us chary of imagining the Franciscan constitutions in great confusion in 1239 simply because Salimbene said they were not ordered.

but not particularly distinguished.[1] That he of all people should have been chosen was perhaps partly the result of a comparative dearth of available talent in the Order—man for man the early Franciscan Ministers General were less eminent than their Dominican counterparts—partly owing to the immediate circumstances affecting the Chapter. The Chapter must have met very shortly after Haymo died. It was probably held at or near Whitsun, which in 1244 fell on 22 May. Sabatier has drawn attention to a series of bulls reissued to the Minors by Innocent IV in the summer of 1244. The most likely occasion for a reissue of this kind was the inauguration of a new Generalate, and as the first of the series was dated 17 June Crescentius was presumably in office by then.[2] There is a bull of 30 April actually addressed to the Minister General, but this is no proof that there was a Minister alive at that moment.[3] In any case for a General Chapter to be held at all that year preparations for it must have been made before Haymo's death, which was expected. He had been seriously ill since the summer of 1243. The matters brought before the Chapter made it painfully clear that the deposition of Elias and the promulgation of the constitutions had been no panacea for the Order's ills. Rather they had in some quarters precipitated a more serious unrest and disaffection. Crescentius, who attended the Chapter as Minister of the March of Ancona, reported that he had had trouble in his province from a group of brethren who refused to respect the official authority in the Order. These rebels, he said, had the impudence to claim the guidance of the Holy Spirit as an excuse for their insubordination. They wore a distinctive dress, cutting their cloaks unsuitably short, and esteemed themselves godlier than their fellows. Crescentius, as Minister, had suppressed

[1] Peregrinus of Bologna, *ap.* Eccleston, 1 ed. p. 142.

[2] Sabatier, 'Fr. Crescentius de Iesi et son généralat (1244-1247)', *Opuscules*, III, 126-34.

[3] Sbaralea, I, 327-8, no. 14, 36 (342) (or 21 April: Eubel's note *ad loc.*). It was normal practice for the Papal chancery to address its letters to an official, omitting his name or initial, so that if he had died or resigned, the letter would automatically go to his successor. Similarly, in the event of a vacancy, a letter might still be addressed to the official, on the assumption that a new one would soon be elected. A letter addressed to a functionary cannot be taken as proof that his chair was occupied.

the misguided unfortunates, and he now brought an indictment
against the *zelanti* for their part in leading brethren to suppose
that the Rule might be obeyed otherwise than as officially interpreted. That night one of the friars had a vision in which Crescentius appeared with shaved head and a flowing grey beard down
to his waist and a voice from heaven said: 'This is Mordecai.'
When told of this Ralph of Rheims remarked, quite probably in
jest: 'He is sure to be elected General today.' He was, and so the
vision and the flippant comment came to be recorded by Eccleston
in all seriousness.[1] It is possible, although it cannot be proved,
that Elias was instrumental, albeit unintentionally, in bringing
this about. The accounts we have suggest that Elias tried at this
juncture to get the friars to take him back. The moment was
quite well chosen. Haymo, his chief adversary, was dead, and
so was Gregory IX, who had consented to his deposition. He
could count on considerable support. Many had accompanied
him to Cortona and thence to the Imperial camp, where he was
in high favour with Frederick II, and there were many more
within the Order who felt they had not done right to depose
him. The brethren had never been unanimously against him.
Even at the Chapter of 1239 when feeling against him had run
highest Gregory IX had been asked whether he might be re-
elected. Elias too had just returned from a successful mission to
the Eastern Empire, and had brought back precious relics, including a fragment of the True Cross, which he hoped would secure
for him a favourable reception. He came to the Chapter and
was allowed a hearing. But he mishandled his audience. Instead
of humbling himself, or seeking forgiveness, he took the line that
the Order and not he had been at fault. He asserted that he had
been unjustly deposed, and his object clearly was not simply to
be accepted back as a brother but to be reinstated in office. His
proud and ambitious speech was answered with contumely and
he was forced to retire in confusion.[2] The incident served to bring

[1] Eccleston, pp. 72–3; cf. also Peregrinus of Bologna, *loc. cit.* pp. 142–3,
A.F. III, 263.
[2] *A.F.* III, 249–50, Salimbene, B. pp. 234–6, H. pp. 160–1; cf. Lempp, pp.
147 ff. Salimbene was a hostile witness, and his informant, Bonaventure of

home to the assembled brethren the seriousness of the differences
that were splitting the Order, and perhaps it was this that led them
to think of Crescentius, who was at that moment in the public
eye for his initiative in stamping out schism in the Marches. Perhaps
they hoped that a policy of firmness and repression might succeed in
restoring harmony and so elected a practitioner of police methods.

Crescentius' Generalate had little constitutional significance. The
Minister himself had little opportunity and seemingly little inclination to contribute new law. The only General Chapter at which
he presided was that of his election. He summoned no General
Chapter while in office, and when after three years had elapsed
the Pope assumed that duty and summoned a Chapter to wait
on him at Lyons in the summer of 1247, Crescentius failed to
attend and was promptly deposed.

The *acta* of the 1244 General Chapter were not very numerous.
This was quite natural and normal; the first Chapter of a Generalate could not be expected to accomplish much—the Chapter of
1239 was exceptional, and the major part of its agenda was prepared in advance. Crescentius was not an obvious candidate and
it is most improbable that he came to Genoa expecting to be
elected and with a programme of legislative proposals already
prepared in his pocket. Nevertheless the decisions that were taken
reflect his interests, and the questions of the moment. Crescentius
was avowedly hostile to the zealots and it is in keeping with what
we know of him that under his auspices a list of leading questions
was drawn up for submission to Innocent IV, calculated to induce
the Pope to relax still further the modified interpretation of the
Rule allowed by Gregory IX in *Quo elongati*. Innocent responded
with *Ordinem vestrum*, on 14 November 1245, which while it
may or may not have satisfied all the hopes of its promoters,
went beyond *Quo elongati* in several important details. There was
no longer any suggestion that the brethren need feel constrained

Forli, may well have embellished his account of how he routed Elias. The
narrative in the *24 Generals* cannot be accurate as it stands, since Innocent IV
arrived at Genoa in June, and the Chapter was probably over by then (the
Chapter of 1244 seems to be indicated, since it was the only Chapter held at
this period in Italy during a vacancy in the Generalate). After the failure of
this appeal Elias tried to get back to Assisi by political means.

by any precepts of the Gospel not explicitly quoted in the Rule; St Francis' Testament was consigned to oblivion; and the brethren were to be allowed to have recourse to their agents for anything that they might find useful, and not just for basic necessities.[1] Some disciplinary measures were almost certainly introduced. Crescentius' main preoccupation when the Chapter opened had been with the need to bring recalcitrant brethren to heel. In *Ordinem vestrum* the Pope approved powers, stated to have been accorded to the Ministers by the General Chapter, to receive back into the Order brethren who had wandered, and in certain circumstances to expel brethren from it.[2] This may refer to some or all of sections 3, 15, 16 and 17 of *Narbonne*, c. VII, *De correctionibus delinquentium*. *Narbonne*, c. VII, 10, which provides that anyone found guilty of participation in an unlawful combination or conspiracy against his superiors was to be deprived of all offices and rights,[3] may be Crescentius' reaction to the lack of respect shown to him by some of his subordinates in the Marches. *Narbonne*, c. VII, 13, threatening excommunication to any who deliberately fostered dissension, may likewise be related to the troubles in the Marches, and also perhaps to Elias' disruptive activities.

Crescentius was also interested in hagiography. He was anxious to preserve a record of miracles and holy living for the edification of his own and future generations. He commissioned a slim volume celebrating the lives and miracles of some of the saintly brethren the Order counted among its sons, and was also responsible for Celano's *Second Life*. With the approval of the General Chapter he appealed to all those brethren who knew anything redounding to the glory of St Francis to send in their reminiscences to Assisi—an appeal which prompted Thomas of Celano to compose a new biography.[4]

---

[1] Sbaralea, I, 400–2, no. 14, 114 (XI).

[2] *Ibid.*: 'Sic vero ministri egressos ab Ordine, cum redierint, ad ipsum recipiant et eiiciant in certis casibus secundum terminationem vestri generalis capituli iam receptos.'

[3] The phrase 'actus legitimus' is quite often used in this chapter (4, 10, 11, 12); it appears to mean 'public activity', i.e. official function.

[4] *A.F.* III, 262, 263, 697; Salimbene, B. p. 253, H. p. 176; *2 Cel.* prologue, *3 Soc.* prol. Moorman, *Sources for the Life of St Francis*, p. 110, has misinterpreted the evidence. He writes concerning the material sent in to Assisi for the new life of St Francis: 'After an attempt by the Minister General, Crescen-

During his short Generalate some repression, envisaged by the 1244 General Chapter and presupposed by the election of Crescentius, seems to have occurred. Angelo Clareno describes these years as the period of the third tribulation suffered by the followers of Francis. His evidence is suspect, but Sabatier has shown cause for supposing that while the interpretation and tone of the passage must be discounted because of the emotion with which it was written the facts it instances may be not so far from the truth.[1] Clareno notes that at that time there were brethren, pre-eminent alike for their virtue and their learning, many of whom worked miracles in their life and after death, who, together with the remaining companions of St Francis, grieved most deeply over the state of the Order, the relaxations that took it ever further from its original perfection, the moving of houses, the building that scandalised the faithful. They grieved too that none gave ear to their admonitions, that rather their rebukes and warnings served only to make matters worse. After conferring together they decided that the situation warranted an appeal to the Pope and a number of them were detailed to put their case before the Curia. Crescentius anticipated their action and represented to the Pope that these men, though seeming outwardly saintly and venerable, were in reality restless, proud and disobedient spirits who were disturbing the provinces with their superstitions and presumptuous assertions. Innocent accepted this view and authorised him to punish them lest they contaminate others and engender schism. The appellants were intercepted on the way, detained and harshly treated, and then banished to the furthermost pro-

---

tius of Jesi, himself to write a biography, the task was entrusted to Thomas of Celano.' There is no suggestion in the sources that Crescentius tried to edit this material before handing it over to Celano. The *Dialogue* attributed to him was not an abortive *2 Cel.* but treated the lives of the holy Friars Minor. The 'opusculum' referred to by Bernard of Bessa (cited by Moorman, *loc. cit.* n.) was this *Dialogue*, as is made clear by the *Chron. 24 Generals* (*A.F.* III, 263) and Bernard of Bessa (*ibid.* p. 697): 'He caused many miracles of St Francis to be sought out and collected, *and* (*necnon*) wrote a book on the lives of the brethren in the form of a dialogue.' In fact this *Dialogue* has survived, and has been printed (ed. Lemmens, 1902; ed. Delorme, 1923). It was not actually composed by Crescentius, but, like *2 Cel.*, inspired by him.

[1] Sabatier, *Opuscules*, III, 109–26.

vinces of the Order with letters declaring their turpitude. The story had a happy ending. Branded as schismatics and heretics and sent among strangers, they were at first detested and shunned, but in course of time their holiness of life belied their reputation and they came to be honoured for their bearing in adversity.[1] The substance of this story is consistent with other evidence. It is in Crescentius' Generalate that for the first time Papal bulls are issued empowering the Minister General to deal with apostates: in the three years that he held office there are no less than four such bulls. With reiterated stringency they authorise him to capture, bind, imprison, and punish apostates, in whatever guise they may be found and whoever's protection they may have invoked. The friars may themselves arrest them or if necessary call in outside help.[2] These bulls were presumably desired; and used. The defamatory letters that Clareno said were sent with the banished brethren to warn others and particularly their Provincial Ministers against them may be related to *Narbonne*, c. v, 17. According to this constitution, if a troublesome brother had to be moved permanently from one province to another the Minister from whose province he was sent was bound to inform his colleague, who from now on would be responsible for him, of his dangerous propensities, so that he could take any necessary precautions. If the Minister General transferred such a one he was to do the same. It is unfortunately not possible to establish the date of this constitution: it may even be earlier than the time of Crescentius. Finally Clareno is not the only author to associate discontent and repression with this period. Salimbene corroborates the fact of this quite incidentally, apropos of an incident he recorded concerning Philip, archbishop of Ravenna. By way of preface to his tale of how this prelate escaped from Conrad, Frederick II's son, disguised as a Friar Minor, he wrote:

He was legate in Germany a long time ago, on account of the landgrave who after Frederick's deposition was made Emperor. At the

---

[1] *A.L.K.G.* II, 256–61.
[2] *Devotionis vestrae* (5 August 1244), *Provisionis nostrae* (7 February 1246), *Cum sicut te* (16 August 1246), *Justis petentium* (9 September 1246) (Sbaralea, I, 349, 410, 422–4, nos. 14, 66 (357), 127 (401), 145 (419), 148 (421)).

time when he was legate there were in Germany three provinces, and in them were some solemn-faced brothers who held the discipline of the Order in contempt and did not wish to obey the Ministers. When they came to seek counsel of the legate he seized them and handed them over to the Ministers that they might do judgement and justice upon them according as the statutes of the Order required. Then it happened that the landgrave died.... [1]

Here we have clearly an account of trouble similar to that which had erupted in the Marches while Crescentius was Provincial. The precise political details enable it to be closely dated. Frederick II was deposed at the Council of Lyons in 1245. Henry Raspe, Landgrave of Thuringia, was elected anti-Caesar in 1246, largely through the efforts of the legate, but died in 1247. It happened therefore while Crescentius was General. The statutes that the legate upheld may have been *Narbonne*, c. VII, 1 and 2, which reaffirm and amplify the requirements of the Rule and *Quo elongati*.[2]

Yet the main impression left by Crescentius was not one of sternness but of ineffectiveness. Rigorous discipline could not still the disquieted consciences of the zealots and so he left the problem that appears to have preoccupied him most essentially unanswered. He had little success in small things as in great. The order that he gave, probably at the Chapter of 1244, that each province was to send two of its brethren to reside in the convent at Rome so that others coming to the Curia might find compatriots with whom to discuss their business, was sterile. Innocent IV fled from Rome in June 1244 and the Curia remained so long at Lyons that the brethren, who had duly come to Rome, were eventually sent back to their provinces.[3] Whatever hopes had been placed in him he hardly justified. Once elected he contracted an aversion to making public appearances, which rendered him ineffectual and unpopular as a leader. Innocent IV summoned

---

[1] Salimbene, B. pp. 571–2, H. p. 397.

[2] Germany was divided into three provinces—the Rhine, Saxony and Cologne—in 1244–6 (above, p. 129 n). The evidence of disturbances in Germany in the mid-1240's is interestingly confirmed by Eccleston, p. 91. Jordan (c. 72) states that the provincial minister of Saxony at this time was a persecutor of singularities.

[3] Jordan, c. 73.

him to his great Council at Lyons, where Frederick II was to be
declared deposed. Salimbene saw the special letters which required
his attendance, but Crescentius was less impressed by them and
did not go. Peregrinus of Bologna alleged that he did not dare.
He excused himself on the ground of his advanced age and sent
John of Parma, and perhaps also Bonaventure of Yseo, in his
stead.[1] He omitted to summon the General Chapter, which was
one of his statutory duties, and Innocent IV, impatient with his
deficiencies and lack of co-operation, convoked one at Lyons for
July 1247. Once again Crescentius chose to stay away and was
released from office, on account, says Peregrinus, of his lack of
eloquence and general uselessness. His behaviour is curious.
Though seemingly too old to travel to Lyons in 1245 he had
not been too old to take on the government of the Order the
year before: perhaps he had an antipathy to Innocent IV; or to
Lyons. His public life was by no means over. No sooner had
the Franciscans deposed him than the cathedral Chapter of Assisi
elected him their bishop. Did they imagine he was in his dotage?
Innocent IV refused to confirm the election and gave the see to
another Friar Minor, brother Nicholas, his confessor. The clergy
and people of Assisi would not at first accept his nominee and
clamoured for Crescentius, but were forced to comply.[2] Crescentius however had not retired. In 1252 he became bishop of Jesi,
and he governed and quarrelled with his diocese until his death
ten years later.

John of Parma who succeeded him was a man of very different
calibre. Between St Francis and St Bonaventure none of the
Ministers General was as well qualified as he to direct and represent
the Order. He was *persona grata* at the Curia.[3] He was acceptable
to most of the friars. The officials elected him, but he could equally
well have been the choice of the *zelanti*. Brother Giles, St Francis'

---

[1] Salimbene, B. p. 254, H. p. 176; Peregrinus, Eccleston, 1 ed. p. 143.
Salimbene says that he sent John of Parma, Peregrinus that he sent Bonaventure
of Yseo; possibly both went.

[2] A.F. III, 697; Eccleston, p. 73; Sabatier, *Opuscules*, III, 121–3; Fortini,
Assisi nel Medio Evo, pp. 188–9.

[3] B. p. 441, H. p. 304.

companion, called out joyfully when he heard of his appointment: 'Well and opportunely have you come';[1] and the rank and
file revered and loved him. Salimbene has left a most vivid and
affectionate portrait of his fellow townsman.[2]

He was of middle height, or rather less. He was shapely in build, of
good complexion and good health, toughly made to withstand toil,
whether on the march or in the study. He had the face of an angel,
gracious and ever cheerful; he was generous, liberal, courtly, charitable,
humble, amiable, kindly and patient—a man devoted to God, mighty
in prayer, pious, merciful and compassionate. He celebrated daily and
with such devotion that the assistants felt as it were a grace flowing
from him. He preached so well and so fervently both to the clergy
and friars that I often saw him move many of his hearers to tears.
He had a fluent address and never stumbled; he was very well learned,
for he was a good grammarian and had been a master in logic in the
world, and in the Order of Friars Minor he was a great teacher of
theology and disputation. At Paris he lectured on the Sentences; in
the convent at Bologna he was lector and also in the convent at Naples
for many years. When he passed through Rome the brothers made
him either preach or dispute in the cardinals' hearing—he was reckoned
by them a great philosopher. He was a mirror and exemplar for all
who observed him, since his whole life was full of goodness and sanctity, and good and perfect were his ways. He was gracious to God and
man. He had a good knowledge of music and sang well. I never saw
so swift a writer, so fair and accurate a hand, nor so legible a script.
He was splendid when dictating in his polished style, and in his letters,
when he wished, grandiloquent.[3]

The Chapter which elected John of Parma was convoked by
Innocent IV and met in his presence at Lyons on 13 July 1247.
Salimbene does not state whether or not John was a member of
the Chapter but it would seem that he was. He was certainly
in Lyons a week later, for on 18 July he signed there, as Minister
General, an agreement between the Order and the Chapter of

---

[1] *A.L.K.G.* II, 263.
[2] B. p. 429, H. p. 295: 'quia familiaris erat michi et intimus valde, utpote
quia de terra mea erat et propinquus propinquorum'.
[3] B. p. 432, H. pp. 297-8.

St Gudule at Brussels.[1] He held three General Chapters during the ten years of his tenure. The first met at Genoa; its date is not given in any of the sources but the circumstantial evidence all points to 1251.[2] The Chapter of Metz was held in 1254. This date, implied by Eccleston, has been established by the discovery of a letter written by John of Parma at that Chapter.[3] The last Chapter of the Generalate met at Rome on 2 February 1257. He presided in person at all three Chapters. His presence at Genoa is attested by Eccleston, who recorded that while all were assembled John called upon brother Bonizo, a companion of St Francis, to bear witness to the truth of the stigmata.[4] His reply, at Metz, to the Ministers and Custodians who suggested they might make some constitutions, is retailed by Salimbene.[5] At Rome he also presided, although no longer General—St Bonaventure, his appointed successor, was not present and he was asked to deputise for him.[6] So he was responsible for all the legislation passed in the ten years 1247–57, up to and including that of the Chapter of 1257.

[1] Gratien, p. 239 n., refers to this document (*A.F.H.* VII (1914), 250 and n.) which proves that the Chapter met at the time stated in a bull of 10 May (Sbaralea, I, no. 14, 193 (445)) and not in August, as Salimbene says.

[2] Chapters were not normally held more frequently than every three years and so no Chapter was due until 1250. In 1249, however, John was sent by Innocent IV on a mission to the Eastern Empire, from which he returned in the autumn of 1250. Had he known in advance that he would be away he might have accelerated the meeting of the Chapter, but in fact the Papal summons reached him early in 1249 when he was visiting the Spanish provinces. He had to go first to Lyons to receive his instructions and then make ready for his embassy. It would have been physically possible for him to have held a Chapter at Whitsun on his way, as Ehrle has suggested, but there is no evidence that he did so, and it would have been difficult to organise. Salimbene was in Genoa at Whitsun that year and had he found a General Chapter in session it would have been odd for him not to mention it. It seems more probable that the meeting was postponed until John's return and took place in 1251: this supposition fits with the triennial pattern of the Chapters which followed.

[3] Eccleston, p. 42 n. The letter is dated from Metz, June 1254 (*A.F.H.* IV (1911), 425 ff.): since it is an original, with the date written in full, there is no possibility of error.

[4] Eccleston, p. 74.   [5] Salimbene, B. pp. 436–7, H. pp. 300–1.
[6] B. p. 449, H. p. 310.

Let us not multiply constitutions [said John of Parma to the Ministers at Metz], but let us concentrate on observing those we already have, for it is written that in the beginning God gave to our first parents but two commands, one positive and one negative, and immediately they transgressed one of them.... Know too that the poor brethren complain of you because you make a multitude of constitutions and impose them on the necks of your subordinates, and you yourselves who make them do not wish to keep them.

On account of these words, concludes Salimbene, they ceased at that Chapter from making constitutions.[1] Because of this incident it has generally been taken that John disapproved on principle of this new practice of making constitutions to supplement the Rule, and that he made few or none himself. In support of this interpretation it can be alleged, on Clareno's evidence, that John accepted as valid and useful aids to the understanding of the Rule only St Francis' Testament and admonitions;[2] and disapproval of the Expositions of the Rule springs from the same basic attitude as disapproval of the constitutions. As Oliger has remarked, however, it is to be feared that the leader of the Spirituals attributed his own ideas to the Minister General.[3] It is dangerous to draw a preconceived picture of John as a Spiritual and explain away anything that does not fit in as done without his knowledge or against his will;[4] dangerous also to assume too readily the opinions of the Spirituals. Hugh of Digne, regarded as a forerunner of the Spirituals, may have helped to draft *Ordinem vestrum*; and his comments, in his own lengthy Exposition of the Rule, on the friars' right to study and make use of all things needful, are in sympathy with the line taken by the Popes and by St Bonaventure.[5] There is good and ample evidence that John of Parma did initiate legislation, some of it at the Chapter of Metz.

John of Parma was a young man when he was made General and he had a young man's energy and determination to put his principles into practice. Since 1239 the Order had had a succession

[1] B. pp. 436–7, H. pp. 300–1.   [2] *A.L.K.G.* II, 274–6.
[3] *4 Masters*, pp. 8–9.   [4] Cf. Gratien, pp. 241–3.
[5] Cf. above, p. 221; *Expositio*, ff. 52 (51)vb (quoted in substance, Bonav., VIII, 334–5), 46 rb–va.

of elderly leaders and in 1247 there was a reaction in favour of youth, similar to that which had led the College of Cardinals in 1198 to elect as successor to a run of elderly Popes the thirty-seven-year-old Innocent III. We do not know the year in which John of Parma was born, but since he lived until 1289 he was appointed probably when in his thirties or early forties.[1] He proved an active and conscientious General, who understood that his position as head of a great religious Order required of him an exceptionally high standard of personal conduct. He sought both in his own life and in his direction of the Order to obey the Rule and the Gospel, and set an example of humility and service. He would not sleep in a bed that had been specially prepared for him in one convent because it was 'fit for a Pope'; in another he rebuked the guardian for always picking a few favoured brethren to dine with him and invited instead brothers who were held of little account, saying that eating was something that all could do with their Minister.[2] His predecessors for one reason and another had done little visiting but immediately after his election John began a systematic visitation of the provinces. In his first two years of office he visited England, France, Burgundy and Provence and had just started on the provinces of Spain when Innocent IV recalled him to Lyons in order to brief him for an embassy to the Eastern Empire.[3] All these journeys were made on foot as John held obedience to the Rule of paramount importance, even if it meant keeping the Pope waiting,[4] and took heavy toll of his own time and energies. His work was so exacting that none of his companions could sustain the labour he imposed upon himself and he had to change them frequently, in the ten years of his ministry employing no less than twelve.[5] Like the Dominican Master General Jordan of Saxony he was constantly on the march and the only certain place of finding him was at a Chapter meeting.[6] Salimbene was so greatly edified in his

[1] Gratien, p. 242, says that he was born in 1208, but gives no authority.
[2] Salimbene, B. pp. 429, 444–5, H. pp. 295–6, 306–7.
[3] Salimbene, B. pp. 432–3, 428, 453, 465, H. pp. 298, 295, 312–13, 321; cf. Eccleston, pp. 73, 98.
[4] B. pp. 465–6, H. p. 321.   [5] B. p. 794, H. p. 553.
[6] Cf. Mortier, *Histoire des Maîtres Généraux de l'Ordre des Frères Prêcheurs*, I, 186.

company that he once exclaimed: 'Father, you do as the Lord taught'; to which John replied: 'It behoves us to fulfil all justice, and that demands perfect humility.'[1]

John took such pains to observe in all matters, great and small, the Rule and the Gospel not simply to save his own soul but because he wished all the brothers to do likewise, and he would not expect of others what he did not undertake himself. 'We never read', he told the Ministers at Metz, 'of Julius Caesar ever saying to his soldiers: "Go and do that", but: "Let us go and do this", always associating himself with them.'[2] From them who have promised much, much is required. The Friars Minor are pledged to a life of evangelical perfection, and it is not enough for them to abstain from sin, for that every Christian ought to do. The very success of the Order in establishing missions through-out Europe and beyond and in multiplying the numbers of the brethren had brought with it a new kind of insecurity. It was threatened with growing hostility from the secular clergy and the universities, jealous of its competition; and within its own ranks criticism, quarrels, even rebellion and apostasy, threatened the continued efficacy of its work. John appreciated the nature of the challenge and set out deliberately to foster the Order's popularity and to restore and maintain its good name.

To encourage the laity to view the Franciscans with favour he introduced the practice of allowing those who befriended them generously to share in the merits of the Order's prayers. He granted benefactors formal letters sealed with his official seal entitling them and their families to spiritual benefits in life and in death and by this means, as Salimbene observed, wondrously stimulated and increased the devotion of the faithful.[3] Another way in which John seems to have courted popularity for his Order was by allow-ing benefactors the privilege of burial in the friars' cemeteries. In February 1250 he obtained a bull enabling him to offer this,[4] and many were eager to take advantage of the opportunity. Until

---

[1] B. p. 448, H. pp. 308–9.   [2] B. p. 437, H. p. 301.
[3] B. p. 433, H. p. 298. So many were distributed that John had them drawn up according to a basic formula. Salimbene quotes a specimen letter in full.
[4] Sbaralea, I, 537, no. 14, 316 (547).

his time the friars had been averse from burying any not of their Order. The count of Provence would have liked to be buried in their church at Aix but the brethren would not let him, said Salimbene, because they nearly always refused burials, both to save themselves the trouble and to avoid offending the clergy, and it was for this reason that they did not want to bury even St Elizabeth of Hungary.[1] Their disinclination for the task and the jealousy it excited among the secular clergy forced John to revise his policy; and he had himself to bring in a new statute instructing the brethren to admit into their cemeteries only those whose claims were such that they could not properly refuse them (*Narb.* c. III, 22). St Bonaventure, in a letter he wrote from Paris shortly after his election, refers to the new statute concerning burials,[2] so it must have been passed before he took over, perhaps in 1257 itself. Henceforward the privilege was to be sparingly given but the stringency thus reintroduced was not immediately fully effective. To prevent any outcry from disappointed licensees St Bonaventure allowed that those who had been promised burial in Franciscan cemeteries before the new statutes were passed were to be duly interred there.[3]

To disarm some of the criticisms brought against the Order by outside observers and by many of the friars John did his best to curb abuses by visiting as many houses as he could himself, and by legislation. When he was in England in May 1248 he ratified provincial constitutions dealing with poverty in buildings and the need for economy,[4] and he may have passed some statutes himself against extravagance in the dimensions and decoration of buildings.[5] He also issued a mandate forbidding any convent to move to new premises without special licence from him. This did not get into the Constitutions of Narbonne, but a similar

---

[1] B. p. 428, H. p. 295.   [2] Bonav., VIII, 469.

[3] 'Explanationes constitutionum generalium Narbonensium' (*Exp. Narb.*), ed. Delorme, *A.F.H.* XVIII (1925), 519, no. 26.   [4] Eccleston, p. 98.

[5] Cf. *Narb.* c. III, 15–18. These are probably earlier than St Bonaventure, who stressed the need to observe existing regulations on these topics; but III, 18 in particular seems later than Hugh of Digne's *Tractatus de paupertate* (cf. *Firmamenta*, f. 106vb), which is probably later than his *Expositio*, i.e. written between 1242 and 1257.

regulation was made by St Bonaventure.[1] In addition to correcting specific abuses of this kind he made a number of statutes designed to safeguard and ensure more positive aspects of the religious life. The regulation declaring that all fasts must be kept with Lenten strictness was his, as may be other of the fasting regulations included in Narbonne.[2] At the Chapter of Metz he issued a letter, to be distributed through all the provinces, ordering the brothers to conform strictly to the rubric of the Ordinals of the missal and breviary 'as corrected by my predecessor brother Haymo of holy memory, confirmed by the Apostolic See and approved by General Chapter'. Among other details he forbade the singing of any hymns, sequences or responses not contained in the Ordinal, with the exception of some antiphons of the Virgin, which might be sung after Compline; regulated the manner in which the *Te Deum* and *Credo* were to be sung; and laid down that the priest celebrating Mass was to put the host on his left and the chalice on his right.[3] Although he ended his letter of instructions with the firm, if hopeful, injunction: 'see that I do not have to repeat it', he had to follow it up at the next General Chapter, his last, held in 1257 at Rome, by promulgating a more elaborate and complete series of decrees, the *Ordinationes divini officii*.[4] These

---

[1] Bonav., VIII, 469: 'Locorum vero mutationem nullatenus concedatis alicui ante capitulum generale. Nam de consilio discretorum, propter scandala vitanda iuxta praedecessoris mei mandatum, hoc mihi reservo districte per obedientiam iubendo, ut nullus deinceps locum mutet sine mea licentia speciali.'

[2] *Narb.* c. IV, 3; Angelo Clareno, *Expositio regulae* (ed. Oliger), p. 91; *Exp. Narb.* pp. 519–20, no. 31. St Bonaventure speaks of constitutions governing fasting as new; they may be partly his own, or, like IV, 3, all John's.

[3] Wadding, *Annales*, III, 208–9. The letter is not dated but its traditional assignment to the Chapter of Metz is supported by a mention of it by Salimbene in the next paragraph to his account of an incident at that Chapter (B. p. 437, H. p. 301), and by a reference to it in the *Ordinationes divini officii* of 1257 (*A.F.H.* III, 68 (no. 29)). Certain provisions in the letter may have been reinforced by separate statute. The *Ordinationes* (no. 24, p. 68) say the *Te Deum* and *Credo* are to be sung as ordained at Metz, and the *24 Gen.* mentions that the Pope gave permission to the friars at Paris to sing certain sequences during votive masses notwithstanding the statute made at Metz (*A.F.* III, 279). These may, however, really just refer to the letter, as do the provisions recorded in *A.F.* III, 275, 697.

[4] *A.F.H.* III (1910), 55–81 (Golubovich), 499–501 (Delorme); cf. Gratien, p. 170 and n.

regulated in detail the way in which the brethren were to conduct their services. As with so much of John's legislation it shows certain affinities and sympathy with Dominican ideas and practices. Like the Dominican constitutions John's *Ordinationes* lay down when the brethren are to stand, kneel, face the altar, bow, genuflect, prostrate themselves; when the bell is to be rung and for how long, how the psalms are to be sung, where the servers are to stand during the Mass, the order in which the various officiants are to enter the choir, and so on—in fact the Franciscan version is now the more precise and detailed.[1] Friendliness towards the Preachers is also shown in the clause stating that the feast of St Dominic is not to be transferred from his day and that his name is to be put into the litanies.[2] It may not be entirely a coincidence that in 1254 Humbert of Romans, the newly elected Master General of the Preachers, was commissioned to put in order and correct their Office, and that his correction was confirmed in 1256.[3] The *Ordinationes* reflect John's personal piety and interest in liturgical ceremony and are in the best tradition of the Order, begun by St Francis and continued by almost all the Ministers General who came after him, which attached great importance to the reverent and properly ordered conduct of Divine Service. His concern for the beauty and dignity of worship, however, leads subtly to a disregard of poverty to which John is not sensitive. His statutes take it for granted that the priest, cantors, acolytes and thurifer will have surplices to wear on festivals, that there will be thuribles and incense, that candles and tapers will generally be available;[4] they permit the epistoler to wear shoes and state that the brothers are to sing the responses in their stalls if they have sufficient books, though if they have only one they are to come

---

[1] *A.F.H.* III, 64 ff.; *A.L.K.G.* V, 535-7.

[2] No. 48, p. 72.

[3] *A.L.K.G.* V, 535-6 and n., *M.O.P.H.* III, 68, 73, 78 (1254-6). Humbert regarded the office of St Francis as more edifying than St Dominic's and in 1254 also asked the Pope to be allowed to delete the phrase 'temporalibus petuntur dari' and replace it with the Franciscan 'spiritualibus proficiat incrementis'. The same year he decided that the number of the *conversi* should be reduced 'exemplo Minorum' (A. Callebaut, *A.F.H.* XX (1927), 213-15).

[4] Nos. 52, 65-9, 77-9, 99, etc.

together in the middle of the choir.[1] The intention of the *Ordinationes* was to enforce uniformity of rite throughout the Order, in which numerous local customs and variations had established themselves, especially in the singing, and this explains the detail and explicitness of the regulations, and the order that all the antiphoners were to be corrected and one good legend of St Francis compiled for use in choir. This order was repeated, and expanded to include a correction of the missals, at the Chapter of Narbonne.[2]

John also agreed to allow the practices permitted by *Ordinem vestrum* to lapse, thus in effect repudiating the bull acquired by his predecessor and making *Quo elongati* once again the standard. The decision to abstain from taking advantage of the more lenient interpretations of *Ordinem vestrum*, first carried at Genoa at the instance of William of Nottingham and Gregory of Bosellis, was reaffirmed at Metz in 1254 and again at Narbonne in 1260.[3] The same two English friars secured at Genoa a similar agreement to abstain from utilising another privilege granted by Innocent IV which threatened to render Franciscan poverty and renunciation of property little more than illusory. This bull, *Quanto studiosius* of 19 August 1247, generalised a licence that Haymo of Faversham had already obtained specially for the Basilica and Sacro Convento at Assisi. It authorised the Provincial Ministers to appoint and dismiss agents empowered to administer all the property held for the friars' use by the Holy See and to do all necessary and advantageous buying, selling, exchanging, bargaining and so forth as the friars should instruct them. As the friars already had the services of 'spiritual friends' acting as agents for their benefactors, which enabled them to receive monetary offerings without technically contravening the Rule, the addition of this further permission to get these same friends, if they liked, to act also as agents for the Holy See gave them virtual control of their properties and

---

[1] Nos. 83, 17. The permission for the epistoler to wear shoes is a corollary to that given to the priest celebrating Mass in a statute of 1242 (*Narb.* c. II, 9; see above, p. 221).

[2] Nos. 73, 74; cf. *Diff. Narb.* no. 2 and n.

[3] *Diff. Narb.* no. 13 gives the repudiation of 1260 as a confirmation of what had been done at Metz; that the repudiation had first been made at Genoa is asserted in Eccleston's circumstantial account (p. 42).

finances.[1] The Papacy was at this time inclined to be extraordinarily
callous and cavalier in its treatment of the Franciscan conscience.
In the winter of 1243–4 Innocent IV deposited the Papal treasure
with the Franciscans at Assisi for safe keeping in the Sacro Convento.[2] In 1253 he authorised the friars to accept money offerings
and sacred ornaments of great price for the Basilica, 'notwithstanding the statutes of the Order to the contrary or the prohibitions of the Minister General or Provincial...or of any other
friar whatsoever'.[3] This suggests that the statute forbidding the
friars to allow valuables to be deposited with them (c. III, 8)
had been already passed, perhaps in 1247 through concern at the
Pope's action. John did, however, occasionally succeed in getting
the Pope to rescind a privilege that had become too accommodat-
ing. According to the Rule the Ministers alone had the right
to admit postulants, and this restriction had been upheld in *Quo
elongati*, but before he died Gregory IX had been persuaded to
allow the Provincials to delegate the right to responsible brethren,
who might accept recruits in their absence. This had become
extended in practice and had led to some friars undertaking missionary journeys being empowered to receive postulants, found
new provinces and appoint Ministers. Such wide powers in the
hands of brothers too remote to be effectively supervised could
easily lead to scandals and abuses, and John had their licences
revoked.[4] It may be he who introduced the statute disqualifying
from office as unworthy any who solicited their own promotion,[5]
and another regulation concerning office, certainly made by him,

---

[1] Eccleston, p. 42; cf. Gratien, pp. 183–8.

[2] Cf. Fortini, *Assisi nel Medio Evo*, p. 177.

[3] *Decet et expedit* (10 July 1253); cf. also *Dignum existimamus* (16 July 1253):
'Non obstantibus quibuscumque statutis vel constitutionibus contrariis ipsius
ordinis confirmatione apostolica vel quacumque firmitate alia roboratis' (Sbaralea, I, 666–7, nos. 14, 489–90 (671–2)). His successor Alexander IV peremp-
torily ordered the Franciscans at Venice to accept a bequest providing for the
permanent provision of food and clothing for a whole convent 'notwithstanding any statutes of your Order or any mandate to the contrary' (19 September 1255, Sbaralea, II, 75, no. A4, 107 (781 n.)).

[4] *Quibusdam ex fratribus* (11 October 1247), Sbaralea, I, 493–4, no. 14, 243
(484).

[5] *Narb.* c. VI, 18; cf. above, pp. 218–19.

was that forbidding a Provincial Chapter to re-elect as its Minister a brother who had just been released from that position by the General Chapter. This was provoked by the action of the English brethren who, hearing that William of Nottingham, who had been their Minister for fourteen years, had been released at the Chapter of Metz, promptly held a Provincial Chapter and re-elected him. John informed them that this was not permissible and ordered them to proceed to another election.[1] As the occasion of this regulation happened after the General Chapter of Metz was over it could not have been immediately inserted among the Order's statutes. Statutes could only be issued by the Minister General in General Chapter.[2] It must have been operative at its first application, in England, as a decree issued on the authority of the Minister General, and so though in a sense dating from 1254 it could only have been incorporated as a statute in 1257, or perhaps in 1260. It is likely that John of Parma issued quite a number of such decrees, some of which may subsequently have been raised to the dignity of statutes and others not. To the general revocation of all his predecessors' edicts that St Bonaventure included among the *diffinitiones* of Narbonne he had later to add a specific note to the effect that none of John of Parma's letters were any longer in force, and this would hardly have been neces-sary if they were insignificant.[3]

But while thus upholding the principles of the Franciscan way of life, insisting on strict observance of the Rule, and putting down abuses, John had at the same time to take disciplinary action against those who within the Order took it upon themselves to criticise and condemn the authorities and their policy and pre-sumed to disobey them. It has sometimes been assumed that only men who were hostile to the *zelanti*, like Crescentius of Jesi, took punitive measures to subdue those guilty of eccentric behaviour, although in fact the maintenance of discipline was a necessary part of a General's duties. John could not hope to safeguard the reputation or the standards of the Order effectively if he failed to keep its members under control, whatever their pretext for

---

[1] Eccleston, pp. 100–1; *Narb*. c.x, 27.   [2] *Narb*. c. vII, 25; see above, p. 242.
[3] *Diff. Narb*. no. 17; *Exp. Narb*. no. 61.

disobedience. The constitution granting to the Provincial Ministers, and even to custodians and guardians where necessary, on the authority of the Minister General powers to excommunicate, capture, imprison and otherwise punish apostates of whatever province found within the territory of their jurisdiction (*Narb.* c. VII, 18), which might well be taken to be one of Crescentius' measures, cannot actually be earlier than 1247. The Papal bull which enabled these powers to be exercised was granted to Crescentius but he held no Chapter at which its substance could have been incorporated into a statute. The bull was reissued to John on 24 April 1250, and that John availed himself of the permission to call in the aid of the secular arm is suggested by the fact that not long after he left England Henry III sent out orders to the bailiffs to seize all apostates from the Franciscan Order, whether clerk or lay, and either to imprison them or hand them over to the friars, whichever the latter might prefer.[1]

The question of learning raised in his time an especial problem, and the way in which John attempted to cope with it reveals many facets of his character and policy. When the friars at Paris, at odds with the University authorities, appealed to Rome against their exclusion from the schools he intervened in person and in a speech before the whole University revoked the appeal and placed himself and the brethren unreservedly in the hands of the Masters. Touched by this unexpected submission his hearers were appeased and reconciled, and his success confirmed John in his conviction that the Minors should trust to public proofs of godliness and meekness to turn aside the anger of prelates and princes rather than to rights or privileges.[2] The statute reminding the friars that their Rule taught them that they should not go to law over any land or goods, or for any injury done them,[3] faithfully reflects his teaching and example and may have been suggested by this incident. The concord in Paris, however, did

---

[1] Eccleston, p. 73 and n.; Sbaralea, I, 542, no. I4, 323, cf. 127, p. 410 (401 and n.).

[2] Salimbene, B. pp. 434–6, H. pp. 299–300; Eccleston, p. 74.

[3] *Narb.* c. III, 24 (also c. VII, 11, which forbade appeals, and was related to a Dominican statute: cf. Appendix III).

not last. The university remained bitterly hostile to the Dominicans and the Franciscans were soon drawn back into the battle. In the very next year, 1254, the university gained notable successes against the friars and her offensive assumed menacing proportions. The Masters pursued the quarrels of the secular clergy in addition to their own, and complaints poured into the Curia. Their leader, William of St Amour, was summoned to Rome and poisoned the mind of Innocent IV to such effect that in July the Pope confirmed the statutes made by the university and in November issued the bull *Etsi animarum*, which to the dismay of the mendicants denounced the excesses of which they were accused and greatly straitened the exercise of their privileges. The Pope was shortly afterwards taken ill. John of Parma sent him brother Hugh Capold of Piacenza, who was a lector in theology and an excellent physician, in the hope that he might induce him to rescind the bull, but the good doctor could neither cure him nor deflect him.[1] The Dominicans, so it was alleged, were less charitable but more effective. Their prayers that he might speedily succumb to his illness were popularly supposed to have killed him, and a new clause: 'From the prayers of the Dominicans good Lord deliver us', was added to the litany of the street.[2] The new Pope, Alexander IV, was Cardinal Protector of the Franciscans, and the tables were promptly turned on the university. *Etsi animarum* was annulled and the Masters were ordered and at last compelled to withdraw their statutes against both Orders and to restore to them their chairs. Another result of the conflict was that henceforward the friars were alive to the advisability of keeping their students under stricter surveillance. One of the factors that had most powerfully contributed to Innocent IV's displeasure had been the appearance of a sensational book, *The Introduction to the Eternal Gospel*, by Gerard of Borgo San Donnino, in which the university had been quick to find thirty-one errors. Gerard was a lector in theology at the Franciscan convent at Paris and he had written and published the book, a garbled, provocative and heretical travesty of the prophetic teachings of Joachim of Flora, without the knowledge of the brethren. The consequences

[1] Salimbene, B. p. 605, H. pp. 419-20.   [2] Cf. Mortier, *op. cit.* I, 465.

were so serious that John of Parma at once put through a statute
forbidding the publication of any new book that had not been
first thoroughly examined either by the Minister General or by
the Provincial Minister and diffinitors in Provincial Chapter.[1]
A further statute imposed heavy penalties on any who dared
to assert or approve any opinion that had been condemned
by the Order, or to defend any 'singular opinion', especially
one contrary to faith or morals.[2] This was all the more
necessary as it was well known that John himself was an ardent
Joachite.[3]

Throughout the crisis John acted in close collaboration with
the Dominicans, who were equally involved and threatened—
the authorship of *The Introduction to the Eternal Gospel* was at
first attributed to a Dominican, and the Preachers were, of the
two, the more disliked by the Paris Masters. In 1255 the two
Generals issued a joint letter to their Orders, and their legislation
has much in common. A statute imposing a censorship on publica-
tions was introduced by the Dominicans in 1254 and its Franciscan
counterpart was probably passed that same year.[4] John of Parma
probably passed a number of other statutes regulating the selection,
conduct and supervision of students and the provision to be made
for them either at the same time or in 1257—possibly the greater
part or all of *Narb.* c. VI, 12–29 and also *Narb.* c. VIII, 24—and
these can be compared to the elaborate *admoniciones de studio* found
in the Dominican *Acta* of 1259.[5] His statutes on other subjects
also sometimes show a verbal connection with Dominican constitutions. The first sentence of the statute depriving friars who
accepted ecclesiastical preferment without licence from enjoying
any of the benefits to which members of the Order were entitled
is almost identical with a Dominican constitution that was proposed in 1252 and confirmed in 1254.[6] His decision to hold

---

[1] *Narb.* c. VI, 21; cf. Salimbene, B. p. 664, H. p. 462.

[2] *Narb.* c. VI, 22; cf. Eccleston, p. 73.

[3] Salimbene, B. pp. 332, 426–7, 438–41; H. pp. 232–3, 294, 301–4.

[4] *M.O.P.H.* III, 69, 73–4, 78; *Narb.* c. VI, 21 (cf. Salimbene, B. p. 664, H.
p. 462); see above, p. 230.

[5] *M.O.P.H.* III, 99–100 (cf. p. 105).

[6] *Narb.* c. VI, 8; *A.L.K.G.* V, 562 (*Dist.* II, 13).

Chapters alternately north and south of the Alps instead of always in the south was likewise probably influenced by Dominican practice, for the Preachers had agreed to do this as early as 1220.[1] Perhaps the immediate occasion for it was suggested to John in 1247, at the Chapter at which he himself was elected. Innocent IV had summoned this Chapter to Lyons and it was the first time a Franciscan General Chapter had been held north of the Alps. He may actually have introduced it then, to the great pleasure of the northern brethren, or else at Genoa in 1251(?) —certainly from 1247 onwards the Chapters were in fact held alternately.

When Gerard's book was condemned as heretical on 23 October 1255 Alexander IV ordered the bishop of Paris to proceed with the utmost circumspection so that no blame or dishonour should attach to the Order because of it.[2] The Pope also forbore to incriminate or condemn along with Gerard's extravagances the genuine utterances of Joachim of Flora that had inspired them. Nevertheless John of Parma's manifest Joachism could not but be regarded now as somewhat discreditable and the Pope intimated to him privately that he wished him to resign. Once this had been said to him John felt he could not continue in office any longer, and he summoned the General Chapter to meet early so that he could lay down his charge as soon as possible. The brothers assembled at Rome on 2 February 1257, in the presence of the Pope, and John announced his intention to abdicate. So popular was he that the Ministers refused to accept his resignation and argued and pleaded with him for a whole day, and at length John had to explain to Peregrinus of Bologna, who was acting as intermediary, that he was not free to accede to their desires on account of Papal objections. The Ministers had then no choice but to release him, but as a mark of their confidence in him they requested him to designate his successor. 'Father, you have visited the Order and know the character and condition of the brethren; assign us one suitable brother, whom we may appoint to this office in your stead.' John promptly nominated St Bona-

[1] *Narb.* c. XI, 2; Eccleston, p. 74; *M.O.P.H.* III, 1.
[2] Cf. Gratien, p. 214 and n.

venture, saying that in the whole Order he knew of none better than he, and the Ministers agreed to elect him forthwith.[1]

St Bonaventure had later to sit in judgement upon John of Parma, who was brought up for trial on account of his continued adherence to the doctrines of Joachim. It was not an enviable role—as Gilson observes, it is doubtful if even a future saint could emerge with credit from the task of judging one who was later to be beatified[2]—and the Spirituals never forgave him for his part in it. Typical of their interpretation of the history of this time is the vision of brother John of La Massa, recorded in the *Fioretti*. The story goes that when John of Parma was appointed Minister General John of La Massa was rapt in ecstasy and the future of the Order was revealed to him in a vision. He saw a great tree with spreading branches: at the very top of it was John of Parma and round about him, grouped on the branches according to their provinces, were all the brethren of the Order. Then he saw Christ give to St Francis a cup filled with the spirit of life and tell him to offer it to each friar, and he did so. John of Parma drained it at a draught, but none of the others emptied it completely. Some did not touch it but poured it all away; some drank a little and tossed away the dregs. Afterwards John of Parma climbed down and hid himself at the base of the tree and another, who had drunk only part of the draught, climbed up into his place. The nails of this brother's fingers grew hard as steel and razor-sharp and he went for John of Parma, intent on wounding him, but he called out to Christ for help and Christ gave St Francis a piece of flint and sent him to cut the nails of that brother.[3] Such stories against St Bonaventure have tended to colour our interpretation of the two men. Professor Knowles writes:

John of Parma, indeed, both in his personal virtues and in his striving to maintain primitive purity of observance, as also in his misfortunes and equivocal relationships, might well have been hailed as archetype

---

[1] Peregrinus of Bologna, *ap.* Eccleston, 1 ed. p. 144; Salimbene, B. p. 449, H. pp. 309–10. Bonaventure was made a cardinal in 1273. In 1274 he resigned his office in General Chapter, and died two months later, on 15 July (Gratien, pp. 315–16 and nn.).

[2] E. Gilson, *La philosophie de S. Bonaventure* (Paris, 1924), p. 25.

[3] *Fioretti*, c. 48.

by all later Spirituals; he was the first and last of his race to hold supreme power in the Order, and the difficulties which led to his resignation, and his designation of Bonaventure as his successor showed clearly enough that the majority even of the most observant friars no longer shared his ideals.[1]

Yet they had more in common than this implies. Like Bonaventure, John was a saintly man and an academic. Both had to deal with the same major problems caused by over-indulgent and over-zealous friars within, and by the attacks of the seculars without. St Bonaventure was more successful: he was not handicapped by a weakness for Joachite prophecies, and he was more constructive in thought and action; but they had, on most essentials, the same mental outlook. Both bore themselves humbly and devoutly, setting an example of dedicated service. Both helped in the kitchen, with preparing vegetables and washing up.[2] But both thought that in their Order learning and virtue should be combined, and in this they agreed together more than did either with Francis. John said that the brethren should build the walls of the Order of goodness and knowledge equally; Bonaventure that the entry of learned men into its ranks and the flourishing of studies were signs that the Order was well pleasing to God.[3] St Bonaventure defended learning as labour, and John, to give an example of labour, copied manuscripts.[4] John was responsible for Bonaventure's advancement. He made him lector at Paris when he was still only a Bachelor of Arts and such rapid promotion was quite unprecedented;[5] and he nominated him for the office of Minister General. Without that nomination it is not very likely that Bonaventure would have been elected.

It was at once St Francis' good fortune and his misfortune that his teaching, directed initially to the ordinary and the uneducated, possessed a content and a profundity capable of challenging and

[1] Knowles, *Religious Orders in England*, I, 177–8.
[2] Salimbene, B. p. 448, H. p. 308; Wadding, *Annales*, IV, 381–2.
[3] Eccleston, p. 74; Bonav., VIII, 336.
[4] Bonav., VIII, 419–20; Salimbene, B. p. 448, H. p. 309.
[5] Salimbene, B. p. 434, H. p. 299.

inspiring one of the acutest intellects of the century. St Bonaventure's philosophy was transformed, deepened and perfected
by what he learnt from Francis, and in his turn he remodelled
Francis' Order. In no other religious Order did two men of such
comparable sanctity and disparate spiritual perception wield so
decisive an influence. St Bonaventure was perhaps one of the three
greatest saints of a century rich in saints. In him it seemed that
Adam had not sinned.[1] He was too great to sink himself utterly
in another's work. It might have been better for his reputation
if he had founded a new fraternity of his own; as it is he is judged
too often for being 'untrue to St Francis' when he is being essentially true to himself. He admired and venerated St Francis, but
as an inspiration rather than as a model. He never nursed the
illusion that the destiny of the movement was to spread throughout the world the greatest possible number of exact imitators of
the founder.[2] Indeed to try to do any such thing would have been
in reality both improper and unfruitful, pointing logically to
brother John the Simple as the ideal Friar Minor, for he had
imitated St Francis to perfection, kneeling when he knelt, weeping
when he wept, coughing when he coughed.[3] To St Bonaventure
the one thing that mattered, the pearl of great price for which
all else should be sacrificed, was the spirit that animated and
informed the Franciscan way of life. This spirit he saw not as
static, still less as tied to the past, to the literal observance of the
teaching, the precepts and desires of a dead man, however saintly,
but as moving forward to the fulfilment of God's purposes,
dynamic and receptive.

Let it not disturb you [he wrote], that the brothers were in the beginning simple and illiterate; rather this very fact ought to confirm in
you a faith in the Order. I confess before God that it is this which
made me most greatly esteem the life of St Francis because it is similar
to the beginning and perfection of the Church, which first began with
simple fishermen and afterwards advanced to the most illustrious and
learned doctors. Thus you will see in the Order of the blessed Francis
that God shows that it was not contrived through human prudence

---

[1] *A.F.* III, 324.   [2] Gilson, *La philosophie de S. Bonaventure*, p. 45.
[3] MS. Perugia, c. 54=19, *Sp. S.* c. 57; *2 Cel.* 190.

but through Christ; and because the works of Christ do not fail but increase, this was shown to be the work of God when wise men did not disdain to descend to the company of simple folk.[1]

Thus in his eyes the influx of educated men was actually the very best thing that could have happened, the positive outward sign of continuing divine favour. The Order in his day was not declining from primitive simplicity but advancing out of it. Consequently he could not subscribe to every article of Francis' faith. In many ways and on many occasions he acted much as St Francis might have done in similar circumstances but there the resemblance ended and had to end. He was accessible to the least of his brethren and thought it his duty to listen patiently to their troubles and requests, however trivial or time-consuming, accounting himself their servant.[2] He welcomed criticism and reproach.[3] But it was not in his nature to renounce his learning.

St Bonaventure was at Paris when the General Chapter met at Rome in February 1257 and elected him General. The distance made it quite impossible for him to be summoned to take over the functions of his office and complete the business of the Chapter, so he was not in a position to introduce any legislation there. When news of his appointment reached him in Paris he sent out a letter to all the Provincial Ministers and custodians outlining the policy he proposed to adopt; and, like St Raymond of Peñaforte, he brought to the first General Chapter over which he presided the draft of a new edition of the Order's constitutions, which he had personally undertaken. His purpose in producing this edition at Narbonne in 1260 is indicated in the letter.[4] Here he called upon the Ministers and their assistants to co-operate with him in defending and enforcing the Rule, 'which we have professed and which, unless we observe, we cannot hope to be saved'. Conscience compelled him to devote all his energies to the eradication of the abuses which disfigured the Order and dulled its splendour, discrediting it abroad and disquieting its own

---

[1] Bonav., VIII, 336.
[2] Z. Lazzari, 'Una piccola vita inedita di S. Bonaventura', *Studi francescani*, I (1915), 130; Wadding, *Annales*, IV, 296-7.
[3] Salimbene, B. p. 447, H. p. 308.   [4] Bonav., VIII, 468-9.

sons. It was not, however, his intention to load the brethren with additional fetters. The abuses he listed were prohibited and denounced in the Rule, and in the ordinances and constitutions promulgated by his predecessors. The chief need was not for more laws, but for more energy on the part of the superiors, who must stimulate their brethren to greater devotion, and see that they knew and understood all the regulations they were supposed to obey. Thus his attitude was identical with John of Parma's,[1] but to promote the chances of making it effective he further decided to clarify the constitutions and make them easier to consult and remember.

St Bonaventure first sifted the constitutions that had been amassed since 1239 and weeded out any that he considered unsuitable or no longer applicable. To prevent confusion he quashed all constitutions, ordinances and instructions, whether written or oral, not included in his collection.[2] A copy of his new edition was to be circulated to every house in the Order and the guardian of each was to be responsible for its safe keeping and for seeing that the entire contents were read out loud to the brethren once a month, with especial emphasis on the first seven chapters which applied to everyone, so that there could be no excuse for a brother to offend through ignorance. All earlier versions, now rendered out-of-date, were henceforth invalid and were to be destroyed so that they could not be consulted or compared.[3] There was to be a single uniform code for all, and no looking back. The constitutions he retained, numbering just over 250, he arranged according to their subject, and divided up the whole into twelve chapters.[4] For convenience he gave each chapter a heading indicating its contents and provided a table listing their numbers and titles at the end of his Prologue.[5] This Prologue was very carefully and

---

[1] Cf. above, p. 258.   [2] *Diff. Narb.* no. 17 (*A.F.H.* III (1910), 503–4).

[3] *Ibid.* no. 1 (p. 502).

[4] We do not know whether this was all his own work or whether any of these chapters existed from the start. Probably some of the grouping of regulations by subject, as for instance those covering elections or visitors, was old, but the idea of creating twelve chapters—comparable with the twelve chapters of the Rule—was probably his.

[5] *Narb.* prol. 4.

elegantly composed,[1] and the style of the constitutions themselves may have been improved by him here and there. *Narb.* c. IX, 17, for example, provides an instance of a word displaced to secure a *cursus* ending. Their presentation too, and the way in which each chapter, except the last of all, was made to open with a reference to the Rule, were probably planned by him. Occasionally he inserted an editorial note explaining or defining the terms of a statute. A transgression could be accounted an 'enormous excess' either by reason of the nature of the sin itself, as for example unchastity or heresy, or by reason of external circumstances, as for example the great value of the object stolen, the notoriety of the deed, or the frequency of its repetition (c. VII, 3). An infringement of the silence rules was 'noisy' if it disturbed those standing near; it was 'extended' if it lasted for longer than it would take to say a 'Miserere mei, Deus' (c. IV, 15). Where punishment included suspension from office the term should be understood to apply not only to prelacy but also to the offices of preacher, confessor, lector, visitor, diffinitor and discretus (c. VII, 9). When used in connection with the election of diffinitors for the Provincial Chapter the term 'subditi' was to include all the brethren subject to the Provincial Minister (c. X, 18).

Apart from these definitions and the Prologue St Bonaventure probably inserted little that was new. Quite apart from Salimbene's statement to this effect[2] and St Bonaventure's own assurance,[3] it is inherently unlikely that a thoughtful chairman would try to direct a General Chapter to consider and approve a major edition of existing constitutions and a major programme of new legislative proposals at one and the same time. The inclusion of many important new regulations would be almost certain to provoke discussion and argument and opposition to them might endanger acceptance of the edition. Approaching the question from the internal evidence of the Constitutions of Narbonne, one

---

[1] Bihl, *A.F.H.* XXXIV (1941), 340–1.
[2] Salimbene, B. p. 231, H. pp. 158–9.
[3] Bonav., VIII, 468–9: '...quae mihi de consilio discretorum visa sunt corrigenda, nec penitus tacens, nec omnino exprimens, nec nova statuens, nec vincula superinducens, nec onera gravia alligans aliis, et imponens....Licet enim non sit mei propositi novis vos vinculis innodare....'

likewise finds very few statutes which can confidently be assigned to him. A bull of 28 August 1260 permits the Franciscans living in the convent at La Verna to wear silken vestments for the celebration of the Divine Office, notwithstanding the constitution and definition of the General Chapter to the contrary.[1] Its date suggests that the statute forbidding the use of gold-fringed or silk vestments (c. III, 19) was either very recent or else at least not previously properly enforced. The statutes on fasting at the beginning of chapter IV are described in the *Explanationes constitutionum* as new ones, and may be his.[2] The statute depriving brothers who accepted bishoprics without licence of the prayers, society and benefits of the Order, which was probably first introduced by John of Parma,[3] is identical in wording with a Dominican statute, except for the addition of the word 'books' to the list of deprivations in the Franciscan version. It is tempting to see in this insertion the hand of St Bonaventure, who was so loath to risk losing track of books that he once produced a veritable 'summa' of reasons for not lending them.[4] By the same token he may have been responsible for the clause providing that any brother transferring to another province and taking with him any books worth more than a quarter of a mark was to make a list of their titles and leave it with the Minister, so that they could be more easily reclaimed on his death by the province which had originally provided them (c. VI, 26; cf. also 25). The penances to be performed for infringements of the constitutions—so many meals or days fasting on bread and water for riding or accepting a lift in a cart, for eating meat, or for burying in their cemetery a layman who had not sufficiently deserved it; seven penitential psalms and seven disciplines for wearing shoes unnecessarily; a probationer's hood to be worn for a week for coming to the place where a General or Provincial Chapter was being held if not a member of it; dismissal from office for frequently consorting with women or persisting in holding opinions that had been

---

[1] Eubel, *Epitome*, no. 1089.

[2] *A.F.H.* XVIII (1925), 519–20, no. 31. They may, however, be John of Parma's (cf. above, p. 262).

[3] *Narb.* c. VI, 8 (above, p. 269.).   [4] Bonav., VIII, 371–2.

condemned, etc.—were in many instances allotted by St Bonaventure.[1] He also probably added the general sections in chapter VII, 'De correctionibus delinquentium' (22-4), providing that no one, from a simple priest to a Provincial Minister or visitor, might absolve a brother who had transgressed constitutions to which fixed penances had been assigned, unless he would undertake to do them; that fixed penances might be changed for equivalent or even arbitrary satisfactions in certain circumstances by responsible superiors; and that no one of inferior rank could absolve an offender from doing a penance imposed by a superior.

Occasionally the allocation of these penances was not made quite clear. The brethren later asked St Bonaventure whether a penance assigned to a part of a constitution applied also to its other clause or clauses, giving for example a statute concerning the guardian's discretion in providing meat dishes for the infirm, and also brethren who caused presents of meat to be sent to them.[2] In one chapter two different penalties were in two separate instances imposed upon the same offence. A statute condemning a brother who crossed the boundaries of his custody or province without an obedience to be deprived of his hood for a week, led on to another saying that the same penance was to apply to any who travelled without a companion, or carried another's money, or took a purse with him (c. V, 10-11). Carrying another's money had already been forbidden on pain of a three-day fast on bread and water, and taking a purse on pain of fasting once on bread and water for each and every meal purchased with money from it (c. V, 6-7). A few other faults can be found with the editing. For example, a similar digression, though not involving a duplication of penalties, occurs in the middle of a group of statutes concerning students, whose sequence is interrupted to say that the same care must be taken in promoting men to be priests or confessors as in selecting students to be sent to Paris or other universities (c. VI, 15-16), and again to say that just as any brother who tried

[1] Salimbene, B. p. 231, H. pp. 158-9; cf. *Narb.* cc. V, 18-19, IV, 4, III, 22, II, 8, XI, 10-11, VII, 8, VI, 22.

[2] *Narb.* c. IV, 5; *Exp. Narb.* p. 520, no. 33.

to get sent to university with the help of outside influence was to be deprived of any office he held, so any who intrigued for his own promotion to office within the Order was to be disqualified from holding any office at all (c. VI, 18). By an oversight the whole of chapter X appears to deal with the Provincial Chapter, but in fact after an opening paragraph on when the Provincial Chapter could be held the regulations turn without warning to the Chapter the Custodian was allowed by the Rule to hold in his custody. *Narb.* c. X, 2 begins: 'Ad istud capitulum...' which should properly refer to the Provincial Chapter mentioned in the preceding paragraph but actually seems to refer to the Custodian's Chapter. Rules for procedure at this local Chapter occupy paragraphs 2–8 and the account of the Provincial Chapter is resumed in paragraph 9. Blemishes of this kind, however, are few and insignificant compared with the positive excellences of the edition. We cannot measure the extent of the improvement, but only judge the result. The work was well done, so well done that it never had to be done again. The brethren showed their appreciation by approving the edition, which came to be known as the Constitutions of Narbonne, and by requesting him to perform the same service for the Lives of St Francis.

3. POSTSCRIPT

The main body of statutes that was to govern the Friars Minor through the succeeding centuries was the combined achievement of the two General Chapters of 1239 and 1242. No single individual was responsible for them but, among the number of educated friars who contributed, Haymo of Faversham stands out as their chief author. He was probably a member of the committee that drafted the original statutes in 1239; he played an active part at the Chapter held that year; and he presided at the Chapter of 1242. The outstanding importance of his personal contribution to his Order's development, for long overshadowed by the greater fame of St Bonaventure, has now been fully acknowledged by scholars. 'He, more than any other single man,' writes Professor Knowles, 'fixed the constitutional and social lines along which the order was to travel during the thirteenth century.'[1] Haymo's achievement shows that the downfall of Elias did not immediately preclude an individual, and a Minister General, from wielding very great influence in the Order, although the days of the greatest opportunities for individual initiative were passing.

The Franciscans had no such pattern for their legislation as the Dominicans had for much of theirs in the Praemonstratensian *Institutes*. In 1239 the Dominican constitutions could have provided a ready-made model if they had cared to avail themselves of it; but it can safely be said that they did not import the Dominican constitutions wholesale. Had they done so, and had St Bonaventure rearranged them without adding to or altering them much,[2] the Constitutions of Narbonne would have been essentially similar to Raymond's collection, the two merely representing two different masters' answers to the same exercise. There is no such identity of content; but in the stages of their compilation we do seem to have a remarkably close analogy—an early collection of statutes that is found in all essentials an adequate expression of the Order's constitutional requirements and only needs serious improvement in its structure. Gerard of Fracheto gives an account of Raymond's work very similar to Salimbene's description of Bonaventure's; and Gerard's can be checked against the documents and found true.[3] This is no proof that Franciscan experience was the same, but it does demonstrate that an evolution of this type was possible, and did in fact occur in a similar religious Order in the same half-century. Raymond's edition represents the 1228 constitutions plus the additions made between 1228 and 1239; and in so far as it can be analysed St Bonaventure's represents the 1239 constitutions plus the additions made between 1239 and 1260. Nevertheless Raymond's edition is likely to have been much closer to 1228 than St Bonaventure's was to 1239. It was more difficult for the

[1] Knowles, *Religious Orders in England*, I, 173; cf. also Gratien, p. 150.

[2] Salimbene tells us that Bonaventure added little of his own 'except that he fixed the penances at some points' (B. p. 231, H. pp. 158–9).

[3] 'Per eius eciam diligenciam constituciones nostre redacte sunt ad formam debitam sub certis distinctionibus et titulis, in qua sunt hodie, que sub multa confusione antea habebantur' (*M.O.P.H.* I, 331; VI, i, 3; cf. VI, i, 1 n. for authorship).

Dominicans to change or annul their constitutions, and the Franciscans probably discarded more on the way than the Dominicans. They possessed a fundamental law in their Rule and they made a clear distinction between it and their constitutions, which in contrast were allowed only a provisional and temporary validity. Also the Franciscans may well not have adhered so strictly to the original wording. St Raymond hardly changed a syllable. St Bonaventure normally showed no such veneration for the written word. When he had composed his own *Life of St Francis* he ordered all the old legends to be destroyed. But his *Life* was not a copy or conflation of these earlier *Lives* and they could not have been reconstructed from it.

The constitutions were at once an answer to particular problems and a statement of ideals; but their multiplication tended to create more occasions for transgression, as John of Parma observed, and explains the increasing preoccupation with fixing penalties for infringement and St Bonaventure's recorded contribution to the collection.[1] It came about in the end that the Franciscans, who had at first been the freer of legal compulsion, set more store by the punctual observance of their statutes than the Dominicans.[2] The Dominicans did not lose sight of the fact that these were intended to serve the Order, not to constrain it. Humbert of Romans stated it as a principle that the statutes should not be kept if they hindered the purpose for which the Order was founded and in the prologue to the Constitutions it is expressly stated that the superiors may dispense from any duty or command that interferes with study, preaching or the cure of souls.[3] The Franciscans were agreed that neither the Chapter nor the brethren had power to change the Rule; but St Bonaventure added the significant gloss that the Rule did not absolve from obedience to the statutes.[4]

---

[1] Salimbene, B. pp. 436–7, 231, H. pp. 300–1, 158–9.

[2] Practice was probably less rigid than theory. Thus three of the nine General Chapters between 1239 and 1260 were not held at Whitsun (probably contrary to the constitutions, certainly to the Rule: *Reg. Bullata*, c. 8; cf. *Narb.* c. XI, 15, IX, 7); and there are various cases of appointments of Provincial Ministers which departed from the letter of the constitutions (Jordan, cc. 68–71, 78; cf. above, p. 205.).

[3] *A.L.K.G.* I, 177 and n., 194, V, 534.   [4] *4 Masters*, p. 160; Bonav., VIII, 432.

The multiplication of statutes also tended to create the impression that they should cover every contingency. Many of the questions which St Bonaventure thought it necessary to answer in his *Explanationes Constitutionum* show that the enthusiasm for constitution-making had fostered a reliance on literal obedience to the statutes rather than on common sense and had given some an amusing academic exercise picking holes in them. They ask if they must sleep in their habits if they are sopping wet; if those can be classed as technically unwell who cannot sleep on other than feather pillows without damage to their heads, though they are otherwise perfectly fit.[1] The constitutions say that no brother may wear shoes habitually, and every time he disobeys and deliberately wears shoes he is to say seven penitential psalms and receive seven disciplines. How can one be 'each time' punishable for 'habitually' wearing shoes, and how can one wear shoes except deliberately?[2] Does the fact that the same penalty is imposed in the constitutions on those who take a lift in a cart as on those who ride mean that carts are to be understood as included in the Rule's prohibition of riding? What is a brother to do if a cart passes him on the road and his companion wants to accept a lift and he does not feel it is necessary? If he mounts the cart he transgresses one constitution, if he abandons his companion he transgresses another![3]

The eleven who had followed Francis in 1210 had with astonishing rapidity become a number reaching into four and then into five figures. Among the constitutions determining the order of procedure at General Chapter meetings is one requiring that on the Monday after Whitsun the brothers are to go into the Chapter after the celebration of the Mass of the Holy Spirit and hear a sermon. Then the number of the friars who have died since the last General Chapter is to be read out. In 1260 this number was 2126.[4] As the preceding General Chapter had been held in 1257 this figure represents the total for three years, an average of about

---

[1] *Exp. Narb.* nos. 15, 17 (pp. 516, 517).
[2] *Ibid.* nos. 9, 14 (pp. 515–16).   [3] *Ibid.* nos. 51, 56 (pp. 523, 524).
[4] *Narb.* c. XI, 21; *Diff. Narb.* no. 26.

seven hundred a year. Unlike figures given in chronicles this should be reliable, and if we reckon the average life of a brother in the Order at twenty-five years, which is probably a conservative estimate, it would suggest that in 1260 the Order numbered somewhere in the region of 17,500 friars.[1] How were the clothing, the needs of the sick—both duties enjoined on the Ministers by the Rule—the feeding, organising and disciplining of so many to be reconciled with taking no thought for the morrow? St Francis had never really answered the problem of running an Order. His way was to put someone else, first Peter Catanii and then Elias, in charge of such things and rebuke him if he worried about it. It is scarcely surprising that his successors were more preoccupied with the cares of administration. Large numbers too entailed a certain dilution of talent and quality. It could not be hoped that all these recruits would be able to follow St Francis perfectly or even adequately. Of those who joined some were fervent, some casual, some conscientious, some fussy, some tiresome, and a few vicious. That some abuses and laxity had gained a foothold was admitted and deplored by all friars of good will. The great majority endeavoured to live worthily. In 1248 John of Parma honoured the English friars for their obedience and uprightness, and as he visited house after house in the province he was so impressed by what he saw that he exclaimed more than once: 'Oh, I wish that a province such as this might be placed in the centre of the world, so as to be an example to all.'[2] Yet the English friars were not absolutely faithful to St Francis' wishes. 'Although the brothers zealously pursued supreme simplicity and purity of conscience in all things, in hearing the divine law and scholastic studies they were so fervent that they did not shrink from going daily, barefoot, in bitter cold and deepest mud, to the schools of theology, however far off.'[3]

St Bonaventure was a keen reformer. His attacks on the

---

[1] Cf. David Knowles and R. N. Hadcock, *Medieval Religious Houses, England and Wales* (London, 1953), p. 363, where it is suggested that the number of Franciscans in the English province ranged from about 1350 (1348) to about 1700 (1702) in the thirteenth and first half of the fourteenth century.

[2] Eccleston, pp. 73–4, 98.   [3] *Ibid.* p. 27.

practices of those friars who were later to form the nucleus of the Conventual party tend to be soft-pedalled because he also had clashes with the 'Spirituals' on doctrinal issues.[1] He was probably aware that there was a danger of schism, and many of his efforts were consciously directed to secure unity. He himself took a middle position, tempering the intolerance of the Spirituals and discountenancing their Joachism, but opposing the lax practices of the Conventuals. Perhaps he was trying to close the ranks of the observant friars against the Conventuals, and perhaps they understood the threat and acted quickly after his death.[2] The Spirituals did not appreciate his services. He was reviled by most of them because they saw him only as the persecutor of John of Parma.

The notion of a radical divergence of policy between John and Bonaventure has led to a misconception of the early history of the Order, to an attempt to read back later history where it has no place, and to too strong an emphasis on the personalities of the Ministers General. Emphasis on character and individuality has notoriously darkened our understanding of Papal history in this period, when the continuing tradition of a great office dominated the personal views of all but the greatest of the Popes. To a lesser extent, already by 1239, the leaders of the Franciscan Order had developed a notion of how the Order should be run and how a Minister General should behave. It was a young tradition and unformed, and it was to be expected that men of the originality and imagination of Haymo, John of Parma and especially St Bonaventure should mould and bend it according to their personal views. But with all the divergences and changes which occurred, we can see a certain unity in the aims and in many of the practices of the Ministers between 1239 and 1274, with the possible exception of Crescentius; and it conforms neither with the Spiritual

[1] On the Spiritual movement see Ehrle, *A.L.K.G.* II–IV, and D. L. Douie, *The nature and effect of the heresy of the Fraticelli* (Manchester, 1932).

[2] Trouble between the two groups first came into the open about the time of the Council of Lyons in 1274, the year of Bonaventure's death; but it did not really come to a head until some years later. The Conventuals made intermittent efforts to persecute the Spirituals from the late 1270's onwards.

nor with the Conventual policies of later days. Haymo's Order and Bonaventure's Order was to be clerical and educated, but humble, ascetic and devout. Through all their vicissitudes the Franciscans of later centuries have remained the most humble of the large communities in the Roman Catholic Church; and the tradition that made this possible owes something to the men who struggled to preserve and extend the life of the Order as well as to the saint who inspired it.

APPENDICES

I. THE CHAPTER OF MATS

It is recorded in the *Verba S. Francisci* (c. 5) that Cardinal Hugolino was present at a General Chapter at Assisi, 'et dictum est capitulum sextoriorum, et fuerunt ibi quinque milia fratres...'; and that it was on this occasion that he tried to make St Francis and his brothers accept an existing monastic rule. It is clear that this incident took place after the meeting of Francis and Hugolino at Florence (see above, p. 62), and it seems likely *prima facie* that Hugolino was already Cardinal Protector. Since this Chapter —traditionally called the Chapter of Mats, on the basis of this and related texts—has sometimes been dated as early as 1218, it has become entangled with the problem of the chronology of St Francis' relations with the cardinal. It is the purpose of this appendix to separate the threads: to show that the meeting at Florence can be dated to 1217 or 1218, and that the Chapter of Mats was a distinctly later event.

The *terminus a quo* for St Francis' meeting with Hugolino at Florence (*1 Cel.* 74, cf. above, pp. 61 ff.) is provided by Celano's information that Hugolino was then legate in Tuscany. He held that office on three occasions, in 1217, in 1218–19 and in 1221.[1] Celano says that the meeting took place after a Whitsun Chapter, when St Francis was on his way to France. In 1219 Francis set out, not for France, but for the East; in 1220 he was still in the East at Whitsun and Hugolino was not legate; and by Whitsun 1221 Francis had obtained from Honorius III the appointment of Hugolino as official Protector (above, pp. 64–6). Formal protection can hardly have preceded informal, and so 1221 is clearly too late for the meeting at Florence. We are thus left with the years 1217 and 1218. There are a variety of other clues, but none of them is decisively in favour of either of these years. In a lengthy article

[1] E. Brem, *Papst Gregor IX bis zum Beginn seines Pontifikats* (Heidelberg, 1911), pp. 26 ff., 111 ff.

Father Callebaut argued for 1217,[1] and his arguments do raise something like a presumption in favour of the earlier year; but not more. 1218 remains a possibility.

The date of the Chapter of Mats is another problem upon which modern scholars have not as yet reached agreement. Sabatier and Moorman chose 1218,[2] Gratien and Attal 1219,[3] and Lempp 1221.[4] The point cannot be established with certainty, and it is difficult to be sure how large an element of legend has entered into the account in the *Verba*; but taking it more or less at face value, I would venture to suggest that the Chapter of Mats was that of 1222.

The name of the Chapter is perhaps the best starting-point. It is generally known as the Chapter of Mats, and Sabatier has pointed out that all the early Franciscan Chapter meetings had an equal right to such a name, as they were all attended by numbers of brethren who gathered round the Portiuncula and lodged under temporary shelters made of rushes.[5] This suggests the possibility that the Chapter has been wrongly called, for it is clear from the wording of the story in the *Verba S. Francisci* and its related texts that the name was intended to distinguish the meeting from others. The best texts, in MSS. Perugia, S. Isidore de Urbe and S. Antonii de Urbe, read 'sestoriorum', 'sextoriorum' and 'sistoriorum', and offer no explanation of the term. In Angelo Clareno's *Expositio Regulae* and the *Speculum Perfectionis* the rendering is 'storiorum', and the latter version is accompanied by a gloss to the effect that it was so called because the only dwellings there were made of rush-matting.[6] A similar commentary is given in the *Actus–Fioretti*.[7] These glosses seem

---

[1] *A.F.H.* XIX, 530–58.

[2] Sabatier, *Sp. S.* (1898), p. LXXXVIII (cf. 2 ed. II, 113 f.), *Vie de S. François*, pp. 248 ff.; Moorman, *Sources for the Life of St Francis*, p. 29.

[3] Gratien, pp. 13–14; Attal, *Frate Elia*, pp. 77–8.

[4] Lempp, p. 47 and n.   [5] Sabatier, *Vie de S. François*, pp. 228 ff.

[6] The various versions of this story are in the *Verba*, c. 5, MS. Perugia c. 17 = 114, MS. Little, c. 114 (*Collectanea Franciscana*, I, 67), Angelo Clareno, *Expositio Regulae*, ed. Oliger, pp. 128–9, MS. St Antonii de Urbe, f. 54 (cf. *A.F.H.* XII (1919), 338–9), *Sp. S.* c. 68.

[7] *Actus b. Francisci*, ed. Sabatier, c. 20: 'Et habebant ibi in campo tecta distincta per turmas de carticinis in circuitu et supra. Unde propter hoc vocatum est capitulum de carticinis vel de store' (cf. *Fioretti*, c. 18).

to indicate that a difficulty of interpretation had arisen. Later scribes were puzzled by the original word they found in their sources and converted it into a form with which they were more familiar, adding a paraphrase for greater clarity. 'Sestoria', etc. may be variants of 'storia' or 'textoria', as the compilers of the *Speculum Perfectionis* and the *Actus* supposed, and mean mats made of woven rushes, or they may be variants of a totally different word, 'consistorium'. There is one piece of evidence which lends support to this emendation, and its possible significance will be discussed later.

The facts about the Chapter that are given in the *Verba* are as follows: it was a General Chapter held at Assisi; it was attended by five thousand brethren, many of whom were learned; Cardinal Hugolino was present; and the question was raised as to whether it would not be better for the Order if St Francis were to adopt certain regulations taken from the Rules of St Benedict, St Augustine or St Bernard. From this information a few definite conclusions can be drawn. It was a General Chapter, and so must have been held at Whitsun. Cardinal Hugolino participated, and as he did not offer St Francis his protection before the summer of 1217,[1] it cannot have been held earlier than 1218. Five thousand brethren were present, and as, once the *Regula Bullata* had been approved, the membership of the Chapter was restricted, it cannot have been later than 1223.

In order to narrow the field further it is necessary to turn to other sources for details about the six Chapters that fell within this period. Of these Chapters, 1221 is the best documented. Jordan of Giano, who was present at it, has left a vivid account of the assembly, which is a useful basis for the discussion.[2] He does not mention any attempt on the part of the learned brethren to persuade St Francis to model his institute on the older Orders of monks or canons, and as the incident recorded in the *Verba* was dramatic, and his memory for a good story excellent, he is unlikely to have omitted it had he witnessed it. Furthermore, his details do not tally with those of the *Verba*. He says that St Francis was sick, and made Elias his spokesman when he wished to address

[1] See above, pp. 286–7.   [2] Jordan, cc. 16–18.

the meeting; whereas at the Chapter of Mats the saint, instead of taking an opportunity to talk privately with the cardinal, chose to speak his mind strongly before all the brethren. Again, the cardinal who was present in 1221 was not Hugolino but the bishop of Sabina, Rainerius Capocci. Lastly, the number of the brethren who attended in 1221 was estimated not at five thousand but at three thousand. Unfortunately the tendency of medieval chroniclers to exaggerate renders deductions from their statistics doubtful. But all, or nearly all, the brethren were present in 1221, and if any reliance at all can be placed upon the estimates then a meeting that contained five thousand must have been held after this date. This conclusion is borne out by Thomas of Celano's remarks concerning the growth of the Order in the *Vita Prima*. He said that when St Francis met Hugolino in Florence, probably in 1217, he had not as yet many brethren, but that when he asked for the Cardinal as official Protector (in the winter of 1220–1) their number was already much increased.[1] It is highly improbable that a small body of men could have so multiplied that in a year or two years they could have reached a figure that would have seemed like five thousand even to the wildest exaggerator.

An additional argument in favour of 1222 may be gleaned from Eccleston's chronicle.[2] He heard tidings of St Francis from Martin of Barton, who had been himself in Italy, and who had a brother who was an officer in the civic guard at Assisi. Brother Martin related that at a certain General Chapter meeting St Francis commanded that a house that had been built to hold the assembly should be destroyed because it was contrary to poverty, and set a bad example. The house had been built by the people of Assisi as a sign of their goodwill, and Martin's brother was among those who intervened to protect the Commune's property. The same story is told in the *Speculum Perfectionis* as an illustration of the saint's love of poverty, but Martin adds one important detail that

---

[1] *1 Cel.* 74, 100; cf. above, p. 66. At a very early Chapter meeting held at Gubbio 300 brethren are said to have been present (*Legenda de passione S. Verecundi militis et martiris*, ed. D. M. Faloci-Pulignani, *Misc. Fr.* x (1906), 7).

[2] For what follows, cf. Eccleston, p. 32, MS. Perugia, c. 48=11, *Sp. S.* c. 7 (for other versions, cf. Moorman, *Sources*, p. 105).

makes it relevant here—the Chapter was attended by five thousand brethren. For such a number to come to Assisi was exceptional, which is the reason why it made such an impression on the popular mind, and it is unlikely that the same figure would have been reproduced for two distinct meetings. The two incidents, Francis' attempt to destroy the house, and the brothers' attempt to introduce monastic legislation, may reasonably be presumed to have taken place at the same Chapter. Through Martin, Eccleston further learned that St Francis wrote a letter to the brethren of the French province, which did not get wet although it was raining, and that the same day his prayers saved from harm a brother who had fallen down a deep well. The saint also predicted the terrible earthquake that destroyed much of Brescia, and wrote a warning to the people in Latin that was ungrammatical. All these reminiscences of brother Martin's seem to date from the same period, and the earthquake to which he referred occurred at Christmas 1222.[1]

If this identification of the Chapter mentioned in Eccleston with that described in the *Verba* is correct, it becomes apparent that the name 'Chapter of Mats' that aptly describes most of the early Franciscan Chapters is inapplicable in this particular instance. The brethren on this occasion did not have to camp out under temporary shelters, but were accommodated in a substantial house of stone and lime. This, as well as the large number that attended, distinguished it from previous meetings, and perhaps the name it was originally given referred not to 'mats' but to the 'house of assembly' (consistorium).

The dating of this Chapter to 1222 does not conflict with any of the details contained in the *Verba*, and such an incident as it describes fits very well into the history of the Order at that period. Between 1221 and 1223 St Francis was engaged in rewriting the Rule, and received much well-meant advice from the learned brethren and from Hugolino. The suggestion that he would do well to profit by the experience of earlier legislators would be more natural and more urgent while the Rule was being revised than at any other time.

Against this date it might be objected that, according to the

---

[1] Eccleston, p. 32 n.

Actus–Fioretti, St Dominic as well as Hugolino was present at the Chapter, and St Dominic died on 4 August 1221. The authority of this version, however, is slight. It says, for instance, that Hugolino came over to Assisi every day from Perugia, where the Curia was then residing, and thus implies that the Chapter was held in 1216,[1] which is impossible. It contains a number of details that do not properly belong in this context, and provides a good example of Sabatier's contention that Franciscan writers tended to telescope the happenings of several years into one glorified event.[2] Like most of the chapters of the collection it tells a charming story, but one which should not be credited with historical accuracy.

II. THE GENERAL CHAPTER OF 1230

The General Chapter of 1230 was eventful: it was held on the occasion of St Francis' translation; it was violently interrupted by a number of Elias' partisans, who made an unseemly and unsuccessful attempt to force the resignation of John Parenti. These stormy and colourful aspects of the meeting have riveted the attention of scholars, and the business that was done, being less exciting, has tended to be ignored or relegated to the background. Little account has been taken of the important constitutional and administrative measures for which the Chapter was responsible, and this has prevented a proper appreciation of its significance. Therefore it seems worth while to set out the various matters that are known to have been included on the agenda, and to reconstruct, so to say, the 'minutes' of the meeting.

　1. Complaints were made against Elias on account of his unauthorised and premature translation of St Francis (Eccleston, pp. 65–6, *Spec. Vitae*, p. 165).

　2. A disturbance was caused by Elias' partisans, who tried to make him General against the wish of the Provincial Ministers (Eccleston, pp. 65–6).

---

[1] *Actus*, c. 20. The only time that Honorius III was at Perugia was from 20 May to 12 August 1216.　　　　[2] *Vie de S. François*, pp. 228 f.

3. Questions were raised about difficult points in the Rule; it was decided to ask the Pope for an elucidation; members were chosen to form a deputation; the result of their mission was the bull *Quo elongati* issued on 28 September (Eccleston, p. 66, *24 Gen.*, A.F. III, 213, Sbaralea, I, 68–70, no. G 9, 56 (IV)).

4. The following constitutions were enacted by John Parenti:

i. The Body of our Lord was to be kept reverently in silver or ivory pyxes (*Catalogus*, A.F. III, 694).

ii. No friar was to be called 'master' or 'lord' (*ibid.* p. 695).

iii. Apostates were not to be readmitted if they were heretical, etc. (*ibid.*).

iv. Novices were not to hear confessions, and the professed might do so only with the licence of their Provincial Minister (*ibid.*).

v. Only one Custodian from each Province was to come in future to the General Chapter, and he was to act as representative for his colleagues (Sbaralea, *loc. cit.*).

5. Provincial business.

i. Breviaries and antiphoners were to be sent to the Provinces (Jordan, c. 57).

ii. The existing Provinces were divided up as follows:

Tuscany	Tuscany Rome Umbria	Germany	Rhine Saxony
March of Ancona	March of Ancona	France and Provence	France Provence Burgundy Tours
Lombardy	Lombardy (Bologna) March of Treviso (Venice) Genoa	Spain	Portugal Aragon Castile
Naples	Naples Abruzzi	Syria	Syria
Apulia	Apulia S. Angeli	Aquitaine	Aquitaine
Calabria	Calabria Sicily	England	England Ireland

(Golubovich, II, 214 ff., 259, and above, p. 129 n.).

iii. New appointments included:

Transfer of John of Piano Carpine from Germany to Spain (Jordan, c. 57).

Appointment of Otto the Lombard as Provincial of the Rhine, and of Simon the Englishman of Saxony (*ibid.*).

Appointment of Richard of Ingworth as Provincial of Ireland (Eccleston, p. 4).

III. RELATIONS BETWEEN THE FRANCISCAN AND DOMINICAN CONSTITUTIONS
(cf. pp. 225–31)

What follows is a table of those sections of the Constitutions of Narbonne which have affinities with earlier Dominican constitutions. They are arranged according to the nature of the link— which varies from a verbal connection to an association of ideas —and the references given are (*a*) to *Narb.*, (*b*) to the Dominican constitutions, by Distinction and section of the two recensions (for 1228, cf. *A.L.K.G.* I, 165–227; for 1241, *A.L.K.G.* V, 530–64),[1] (*c*) by date to the Dominican Chapters which passed individual constitutions (for these, cf. 'Acta Capitulorum Generalium Ordinis Praedicatorum', I, *M.O.P.H.* III), (*d*) by page to a discussion in the text of this book; to these is sometimes added a note of whether the Franciscan or the Dominican is the debtor, and which of the

---

[1] References are given to Denifle's editions because they are more available and more convenient for the present purpose. Where necessary his text has been checked against later editions (for 1228, P. Mothon, *Analecta sacri Ordinis Fr. Praedicatorum*, III (1896), 621 ff.; H. C. Scheeben, *Quellen und Forschungen zur Geschichte des Dominikanerordens in Deutschland*, XXXVIII (1939), 48–80; French transl. by M.-H. Vicaire, *S. Dominique de Caleruega d'après les documents du XIIIe siècle* (Paris, 1955), pp. 137–84; for 1241, R. Creytens, *Archivum Fratrum Praedicatorum*, XVIII (1948), 1–68). Denifle's edition of the second recension is based on a copy drawn up *c.* 1256; that by Creytens on a MS. which reveals the state of the constitutions in 1241–2, which makes the reconstruction of Raymond's text more secure. The first recension is known only from a fourteenth-century MS. which gives, though imperfectly, the state of the constitutions *c.* 1238. In his edition Denifle attempts to reconstruct the text of 1228 (which was itself, as we now know, closely based on earlier versions: cf. Vicaire, *op. cit.* pp. 113 ff.).

two Dominican versions is closer to the Franciscan. Where there is a connection with the earlier Dominican recension (whether directly or through that of 1241), the Franciscan must normally be derived from the Dominican, since with very few exceptions the Franciscan constitutions are later than 1228;[1] this point is not noted by each item which it affects in the following analysis.

A. *Constitutions showing verbal connection*

Narb. c. IV, 20–1; cf. 1228, I, 20 (very slightly closer than 1241, I, 11) (for *intra* read *inter*: Creytens, art. cit. p. 37); above p. 228.

C. VI, 8; cf. addn. to 1241, II, 13 (passed 1252–5); above, p. 269.

C. VII, 11; cf. 1241, II, 8 (slightly closer than 1228, II, 8).

C. VII, 12; cf. 1228, II, 14, 1241, II, 8 (probably from 1228, in spite of a minor agreement in word order with 1241. The reading *diffinitiones* in Denifle's edition of 1228 is a scribal error.)

C. VII, 13; cf. 1228, II, 14 (closer than 1241, II, 8); above, p. 227 n. (Franciscan presumably derivative).

C. IX, 2, 4; 1241, II, 4 (closer than 1228, II, 11) (Franciscan derived from 1241 edition).

C. IX, 7, 8; cf. 1228, II, 13, 1241, II, 4 (*Narb.* and 1241 have *nuntietur* for *denuntietur* in 1228).

C. XI, 6; cf. 1241, II, 5 and addn. (passed 1242–4).

C. XI, 21; cf. 1241, II, 9, as emended in 1252–5 (closer than 1228, II, 17).

C. XI, 24; cf. 1228, II, 16, 1241, II, 7.

C. XI, 28; cf. 1241, II, 9 (very slightly closer than 1228, II, 21—*fiat communis* for *communis fiat*).

B. *Constitutions showing slight verbal connection[2] and definite association of ideas*

C. I, 8; cf. 1228, I, 13, 1241, I, 14; above, p. 244.

C. IV, 11; cf. 1228, I, 17, 1241, I, 12; above, p. 227.

C. IV, 13; cf. addn. to 1241, I, 12 (passed 1246–8); above, p. 227. (Dominican possibly derivative, because Franciscan probably passed in 1239; cf. above, pp. 234–5).

[1] This argument is only slightly affected by the possibility that some of the constitutions in our text of the recension of 1228 were in fact passed between 1228 and 1238—there was no considerable body of Franciscan legislation before 1239.

[2] The verbal connection is usually too slight to prove a direct link by itself; but the combination of ideas and words is sufficient to establish that in most of these cases the constitutions are in some way linked.

C. IV, 19; cf. 1228, II, 34, 1241, II, 13; above, p. 230 n.

C. V, 13; cf. 1228, II, 36, 1241, II, 13.

C. VI, 21; cf. addn. to 1241, II, 14 (passed 1254–6); above, p. 269 (probably the fruit of joint action to meet the crisis of 1254).

C. VI, 25; cf. addn. to 1241, II, 14 (passed 1240–2).

C. VIII, 6; cf. 1228, II, 19, 1241, II, 11.

C. VIII, 14; cf. addn. to 1241, I, 17 (passed 1254–6).

C. X, 6; cf. addn. to 1241, II, 9 (passed 1252–5).

C. X, 8; cf. 1228 (?corrected 1236), II, 1 (closer than 1241, II, 5, 6).

C. X, 13; cf. 1228, II, 1, 1241, II, 5.

C. X, 16; cf. 1228, II, 2, 1241, II, 7.

C. X, 21; cf. 1228, II, 3, 1241, II, 7.

C. XI, 23, 25; cf. 1228, II, 17, 1241, II, 9.

C. XII, 1, 3, 4, 6, 7; cf. 1228, II, 22, 1241, I, 3 (several of the instructions on prayers for the dead are similar).

C. *Constitutions showing some association of ideas*

(See above, p. 228: many of these may be due merely to similar problems leading to similar solutions, or to both orders following the same tradition.)

C. I, 6; cf. 1228, I, 14, 1241, I, 13; cf. above, p. 244.

C. III, 15, 17; cf. 1228, II, 35, 1241, II, 1; cf. above, p. 228.

C. IV, 4; cf. 1228, I, 12, 1241, I, 8.[1]

C. IV, 16; cf. 1241, I, 9 (not in 1228).

C. V, 9, 10; cf. 1228, II, 34, 1241, II, 13.

C. VI, 6; cf. 1228, II, 27, 1241, II, 1.

C. VI, 11; cf. 1228, II, 37 (not in 1241).

C. VII, 25, 26; cf. 1228, II, 6, 1241, prologue, II, 9.

C. VIII, 18, 20; cf. 1228, II, 18, 19, 1241, II, 11.

C. IX, 10–15; cf. 1228, II, 15, 1241, II, 3 (Mandonnet, *S. Dominique*, II, p. 250 n., suggests that the Franciscan is partly a résumé of the Dominican of 1228, on the ground that it is closer in order to 1228 than to 1241).

C. IX, 20–2; cf. 1228, II, 23, 1241, II, 1.

C. X, 2, 7; cf. 1241, II, 7 (not in 1228).

C. X, 18; cf. addn. to 1241, II, 5 (passed 1249–56).

[1] Mandonnet, *S. Dominique, l'idée, l'homme et l'œuvre* (Paris, 1938), II, 258 n., argues for a connection between c. IV, 4 and 1228, I, 8, 1241, I, 5; but there seems no reason to suppose that these constitutions are not independent.

C. XI, 3, 12; cf. 1228, II, 5, 1241, II, 5.
C. XI, 4, 5, 14; cf. 1228, II, 7, 1241, II, 8.
C. XI, 15–20; cf. 1228, II, 9, 1241, II, 8.
C. XI, 26, 27; cf. 1228, II, 21, 1241, II, 9.

D. *Franciscan constitutions related to Dominican Acta*

(The *acta* included in this section are only those which were not incorporated into the Dominican constitutions.)

C. III, 19; cf. *Acta*, 1239, revoked in 1240 (slight verbal connection); above, p. 226 n.

C. IV, 22; cf. *Acta*, 1249, 1250, replaced by a new *inchoacio* in 1252, then dropped (connection of ideas); and see above, p. 229.

C. VI, 2; cf. *Acta*, 1249, 1250; above, p. 226 n.

C. IX, 5; cf. *Acta*, 1250.

(For other relations, see above, pp. 228, 269.)

IV. THE CONSTITUTIONS OF NARBONNE

What follows is an index of references to the Constitutions of 1260, with an indication of the original date of those which can be dated, and brief notes on a few not discussed in the text of this book. The principles of dating have been discussed above (esp. pp. 212 ff.); pages containing evidence for the dates of individual constitutions are given in italics here. Some even of those most securely dated may, of course, have been later revised, and many of the dates are extremely tentative (but see p. 213). Two points should perhaps be emphasised. (1) Constitutions could only be passed in General Chapter, and so virtually all the constitutions must belong to the years 1239, 1242, 1244, 1247, 1251 (?), 1254, 1257, 1260. Thus if a constitution was probably later than 1252 but earlier than 1260, it can be dated tentatively 1254 or 1257 (cf. c. XI, 21). (2) Constitutions more closely connected with the earlier than the later Dominican recension were probably passed in 1239 (see pp. 227–8). Where the Franciscan texts agree with slight revisions made by the Dominicans in 1239–41, the Franciscans were probably again the borrowers, and the debt was incurred in 1241 or later.

For editions of *Narb.*, see pp. xii, 210 nn.

Constitutions passed before 1260 but not incorporated in *Narb.* are referred to on pp. 110, 156–7 (1223–4; cf. p. 114); 127, 156–7, 228 n., 292 (1230); 156–7 (1232–9; cf. p. 52); 215, 233–5, 237–8 (1239); 246 (1242).

Prol.: 275–6.
I, 3–4: 228.
I, 3: *243–5* (prob. 1242).
I, 4: *245* (prob. 1242).
I, 6: *244*, 295 (? 1242).
I, 7–11: *244* (? 1242).
I, 8: *244*, 294 (? 1242).

II, 1: *220–1*, *241* (1242).
II, 5, 6: *233* (? 1239).
II, 8: *277–8* (? partly 1260).
II, 9: *221*, 245, 264 (1242).
II, 11: *234–5* (? 1239).

III, 1, 2: 233 (1239: cf. p. *220* for 2, which presupposes 1).
III, 4: *221*, *241* (? 1242).
(III, 5 on collecting-boxes might be connected with Elias' collections for the Basilica; but see pp. 121–2, 150.)
III, 6: *222* (after 1242).
III, 7: *245–6* (before 1257; ? 1242).
III, 8: *265* (before 1253; ? 1247).
III, 11: *220–1*, *241* (1242).
III, 15–18: 228, *261* (before 1257, but 18 in particular probably later than 1242; possibly all 1247–57; for 15, 17, see also p. 295).
III, 19: 224, *226*, 277, 296 (1239–60, ? c. 1260).
III, 20, 21: *246* (? 1242).
III, 22: *261*, *278* (1257 or shortly before; perhaps partly 1260).
III, 24: *267* (? 1254–7).

IV, 1 ff.: *277*, cf. 262 (? 1247–57 or 1260).
IV, 3: *262* (1247–57).
IV, 4: *277–8*, 295 (? partly 1260).

IV, 5: 278.

IV, 7: *213–15*, 235 (prob. 1239).

IV, 10–14: *234–5* (? 1239; on 10 see also pp. 215, 222, on 11, 13, pp. 227, 294).

IV, 15: 276 (? partly 1260).

IV, 16: 295.

IV, 18: 215.

IV, 19: 230, 295.

IV, 20–1: 227, *228–9*, *294* (prob. 1239; for 21 see also p. 234).

IV, 22: *229, 246*, 296 (? 1242).

IV, 23: *246* (? 1242).

V, 3: *216* (? before 1249).

V, 6, 7: 278.

V, 9, 10: 295.

V, 10, 11: *216*, 278 (10, ? before 1249).

V, 13: 295.

(V, 16, on brothers forced to leave their convents in large numbers, may have been occasioned by the Mongol invasion of 1241 which devastated Poland and Hungary (cf. Jordan, pp. 72–5), or (less probably) by the persecutions of Frederick II's later years.)

V, 17: 253.

V, 18, 19: *222–3*, 224, *233*, *277–8* (18, ? 1239 with penalties ? 1260; 19, after 1242, ? 1260).

VI, 2: 226, 296.

(VI, 3: on licence for hearing confessions, cf. constitution of 1230, p. 292.)

VI, 6: 295.

VI, 8: 225, 228, *269, 277, 294* (prob. 1254 or 1257, ? with addition in 1260).

VI, 9: *218* (applied by John of Parma; i.e. before 1257, possibly before 1247).

VI, 11: *295* (probably early, because parallel with earlier Dominican recension only; ? 1239).

VI, 12–29: *269* (? all 1254–7; but 12–16 may be earlier, see p. *217*. For further references see below).

VI, 12–13: 223.

VI, 15–16: 278.

VI, 18: *219*, 265, 279 (? 1247–57).

VI, 21: 230, *269*, 295 (1254).

VI, 22: *269*, *278* (prob. 1254; ? partly 1260).

VI, 25–7: *225*.
VI, 25–6: *277* (? 1260).
VI, 25: *295*.

VII, 1, 2: *254* (prob. before 1247).
VII, 3: *251*, *276* (? 1244; ? partly 1260).
VII, 4: *251*.
VII, 8: *278* (? 1260).
VII, 9: *276* (? 1260).
VII, 10–12: *251*.
VII, 10: *251* (? 1244).
VII, 11: *267*, *294* (prob. later than 1241; ? 1253–7).
VII, 12: *211*, *294* (prob. 1239; for VII, 12–13, see also p. 234).
VII, 13: *227–8*, *251*, *294* (? 1239; but just possibly 1244).
VII, 15–17; *251* (? 1244).
VII, 18: *267* (1247 or later).
VII, 20: *214–15*, 235 (prob. 1239).
(VII, 21: the reference to laymen having the Rule and Constitutions
   expounded to them in the vernacular suggests an early date. A con-
   stitution on the visiting of custodies by Custodians seems presupposed
   in Grosseteste's *Ep.* cxxvII, ed. Luard, pp. 377–8, written in 1239
   or later, perhaps as late as 1245.)
VII, 22–4: *278* (? 1260).
VII, 25: *242*, *266* (? 1242).
VII, 25, 26: *295*.

VIII: *232* (prob. largely 1239).
VIII, 6: *295*.
VIII, 14: *295* (connected with a Dominican constitution passed 1254–6).
VIII, 18, 20: *295*.
VIII, 24: *269* (? 1254–7).

IX, 2, 4: *227*, *240*, *294* (? 1242).
IX, 7, 8: *195*, *240*, *294* (? 1242, but possibly 1239).
IX, 7: *281*.
IX, 10–15: *234*, *295* (1239).
IX, 17: *276* (? revised 1260).
IX, 18–22: *237–8* (prob. mainly 1242)
IX, 20–2: *295*.
IX, 23: *233* (? 1239).

X: 279.

X, 2: *232*, 295 (? 1239).

X, 6: 295 (connected with a Dominican constitution passed 1252–5).

X, 7: 295.

X, 8: 234, *295* (prob. 1239, because closer to earlier Dominican recension).

X, 13, 16: 295.

X, 18: *276*, *295* (possibly connected with a Dominican constitution of 1249–56; ? partly 1260).

X, 21: 295.

(x, 26: before 1260, cf. *Diff. Narb.* no. 15; the curb on the powers of Provincial Ministers, as also the reference to the reception *inutilium*, perhaps suggests Haymo, i.e. 1242.)

X, 27: *265–6* (prob. 1257).

XI, 1: *241–2* (prob. 1242).

XI, 2: *269–70* (1247 or 1251 (?)).

XI, 3: 227, *237*, 295 (prob. 1242).

XI, 4, 5: 296.

XI, 6: 294 (connected with a Dominican constitution of 1242–4).

XI, 7: 294.

XI, 10, 11: *277–8* (? 1260).

XI, 12: 227, *237*, 295 (prob. 1242).

XI, 14: *232*, 296 (? 1239).

XI, 15–20: 296.

XI, 15: 281.

XI, 21: *240*, 282, *294* (prob. after 1252, i.e. 1254–60; but probably 1254 or 1257, because it was acted on in 1260: cf. p. 282).

XI, 23: 295.

XI, 24: 211.

XI, 25: 295.

XI, 26–7: 296.

XI, 28: *240*, *294* (1242 or later).

XII, 1, 3, 4, 6, 7: 295.

(XII, 3: masses for a Minister General dying in office may have been ordained in 1242 for Albert of Pisa, the first to do so after 1226.)

(XII, 4: earlier than 1260: cf. *Diff. Narb.* no. 27.)

(XII, 6: earlier than 1257: cf. *Ordinationes divini officii*, no. 36, *A.F.H.* III, 70.)

INDEX

All friars are designated br[other]. Dominicans are distinguished by the letters O.P.; the rest were Franciscans